GOD'S LAW AND ORDER

God's

THE POLITICS OF PUNISHMENT IN EVANGELICAL AMERICA

Law
and
Order

Aaron Griffith

HARVARD UNIVERSITY PRESS

Cambridge, Massachusetts & London, England

2020

Publication of this book has been supported through the generous provisions of the
Maurice and Lula Bradley Smith Memorial Fund

First Printing

Library of Congress Cataloging-in-Publication Data

Names: Griffith, Aaron, 1985– author.
Title: God's law and order : the politics of punishment in evangelical
    America / Aaron Griffith.
Description: Cambridge, Massachusetts : Harvard University Press, 2020. I
    Includes bibliographical references and index.
Identifiers: LCCN 2020016859 I ISBN 9780674238787 (cloth)
Subjects: LCSH: Evangelicalism—United States—History—20th century. I
    Criminal justice, Administration of—United States—History—20th
    century. I Church and state—United States—History—20th century.
Classification: LCC BR1642.U6 G75 2020 I DDC 261.8/33609730904—dc23
LC record available at https://lccn.loc.gov/2020016859

For Eliza

CONTENTS

GOD'S LAW AND ORDER

INTRODUCTION

"Get ready to see Jesus's face.... The chariot's here to get you."

Lying on his deathbed, Antonio James listened to these comforting words from a caring Christian friend. James calmly welcomed the words, whispering "Bless you" in reply. Yet immediately after the soothing friend spoke, he motioned to some technicians standing nearby. This was the sign that they could begin injecting poisonous chemicals into James's body, which had been strapped down to prevent resistance. These chemicals would sedate James, relax his muscles, and finally stop his heart, abruptly ending his earthly life even as they began his heavenly rest.

It was Burl Cain, the warden of the famed Louisiana State Penitentiary, better known as Angola, who had been James's spiritual confidant at the end of his life. Cain was proud of this role. It was his opportunity for a second chance, he confessed to a crowd at Wheaton College, after he had failed to minister to another condemned prisoner. In this earlier case, Cain had ignored the man's fear, callously signaling the technicians to begin the injection process without offering an evangelistic word or spiritual support. As he spoke in Wheaton's chapel service, Cain admitted to students that he was later horrified by what he did: "Not that we had executed him so much but because [I] didn't use the opportunity to do the right thing."[1]

Even before resigning his post in 2016 after allegations of suspicious real estate dealings came to light, Cain was a very controversial figure.[2] Journalists complained of secrecy shrouding Angola, and the American Civil Liberties Union sued him for improperly favoring Protestant expressions of faith in his capacity as a state official.[3] One Angola inmate wrote a popular memoir that criticized aspects of Cain's reign and decried his paternalism.[4] However, Cain has also been regularly praised by American Christians, and other prison officials and politicians from both parties

1

have lauded his correctional approach, which included establishing a branch of New Orleans Baptist Theological Seminary at Angola.⁵ Democratic New Orleans mayor Mitch Landrieu (who regularly visited Angola) feted Cain in the *Atlantic:* "The warden has some very progressive ideas. He knows that we're all about the quick fix—more guards, more prisons, more punishment. He knows that something is seriously messed-up in the way we do things."⁶ Cain has also noted that his behavior toward death-row inmates was apparently sympathetic enough to have gotten him in trouble with the families of murder victims: "They say that I seem more interested in their loved one's killer than I do in the victim."⁷ The gathered evangelical community at Wheaton was either unaware of any controversy regarding Cain's work or simply did not care. Students offered him a standing ovation at the conclusion of his message, while the college's Christian outreach office continued to send students on spring break mission trips to Angola.

This is not a book about Burl Cain and the unique evangelistic disciplinary regime at Angola. Cain has been the focus of other works, and as a state warden who used his official position to evangelize and pray with prisoners, he is largely exceptional.⁸ Instead, this book is about the history behind the deeper sentiments underlying his message and its reception. It is about a quintessentially American gospel and law amalgamation, the work of soul-saving witness and spiritual concern within the context of severe punishment, all of which characterized evangelical influence in prisons and criminal justice in the twentieth century. Indeed, this book is just as much about the enthusiastic applause from the Wheaton students assembled to hear the grizzled, plainspoken warden preach as it is about the conceptual framework that informed him. There was something in Cain's message about gospel and law that confirmed what the young evangelical vanguard at the "Harvard of Christian schools" knew to be true about their inherited faith, a conceptual affinity that united American evangelicals across generations, culture, theology, and region.

This book is a religious history of mass incarceration. It charts the influence of evangelicals in American criminal justice from approximately the end of World War II to the present (though with important roots in preceding decades). This was a time when arrest and imprisonment rates rose exponentially, the result of new "law and order" currents in American culture; more aggressive policing, prosecution, and sentencing strategies; and the abandonment of rehabilitative penal practices for more retributive ones. The shift can be seen in a comparison of imprisonment rates from 1972, when 161 US residents were incarcerated per 100,000 population, to 2010, when 767 were incarcerated per 100,000. This resulted in a prison and jail population that now numbers as many as 2.23 million people (and the world's highest incarceration rate).[9] The growing number of African Americans behind bars has been even more dramatic. Black men today are imprisoned at a rate 6.5 times higher than white men, and since the late 1960s are more likely to have been imprisoned than to have graduated from college with a four-year degree.[10] All of this was occurring at the same time that evangelical religion in America was surging in popularity and influence, though also with important roots in the preceding decades. Therefore, this book is also a history of modern evangelicalism, explored through the lens of concern about crime and punishment. This book's broad task, then, is to analyze how two parallel developments, the rise of both the "age of evangelicalism" and the carceral state, overlap and connect.[11]

Crime and punishment mattered so much for evangelicals because their religious outlook meshed well with important aspects of America's penal culture. Simply put, there were historical reasons why Wheaton students applauded Cain so vigorously. For example, early postwar evangelicals saw religious value in emerging conceptions of crime, as when Billy Graham denounced American sin with reference to rising public concerns about juvenile delinquency. They channeled broader shifts in American religious culture into daily prison life, through evangelistic literature given to inmates and inspirational sermons preached by visiting prison missionaries in the 1970s. And their robust sense of God's forgiveness and grace led certain evangelicals to champion inmate restoration and prison reform programs in the 1980s and 1990s. In some ways this compatibility was a return to form, as evangelicals ranked as America's original criminal justice pioneers in their antebellum penitentiary construction and reform. And like evangelical social engagement in antebellum prisons, this present consonance has a complicated legacy: evangelicals have simultaneously proved complicit in the American justice system's most grievous problems even as they have also been pioneers in humanitarian engagement with modern prison life.

Though this book charts the story of modern evangelical crime and prison concern through several chronological and interpretive lenses, it presents three broad arguments about the intersection of evangelicalism and mass incarceration. These arguments try to make sense of the confluence of sympathetic piety and punishment as seen in figures like Burl Cain, and the striking correspondence this seemingly paradoxical integration had with broader evangelical culture.

First, crime and punishment simply *mattered* for evangelicals in the latter half of the twentieth century and were central to their entry into American public life. Evangelicals were on the cutting edge of engagement with American criminal justice, prisons, and reform, outpacing nearly all other American religious and social constituencies in their interest, intensity, and influence. They used crime as a rhetorical frame, led the way on all sides of the political battles around mass incarceration, and were very active in shaping the religious culture of prisons themselves. One cannot understand the creation, maintenance, or reform of modern American prisons (or how someone like Burl Cain could have appeared on the scene) without understanding the impact of evangelicalism. Each facilitated the rise of the other.

Second, evangelicals not only lobbied for policies and voted for politicians who helped build America's carceral state, they also helped make these changes appealing to other citizens. Unlike much of the previous work on twentieth-century evangelicalism (particularly their influence in politics), this book frames the movement less as a divisive culture-warring crusade and more in terms of consensus. Postwar evangelicals increasingly framed their own religious movement as reputable, racially moderate, and politically savvy, and they helped to do the same for the cause of punishment, bolstering law enforcement's "neutral" quality, color-blind aspirations, and respectable status. Though they argued for conservative notions of limited government and the strengthening of family values over progressive social programs, they did so while supporting the massive expansion of the state via its work of policing and imprisonment. They were, as Axel Schäfer has argued, "antistatist statists," a flexible identity that aided their political and cultural ascendance.[12]

Race was a key factor in this particular brand of Christian respectability politics. Throughout the nation's history, race has been a crucial backdrop for American thinking and policymaking on criminal justice. Sometimes ideas and policies were formulated by whites with clear racist intent, such as the convict leasing systems that developed in the post–Civil War South. Other times, reformist and radical advocates contended for systems with aspirations of racial justice. Somewhere in the middle were forms of criminal justice that mobilized the rhetoric of racial neutrality in service, sometimes unintentionally, of racialized aims and outcomes. This particular mode of mobilization depended on a "color-blind" frame,

4

one that opened up the possibility of "racism without racists" in unfolding views of criminality and law enforcement strategy.[13] Often this approach, in the words of Keeanga-Yamahtta Taylor, is "deployed to hide or obscure inequalities and disparities between African Americans and whites" and ultimately serves to "amplify politics that blame Blacks for their own oppression."[14] Religious ideas and actors proved influential in all of these formulations, providing them a sacred valence that helped broaden and deepen their appeal. And when reforms went off the rails or ended up exacerbating inequality, the influence of religious ideas and actors often made the problems all the more difficult to untangle.

Analyzing the ways evangelicals thought about race's relationship to crime and punishment is challenging because it so often went unacknowledged. This was not true of black evangelicals, who regularly focused on matters of race, discrimination, and the prospects and perils of American criminal justice for their churches and communities. Neither was this true of white racist Christians, who hardly concealed their blatant beliefs that law and order should subdue unruly black people as slavery had in past generations. But for many moderate white evangelicals, analysis of race was regularly missing in their sermons, writings, and ministry campaigns. Sometimes this was intentional, because white Christians aspiring to racial neutrality believed the best course of action was avoiding controversial matters in their public engagement. Other times it was simply overlooked by white Christians as a topic of discussion, a significant omission given the ways that criminal justice in America has always intersected with racial formulations, with disproportionate effects on people of color. This book zeroes in on these peculiar lacunae, the ways racial formulations were produced with reference to criminal justice without direct address. Cain did not make reference to the clear racial dynamics at play in Angola in his Wheaton address, despite the fact that James, like the vast majority of the prison's inmates, was black. The elision or smoothing over of racial complications, however unintentional, was a regular theme of postwar evangelical crime concern.

Third, this book argues for the political import of evangelical soul saving, often overlooked by scholars who characterize the movement's conversionism as neglectful of issues of social change. I show how, though individualistic and unapologetically spiritual in focus, evangelicals' concern with conversion influenced their politics of crime and punishment. Sometimes it offered cover for punitive politics. But other times conversion opened evangelicals' eyes to the needs of juvenile delinquents and prisoners, leading them to solidarity with offenders and new forms of reform work. The lines between these two positions were often blurred, the political implications of conversion serving as contested terrain.

This book is a work of cultural history. It places at the forefront of its analysis "the viewpoint of the motives and meanings that individual and collective and historical agents from the past gave to whatever they were doing, and to the contexts in which they operated."[15] These motives and meanings were almost always politically and religiously charged, but not in ways best explained solely through legislative developments or traditional doctrinal formulations. In the vein of one important work of American religious cultural history, this book therefore "comprehends a range of actions and beliefs far greater than those described in a catechism or occurring within sacred space."[16] To put it another way, it attempts to interpret a range of actions and beliefs beyond those listed in the formal doctrinal standards of a prison ministry or the penal codes of a particular congressional bill. However, each chapter incorporates a variety of tools in order to explain certain developments and to enliven the overall narrative. At some points the book depends on a more straightforward political account, while elsewhere it follows the lead of recent histories of evangelical intellectual life. But taken as a whole, it is a historical attempt to make sense of the overlapping American evangelical and penal cultures.

This book builds on important currents in both the historiography of twentieth-century evangelicalism and criminal justice. Recent studies of varieties of evangelical influence in American politics and culture, such as works by Kate Bowler, Darren Dochuk, Steven Miller, David Swartz, John Turner, Grant Wacker, Daniel Williams, and Molly Worthen, are all important for framing various aspects of the "age of evangelicalism" in the second half of the twentieth century. This was the broader context, as Miller argues, for evangelical faith to develop in American politics and culture as a "language, medium, and foil," a powerful reference point for those who championed it, opposed it, or fell somewhere in between.[17] The history of this reference point, however, has yet to be detailed with reference to what Elliott Currie called the "most thoroughly implemented government social program of our time," America's massive prison system.[18] Besides highlighting an understudied issue in American religious history, this book's focus on criminal justice also helps to reframe common understandings of evangelical influence in public life. Understanding evangelicals' roles in relationship to this peculiar formation of state power (whether supportive, ministerial, or critical) requires movement beyond a simplistic "backlash" thesis, the idea that the evangelicals who gained cultural and political power in the latter half of the twentieth century were simply reacting negatively to threatening modern trends.[19] Postwar evangelicals were not reactionaries who found their conservative theology in conflict with developments in modern life, such as mass incarceration. As Ruth Wilson Gilmore has pointed out, modern prisons are not marginal spaces but sit in the "middle of the muddle" of American political, social, and cultural life.[20] So too with evangelicals, who were likewise products of their time and who bolstered the mainstream appeal of concern about punishment.

While commentators on modern American crime and punishment have named a variety of contributing cultural and political factors in the rise of mass incarceration, they have rarely discussed the relevance of evangelicalism (or even religion more broadly) to the history of the simultaneous rise of America's carceral state. The book-length scholarly works that do analyze religion's import to mass incarceration in the United States, such as those by Tanya Erzen, Winnifred Sullivan, Joshua Dubler, and James Logan, largely focus on the contemporary landscape.[21] *God's Law and Order* is distinctive in that it shows how religion must be understood as a key feature in the longer history of mass incarceration (and, at times, of its discontents).

A word about definitions. This book does not directly wade into the seemingly endless interpretive debates about defining evangelicalism, though I do chart commonalities and shifts in evangelical self-understanding over the course of the twentieth century regarding crime and prison concern. I find Douglas Sweeney's definition of evangelicalism as a "movement of orthodox Protestants with an eighteenth-century twist" to be a helpful starting point in showing what grounds evangelical identity over the course of my book's chronological scope, and American history more broadly.[22] "Orthodox" here references evangelicals' regular concern with conserving what they saw as biblical Christian doctrine. In the twentieth century, evangelicals often framed such concerns in terms of a battle against secularism and forms of liberal Christianity that they believed accommodated it. The "eighteenth-century twist" phrase (a reference to the transatlantic series of revivals that came to be known as the Great Awakening) indicates the recurring importance of conversion, regularly in direct contrast to established church structures. Conversion was a key theological marker of postwar evangelicalism, one that had consequences for evangelicals' engagement of issues related to crime and prison. The Christians who could be counted as evangelicals came from a wide array of Protestant traditions and denominations. Many downplayed denominational labels. Conservative Protestants' doubling down on orthodox and conversionist distinctives (sometimes with reference to crime and prison concern) put them at odds with liberals in their own denominations. This development, along with the regular usage of descriptors like "Bible-believing," helped to solidify "evangelical" as a standalone religious category by the mid-1970s.

When I use the term "evangelical" in this book, I am usually, though not always, referring to white conservative Protestants. Whether or not all conservative African American Protestants should be counted as evangelicals is a matter of significant debate.[23] I do discuss black Christians who I believe should be counted as evangelicals, not only for their theological dispositions but also for their clear connection to avowed evangelical figures and organizations. However, I also show how black evangelicals' engagement with issues of crime and punishment sometimes deviated from their white counterparts' or was justified with different rationale.

One other note regarding terminology. I regularly use the vocabulary of my subjects; often this means deploying common phrases in evangelical parlance, such as characterizing a religious conversion as someone being "led to Christ." Other times it means using terms like "prisoners," "criminals," "offenders," and "inmates." I am highly aware of the scholarly and moral hazards here. People who have been arrested or incarcerated are people, and their humanity risks being minimized or erased by terms like these.[24] However, I have made the difficult decision to generally not use terms that are often posited as more humanizing referents, such as "incarcerated persons." I found that terms like these sometimes obscure the various ways that evangelicals, law enforcement officials, and incarcerated people themselves (all of whom used terms like "criminals") spoke and thought about the world around them in their own time and place. For evangelicals in particular, "criminal" was indeed a word with negative connotations. But that was the point. Criminals, like all sinners (another negative term), were loved by Jesus and could choose to follow him. Whether or not that belief redeemed their use of the term is a decision I leave to the reader.

The book begins by exploring the history of religious interest in crime and punishment in the interwar period. Though most discussions of crime concern in the twentieth century focus on the law and order politics of conservatives in the 1960s and after, the broad religious influence on crime from an earlier generation is instructive. A wide array of Protestants, Catholics, and Jews (liberal and conservative, black and white) expressed sharp concern about the downward spiral of their lawless land. Religious debates about crime paralleled the divides between modernism and fundamentalism, with liberals arguing for attention to criminals' social conditions and conservatives pushing for harsher punishment. This divide was crystallized in the public religious rhetoric around one famous courtroom drama: the 1924 "trial of the century" of Nathan Leopold Jr. and Richard Loeb for murder. Whether regarding this trial or other crimes, these disagreements were significant, but there was common ground on two points: the beliefs that rising crime reflected growing secularity and that disciplinary state power was ultimately responsible for addressing the problem. Political leaders drew on these shared sensibilities as they built national support for the expansion of tougher law enforcement efforts. This broad consensus meant that future religious movements that wanted to exert widespread cultural influence would need to take crime seriously.

One such movement was evangelicalism in the early postwar era. The postwar evangelical surge has often been narrated in terms of its members' self-understanding (that it possessed the savoir faire of other cultural and intellectual movements) or its political engagement that helped spark the culture wars (on such issues as prayer in schools, communism, or family values). But crime was also a frequent reference point. It offered conceptual common ground with millions of other Americans and served as a cipher for a variety of other issues (from secularism to civil rights to parental responsibility). Most important, it allowed the new evangelical movement to chart a distinct path away from their fundamentalist forefathers and liberal Protestant rivals. Evangelical leaders in the early postwar era like Billy Graham and David Wilkerson used concerns about crime and delinquency to sharpen their messages about Christian conversion over and against the fundamentalist and liberal alternatives hashed out in the interwar period. In sum, their crime-inflected conversionism gave them a way to reach America and appeared to provide a path between the punitive and progressive paradigms.

In charting this path, however, these leaders set the stage for later evangelical enmeshment with a new form of punitive politics in the 1960s and early 1970s. As postwar evangelicals gained cultural cachet, they became more comfortable moving away from strict conversionism as the solution to social ills, and allying with the state. This move meant endorsement of one of the state's key functions: protection of the social order. Since public decorum seemed to evangelicals to be increasingly under threat in the mid-1960s and beyond, evangelicals moved to promote the state's just use of violent force and confinement. However, evangelicals did not see this as a recapitulation of fundamentalist backlash. Instead, they saw their ramped-up support for the expansion of policing, the streamlining of sentencing procedures, and the lengthening of prison sentences as fully in the main-stream. They saw it as a reflection of American values and, crucially, a sign of racial equality and color blindness. We will examine the broad in-tellectual and cultural shifts that underpinned evangelical law and order, as well as their political consequences on the federal, state, and local levels.

The widespread escalation of evangelical prison ministry efforts par-allels the story of evangelical influence in the rise of mass incarceration. At midcentury, religion in American prisons was largely directed by state-funded chaplains who served as therapeutic coordinators of "religious diversity." But beginning around the 1970s, evangelicals jumped into various types of prison ministry work: they founded ministries, produced vast quantities of spiritual literature for inmates, launched prison radio broadcasts, and led evangelistic crusades at prisons nationwide. In doing so, they dramatically changed the practice of religion in prisons. Focusing on several key evangelical prison ministries and leaders, we will explore the stories of each ministry's founding with particular attention to their commonalities, the shared attributes that provide insight into why this widespread revival of prison ministry occurred. We will also examine the tensions that evangelical prison ministers frequently were caught within as they negotiated pluralistic spaces and broader "law and order" cultural currents.

Finally, the book will discuss the conservative evangelical activism that arose in the 1980s and early 1990s in response to the oppressive realities of American criminal justice. This activism was pioneered by former in-mate and prison minister Charles Colson, whose personal encounters with inmates led him to understand the problems inherent within the criminal justice system and the need for social change (often putting him at odds with other evangelicals who espoused "tough on crime" rhetoric and championed policies accordingly). The "compassionate conservative" ac-tivism of Colson and his allies was marked by failures and compromises but gradually produced models for criminal justice reform that allowed for bipartisan responses to the evils of mass incarceration. Colson's reform work was an attempt to mitigate the harshness of American criminal justice with appeals to the same evangelical concepts and constituencies that had contributed to the law-and-order regime.

The book concludes with a brief word on the present state and potential future of evangelical crime and prison concerns. As evangelical luminaries exit the scene, they offer powerful reminders of the importance of these concerns to their public ministries. For example, upon his death in early 2018, Billy Graham was buried in a casket crafted by inmates at Burl Cain's Angola prison. New leaders with evangelical connections and audiences are taking their place in contemporary American conversations about crime and prison. Some, like the popular lawyer and author Bryan Stevenson, make arguments that build on past evangelical emphases of justice, mercy, and the Christian duty to seek close proximity to prisoners. But they also chart new ground, placing concern about the oppression of people of color at the center of their activism and highlighting the racial injustices at the root of America's system of mass incarceration.

A final note about my own background. As a student at Wheaton College, I attended the 2005 chapel service when Burl Cain came to speak. This book is born out of my scholarly interests in the histories of mass incarceration and American religion. But, as with many book projects, part of the impetus for exploring this history stems from my own experiences. I have volunteered in prison ministry work and research and write with these experiences in mind. Like some of the figures I write about, my own conscience has been pricked by what I have seen while working in prisons: the poor conditions, frustrating procedures, and obvious racial and economic inequalities. I have also been struck by the ministry of evangelicals (who are everywhere in prison work). Their sincerity and clear concern for incarcerated people are evident and often appreciated by the people they serve. But I also have wrestled with the fact that evangelicals, formed in the same traditions and churches, are often enthusiastic about punishing wrongdoers and getting "tough on crime." Many possess deep comfort with the state's capacity to surveil, constrain, and take life, even as they remain highly attuned to the spiritual well-being of those caught in the grips of the state system. I hope the history I chart in this book is instructive and helpful, not only for historians and readers interested in religion or criminal justice but also for those in prison ministry or reform work who want to reckon with the complications and historical contingency of their vocations. This contingency can seem threatening to some Christians, as it may seem to downplay one's calling or the timeless message of Jesus's command to visit prisoners (Matthew 25:36, New International Version). But I have come to see this contingency as a gift, as it invites us to imagine new possibilities of more faithful and devoted service to incarcerated people and of a world beyond prisons.

1

CHURCHDOM'S WAR ON CRIME

On a cloudless May afternoon in a wealthy South Side neighborhood of Chicago in 1924, fourteen-year-old Bobby Franks was kidnapped off the street near his home. Almost immediately after luring him into their car, the perpetrators killed Franks by beating him with the blunt end of a chisel and suffocating him with a rag. They dumped his body in a nearby forest preserve. The killers attempted to deceive Franks's wealthy father into paying a ransom, but a passerby happened to discover the boy's lifeless corpse when he spotted some feet protruding from a drainage culvert. The crime seemed to many to be unsolvable, but investigators had a lead from a set of eyeglasses found lying near Franks's body. After some sleuthing, they discovered that the glasses' manufacturer sold this particular model through only one Chicago optician, whose records showed that the glasses had been purchased by Nathan Leopold Jr., a nineteen-year-old University of Chicago law student. Upon questioning by police, Leopold maintained that the glasses had fallen out of his pocket during a birding expedition, and presented his friend Richard Loeb as his alibi for the afternoon of Franks's kidnapping. But after further police interrogation that highlighted inconsistencies between their accounts, a search of Leopold's apartment that turned up suspicious items, and the matching of Leopold's typewriter to the print on the ransom note, the duo's story fell apart.

Leopold and Loeb soon confessed their guilt, and their trial that summer was primarily a forum for debating their punishment. The duo's wealthy families enlisted the famous attorney Clarence Darrow to lead their defense, hoping he could save them from the death penalty. Darrow's defense was made all the more difficult by the answers that Leopold and Loeb had given in interviews with investigators after their confession of guilt. In no need of money, they had committed the kidnapping and murder simply "for the thrill of it." Not only that, their literary encounter at the university with Friedrich Nietzsche's *Übermensch* had led them to believe that their intellectual superiority absolved them of moral blame. Leopold had reportedly told investigators that he "did [the murder] as easily as he would stick a pin through the back of a beetle."[1] Darrow pursued a defense strategy that highlighted the duo's mental instability, presenting the testimony of medical professionals who discussed the traumatic childhoods that made Leopold's and Loeb's actions possible. Though the prosecution presented its own psychiatric evidence that stressed moral culpability, the judge ruled in favor of the defense and sentenced both Leopold and Loeb to life in prison.

Because of the gruesomeness of the crime, the wealth of the families, salacious rumors surrounding Leopold and Loeb's homosexual relationship, and the pair's noxious justification of their actions, the court proceedings garnered an immense following on a national scale. Media played an important role not only in sensationalizing the case but also in solving the mystery of Franks's death: the connection between Franks's body and the kidnapping, as well as Leopold and Loeb's possible connection to the case, was made by *Chicago Daily News*'s reporters. They won a Pulitzer. Beyond reporting the case's lurid details, media commentators also used the trial as a platform for debating topics like the moral well-being of American children and the merits of psychiatry.[2]

The Leopold and Loeb tribunal occurred one year before another famous courtroom drama, the 1925 "monkey trial" that transpired in the sweaty confines of a courthouse in Dayton, Tennessee. In this case, high school instructor John Scopes was found guilty of teaching evolution in violation of the state law. Other than the crimes, the two trials had a great deal in common. Both saw Darrow occupying the role of defense attorney, both had fervent courtroom speeches, both drew enormous amounts of public attention from press and public alike, and both inspired later retellings of the dramas on theater stages and movie screens. But more important, both trials were seen as battles between the godless ideology of modernist elites and traditional values, referendums on the legitimacy of religious faith in an increasingly secular age. The cases crystallized the internal clashes of the time in American denominations between fundamentalists and modernists, over issues like evolution, the reliability of scripture, and the unique truth of the Christian gospel. Though Billy Sunday just as well could have been referring to the Scopes trial, the famous revivalist framed the Leopold and Loeb case in precisely these terms as he traveled through the Chicago area around the time of the trial. The murder that precipitated the trial could be "traced to the moral miasma which contaminates some of our 'young intellectuals.' It is now considered fashionable for higher education to scoff at God. The world is headed for Hades so fast no speed limit can stop it."[3]

Pastors spoke to their congregations about the Leopold and Loeb trial as well, and their sermons frequently appeared in national newspapers. Their reactions diverged sharply, with fault lines paralleling those of the Scopes trial. Conservatives assailed the modernist intellectual culture that produced Leopold and Loeb and urged capital punishment. Liberals argued against application of the death penalty and pointed to the need for a more compassionate and "scientific" spiritual approach. But despite their strenuous disagreement, the shared concern of these warring camps of clergy symbolized the broader denotation of crime as a distinctly *religious* national issue. And it was this religious concern with crime, more than the question of evolution, that would ultimately have a deep impact on the landscape of American politics and culture.

Long before the law-and-order years of the 1960s and after, the era of Leopold and Loeb saw the unfolding of a new politics of crime and punishment. And before postwar evangelicals became key religious authorities on issues of crime and punishment, they were preceded by a wideranging swath of Protestants, Catholics, and Jews (liberal and conservative, black and white) who were worried about lawlessness and who framed their concerns as part of the battle against encroaching secularism. This religious "war on crime" of the interwar period was itself the culmination of a longer history of the intermingling of religion and criminal justice in the late eighteenth, nineteenth, and early twentieth centuries. This war was fought in speeches, newspapers, and magazines, both religious and secular, and the shared rhetorical culture that emerged was powerful. It not only made intelligible the dramatic changes in crime policy (often in response to heinous crimes like Leopold and Loeb's) but also reflected the religiously infused views of policy makers and law enforcement officials themselves.

Prison Religion and Police Missions

From the nation's founding to the early twentieth century, religious conceptions of crime and punishment underwent shifts in aims and scope, each of which laid important groundwork for the emerging anticrime consensus. Religious influence in prison work, support for policing, and, most importantly, the racialization of crime helped set the stage for the sacred crime war to come.

Before the nineteenth century, American responses to lawbreaking were largely disorganized, decentralized, and regularly ineffective. Offenders might be caught and punished, but few people expected that crime could be fully curtailed by policing or ramped-up criminal codes, both of which were often negatively associated with the overweening power of the British monarchy.[4] When crimes did occur in the colonial era, official forms of punishment were typically ad hoc and limited to the local level. As there was little criminal justice infrastructure, few prisons, and few personnel (solitary lay magistrates and constables were largely responsible for law enforcement), penalties were swift and low cost. Fines, public humiliation (such as confinement to the stocks), banishment, and capital punishment found favor, all of which had deterrence of future crimes, swift retribution for the moral debts created, and quick restoration of public order as their primary aims.[5] The postrevolutionary and antebellum periods saw growing public concern with crime and violence, and reformers organized campaigns to combat the various forms of deviance that threatened social cohesion in the new republic. Penitentiaries were built with the aim of reforming wayward offenders, a conscious movement away from the more haphazard, retributive, and localized forms of punishment that had characterized the response of previous generations.[6]

Religious justification helped provide punishment's underlying logic during the eighteenth and early nineteenth centuries. Capital punishment in puritan New England often bore an explicitly theological component, with ministers preaching sermons at the gallows on the wages of sin and the law-keeping function of civil authority.[7] The postrevolutionary and antebellum reformers who pioneered the penitentiaries were primarily Christian leaders in the emerging Protestant "benevolent empire," and the various prison models (from Quaker "gardens" to Calvinist "furnaces") reflected their different theological sensibilities.[8] In their nearly yearlong national study of American prisons, Alexis de Tocqueville and Gustave de Beaumont praised this rehabilitative and reformist approach: "In America the progress of the reform of prisons has been of a character essentially religious. . . . It is [religion's] influence alone which produces complete reformation."[9] However, though penitentiaries served as a symbol of important shifts within penology and reformers were optimistic about their potential, their significance was checked by their lack of public support and governmental backing. As Jennifer Graber has shown, they largely remained the projects of ambitious activists who often found their pioneering hopes for inmate rehabilitation frustrated by overcrowding, budget cuts, and the absence of broader sympathy for their humanitarian motives.[10] Similarly, police forces throughout the rest of the nineteenth century remained decentralized, unprofessionalized, and unreliable.[11]

As penitentiaries floundered in achieving their original humanitarian and religious aims, a generation of evangelists began work in prisons in the second half of the nineteenth century. They preached the gospel with the hope of reducing crime and reforming prisons, one soul at a time. Methodists, whose numbers increased exponentially throughout the nineteenth century, regularly evangelized prisoners (following the lead of John and Charles Wesley, who had preached in prisons in England in the 1730s). The popular Methodist minister James Finley took up a chaplaincy role at the Ohio Penitentiary after critics began blasting it for its brutality. Finley paired proselytism, what he called "the work of spreading the spirit of evangelical religion among the prisoners," with a message to the public of the need to treat inmates with dignity.[12]

The Salvation Army was another such effort. An organization that originated in Britain in the mid-nineteenth century before taking root in the United States in the 1880s, Salvationists quickly became known for their work among the poor, building soup kitchens and shelters in America's urban slums. They also had a significant presence in prisons and among former inmates. William Booth, who cofounded the movement with his wife, Catherine, regularly saw ex-prisoners converted under his preaching. Various organizations within the Salvation Army focused on prisoner needs, such as the Prisoner's Hope Brigade and the Brighter Day League. Salvationists helped inmates with reentry into society, ministered to families of the incarcerated, and distributed religious literature and Bibles in prisons. More generally, they attempted to develop friendships and empathy with those behind bars. Maud Booth (daughter-in-law of William and Catherine) pledged to one of her "boys" at Sing Sing prison that she would be "a friend in your hours of loneliness and need and a faithful representative to champion your cause with the outside world."[13]

Other prison evangelists operated independently. This generation of prison evangelists largely arose from churches associated with the radical Holiness tradition, a movement of "come outers" who broke from mainline Methodism in the late nineteenth century because of their worries about the denomination's increasing theological liberalism, wealth, and aspirations for social respectability. Elizabeth Wheaton had grown up in the Methodist church in antebellum Ohio but felt convicted by God of her own nominal faith and "high society" desires. Fleeing lukewarm faith and respectable social aspirations, she underwent "entire consecration" through the baptism of the Holy Spirit in 1883. Not long after, she felt called to prison work when she encountered three handcuffed inmates in a rail car. "My heart was moved with deep compassion for them," she wrote later in her 1906 memoir *Prisons and Prayer.* Others on the train were "curiously inspecting them, as if they thought they had no tender feelings." Wheaton felt moved to say something. She offered them her hand and said, "I am sorry for you, but God can help you in this hour of trial." Promising to visit the men in prison, she did not know that this would be the first of many times she would attempt to bring inmates spiritual comfort. "But the burden of those in prison kept coming heavier upon me," she wrote. "I told my friends I must go and preach the gospel to prisoners."[14] For the next twenty-two years, she would travel the country via railroad to preach in jails, in prisons, and on death rows.[15]

In addition to their prison work, Protestants developed another ministerial focus: law enforcement. In the late nineteenth century, Christian leaders began speaking in increasingly laudatory tones about the work of policing and crafted outreach efforts to officers. This development also had British connections. In 1883, at a parlor meeting in London, a small group of women and policemen established the Christian Police Association. Led by Catherine Gurney, the association built convalescent homes and reading rooms for officers and founded a journal entitled *On and Off Duty.*[16] It was not long before over 120 branches of the association appeared across England, Scotland, Ireland, and Wales, with North American branches in Washington, DC; New York; Philadelphia; and other cities emerging a few years later.[17] The association also had an outward function to convince the public of the spiritual validity of policing. Many people believed policing and Christian work to be at odds, one British account noted, but "if this Association has done nothing else, it has brought out the fact . . . that there can be as bright Christian men in the police force as anywhere else."[18]

The New York branch of the Christian Police Association was endorsed by Christians from across the Protestant spectrum, with the *New York Times* calling it "quite undenominational."[19] Meetings for prayer and Bible study occurred four times each week.[20] J. L. Spicer, the first secretary of the association (and former employee of the American Sunday School Union), proudly noted the presence of one member who moonlighted as a Methodist preacher when he wasn't on patrol.[21] Spicer reminded his fellow Christians that Saint Paul prayed "for all in authority," and that they would do well to similarly hold law enforcement in high regard by paying them higher wages. On the wall of the meeting space, accompanied by emblems of cross, crown, and a police officer's helmet, were emblazoned biblical words meant to encourage patrolmen: "God is our refuge and strength."[22]

Baptized in religious waters, American criminal justice around the beginning of the twentieth century was also immersed in a racialized imagination. African Americans were no longer enslaved, but their skin color marked them as criminals in the eyes of many white Americans, who justified their treatment as such. This imagination expressed itself in several ways, some blatantly racist and unswervingly violent, others scientifically minded and paternalistic. At every stage of racialization (and resistance to it), religious influence proved crucial.

In the American South, the practice of convict leasing emerged after Reconstruction as a system of racial control by which southern states used black prisoners (often arrested for minor offenses or false charges) as forced labor. It was an opportunity to replace the labor pool lost in emancipation, a kind of "slavery by another name."[23] Convict leasing had prominent religious advocates, such as Joseph E. Brown, the chair of the board of trustees at Southern Baptist Theological Seminary in Louisville, Kentucky, and its most important donor. Brown's horrific coal mines and furnaces were filled with black convict laborers, whose backbreaking work under threat of corporal punishment enriched Brown and allowed him to donate $50,000 to the seminary and save it from financial ruin. The continued ministerial preparation of Baptist pastors was made possible by forced black labor.[24]

Black Americans also faced the specter of an informal, yet no less horrifying, form of southern criminal justice: lynching. Though whites had been subject to lynchings for much of the nineteenth century, after Reconstruction the violent form of mob punishment became a way for whites to punish African Americans for real or perceived violations of the law and the Jim Crow social order. By the 1880s, the number of black lynchings overtook that of whites.[25] Of the 4,743 lynchings recorded between 1882 and 1968, 3,446 of the victims were black men and women.[26]

Lynchings were white supremacist rituals that held a mystical quality for perpetrators. A black person would be accused of a crime, a mob would form, and the victim would be killed in a painful manner, often with large crowds observing. Though technically extralegal violence, lynchings often occurred with sanction from local authorities. As historian Donald Mathews has shown, sacred concepts like sin and atonement were pervasive in white justifications of lynchings, with perpetrators shouting "Glory!" as they tortured black victims. This was why, as one southern newspaper proclaimed, lynching was a matter of Christian duty, "part of the religion of our people."[27]

American Christians, both black and white, took a particular interest in lynching because it was an act so obviously laden with sacred meaning. While some African Americans depicted lynching simply as godless and evil, others saw potential in reframing the act as a theological weapon against white supremacy, pointing to Jesus's own status as a kind of lynching victim as evidence of divine solidarity with their race.[28] Some white Christians, particularly leaders of mainline Protestant denominations and churches, critiqued lynching as well. But while black Christians typically protested racist mob violence by pointing to lynching's harmful effects on black well-being, white Protestants zeroed in on the threat that lynching posed to law and order more broadly.[29] For these Christians, like other middle-class Americans, lynching was an outmoded, anarchic form of "rough justice" that threatened lawfulness and rational legal procedure.[30] In the wake of lynchings and rioting that targeted black people in the early twentieth century, white Christians regularly lamented how mob violence primarily endangered, as one ministers' group put it in the wake of the 1906 Atlanta riots, "the spirit of obedience to the law."[31] In this case, white mobs in the city had killed or wounded dozens of black people and destroyed black-owned property, justifying their actions with racial stereotypes about black men's predations of white women.[32] Some white pastors lamented the violence even as they concurred with the mob's racist opinion about black men's "unregenerate hearts thoroughly inflamed with lust."[33] Others framed their commentary on the events with a nod toward America's colonial forms of justice and the hope of a modernized future. As a group of Episcopal clergy stated, "The history of our civilization is largely the history of the process by which private vengeance has been replaced by public justice." Lynchings were akin to frontier barbarism, hardly fit for a modernizing city and nation. The key, the Episcopalians contended, would be to convince the public that "the taking of the law into their own hands by unauthorized men is far worse in its essential nature and in its ruinous results than any crime committed by one individual against another." Crime was a problem, "but lynching is the murder of law itself."[34]

This well-intentioned critique of lynching as a threat to law and order was repeated with regularity by white Protestants, eclipsing concern about the suffering of black people and the racialized quality of the crime. A Presbyterian pastor named Edwin T. Wellford authored an entire book on the matter in 1905, entitled *The Lynching of Jesus*. Though Wellford cited statistics early on about how black Americans were affected disproportionately by the crime, the rest of the book lacked any discussion of race or reference to African Americans. Instead, Wellford contended that "the real victim of lynch law is the *Government*" (italics in the original).[35] As the book's title indicates, Jesus was a victim of mob violence too. But in contrast to the black Christians who likewise stressed this point in order to show their Savior's solidarity with their suffering, Wellford spent most of the book lamenting how the trial and execution of Jesus was morally outrageous because it violated established legal procedure. But, Wellford believed, American Christians were also a people who could come to believe in the righteous power of public safety. He offered a challenge to fellow believers: "All who would be lovers of law and order must be lovers of Jesus."[36] This elision of lynching's racialized threat to African Americans, in favor of a generalized critique that foregrounded lynching's threat to public order and the need for lawfulness more broadly, would persist among American mainline Protestant leaders for the next few decades.

Paralleling Jim Crow–era lynchings were regular exchanges about the significance and interpretation of black crime rates. In 1896 Frederick L. Hoffman, a German who immigrated to the United States twelve years earlier, published *Race Traits and Tendencies of the American Negro*. Hailed by many in its day, this text would be influential for decades to come in shaping public understandings of race and crime. In the words of Khalil Gibran Muhammad, Hoffman's book emphasized "the innate self-destructive tendencies of black people" and argued that their challenging socioeconomic status "had absolutely nothing to do with black criminality." Hoffman presented data that showed black crime rates in liberal northern cities rivaling those in the Jim Crow South.[37] He believed that the criminality of white Americans (including new immigrants from Europe) could be ascribed to problems stemming from a modernizing society, such as economic inequality and challenging industrial working conditions. But he did not extend the same progressive courtesy to black

Americans. In contending that crime was endemic among emancipated black people (as opposed to enslaved black people, who had exhibited "neither crime [nor] pauperism") while ignoring the innumerable limitations and injustices they faced during Jim Crow, Hoffman firmly linked criminality to blackness.[38]

Hoffman had previously considered becoming a Unitarian minister. Though he turned to statistical analysis instead of ministry, *Race Traits* still showcased Hoffman's own interest in religion.[39] Alongside education, economics, and physical health, religion worked as an analytical lens through which to interpret black criminality. Hoffman presented statistical evidence for high rates of black church attendance and religiosity after emancipation, which, in Hoffman's mind, bolstered his argument. The fact that black people attended church in larger numbers than white people and yet were seemingly still more prone to crime and immorality was, for him, evidence of their natural inferiority. To drive home this point, he cited missionary accounts from Jamaica that showed how emancipated black people persisted in both Christian worship and immorality. Hoffman explained this tension with reference to inherent racial difference, quoting British historian James Anthony Froude at length: "Morals in the technical sense they have none, but they cannot be said to sin, because they have no knowledge of a law. . . . They sin only as animals sin, without shame because there is no sense of wrong doing. . . . In fact these poor children of darkness have escaped the consequences of the fall, and *must come of another stock after all*" (italics in the original).[40]

For Hoffman, reflecting the prevalence of "scientific racism" in his era, the high point of black Americans' civilization was their enslavement; at the moment of emancipation, black people began moving on a "downward grade."[41] The offerings of benevolent white people to black people— "education, philanthropy, and religion"—had "failed to develop a higher appreciation of the stern and uncompromising virtues of the Aryan race." In his hailing of slaves' moral virtues, his indictment of liberal magnanimity, and his arguments for recognition of black people's criminally prone nature, Hoffman opened the possibility that the only effective social response to black lawbreaking was their control.[42]

Hoffman had a devotee in John Roach Straton, a Mercer University professor and Baptist minister. In 1900, the year of his ordination, Straton channeled Hoffman's ideas into an article for the *North American Review.* He pointed to the increasing numbers of lynchings as proof, not of rampant white supremacist violence, but of rising black criminality "against female virtue." And, citing Hoffman regularly, he identified attempts at black uplift "to the plane of the Anglo-Saxon" as part of the problem. Whites had striven for centuries, Straton contended, in order to arrive at their present state of achievement. But "we take these savages from their simple life and their low plane of evolution, and attempt to give them an enlightenment for which the stronger races have prepared themselves through ages of growth. . . . Like little children in a tropical garden, they eat all fruit merely because it looks pretty or tastes sweet." Straton believed that the black industrial education programs of Booker T. Washington were admirable. But he doubted that they could truly address the pathology unique to black Americans. Segregation was likely necessary, as was a campaign for moving them abroad to a distant country. In the meantime, however, Straton urged whites to treat black people with "sympathy, tolerance, justice and absolute fairness. . . . We must lead this weaker people's steps aright."[43] Washington would reply to Straton later that year, arguing for continued black education and recognition of systemic discriminatory factors that led to black criminality.[44]

Straton was a theological and political conservative, and he would later become a leading fundamentalist. But progressive white Protestants could propound similar ideas. James G. K. McClure, the president of McCormick Theological Seminary in Chicago, remarked to an audience in a talk titled "The White Man's Burden" that "even here in Chicago, which is a black man's heaven, although he is less than 3 percent of the population, last year he furnished 10 percent of the crime." Civil rights and antilynching activist Ida B. Wells was in attendance. Worried that "race prejudice seemed to be growing in Chicago if that was the sort of address being given," Wells challenged McClure directly. In her address, she pointed to the misleading nature of the statistics. Far from being an indictment of black criminality, Wells contended, figures like these were simply indicative of how underserved black people were by city social work institutions.[45]

White Protestants on the front lines of prison ministry at the turn of the century sometimes saw things differently from Hoffman, Straton, and McClure, channeling instead the witness of Wells. In her memoir, Elizabeth Wheaton highlighted the practical results of a system that condemned blackness more often than not: "Judges often sentence men and women to years of hard labor in prison for the slightest offenses. An old colored man employed in a store took a box of cigars, but regretting the act, returned them and confessed his wrong, and asked forgiveness. He was arrested and sentenced to twenty-five years in the stockade; one year for each cigar."[46] In 1907 the Pentecostal Era Company published Clarissa Olds Keeler's *Crime of Crimes; or The Convict System Unmasked.*[47] Keeler, a copublisher with her husband of a religious paper, the *Banner of Love,* had originally presented part of this work at the National Convocation for Prayer in Saint Louis in 1903, a large tent revival meeting (which Wheaton also attended).[48] Her text was an eviscerating exposé of convict leasing. Laced with references to scripture and criminological statistics indicating the injustice of convict leasing, her presentations and writing "call[ed] the attention of the Christian people to the present condition of convicts, most of whom are colored, and many of whom are guilty of but trifling offences and some of them none at all."[49] Her work was a sharp indictment of the powers and principalities of the age, a way to, as she wrote in a letter to W. E. B. Du Bois, "*Expose it; expose it; agitate* the matter" (emphasis in the original; Du Bois wrote her back to thank her for her "work for [his] people").[50] As long as the south reenslaved its black men and women in labor camps, Keeler argued in capitalized letters, "THERE IS NO SUCH THING AS JUSTICE IN THE UNITED STATES IN THE PUNISHMENT OF CRIME."[51] As the century wore on and the national crime war began in earnest, race would remain a contested legal and religious site.

A New (Religious) Crime War

The 1920s through the 1940s saw the beginning of an expanded national vision and toughening attitude of policy and public opinion on crime. The moral crusades of the Progressive Era helped assuage worry about state involvement in crime fighting, and law enforcement expanded to address criminalized vices like drunkenness and prostitution. Concerns about vice lessened by the end of the 1920s, but worry about crime in general remained, and for good reason. Between 1900 and 1925 the national homicide rate grew by 50 percent (peaking in 1933), and in the first half of the 1920s violent crime rates doubled in several cities.[52]

Accompanying the rising concern over these increases was a shift in the public expectations of law enforcement. Incarceration rates had failed to track with the growing crime spree (in Chicago, for instance, less than a quarter of murderers were convicted from 1875 to 1920).[53] After World War I, Americans began to demand more from their politicians, prosecutors, and police officers. President Calvin Coolidge delivered public appeals on the need for law observance in response and formed the National

Crime Commission to study the problem.[54] President Herbert Hoover launched the first real federal policy broadsides on crime.[55] Often new crime-fighting efforts undertaken during his administration were responses to particular offenses that had engendered alarm. For example, the famous kidnapping and murder of Charles and Anne Lindbergh's young son in 1932 (one of several kidnappings of the children of wealthy families at the time) drew public outcry and led to the enactment of the Lindbergh Law by Congress, making kidnapping a federal offense. Though Hoover was initially reluctant to increase the government's law enforcement capacities at the expense of the rights of individual states, he eventually signed this law and others that formed the foundation for the immense enlargement of federal, state, and local crime-fighting efforts. Under Hoover, federal law enforcement began to be professionalized, and new governmental agencies were assembled to fight crime in its various forms, such as the Federal Bureau of Narcotics. President Franklin Roosevelt (who had previously served on Coolidge's National Crime Commission) went even further, increasing federal law enforcement powers by linking the fight against crime with the New Deal. Roosevelt entrusted Attorney General Homer Cummings with this expansion. Cummings did not disappoint, enacting policy and justifying newly expanded law enforcement powers to the media. It was in this climate that a young J. Edgar Hoover transformed the Justice Department's small Bureau of Investigation into an innovative and bellicose beachhead against organized crime, a band of "G-men" who battled (and sometimes killed) high-profile gangsters such as John Dillinger, Bonnie and Clyde, and Baby Face Nelson.[56]

The result of these efforts was that from the 1920s through the 1940s, crime began to be cast primarily as a *law enforcement* issue, not simply a problem to be addressed through social reform measures, whether by the penitentiaries themselves, via prison ministry reformers like those in the Salvation Army, or through changes in penal philosophy. In the years following World War I, criminals were increasingly portrayed as cancerous outsiders to American society, not the natural result of its economic or racial dislocations.[57] Crime was also progressively understood as a problem with a universal geography, one that deserved *national* attention. Prohibition (which was enshrined in a constitutional amendment in 1920) foreshadowed this universalized approach to crime, and lawmakers, police, and prosecutors in county, state, and federal agencies began directing attention to suspects beyond the neighborhood level.[58] The results of these efforts can be seen in the dramatic rise in nationwide imprisonment rates.

After a brief, sharp rise in the 1880s, imprisonment rates grew only slightly from 1890 to the early 1920s, from 72 to 74 prisoners per 100,000. From 1923 to 1930, however, the rate jumped from 74 to 98 per 100,000, and the decade after that from 98 to 125, a 69 percent increase.[59]

At a 1934 anticrime conference, President Roosevelt summarized the recent expansion and heightened intensity of American criminal justice. He began his remarks with reference to the necessity of increased governmental intervention in the nation's economy in order to address the poverty of the Great Depression. But simply clothing the naked and feeding the hungry was not enough. The New Deal needed guardians. With typical oratorical prowess, he argued, "As a component part of the large objective we include our constant struggle to safeguard ourselves against the attacks of the lawless and criminal elements of our population. Relentlessly and without compromise the Department of Justice has moved forward in its major offensive against these forces. With increasing effectiveness, state and local agencies are directing their efforts toward the achievement of law enforcement; and with them, in more marked degree than ever before, the Federal Government has worked toward the common objective." But Roosevelt also knew that expansion of the anticrime cause needed strong cultural footing if policy changes were to gain any long-term traction. He went on: "Widespread increase in capacity to substitute order for disorder is the remedy. This can only come through expert service in marshaling the assets of home, school, church, community, and other social agencies, to work in common purpose with our law enforcement agencies. . . . I ask you, therefore, to do all in your power to interpret the problem of crime to the people of this country."[60] The American home and school could run parallel to law enforcement, creating a culture where the intensification of crime fighting was both intelligible and expected. Indeed, both these institutions were frequent reference points in public discussions about crime, particularly juvenile delinquency. In this way, home and school were simply analogues of the federal government's increased entry into the nation's economy. The threat of a smack of the disciplinarian's ruler, whether on the mischievous mitts of youngsters or the invisible hand of the market, was essential for the nation's greater good.

But the import of religion—or "church," to use Roosevelt's term—to the crime problem was a different matter. Religion had already proved a capable tool for "interpreting" crime for Americans in decades past. And the present "church" boasted a slew of willing and able interpreters: the bishops, pastors, and rabbis who were willing to speak about issues of public concern from their pulpits and in their respective denominations. It was no surprise then that, during the 1920s, 1930s, and 1940s, religion was an ideal complement to crime's expanded geography and newly sharpened diagnosis. This religious affinity maintained the past framing of crime and lawlessness in sacred terms while also extending the cultural roots of American law and order. Police officers themselves had been named as objects of Christian concern, but there was hope that the work of officers of the law might be seen as a sacred task itself. This sacralization was literal: the very crime conference at which Roosevelt spoke (which had been organized by Attorney General Cummings) had begun with a "special inspiration service" at the Washington Cathedral and closed with an address by Methodist bishop Francis J. McConnell.[61]

Rhetoric about crime around this time generally took two forms. The first was a punitive perspective, which painted crime in terms of moral decline and individual culpability while arguing for a tough crackdown in response. The second form championed a progressive approach, pushing for the recognition of social factors in understanding the causes of crime, such as poverty or the negative influence of the entertainment industry. But though progressives recommended that part of the answer to crime was addressing these influences, they insisted on making *crime* (not poverty or other social ills) the primary problem to be solved and therefore argued alongside conservatives for the strengthening of law enforcement capabilities. Each of these perspectives had roots in broader currents in American life, including concerns about race. Both perspectives also had religious proponents and helped lead to the development of important changes in modern American criminal justice.

Preaching Punishment and "the Sword of Justice"

The punitive anticrime cause framed lawlessness as a threat facing America, and harsher punishment as the answer. Religious concern with crime was not new, but until this point there had been some hesitancy about how to best frame a response to the problem theologically. For instance, in the years following the Civil War, some conservative Protestants had even stressed the futility of police action or the fact that crime was an unavoidable sign of the impending end times. A massive, coordinated state response therefore was as undesirable as it was unlikely.[62] By the 1920s, however, many ministers (especially conservative Protestants) would eschew peaceful pacification and pessimism alike for the state's use of violent force as the default, even righteous, response to criminal acts.

The punitive approach generally saw crime as rooted in human sin, whether in the criminal act itself or in broader contempt for America's laws. Sin as an explanatory category was a powerful way to universalize wrongdoing, and preachers who needed a convenient shorthand to illustrate total depravity began relying on crime as a generalizable example. This sin was seen in individualistic terms that imbued crime with, in the words of one Baptist newspaper, "moral accountability." Criminals like Leopold and Loeb make a clear choice to commit murder as a means of thrill seeking, the piece argued. Though this act was a symptom of a spiritual disease afflicting the entire social order, "such crime is always deliberate and willful." If criminals were morally accountable as individuals, then the response was clear: punishment, and more of it.[63] Punishments for lawbreaking were increasingly seen by religious figures as being too lenient, and police efforts to stop crime as lamentably, but not inevitably, anemic. One New York Presbyterian pastor illustrated both of these dynamics in a sermon excoriating the citizenry and courts because of the "weak and sickly sentimentality" that prevented executions from going forward. "Some say [crime] is a phantasy, an idea of the subjective self, a disease," the preacher thundered. "But the Church says it is sin, and that the Bible is right when it says: 'The wages of sin is death.'"[64]

These advocates usually (though not always) came from the conservative side of the religious spectrum, with the most ardent rhetoric originating from fundamentalists and other Protestants worried about the encroachment of modernism. In their minds, the fact that the affluent Leopold and Loeb had been enrolled at the University of Chicago (a bastion of liberal Protestantism), revered the atheist Nietzsche, and were defended by the agnostic Darrow was no coincidence. Indeed, this trial provided a convenient slippery slope–style argument for modernism's inevitable end. Billy Sunday's jeremiad about the case continued in this vein: "Precocious brains, salacious books, infidel minds—all helped to produce this murder."[65] William Jennings Bryan suggested at the Scopes trial that an evolutionary worldview was a motivating factor in the boys' crime, hence Darwinism's danger.[66] The southern Methodist bishop Warren A. Candler found the Leopold and Loeb trial more significant than that of Scopes, writing that the murder showed the futility of materialistic self-indulgence, the logical outcome of the evolutionary worldview that the University of Chicago propagated.[67] John Roach Straton, who had voiced worries about black lawlessness twenty years earlier, had a more direct response to the Franks murder. It was in keeping with the fundamentalist movement he was now firmly allied with, as pastor of New York's Calvary Baptist Church: "[Leopold and Loeb] are simply Modernists who have let their Modernism go to the full and logical limit of utter unbelief in God and heartlessness toward man."[68] Though it did not mention the Leopold and Loeb trial, a 1925 issue of the fundamentalist magazine *King's Business* rendered these refrains with artistic embellishment. On its cover, an illustration of an "unbelieving preacher-professor" faced a judge, who named the modernist intellectual responsible for "destruction of faith in the Bible as the Word of God" and "the tidal wave of vice and crime."[69]

If modernism was the problem, swift lethal justice was the answer. Chicago pastor Arthur Kaub lamented, "When notorious criminals are found guilty of atrocious crimes deserving the death penalty, a host of sympathetic people intercede for them, urging pardon or lesser sentence." Instead, the clergyman argued, "we must not shirk responsibility. . . . We must have the law upheld, justice meted out and proper punishment executed upon the evildoer."[70] Upon hearing the verdict that Leopold and Loeb would receive prison sentences and not death, other pastors launched critiques of the "weaklings" on the bench who threatened to "undermine the philosophy on which our civilization is based" by allowing the two to "escape the sword of justice."[71] Pastor Simon Peter Long, who defended capital punishment as a "means of grace" earlier in his career, offered what he saw as a more humanitarian gloss that reinforced the connection of law with gospel. He told the gathered faithful at Wicker Park Lutheran Church in Chicago that execution was the boys' best eternal hope, as it would give them impetus to repent. As the headline of the *Chicago Daily Tribune* article featuring Long declared, the noose was the duo's "only salvation."[72]

In the years following the Leopold and Loeb trial, conservative Protestants continued their assault on crime as a broader symptom of modernist indulgence. Carl McIntire, one of the most influential fundamentalists of the twentieth century, made crime part of his first foray into public life in 1927. Though better known for his later assaults on communism and ecumenism, McIntire's very first public speech focused on lawlessness. "America is the greatest criminal nation on earth," he said. "Crime is an ever-flowing tide, engulfing our entire nation, claiming our freedom, crippling our democracy, never ebbing." After painting a chilling portrait of corrupt courts and the murders and robberies befalling American cities, McIntire called on citizens to demand justice and meet the "army of one million criminals marching up and down our land tonight" with the same force that they might meet an invading army. His closing lines were commanding: "Will we permit law violence that will ultimately mean the undermining of our democratic system? No! We will rally to the fight in the name of democracy, in the name of humanity, in the name of the unborn children, in the name of God return the verdict of public opinion. 'Guilty, Guilty Criminal!'—and then our courts will pronounce the sentence, 'Criminal thou shalt not pass.'" This final phrase indicated some restraint on McIntire's part, as "not pass" was scribbled over the original typewritten wording that read, "Criminal thou shalt die." But the underlying sentiment was still the same: God-fearing citizens must stand strong and take drastic measures against the chaotic menace of criminality.[73]

This speech was remarkably secular compared with McIntire's later preaching, focusing primarily on social change and civic involvement over evangelism. However, the spiritual significance of crime was apparently so compelling that McIntire soon abandoned his plans to pursue a career in law and enrolled in seminary. Defending America from her enemies within and without would become his ministerial vocation, and castigation of criminal activities was a perfect entry point into this work.[74]

In the Scopes trial, conservatives won the legal judgment but lost the sympathy of many Americans. With Leopold and Loeb's case, however, conservatives lost their death penalty appeals but nonetheless realized that their insistence on crime as a national issue of religious significance could have deep affinities with broader mainstream culture. The most obvious example was the presence of religious figures and rhetoric in law-and-order-style crime conferences that proliferated in the late 1920s and 1930s. The 1933 National Anti-Crime Conference was a prominent example. Convened by the United States Flag Association in Washington, DC, the conference was marketed as a response to the "present frightful crime situation." Though the Flag Association had been incorporated nine years earlier to help youths resist communism and anti-American ideologies, the organization now focused its energies on crime—"the gravest moral issue that the Nation has ever had to face." The association, with representatives from governmental, educational, and religious organizations, gathered "to formally mark the awakening of American people as regards crime." The conference's organizers were not shy in proclaiming the greatness of this particular awakening, contending that "the National Anti-Crime Conference will go down in history as one of the most important and far-reaching conferences in the annals of the Nation."[75]

The organizers could be forgiven for their ambitious self-assessment. They had received a public endorsement from President Roosevelt (who, along with two previous presidents, served as honorary chair of the Flag Association) and their organizing committee included prominent law enforcement officials, senators, and judges. As if to prove the lethal seriousness of crime and the need for an all-out assault against it, leaders from the US armed services lent their expertise to the campaign, with former secretary of war Patrick J. Hurley serving as lead organizer.[76]

Conference speakers proposed a variety of practical responses to the crime problem. Some called for modernizing and sharpening law enforcement practices, such as by standardizing a universal process of fingerprinting and changing laws to permit police to frisk suspects without warrants. Others decried broader cultural sympathy with criminals, brought on by crime's glamorization in newspapers and movies.[77] Judge Marcus Kavanagh of Illinois, who had previously written a book on the dangers of crime and the need for tougher enforcement entitled *The Criminal and His Allies,* called for a return to flogging prisoners convicted of serious crimes.[78] Attorney General Cummings saw the conference as the perfect venue to announce the acquisition of a new, secure prison from the War Department "for confinement of defiant and dangerous criminals." Popularly known as Alcatraz, this prison served as the perfect encapsulation of the federal government's new push for domestic security, a national beacon for law and order in the middle of San Francisco Bay.[79]

Religion was also part of the conference proceedings, an attempt to rectify what one speaker saw as "the apathy of preachers and church leaders" on crime.[80] Judge Kavanagh, a noted Catholic who had dedicated an entire chapter in his book to "the church and the criminal," argued in his conference address that the answer to crime was fundamentally a "return to the old-time reverence of Almighty God."[81] In an address tellingly entitled "The Church and Crime," the Jesuit priest and anticommunist crusader Edmund A. Walsh diagnosed the crime problem in a similar manner, albeit with more sophistication. Though he had elsewhere celebrated the judge and "courageous jury" that convicted Al Capone, Walsh was not quite as retributively minded as Kavanagh, decrying the idolatry of "Law" if it was executed without reference to divine guidance. But Walsh did point out how the rising tides of secularism obfuscated criminals' recognition of the justice of their punishment.[82] The problem with law enforcement, he argued, was not that it was forceful but that it increasingly lacked a transcendent reference point.

As the conference closed, a resolution offered by the Right Rev. J. E. Freeman, the Episcopal bishop of the diocese of Washington, DC, was adopted. Freeman served along with Catholic and Jewish representatives on the Flag Association's board of founders. He called on Protestant, Catholic, Jewish, and Greek Orthodox congregations to set aside two days in November for consideration of crime conditions and "awakening of the people to the imperative need of rededication to patriotic ideals and principles." Indeed, the cause of crime was so tied to the mission of the church, Freeman argued, that "unless the church is aroused to a more militant attitude on these matters it will experience a great loss of interest in years to come. The church can hardly hope to survive unless it assumes its parts and responsibility in these campaigns."[83] A few months after the conference, the Flag Association formed the Washington Church Committee, composed of clergymen from the District of Columbia, to, in the words of the *Washington Post,* "formulate a program for immediate unification of all religious forces in the fight on lawlessness . . . to make churches a strong arm in the attack."[84] As with any successful revival, awakened hearts needed unity, accountability, and a sense of mission if they were to persist in faithfulness.

With the blessing of religious leaders and language at gatherings like this, an American crime-fighting culture was being constructed in Washington. This culture helped sustain the expanding and toughening crime policy charge that Hoover, Roosevelt, Cummings, and others were leading.[85] On the local level, leaders were similarly vocal about the connection of faith to public life and contributed to crime commissions and conferences in states and cities nationwide. The Chicago Crime Commission had as one of its founders a man named Frank Loesch, a prominent lawyer and elder and Bible-study leader at the city's Fourth Presbyterian Church, and counted the president and secretary of the Moody Bible Institute as members and trustees. Loesch regularly hailed the need for a "Christian approach" to public service and was a constant presence in the fight against the city's violent and influential gangsters. After some early setbacks in failed mob prosecutions, Loesch won the day with his innovation of a "public enemy" list, with Capone in the top slot. The list and accompanying media campaign turned the formerly ambivalent tide of public opinion against the mobsters and helped push federal investigators to prosecute Capone for tax evasion. As the "pioneer of the crime commission movement," the Chicago effort also successfully pushed the city to eliminate unwarranted continuances in criminal cases and helped obtain convictions of murder suspects who had been "unjustifiably exonerated."[86] A similar Los Angeles commission garnered the support of the city's Church Federation, which publicized its endorsement of proposed legislation to lower the criminal convictions threshold from a unanimous jury vote to a simple majority.[87]

White elites in America's halls of power were not the only ones championing the sacred cause of law and order. African Americans had endured high crime rates in their own communities for generations, a result of limited economic opportunities and whites' ability to harass or even lynch black people with few legal consequences. Black ministers and churches were frequent anticrime advocates along these lines. The Harlem pastor and civil rights leader Adam Clayton Powell Jr., who would later lead the famed Abyssinian Baptist Church and serve in the US Congress, attacked the "crooks, racketeers, bootleggers, kidnapers, and lynchers, abetted by politicians," who were "flaunting themselves in the face of decent society."[88] Black leaders actually saw antilynching and anticrime as complementary enough to criticize the National Anti-Crime Conference *not* for its inflated rhetoric but for failing to consider lynching as a worthy issue in its proceedings.[89] In a 1931 sermon, one black Ohio minister lambasted the apparent effects that Clarence Darrow's work on behalf of Leopold and Loeb was having in American life: "Darrow's defense . . . [has] done more to animate and perpetuate the crime wave in America than any hundred cases combined. . . . Such lawyers are largely responsible for the criminal conditions confronting the nation and for the apparent breaking down of all law and order."[90] A coalition of black ministers from Chicago joined in 1935 to promote "churchdom's war on crime," addressing the police department's indifference to corruption, prostitution, illegal liquor trade, gambling, theft, and juvenile delinquency in their South Side neighborhoods.[91]

Some of these appeals reflected the tendency of more conservative black leaders to attack lawbreakers from their own communities even as they criticized lynching and other racially motivated crimes committed by whites. Though often evidence of the prejudices that black elites had against lower classes in their midst, it possibly reflected a pragmatic consideration as well, as black leaders striving for broader respectability knew they had to echo the anticrime sentiments that normally came from white leaders.[92] At a "War on Crime" gathering in Louisville, one black pastor denounced the killing of black people. But in the words of a journalist covering the event, "there were white folks present and Rev. Huglette had to show them that he hated all murderers—even those who kill white folks." According to the journalist, Huglette even condemned recent efforts to give a black man convicted of the murder of a white man a life sentence instead of the death penalty. He said "he should burn until he was blue in the face," a comment that led the journalist to note, "These were strong words coming from a preacher standing in his pulpit where weekly he no doubt recites 'Thou shalt not kill.'"[93] Yet these were exactly the kind of sentiments to be expected of any preacher who wished to join America's religious crime-fighting consensus, a reflection of similar exhortations by many white preachers at the time.

Crime and Progressive Religion

The alternative to the punitive approach was a progressive paradigm championed by a broad coalition of liberal Protestants, Catholics, and Jews. Advocates of this perspective often critiqued the rhetoric of those advocating harsher punishment and expanded police presence. Some went on to work inside prisons with convicts themselves, bringing a new perspective to prison ministry through the cutting-edge tools of modern social science. However, this progressive, "sociological" approach also helped fuel the broader war on crime in its own way, as it further defined the issue in religious terms and increased the state's scope and influence in addressing lawbreaking.

The sociological approach to crime had its roots in Progressive Era discussions about the root causes of social ills. Activists and thinkers in this period challenged the American "bootstraps" mythology by pointing to the *environmental* factors that led to poverty. Similarly, Progressive Era prison reformers problematized assignment of clear-cut moral blame to criminals. Crime, these reformers and advocates of the "new penology" argued, was the result of any number of social, psychological, cultural, and economic factors, from poor sanitation to urban overcrowding to job loss to mental trauma.[94] Not unlike the humanitarian prison campaigners of the antebellum era, these reformers also emphasized the need to transform punitive punishment and ghastly prisons into therapeutic havens.[95]

The religious parallel to the progressive environmental emphasis was the social gospel, with late nineteenth-century roots in both lay organizing efforts on behalf of the working class and leaders' published pleadings for Christians to address the "social crisis" of industrializing urban centers.[96] By the turn of the twentieth century, the overarching message of the social gospel, that a truly Christian response to issues of poverty and injustice necessitated the dismantling of the unjust economic structures (and not simply a spiritualized gospel, calls for individual responsibility, or nominal displays of charity), had achieved official recognition in many of the denominations of American Protestantism.[97]

The temperance crusade was a major outgrowth of the social gospel coalition, one that helped initiate the expanded reach of law enforcement while also garnering support from more conservative Protestants.[98] But it also alienated Roman Catholics and Jews, many of whom saw Prohibition as little more than concealed Protestant bigotry against European immigrants of both faiths who had fewer qualms about alcohol use.[99] The anticrime cause, though it had conceptual affinities with Prohibition, proved far more compelling to a broad religious audience. By the mid-1920s this cause had coalesced into a definable progressive movement, with criminologists and politicians joining with religious leaders to call on the nation to address broader social ills in order to combat crime. The *Christian Herald*, an ecumenical Protestant newspaper that at the turn of the twentieth century had nearly a quarter million subscribers (the most widely read religious periodical in the world), widened its strident anti-alcohol stance into a much broader 1925 campaign it called the Christian Conscience Crusade.[100] The crusade was a general call for American Christians to practice good citizenship and to pray for their country, but the *Herald* regularly framed it as a spiritual assault on crime and lawlessness. A variety of politicians voiced their support of the crusade for its wide-ranging appeal beyond the temperance issue with its attention to crime. It was good, the governor of Vermont wrote in a letter to the *Herald*, that the crusade was "not only about the Prohibition law enforcement but also about all law enforcement." It meant, as later issues of the *Herald* showcased, that northern Catholic politicians like New York governor Al Smith (who opposed Prohibition) could support the crusade and its broader campaign for national "reverence and obedience."[101]

The Leopold and Loeb trial provided an opportunity for liberal religious leaders to contrast their perspective with that of law-and-order conservatives. Their key appeal was the impropriety of capital punishment. The Rev. Charles Francis Potter of the West Side Unitarian Church in New York City (and occasional theological sparring partner of John Roach

Straton) noted that "the most vehement protestors against [the judge] giving life imprisonment, instead of death, have been Christian ministers," owing to the fact that a literal reading of the Bible would naturally lead one to support capital punishment: "Orthodox religion opposes progress as usual." Instead, he argued, "exact justice cannot be secured unless a careful study of the mentality of the prisoner is made."[102] The Rev. Dr. Edward Taber assailed the death penalty sentence of a different murder case before telling his Baltimore Baptist congregation, "In imposing life imprisonment upon Leopold and Loeb I think the judge exercised the right decision." Yet, adopting the modernist mantle himself, Taber acknowledged his chief complaint regarding criminal justice at the time: it "is very unscientific."[103] Few defendants could afford to draw on such an array of psychiatric experts, as Leopold and Loeb had, and most other criminal cases unfortunately proceeded with little reference to the troubling backgrounds or stilted development of the accused.

As crime became a broader issue of public concern in the late 1920s and early 1930s, clergy increasingly echoed arguments made by advocates for the progressive position. For example, in a 1932 convention held at Columbia University by the Religious Education Association, more than one hundred Protestant, Catholic, and Jewish educators (including representatives from Catholic law schools and the Federal Council of Churches [FCC]) gathered to consider the problem of crime. The conclusion of the conference was that "maladjustment" of individuals to their social environment was crime's root cause. Though there was argument among participants over the best way to address this fact, one participant reported, "We agreed that the behavior of a child is determined to a great degree by the locality—the social matrix. Moral conduct is a function of the situation and in order to do something for the individual, something must be done for the situation in which he lives."[104] Crime's true reference point was not found exclusively in an individual's moral consciousness, but also in the living conditions that made unsavory choices more likely.

Criminological and legal specialists themselves invoked religious concepts to articulate the progressive position. Sanford Bates, president of the American Prison Association and future director of the US Bureau of Prisons, wrote an article for the *Christian Register* (later reprinted in booklet form) entitled "Crime and Christianity: What Can the Church Do about It?" Bates challenged the notions that the recent crime wave was the result of lenient judges, blundering police officers, or the lack of a punitive deterrent. Instead, he cited eight real causes of crime, including the country's failure to assimilate "various racial strains" and unregulated possession of firearms. But the final cause Bates cited was that "the church, having largely relieved the individual from the pressure of fear as to the hereafter, has not yet replaced it with a religion of performance." The church had lost its way on the crime issue because it had not stressed enough "the comprehensive moral and social program of education and social co-operation" to change criminals' hearts and minds. The correct response to the crime from "any Christian government" should not be to "punish people into obedience," for "only good will, education, tolerance, and the power of a good example can lift a community out of crime into a state of peace and good conduct." Concluding with a word directed to "the Liberal Christian church," Bates called for engagement with scientific learning and a revival of the belief that "by their works shall ye know them." When the church remembers the divine power of knowledge and deeds, "there will be no crime."[105] Bates knew his audience well. His scientism, optimistic anthropology, and trust in the salvific power of Christian works crystallized key aspects of the broader modernist Christian project that sought to adapt religion to human culture.[106]

"The Liberal Christian church" found another capable ally in the pursuit of a crime-free nation in Charles Tuttle, US attorney for the Southern District of New York and a prominent Episcopal layman. Well known for his battles against political corruption and mobsters since being appointed to his post by President Coolidge in 1927, Tuttle frequently called for "an organized study of the crime problem and of the duties of the Church with regard thereto."[107] Tuttle hoped that such an effort could be launched by the FCC, and less than one year later he served as "toastmaster" at the twenty-first annual dinner of the council. Speaking from a stage with religious luminaries like Bishop Francis J. McConnell and Harry Emerson Fosdick, Tuttle proposed to the crowd that the church had to address the "greatest problem facing America today, that of crime." But the answer to this problem, Tuttle argued, comes "from within, and not by outside legislation," through the church manifesting a "spirit of peace."[108] He also argued in a radio address as an interfaith representative that individuals were not the only ones culpable for criminal acts, but society as well: "Crime is a problem for education and for the church as well as it is one for government." To truly combat crime, the church needed to do its part to address the "spiritual illiteracy" and "blatant materialism" endemic to American society.[109] Tuttle later echoed these themes as a Protestant representative at a large prison convention in Baltimore.[110] The other speakers at the convention were a mix of religious, legal, and criminological professionals, including US attorney general William Mitchell, Sanford Bates, law school deans from Northwestern and Duke, Sing Sing prison warden Lewis Lawes, and Rev. Christian Reisner of Broadway Temple Methodist Episcopal Church in New York. In his address, Tuttle criticized the inability of harsh American prisons to address crime: "The permanent solution of the crime problem does not lie in force and punishment" but in tackling America's spiritual deficit. Many of the conference's speakers also fanned out to preach at over twenty Baltimore congregations in honor of "Prison Sunday."[111] Baptist, Brethren, Presbyterian, and Methodist churches all hosted these guest preachers, guaranteeing that the connection of crime and religious concern would transcend more narrow denominational loyalties.[112]

The ministerial role that emerged as a direct result of this approach to the crime problem was that of the clinically trained, state-sponsored prison chaplain. The prison chaplain's role was to highlight the "social matrix," to bring the latest tools of psychological and social scientific investigation to bear in the ministry, and to exhibit sensitivity to religious diversity. This was a significant break with past prison ministry paradigms, such as that of evangelists Maud Booth and Elizabeth Wheaton. Historian Stephanie Muravchik tells the story of an encounter in 1939 between enterprising pastor Stephen T. Wood (who regularly visited inmates at an Illinois prison) and Arnold Dunshee, a professional prison chaplain. Wood related his ministry experiences at the prison to Dunshee, in hope that he might be hired on at the facility full time. He told of his time praying with prisoners and of his ultimate goal: to "bring men to Christ." But Dunshee would have none of it. Dunshee's striking response, Muravchik writes, was to "declare the man utterly unfit to be a chaplain anywhere." Wood had failed Dunshee's informal test because he "was thinking and behaving exactly as Protestant ministers had long done." By contrast, Dunshee noted later in a training brochure, he was looking for prison workers who would approach their work with a different professional bent: "first-hand knowledge of problems of physical health, mental hygiene, and penology," acquired through "supervised clinical training."[113]

As Dunshee's requirements indicated, in the years around World War II, growing numbers of penal and religious authorities began to see innovations in social scientific investigation and psychological treatment as key to prison chaplains' religious mission and the prison's rehabilitative goals. This kind of work required significant training. Chaplains were increasingly required not only to have graduated from seminary and receive denominational endorsement but also complete units in clinical pastoral education (CPE). CPE was a certification system rooted in several historical streams: growing interest in connecting psychology with religion (as seen in the work of thinkers like William James), John Dewey's experiential philosophy of education, and the broader emergence of clinical and "case study" educational forms in legal and medical training.[114] CPE eventually formalized into a type of ministry that emphasized patient-centered pastoral counseling through practices of presence, listening, and moral guidance.[115] It was not missionary work, as prison evangelists had practiced in years past. Instead it was, as Anton T. Boisen (later called the "father of clinical pastoral education") put it, attention to "living human documents."[116]

Students of Boisen innovated clinical training programs and by 1932 had developed programs in mental hospitals, general hospitals, and a prison.[117] Not long after, two prison chaplaincy organizations based on CPE philosophy and training requirements formed, the American Correctional Chaplains Association and the American Protestant Correctional Chaplains Association.[118] This new paradigm was increasingly preferred by prison administrations because it was adaptable to the prison environment. Chaplains could be hired and evaluated with reference to set professional standards and guilds, and their work was intelligible to the progressive correctional ideals that administrators saw as characteristic of modern penology. Prison administrators increasingly saw nineteenth-century evangelical penal projects as failures, but there was a sense of optimism that prisons could still be redeemed and crime could be reduced. Chaplains would be their key allies in mobilizing the tools of modern science, particularly with new empirical methods for classifying and treating deviance.[119]

One Problem, One Solution

The punitive and progressive perspectives diverged in their analysis of America's crime problem. But two beliefs they shared would prove far more influential in the grand scheme of the history of the relationship of religion to modern American criminal justice: the belief that rising crime reflected growing secularity and the belief that disciplinary state power was ultimately responsible for addressing this problem. Race would remain an important, if sometimes unstated, framing concern for this consensus.

The pastors who called Leopold and Loeb modernists were the most assertive exponents of secularism's connection to crime. But they were in good company, as indicated by the frequent references to the travails of irreligion by other anticrime advocates. Rabbis who spoke out on crime generally leaned in the direction of the progressive diagnosis and were less worried than conservative Protestants about the rise of modernist tendencies in American intellectual life. But like so many of their Protestant and Catholic contemporaries, they were no less willing to connect crime to rising secularity. In a 1926 Yom Kippur sermon, New York rabbi Samuel Schulman assailed the conscious and unconscious forms of atheism in modern life, blaming the surge of lawlessness on the "inner contempt of law . . . that denial of any compelling authority to moral ideas." Just blocks away, on the same day, Rabbi Rudolph Grossman noted how crime was not limited to the lower classes but was spread throughout modern society: "This lawless spirit does not confine itself to the illiterate and the depraved. It manifests itself in other forms, among the enlightened, the well-situated and socially respected." It was truly an "epidemic," a secular social contagion that showed no concern for class, color, or creed.[120]

At a time when acceptance of the religious "other" by the Protestant establishment was by no means a guarantee, the crime issue allowed Protestants, Catholics, and Jews to all seek state protection of what Will Herberg would later call the "common religion" of "the American way of life."[121] The emergence of "tri-faith America" has been framed as a product of a pluralist vision that emerged in the 1930s through common critique of international fascism and communism.[122] But the anticrime cause helped provide *domestic* fuel for the manufacture of another "Judeo-Christian" consensus, in terms of shared rhetoric as well as organizational unity. "Why can't we all stand together, no matter what our denomination or creed?" wondered Asa Keyes, the district attorney of Los Angeles, before a packed crowd of 5,300 people at Aimee Semple McPherson's Angelus Temple, as part of an address entitled "The Part of the Church in Law Enforcement." Police, prosecutors, and a wide spectrum of religious folk all had a common task, he argued: "We are all engaged in making this country of ours a better one in which to live."[123] At a Catholic gathering in New York focused on youth crime, Cardinal Joseph Hayes welcomed Protestant and Jewish partners in the fight against delinquency: "You have given me an experience of encouragement, inspiration and consolation. . . . This cannot be called a 'Catholic conspiracy' today, because we have you in the boat with us." He later praised a Presbyterian judge's address about youths' need for religion, saying his speech contained "the Catholic spirit."[124] The same ecumenical disposition was on full display at another crime conference held in Albany, New York, where Protestant, Catholic, and Jewish ministers each led sessions on religious approaches to the harmful social environments that led to crime, and took turns opening the other conference sessions with prayers.[125]

State-sponsored chaplains were exemplifications of this ecumenical consciousness. Not only had they relinquished a conversion-centered paradigm, they also moved ministry to incarcerated people away from association with particular religious traditions. Part of this was a response to new demands by prisoners, as religious minorities such as Jehovah's Witnesses and Muslims increasingly pushed for recognition in the years around World War II. The military chaplaincy paradigm that had emerged during World War I was also no doubt influential as a parallel site of patriotic cultivation of a flexible "moral monotheism" that could manage difference in broader service to the state's use of force.[126] Based on these demands and the ecumenical sensibilities of practitioners, prison chaplaincy developed into a *maintenance* role, a "ministry of presence" to help prisoners avail themselves of the "free market in religion."[127] Chaplains still came from particular religious backgrounds. But they did their best to operate as neutral spiritual leaders: they were to be addressed as "Chaplain," not "Reverend," "Rabbi," or "Father."[128] These perspectives and policies took some time to filter down into state prisons, but by mid-century it was clear they were having an effect in forming a new generation of prison workers. At a meeting sponsored by the American Correctional Association, the associate secretary of the Methodist church's commission on chaplains (which oversaw five hundred chaplains) noted to the gathering, "A narrow-minded Methodist can be of no earthly use to a Jew or a Catholic, or vice versa."[129]

Liberals and conservatives within religious traditions also found common cause in framing crime as a religious issue. Though they would have disagreed on any number of other doctrinal points, they could both assent to the proposition that, in the words of the conservative *Moody Monthly,* "causing this wave of crime there is a wave of anti-theism."[130] Or as the more liberal Tuttle put it, crime was "a symptom of widespread paganism" found in a "purely acquisitive and secular" society.[131] Even Clarence Darrow (not known for religious convictions) concurred with the prevailing Christian opinion during the Leopold and Loeb trial that Nietzschean secularism was to blame for his client's moral blindness. "Is any blame attached because somebody took Nietzsche's philosophy seriously and fashioned his life upon it?" he pleaded fervently. "It is hardly fair to hang a 19-year-old boy for the philosophy that was taught him at the university."[132]

The religious valence of crime was recognized by the new class of penal experts who contributed to the emerging field of criminology. Over the course of the nineteenth and early twentieth centuries, various theorists had increasingly approached the problem of crime with the tools of evolutionary biology, economics, phrenology, and psychiatry. A common thread among these approaches was a social scientific disposition that sought answers to deviance beyond simplistic explanations of human selfishness (much less theological definitions like "sin").[133] But some early theorists, such as Cesare Lombroso, known as the father of modern criminology, still analyzed the social effects of religious tradition on crime rates (Lombroso concluded that religions that prevent crime tended to be new, "fanatical," or "passionately moral").[134] Into the 1920s and 1930s, other theorists in the field regularly debated religion's role in reducing crime. Since currently "crime pays so well" given that criminals typically escape punishment and maintain respectability, a lasting, more transcendent deterrent was needed: "There can be but one great deterrent and that is the power of religion."[135] Other pieces questioned the helpful connection of religion to crime, using statistical analysis to show how church affiliation did not prevent crime, or critiqued the theological rationale for retributive definitions of punishment.[136] The Italian criminologist Raffaele Garofalo, a student of Lombroso, argued for a balanced perspective, one that recognized religion as a "moralizing force" and "restraining influence" for potential criminals even as it acknowledged its limitations for serious offenders.[137] Either way, religion was recognized as a worthy topic of debate for understanding common responses to crime, even if some criminologists ultimately discounted its significance. Whether crime was truly "our crown of thorns," as the title of a 1932 piece in the *Journal of Criminal Law and Criminology* put it, the fact that many Americans believed that "democracy is being crucified on the cross of crime" meant that the famously secular criminological profession was cognizant of religion's import for its area of study.[138]

The frequent presence of clergy at anticrime gatherings, pastors' willingness to preach on crime in their church and synagogue services, and the frequent discussion of faith in criminological journals guaranteed that the issue would be framed as a religious one. Pastors saw the blessing of the anticrime cause with their prayers and presence as a civic obligation. As the spokesman of sixty ministers of Nashville preached in a sermon entitled "Christian Citizenship," "We have represented from our pulpits the Community Chest, the Red Cross, the March of Dimes; we feel the time has come for us to speak for the protection of our wives and children and businesses against crime and lawlessness."[139] Christian pastors linked the gospel and governmental obedience even more closely. One African American pastor in Atlanta encouraged the church to evangelize not only the lost souls who "never attend church" but also those who "oppose law and order," while the head of the FCC, in an attempt to rouse "militant public opinion" in the fight against organized crime, urged readers of the *Christian Herald* to push the demands of the law even as they preached the gospel: "Remember Sinai, as well as Calvary!"[140]

Though these civic-minded conservative and liberal religious leaders may have disagreed about how crime should be diagnosed and treated, they shared assumptions and policy proposals that evinced practical overlap where it really mattered: the bolstering of the disciplinary, law enforcement power of the state. The law-and-order side's contribution here was rather clear-cut. But despite the progressive approach's contrasting diagnosis, its effects were in keeping with the aims of advocates for a tougher and expanded state response. The first effect was rhetorical. Even when Charles Tuttle was denouncing the national tendency to "seek salvation in the passage of laws and deal with sins by statutes," he was still calling criminals a "Black Army," a term Judge Kavanagh also used in his writing. For Tuttle, criminals were "the host of darkness, who through stratagem, perfidy or force have placed on American soil a hostile warmachine more formidable in size and efficiency than any that before the World War ever invaded a civilized country."[141] The liberal *Christian Century*, though avowedly pacifist during the 1930s and 1940s in terms of American engagement with Nazism, nonetheless argued for an expanded federal criminal code and nationwide campaign against crime: "No 'recovery' is more important than a recovery of law-enforcement."[142]

Other liberal Protestant leaders with well-known social gospel or pacifist leanings made similar appeals, or at the least offered distinctions between policing and militarism. Harry Emerson Fosdick was quick to distinguish between the "satanic" temptation of war and the virtuous possibilities of local law enforcement, what he called "the salutary nature of coercion communally applied for the good of all."[143] As dean of the liberal University of Chicago Divinity School, Shailer Mathews urged

Figure 1.1 The popular *Christian Herald* newspaper named crime as a major area of concern and promoted a humanitarian form of Christian "missionary" policing as one solution. *Christian Herald,* March 11, 1903.

Christian laypeople to show "constant and expressed support" for law enforcement and held a Chicago Church Federation event with a district attorney to combat gangster influence.[144] Charles Sheldon, author of the best-selling novel *In His Steps* (which popularized the phrase "What would Jesus do?"), was fond of calling police "missionaries" and urged Christians everywhere to partner with the state in order to "abolish crime and establish law and order and decency."[145] Other interreligious groups paired punitive appeals with calls for recognition of the poverty that plagued their neighborhoods, putting themselves "on record behind a definite program of attack on crime."[146] With statements like these, liberals consistently framed crime as an issue of national concern that necessitated "war." This not only matched the rhetoric of more punitive voices but also engendered the same public expectations that *crime* itself (and not simply poverty or lack of education) was a distinct issue to be dealt with.

The expanded national scope of the crime war, the disconnection of criminal justice from other social reform measures, and the blessing of religious civic concern all coalesced at an FCC anniversary celebration in December 1933. This time, however, Tuttle, McConnell, and even Fosdick were outshone by the enormous celebrity that the FCC had secured as the keynote speaker: President Franklin Delano Roosevelt. The president congratulated the representatives of the twenty-five denominations present at the event and the FCC for twenty-five years of faithful service. More work needed to be done, but "your churches and the other churches— Gentile and Jew—recognize and stand ready to lead in a new war of peace—the war for social justice." This new war, in which government and churches were allied, entailed seeking out economic justice, advocating for fair wages, and "social planning . . . wholly in accord with the social teachings of Christianity." The war also entailed meting out justice to the violent oppressors who practice "lynch law." But, Roosevelt continued, "a thinking America goes further. It seeks a government of its own that will be sufficiently strong to protect the prisoner and at the same time to crystallize public opinion so clear that government of all kinds will be compelled to practice a more certain justice. The judicial function of government is the protection of the individual and of the community through quick and certain justice. That function in many places has fallen into a sad state of disrepair. It must be a part of our program to reestablish it." Though he had briefly mentioned the needs of prisoners, the overriding message was clear: a prosperous and fair America was an America safe from crime.[147]

It was not a stretch to imagine the punitive effects of rhetoric like this, even as it came from exponents of a more balanced approach to crime; a war cannot be fought without an army, and "quick and certain" victory was unlikely if its soldiers remained ill equipped. The following month, Roosevelt demanded legislative adoption of Attorney General Cummings's Twelve Point Crime Program (which expanded federal jurisdiction on crimes like bank robbery and extortion), and lawmakers responded by adding more provisions to the federal criminal code than all previous congresses.[148] Christian progressives also directly pushed for the expansion and toughening of criminal justice policy even as they pointed to the need for broader social improvement. Though he called the lawyers and the public to recognize the roots of crime in "maladjustment," Tuttle's "Black Army" became a key reference point in his calls for the modernization of police forces, streamlining of prosecution efforts, and centralization of states' law enforcement efforts in departments of justice.[149] He directed these policy recommendations at the legal professionals of the American Bar Association, and the organization responded positively, making them part of its public platform.[150] Tuttle himself was also a proponent of tougher penalties for perjury ("Treat 'em rough," he argued in one piece) and a law to send drug dealers to prison for life after a second conviction.[151] Confident, streamlined, and expanded criminal justice was the only way to win a war with such high stakes.

Race had framed earlier forms of religious law and order, such as in debates about black crime rates and lynching. This framing continued as the national crime war unfolded. The place of race in the crime war was complex. Both white and black religious leaders made anticrime appeals, often in generic terms that seemingly transcended race or ethnicity. White appeals in particular could appear color blind, as leaders spoke in harsh tones of lawbreakers of any and all stripes, from any neighborhood or town. But discourse and policing strategies that assumed black criminal pathology remained common into the 1940s and beyond.[152] And there were indications among religious voices that the national war on crime was unfolding in a manner that would continue to reify racial categories and affect black Americans disproportionately.

Voices that were missing in the ecumenical anticrime cause indicated the racial limits of the Judeo-Christian consensus. Most obviously, black Muslims emerged as a key focus of law enforcement around this time. Adherents of groups like the Moorish Science Temple underwent FBI surveillance and harassment soon after the religious movement's official launch in the mid-1920s. At the urging of J. Edgar Hoover, the FBI painted the group as subversive and a threat to the social order, despite the fact that investigations regularly showed no public danger. As Sylvester Johnson has written, "The Islamic, Asiatic nature of the diaspora that Moorish Americans signified was inevitably in conflict with the imperatives of racial Whiteness . . . the symbolic and material realities of the United States as a racial state."[153] This story repeated itself with the Nation of Islam in the 1940s and after. If Protestants, Catholics, and Jews were able to find common ground as faithful citizens concerned about crime, black Americans who claimed alternative allegiances and religious profiles that championed the cause of their race could be not only marginalized but targeted.

Frederick Hoffman's racialized crime statistics remained profoundly influential into the 1930s, when they were replaced by the FBI's *Uniform Crime Reports*.[154] In religious discussions, Hoffman's work could be cited in race-neutral terms, such in a 1929 Southern Baptist report on the "frightful homicide record" that reprinted his murder statistics.[155] But the argument of Hoffman, that high black crime rates indicated a unique black pathology, remained a common trope. Marcus Kavanagh, the outspoken Catholic judge from Chicago who had urged tough, prayerful justice at the Flag Association conference, mobilized forceful black pathology discourse in his anticrime rhetoric around the time of the Great Migration of southern African Americans to northern cities. He removed systemic or discriminatory factors from consideration of what he termed "negro criminal forces"; instead, the "chief enemy" of the black race was "the negro criminal."[156] If African Americans did not get their own house in order, Kavanagh said, law-abiding whites would have no other choice but to subdue black people who "continue to ravage and destroy."[157] To be sure, he did not believe in black people's innate inferiority, arguing in *The Criminal and His Allies* that God "could never create an inferior race" and made humans "of all colors" in "one family." But Kavanagh understood black Americans to have a massive *cultural* deficiency: they valorized criminals, they lacked self-reliance, and their advocacy organizations (likely referring to the NAACP) were unwilling to address the issue of black crime. Kavanagh cited Hoffman's black crime statistics and parroted his arguments on black pathology, contending that black people were more law abiding when under the influence of whites and less so when they lived in their own communities. In contrast to his own home of Chicago, with its high crime rates, growing black neighborhoods, and loss of moral and religious character, Kavanagh posited the city's northern neighbor of Wisconsin as the ideal: as part of its German heritage, the state had "good racial stock," "God-fearing traditions," and streamlined criminal procedure. And as a result, its crime rate was quite low, a model for the nation.[158]

Rhetoric like this had consequences. Not long after, Kavanagh sentenced two black men to death following their convictions for murder in a drugstore robbery. In a speech before the state parole board (urging denial of clemency), Kavanagh took the opportunity to remark on black crime in Chicago: "There are no fewer than 500 young Negroes south of 22nd St. whose business is robbery and whose instrument is the gun. . . . These men will murder anyone for the princely sum of $10." Discounting the possibility that black migrants were coming to the city to escape Jim Crow racism and southern poverty, Kavanagh claimed that "desperadoes" were "pouring into Chicago from the South to make robbery their business" and were a particular threat to "well-dressed white men." One answer, he proposed, would be to adopt new statutes that allowed the use of a whipping post.[159]

The contrast between the conclusions drawn by religious conservatives at the Leopold and Loeb trial a few years earlier (who blamed the influence of modernism) and Kavanagh's words about this trial of two black men (indicting their blackness) was a practical manifestation of a racial double standard. The *Chicago Defender*, the city's popular black newspaper, understood this and blasted the judge not for his verdict but for his racial prejudice. "It is the first time that a judge, sitting in a Chicago court, has taken it upon himself to label Chicago's crime black. It is the first time that one has dared to say openly that Chicago's dark citizenry is any more violently criminal than Chicago's white citizenry." Almost as if rebutting Hoffman alongside its critique of Kavanagh, the newspaper pointed to the presence of dangerous Italian and Irish gangsters and troublemaking white teens in the city, who all escaped Kavanagh's racial ire: "Will Judge Kavanaugh [sic] indict the white race because these murderers are white?" The newspaper blasted the state of criminal justice in the city more broadly, the ways that black Americans were unfairly blamed for crime and the horrible conditions they faced in jails. Equality before the law was needed—"less color-justice and more real justice." Only then would crime and lawlessness subside.[160]

There were other forms of anticrime advocacy that did not mention people of color at all but nonetheless had racialized effects precisely because of this omission. Southern Baptist Convention (SBC) resolutions from 1900 to 1940 reflected this sensibility. At this time, the SBC, which had emerged in 1845 as a result of the sectional split among American Baptists over slavery, was largely conservative. But the SBC did count a wide range of theological and political outliers among its members, from aggressive fundamentalists like J. Frank Norris to progressives in the denomination's social gospel–style Social Service Commission. Many in the SBC were segregationists, though there were some outspoken dissenters and critics of racial inequality.[161] The wide array of voices meant any cause that the SBC promoted would have to pass muster for the whole of the denomination and its diverse constituencies.

Crime was one such cause. From 1906 to 1941 the denomination passed several resolutions on matters of crime and law enforcement. The earliest resolution, authored by Georgia judge and former Atlanta mayor George Hillyer, critiqued the "weak and imperfect" state of the law, which ultimately was to blame for the surge of lynchings. Urging "substantial improvement" in criminal justice, it condemned both lynchers and, "with equal emphasis, and in many cases with much greater emphasis[,] . . . the horrible crimes which cause the lynchings."[162] As the national crime war began in earnest in the 1920s, resolutions spoke in increasingly critical terms of lynching and "mob violence" while also urging commitment to the "orderly" and "impartial" administration of criminal justice in order to protect the "sanctity of human life." By 1939, resolutions noted declines in lynching or simply abandoned the issue. Instead they focused attention on crime in general, the "4,600,000 criminals" causing $15 billion of damage yearly, and urged support for state crime fighting and the "maintenance of law and order."[163]

Racial elision in service of antilynching had likewise been present in Edwin T. Wellford's 1905 *Lynching of Jesus*. But now, in the midst of the national crime war, the book took on new meaning with its 1930 reprint. Wellford titled this new edition *Crime and Cure: A Review of This Lawless Age and the Mistrial of Christ,* revamping a book that was formerly focused on mob violence into an anticrime volume. "Judge Lynch" had been succeeded by "Judge Homicide," with criminals creating a "Reign of Terror" across the nation.[164] Wellford hailed new federal anticrime efforts and the modernization of law enforcement as answers. But, as in his earlier book, Wellford avoided discussion of race or the disproportionate effects of lynching or crime on black Americans.

Antilynching advocacy had been refashioned into an anticrime effort. Streamlined, well-funded, and tougher law enforcement had tackled the problem of mob violence and now could be directed toward other criminal ills in order to secure the social order. But as the SBC resolutions and Wellford's book indicated, what was perhaps most racially significant about these efforts was what they did not mention: white supremacist violence that African Americans faced with regularity, often by police themselves, and the extent to which Jim Crow deeply undergirded American society.[165] The focus in most of these efforts was not directly on black pathology and criminality. But there was a clear omission of the struggles African Americans faced, an elision that would remain significant as America's criminal justice system expanded in later years under the guise of race neutrality and color blindness. Criminologist Thorsten Sellin realized this in the 1930s, arguing for the recognition of the racially disparate effects of the allegedly neutral criminal justice system. Though "the blind goddess of justice is assumed to weigh all men in her scales, regardless of their color nationality, economic status, or religion[,] . . . ideals are difficult to live up to." Pointing to disparities in sentencing from statistics he gathered in 1931, Sellin showed that black people received far harsher treatment in this system. He argued that the justice system could not help but be enveloped in racial bias, given that the judiciary was composed almost entirely of old stock whites. "Equality before the law," he wrote, "is a social fiction."[166] Sellin perceived the problem in his own day and intuited the long-term racialization that would be further exacerbated in future decades.

Black Christians seeking white allies in the crime war were in a tough spot. They shared many of the same general concerns about lawbreaking with their white brethren and often endorsed punitive solutions alongside communal uplift.[167] But engaging in the anticrime cause also risked the dilution of black struggle or even the endorsement of racist sentiment. Some believed it was worth the risk. In 1922 the National Law Enforcement Conference of Negro Leaders invited John Roach Straton to deliver an address. In his speech, Straton avoided the overtly racist language from his endorsement of Hoffman two decades earlier, instead focusing on the shared concerns of lawlessness and cultural decline. Straton still managed to propound black stereotypes in his talk, speaking of his "Negro Mammy . . . one of the best and most consistent Christians" he "had ever known." This was the same kind of paternalistic sentiment that had led Booker T. Washington to critique Straton years earlier, but here black attendees were apparently satisfied enough with the speech to praise its overall message and reprint it in the *National Baptist Voice*.[168] Elsewhere Straton denounced the Ku Klux Klan for its "divisive evils." But though his comments on the Klan indicated his opposition to the organization, it was primarily because their clandestine methods undercut orderly administration of the law, and less because of their motives.[169] For black Christians facing rising crime rates and the threat of racist mob violence, an alliance with Straton was a risk some were willing to take.

Tasked with caring for the growing number of prisoners, prison chaplains played a key role in the religiously rooted state crime-control effort. Liberally minded prison ministers could be compassionate and directed toward inmate betterment, but they also served as extensions of the disciplinary arm of the state. If someone wanted to join in this ministry work, they would have to play by the state's rules. One mainline Protestant ministry to prisons, hospitals, and children's homes in Louisville, Kentucky, exemplified this approach. The chairman of the Louisville Council of Churches authored the ministry's promotional booklet, tellingly titled *The Layman Helps the Warden*. On the very first page, the booklet listed the ministry's single guiding rule: "There is to be no unfavorable public criticism of the management of the institutions which we study and seek to help." The rest of the booklet continued in this vein, along with stress on the goal of inmate rehabilitation. Besides the "religious counseling and services" the ministry realized through the hiring of a "clinically-trained chaplain," it also pushed for "a balanced diet of appetizing food," support for the inmate newspaper, and inmate education. The *Christian*

Century hailed the ministry for providing "constructive channels" like these. More importantly, however, the ministry was praised for focusing on inmates and avoiding criticism of the prison. *Time* and the Associated Press noted approvingly that "the committee avoids public crusades or reform waves" and the "traditional 'view with alarm' attitude." Illustrating that this brand of ministry was complementary with the work of the modern prison itself, the Kentucky State Reformatory warden happily reported, "They do not make destructive criticism or try to run the prison. On the whole, these men are the civilian eyes, ears, and mouthpiece of this institution."[170] Becoming a part of the prison's surveillance measures (or even receiving endorsement from punitive anticrime crusaders like Marcus Kavanagh) did not mean that there was a lack of passion or concern for criminals among chaplains. There was.[171] But their very position as state employees prevented them from turning compassion for inmates into substantial critique of the criminal justice system itself. Too much critique, and one would lose one's job (and with it, access to prisoners altogether).

The utilization of a consensus history interpretive model to show the common contributions of a wide range of historical actors to the development of American mass incarceration is a recent historiographical development, yet one that has made important contributions to understanding the roots of modern American criminal justice.[172] Whether locating the foundation of mass incarceration in the immediate postwar era or in later Great Society social programs, these consensus accounts point to the limits of the "backlash" thesis, the notion that America's high incarceration rates arose as post-1960s Republicans utilized racially coded law-and-order appeals to construct a "new Jim Crow."[173] Instead, as the provocative subtitle of Naomi Murakawa's book puts it, "liberals built prison America" through well-intentioned efforts to address lynchings or crime problems in poor inner-city neighborhoods. Liberals proposed the creation of a criminal justice system that emphasized professionalization and codification, and named safety and security as essential American rights in the postwar era. Though backlash-driven appeals were significant in their own right in the creation of modern American criminal justice, liberals were always there along the way, laying "the scaffolding beneath our explanations for the rise of mass incarceration."[174] This interpretive lens helps make sense of the seeming conceptual incongruity between the sociological and punitive religious perspectives. Though they may have disagreed at times on the proper response to crime, they all agreed that it was truly a *war*, and one worth *fighting*. If the scaffolding of mass incarceration was erected in the postwar era, the materials for construction were being provided by the diverse crime-fighting coalition of the 1920s, 1930s, and 1940s. And because this coalition received the blessing and support of a panoply of religious leaders, and because the cause was so often framed explicitly as a struggle against secularism, this first "war on crime" was a religious war. The crimes in question may not always have been as horrific or famous as Leopold and Loeb's, but religious and law enforcement leaders would be no less willing to frame the issue in similar terms. Indeed, the connection of religion to crime fighting at this time has been difficult for scholars to perceive, perhaps because, in the words of Attorney General Cummings in 1935, "the role of religion in crime prevention seems such an obvious one that it is taken for granted."[175]

The crime crusade was analogous to the religious influence in the twentieth-century campaign against communism, as politicians and law enforcement also sought alliances with clergy. But it also followed the pattern of the pre–World War II Red Scare and Cold War in another sense: though anticrime and anticommunism enjoyed broad religious support early on, one particular group of Christians made both causes their own as they ascended in numerical and cultural influence in the postwar era.[176] These Christians were the "new" evangelicals. Like communism, crime would become a wedge issue that distinguished conservative Protestants of various stripes from the more liberal mainline, who increasingly championed civil rights and Great Society social uplift *without* referencing crime as they had in earlier years. This divergence reflected a broader "restructuring of American religion" from the postwar era onward. As the scope of governmental power remained permanently enlarged in the generations after its explosive increase during the New Deal and World War II, religious denominations found their cultural cachet diminished. They were forced to restructure by aligning with a variety of new special-interest groups vying to influence the direction of state power, and largely broke along liberal and conservative political lines to that effect.[177] The crime war of the 1920s, 1930s, and 1940s foreshadowed this emerging divide even as it showcased one of the final examples of religious unanimity around the expansion of the state's reach. By contrast, in the following decades African American and liberal Protestants, Catholics, and Jews made arguments for state influence in securing civil rights and economic welfare, while white evangelicals championed the law enforcement function of the state to address what they deemed social disorder.

As evangelicals began to exert more influence in American public life in the postwar era and the following years, they helped further the idea of crime as a sacred national issue by *continuing* to define it in religious terms. They did so by sermonizing about crime's ongoing threat to the order of American society and Christian civilization, by engineering new evangelistic efforts as a form of crime prevention, and eventually by backing political leaders who championed the law-and-order cause (or critiquing those who did not). These efforts had far-reaching effects in the development of American criminal justice into a system of mass incarceration, one made all the more impossible to deconstruct because of law and order's hallowed cultural cachet. But evangelicals were only working with the tools that they had been given, the legacy of the sacred crime crusade of an earlier generation.

2

JESUS CHRIST IS THE ONLY CONTROL

Just before the tall, handsome, but largely unknown evangelist Billy Graham stepped onto the stage inside a Los Angeles revival tent in 1949, he received a warning. One of the most cunning criminals of the day was in the audience, the anxious revival committee informed Graham. "We don't know why he's here. He may be here to be against you, or he may be here out of curiosity. We don't know why he's here." The committee's worries initially proved to be justified. As Graham preached, an overeager usher approached the feared criminal—named Jim Vaus—and asked him whether he wanted to respond to the invitation. "If you speak to me again," the surprise guest responded, "I'll take my fist and knock you down."[1]

But a few minutes later, something changed. As Graham continued his sermon on the need for repentance, tears began to well up in Vaus's eyes. He said to himself, "I'm through, I realize that my only hope of salvation rests in Jesus Christ." As a visible sign of his decision for Christ, Vaus tore up a plane ticket that had been stuffed in his pocket, a ticket that would have taken him to an eastern city where he could ply his illicit wiretapping trade for another criminal syndicate. "There is destroyed the last link between myself and the underworld and crime," he declared. "For years I've drifted away from Christ to serve politics, politicians, criminals and crime. . . . I am now convinced that my salvation rests with the Lord." As if further to prove his newfound faith, Vaus later went voluntarily before the Los Angeles County Grand Jury and told them he was prepared to serve a prison sentence for perjury. He connected Graham with his boss, famed mobster Mickey Cohen, and the evangelist and gangster met for conversation and Coca-Colas soon after.[2]

Graham's remarkable accomplishment in winning Vaus to the Christian faith was such a powerful story because it seemed to be such a bombshell. But the contrast played up by the Billy Graham Evangelistic Association, by news reports of Vaus's conversion, and by Vaus himself (all symbolized by the puzzlement of the Los Angeles revival committee—"We don't know why he's here") should have been the real surprise, given the content of Graham's preaching at the time. On his very first night preaching in the Los Angeles revival, Graham described why the city needed spiritual renewal in terms that indicated that a man like Vaus was the *expected* kind of convert: "We see a crime wave in this country that is unchecked," he thundered. "Crime in Los Angeles is out of hand. . . . We need revival! 800% increase in crime in the last ten years!"[3] Here was an enterprising preacher on the cusp of fame, identifying crime as an important public concern, with a criminal responding with a life-changing decision for Christ.

As in the Los Angeles revival, Graham's ministry in the following decades and the various forms of evangelicalism he represented were marked by concern about crime and lawlessness. These were key issues for American evangelicals seeking cultural influence in the early postwar era (from roughly 1945 to 1965), and they moved to address it by emphasizing personal conversion, not punishment. As leaders like Graham, ex-criminals like Vaus and former gang leader Tom Skinner, and the Pentecostal preacher David Wilkerson stepped into the public eye and into new forms of ministry, their focus on the conversion of criminals avoided a punitive approach. But the way they spoke about crime planted seeds for later evangelical enmeshment with law-and-order politics from the mid-1960s on.

Graham's 1949 Los Angeles revival has been understood as his stepping-out party, the beginning of his tenure as "America's pastor."[4] More broadly, this was, in the eyes of observers then and now, one sign that a "new evangelicalism" (or neo-evangelicalism) had arrived on the American scene. This movement consisted of conservative Protestants who were willing to shirk fundamentalist isolationism and engage American culture, politics, and media anew. Institutions and scholarly figures often associated with this movement included the National Association of Evangelicals, Fuller Theological Seminary, and theologian Carl F. H. Henry.[5] But there was also a popular side to the movement, the sermons, films, and easy-reading paperbacks indicative of evangelicalism's status as a "folk" religion.[6] Focus on this popular side is necessary, given how important crime and delinquency were in debates about American mass culture at this time, particularly television and film.[7]

Inclusion of the plainspoken preacher Graham in the new evangelical category, even as he interfaced with its more highbrow forms, is uncontroversial. Some explanation is needed regarding the assumption that a Pentecostal like Wilkerson could be considered a part of this movement as well. As Molly Worthen has shown, participating in this midcentury movement's theological conversations "required fluency in the Reformed tongue," and debates raged in the early days of the National Association of Evangelicals as to whether Pentecostals should be included in the emerging coalition.[8] Many Pentecostals eventually came to identify with the new evangelical cause through mutual concerns about America's destiny and fears about Catholicism, modernism, and communism.[9] More complicated is the question of why Skinner and like-minded African American Christians should also be included in the new evangelical movement, which was predominantly white. Some of the complications of this connection will be explored later. For now, however, we shall view them in common cause if for no other reason than that Skinner (and others, such as Howard O. Jones and E. V. Hill) embraced the label and its associated access to evangelical institutions and networks.

More important for both white and black evangelicals was the shared stress on the need for personal Christian conversion within the context of cultural engagement. Long considered one of the hallmark qualities of evangelicalism, conversionism as a descriptive category is complicated by shifting contexts and differing evangelical views on its mechanics and ends.[10] In the early postwar era, however, broader worries about crime and delinquency provided a common frame for evangelicals to narrate the need for conversion. This inflection of conversionism served as a conceptual bridge between various conservative Protestant groups and to mainstream American culture more broadly, laying the foundation for evangelical influence in the "born again" 1970s and after.[11]

The interest of evangelicals like Graham in lawlessness signaled important developments. Evangelicals defined crime and lawlessness in terms of their direct connection to, or equality with, *sin*. This was in keeping with the earlier history of American evangelical work in prisons. But now their focus was on youth crime. The implication was that juvenile delinquency was primarily an issue of salvation, not social conditions. Though this understanding of delinquency was not as holistic as it could have been, it also meant that the ideal result of criminal encounter with the gospel was salvation, not punishment. Many new evangelicals (including Graham) would embrace the law-and-order mantle later on, but their early ministries indicated a different frame of reference for how crime should be understood and criminals should be treated.

This form of evangelical crime concern in the 1950s and early 1960s had two general manifestations. The first, as seen in Graham's reference in his 1949 crusade, was rhetorical. Crime provided a useful tool for sharpening evangelical messages about sin and salvation. The second was institutional. The converted Vaus was among a coterie of evangelicals at this time who formed ministries around the goal of reaching criminals and delinquents. These ministries built on iterations of evangelical work among criminals from generations past but also charted new territory in terms of public engagement.

Graham was not the only minister who made crime concern a topic of his evangelistic outreach. However, he was the most popular voice, and he exemplified an important point: for evangelicals in the early postwar era, the ideal outcome for criminals was their *conversion,* not conviction. Evangelicals like Graham spoke about lawlessness in dire terms, but they generally believed the best way forward was for criminals to be embraced by the nail-scarred hands of Jesus, not the long arm of the law. Evangelicals worked out more intensified versions of this concern in localized ministry to gangs in America's urban slums. This work was significant in its own right, but it became a markedly public form of evangelical outreach as its practitioners used their platforms to speak to the nation through popular media, most prominently in Wilkerson's best-selling account of gang ministry in New York, *The Cross and the Switchblade.* At every point, evangelicals' efforts were marked by assumptions that set the terms for shifts in their engagement with matters of crime and punishment in future decades.

Youth for Christ, Billy Graham, and the Conversion of Criminals

Graham was the most prominent face of evangelical crime concern in the early postwar era. Youth for Christ (YFC), the site of his first national ministry work, made juvenile delinquency a signature issue in the mid- to late 1940s. Graham continued the crime crusade as he launched his own ministry soon after, speaking to matters of delinquency and lawlessness more generally as he preached the gospel worldwide. He touched a nerve. Americans shared this concern with crime, and media sustained coverage of Graham in large part because they saw the evangelist's relevance to this public issue.

Graham began his national ministry as an evangelist with YFC. This ministry coalesced in the early 1940s as a form of evangelistic outreach to America's teens, achieving broad popularity in the mid-1940s as a result of its radio outreach and giant rallies that attracted thousands.[12] One estimate put weekly attendance at YFC rallies at one million people by the end of the decade. YFC was a sign that American evangelicals were "coming in from the cold," abandoning fundamentalist seclusion and achieving mainstream cultural success through clever forms of media outreach and by capitalizing on the patriotic civic religious ferment left over from World War II.[13] The organization promised to form a legion of youths devoted both to the gospel and to a godly, democratic America's unique place in the modern world, over and against godless communism.[14]

Another issue also prompted YFC's rise: juvenile delinquency. Americans had been concerned about crime for years, but teenage crime was widely reported to have risen dramatically in the immediate aftermath of the war and captured the country's attention. To what extent youth crime rates actually rose was a matter of debate and definition. For example, rates of "status crimes" (acts defined as criminal because of age, such as underage drinking) rose in many cities in the postwar years, but this may have reflected more willingness on the part of law enforcement to press charges. Rising or not, the severity of youth crime was regularly exaggerated.[15] Nevertheless, YFC's rallies, Joel Carpenter has noted, "enjoyed their greatest expansion during 1943–1946, the years when juvenile delinquency emerged as a national problem."[16] In early planning sessions and marketing materials, YFC leaders regularly discussed the import of the organization's work regarding delinquency. In 1944 Chicagoland director Torrey Johnson and advisory council member Bob Cook characterized regional YFC meetings as geared toward the "salvation of the thousands who are tagged with the dreadful word, 'delinquency.'"[17] In his opening address to the second annual YFC convention, Johnson (now the ministry's president) and field representative Cliff Barrows told stories of how YFC had succeeded in combating delinquency in their crusades, including that of one young armed robber who "at seven o'clock was a potential criminal, at nine o'clock was kneeling at the foot of the cross and receiving Jesus Christ as his personal savior."[18] Later YFC promotional materials were emblazoned with shocking headlines and stories of teenage crimes, and proposed the ministry's High School Bible Club program as "an answer" to the "hellish nightmare of delinquency." Bible club attendees "aren't going around trying to kill anybody! They are too busy winning their pals and buddies to Jesus Christ."[19] YFC leaders like Billy Graham made the case to business and educational leaders that their evangelism to teenagers was an essential part of the shared national struggle against delinquency.[20] A college president reportedly told one YFC employee, "There is a terrific crime wave and fact of delinquency. But you fellows in Youth for Christ are helping us in our churches by sticking to the one essential of getting them saved by proclaiming a positive message, and letting us indoctrinate them after you turn them over to us."[21] Governmental and law enforcement authorities agreed. State governors praised YFC's meetings as "tremendous forces" in the fight against youth crime, while the chief of police in Charlotte, North Carolina (who also agreed to serve as director of the city's rally), said, "Youth for Christ is doing more than anything else I know to stop juvenile delinquency."[22]

Though it had the endorsement of police and governmental leaders, YFC wanted to fight delinquency not through law enforcement action but by leading teens to Christ, either by preventing them from engaging in troublemaking in the first place or by rescuing active ne'er-do-wells from the clutches of sin. Johnson and Cook described this approach in an early promotional book. Though a "prominent social worker" had told them that "there is nothing that we can do about a delinquent until after the case is brought into court," Johnson and Cook contended that "there are a multitude of things that can be done. . . . Thank God, 'the gospel of Christ . . . is the power of God unto salvation to everyone that believeth.'"[23] This paralleled conversionist proposals to solve the problem of delinquency from other youth-centered Christian organizations emerging at the time. For example, Jim Rayburn, the founder of Young Life, regularly spoke about delinquency in similar terms: "The Gospel of our Lord Jesus Christ is the only solution."[24]

This solution was, as Graham put it in his 1947 book *Calling Youth to Christ*, a "spiritual call to arms. . . . America cannot organize her way out, nor buy her way out. She must *pray* her way out."[25] In the same volume, Graham told a modified story of the biblical figure Barabbas to prove the depths of God's grace. In the biblical account, Barabbas was the murderous criminal who was released without penalty by Pontius Pilate in the place of Jesus, who would go on to be crucified. Graham embellished the story by describing a fictionalized version of the conversation Barabbas might have had with the jailer upon being released. He wrote, "'Barabbas, have you heard the Good News?' It was the warden's voice, jubilant and strong. 'What Good News?' retorted the condemned man in a bitter tone. 'All I know is that this is the day of my execution, and that you have come to lead me out to be crucified for my crimes.' And he shrank farther back against the cold, wet wall. 'Ah! but you don't know,' replied the warden in the same triumphant tone. 'Listen, Barabbas: Somebody died for you!' "[26] Graham used this story to drive home his gospel presentation, but it also served as a theological gloss that relativized the punishment of lawbreakers (just as the story relativized the injustice that most readers of the original passion narrative might have sensed in the exchange of the sinless Jesus for Barabbas). Sermons like this led one observer writing in 1945 to note that the evangelism of YFC did "more to discourage juvenile delinquency than all the curfews, threats and even punishments could accomplish."[27]

One 1949 article from the YFC magazine described an idealized result of this spiritual strategy. A fifteen-year-old "skid row hoodlum" prone to knife fights attended a YFC rally, went forward at the invitation, and was counseled in a private prayer room by a Christian businessman. "When I left the room . . . ," he recounted, "I knew Christ in a way that has completely changed [my life]." The teen left his life of crime and eventually became the president of a YFC chapter and Sunday school teacher.[28] Streamlined stories like this, of escape from crime, and the punishment that could accompany it, were compelling fare to evangelicals who shared YFC's outlook. To some critics, they could be frustrating. One journalist from the liberal *Christian Century* covered a huge YFC rally in Chicago and voiced his displeasure at the spectacle. The revivalists, he argued, oversimplified Christianity with "milky abstractions." YFC speakers never clearly defined the salvation they spoke of, and never made reference to Christianity's ethical demands. This threatened to veer into antinomian cheap grace. "Repentance is not mentioned," he observed. "Religion is purely a matter of perpendicular relationships, so restitution for wrongs done is not referred to."[29] Though this critic may have been overstating the lack of a call to repentance from sin (a call Graham and other evangelical preachers frequently made elsewhere) or a concern with ethics, in noting the absence of a call to temporal "restitution," he was correctly zeroing in on an important implication of this movement's spiritualized focus.

The *Century*'s reporter was not impressed by YFC, but that was of little consequence when the most powerful newspaperman in the country was: William Randolph Hearst, owner of numerous media outlets nationwide. Part of the reason YFC became so popular was its appeal to the media magnate, who ordered his newspapers to cover the organization continually. He justified this decision with reference to concern about juvenile crime. "If we make the movement popular in one or two churches," he told his editors, "it will probably be adopted by all the churches in some form or other and it will be one of the most valuable influences in overcoming juvenile delinquency."[30] Delinquency was a problem that YFC could help solve, and Hearst was willing to evangelize for the evangelists to accomplish this task (and selling a few papers along the way would not hurt).

YFC gave Graham an opportunity to exploit the national stage, but it was not until the evangelist held his own series of revivals in Los Angeles in 1949 that he began to emerge as a bona fide celebrity. Whether he literally gave the famous order to his staff to "puff Graham" is debated, but Hearst almost certainly guided his papers to push Graham into the national spotlight.[31] Again, concern about crime was key. Hearst characterized the 1949 Los Angeles revival as "restoring and strengthening the spiritual communion with God which is the essence of civilized freedom and law." This was a crusade against the paganism and materialism that informs "crime, vice and graft, all the ways in which men and women torment themselves and each other to injure the welfare of their community."[32]

The revival setting as a site of evangelical crime concern was significant. Graham was not heading up a crime commission or making specific political pronouncements on issues of delinquency. Instead, it came through his gospel presentation, the evangelistic message he propounded with great consistency in preaching and print. This message was simple: all people were sinners, separated from God by virtue of their selfishness and immorality. Most people had a sense of this sin, often through feelings of emptiness or purposelessness. Nothing could save people from their sin except Jesus, who desired a personal relationship with everyone. This personal relationship commenced when individuals made a decision for Christ, laying down their sin and asking Jesus into their hearts.

Graham did not invent this evangelistic form so much as he perfected its presentation. He was particularly skilled at connecting this gospel to the anxieties of middle America, putting broader social trends in personal terms that everyday listeners could understand and relate to. For example, he connected the global threat of communism to the more narrow worries of crusade attendees about their personal sins, linking the disorder of the world to the chaos of individuals' moral lives.[33] Graham estimated later that he mentioned communism in his preaching more than any other topic (other than the gospel message itself).[34] But crime and lawlessness were also regular homiletic themes. Juvenile delinquency was "so serious," Graham warned reporters, "that it almost equals Communism in the problems we face today."[35] And like communism, crime helped to explain and frame other forms of sin. "Lawlessness has become the spirit of our age," he wrote in a *Washington Post* feature promoting his 1957 Madison Square Garden crusade, before listing multiple ways people were rebelling through sexual immorality and divorce, as well as crime and delinquency.[36] Lawlessness here was an existential gloss, a way to characterize the widespread lack of respect for divine and human authority.

Graham expanded on this sentiment in his sermons at this New York crusade. On the first night, he characterized crime and delinquency as part of America's spiritual ailment that could only be solved through faith in Christ.[37] On the second night, in a sermon entitled "What's Wrong with New York," he developed this idea with a message based on Matthew 9:12, "They that be whole need not a physician, but they that are sick." The symptoms of sickness he referred to were apparent in the "murders, rapes, and robberies" that cities like New York face constantly. "Nearly a million crimes were committed here last year." But then he pivoted to generalizing this lawless condition for his audience in terms of the evangelical gospel presentation: "What's wrong with the human race that allows crime, social injustices, racial prejudice? It seems we can't control it. We are sick with a moral disease the Bible calls sin."[38] The answer to this universal human problem was the healing balm of salvation, the work of the Great Physician, who could restore souls and, through that, end the social scourge of crime.

The rest of Graham's sermons during his sixteen-week Madison Square Garden residency were filled with references to crime. Though he had mentioned the issue before in his preaching career (like in the Los Angeles revival), he now devoted sustained attention to it. Graham brought crime up in some way in nearly thirty of his Madison Square sermons. Often it was only a passing allusion, such as mentioning crime as part of the broader national crisis of sin facing America that necessitated the nation's spiritual revival. Other times it was a major theme, such as when Graham preached a sermon entitled "Samson—God's Delinquent." He began this message with a catalog of the problems of juvenile delinquency: "Newspapers are filled with stories of teen-age violence and crime. . . .

41 percent of all arrests for serious crime in New York were under 21 last year." He then turned to the example of the Old Testament figure Samson to diagnose this situation. Samson had significant social advantages—strength, good looks, caring parents—but he still found his way into trouble. Likewise, Graham argued, today's youths are not primarily led to commit crimes because of environmental factors, such as poverty or trashy television. Instead, the "cause of all causes" is sin, the all-encompassing category that signified a conscious turn to the ways of the flesh. Sin bound Samson to a life of blindness and boredom. Similarly, Graham lamented, "When I see the wayward lawless youth walking the streets of this city, I can picture them a few years hence: ill-clad, sin-marked, Bowery bums, living out of the garbage cans and embalming their weary bodies with alcohol." The concluding moment of decision was less an altar call and more of an exhortation to the gathered crowd to exercise their God-given wills to stay out of crime.[39]

Graham delivered this sermon twice during the Madison Square crusade, once on June 6 and once on August 11. The second time it appeared, it was a part of Teen Week, an intentional outreach to New York City's youths. Teen Week utilized tried-and-true youth evangelism techniques, such as enlisting celebrity athletes to serve as platform guests. But it was also an attempt at spiritual crime control. Teen Week was initiated as a reaction to a rash of highly publicized crimes in the city that summer. Graham led the week off with a press conference featuring converted youths, as one account put it, "with doubtful backgrounds." His preaching dwelled on the terrible criminal consequences of sin ("boredom, mischief, gang wars") and positive benefits of parental discipline and corporal punishment. The results of Teen Week were two thousand youngsters newly dedicated to Christ, a pair of pistols that converted gang members had handed in, and a host of newspaper headlines that trumpeted the disciplinary possibilities of the crusade: "Graham Raps Parents for Teen Evils"; "Young People Need Control, Graham Says"; "Teeners Coddled, Bored, Need Dedication to Christ"; "Graham Urges Teen Gangs for Christ."[40] The story was similar during a New York visit a few years later when Graham traveled to East Harlem to meet with teenage gang members. At the behest of Jim Vaus, who now ministered to Harlem's youths, Graham shared the gospel to gangs like the Untouchables, the Turbans, and the Dragons. "Jesus Christ is the only control," he preached. "He alone can help you live a clean life." The New York Times reported that the message motivated twenty of the seventy gathered teens to accept Christ, and that one gang leader (known as Flamingo) pledged that his gang members would go to church the following day, "or else."[41]

During the 1950s Graham frequently played up crime's immense danger to the American way of life. But he was remarkably consistent in defining the truly Christian response to the issue as spiritual heart change, not harsher law enforcement. This paralleled Graham's broader Cold War framing of communism as an existential threat, but differed from his hawkish views about the just use of military force against America's foreign enemies (even as it tracked with his later, dove-like focus on communists as potential friends and converts, and warnings about the dangers of unchecked militarism after the 1970s).[42] It also was a marked departure from many of the conservative Protestants who, in the 1920s–1940s, had urged tough responses to criminal acts. Graham was not naïve, nor was he pacifistic; he still believed in the need for policing, incarceration, and especially the tough love of parental discipline. But ultimately these measures were insufficient. In a 1956 sermon on crime on his *Hour of Decision* radio program, Graham asked rhetorically, "Do we need more laws, heavier sentences, streamlined administration? No! All of these are surface remedies that don't get to the root of the problem."[43] Just three weeks after the conclusion of the 1957 New York crusade, in another radio sermon, entitled "God, Crime, and the Devil," Graham argued that by focusing on law enforcement alone, "we are treating symptoms of crime, not the source." "Out of the heart of man is where the problem is. . . . We must recognize who the author of crime is: the devil." Graham then spoke of a career criminal who had been converted at the Madison Square Garden crusade. "Nothing seemed to work, everything went wrong," Graham reported the man saying in a letter. "Then I came to Madison Square Garden. I came five nights in a row. One night I walked down the aisle with tears streaming down my face. My whole life is different now. I cannot describe the peace and joy. I have a new power to resist temptation. Next Sunday I am joining a church. I am convinced that I have found a totally new way of life, but like you said, Christ had to change my nature before I could change my way of living." *Conversion* was the ideal outcome for the criminal, not prison.[44]

To be sure, Graham had high, practical hopes for this conversionist strategy in terms of crime reduction. In 1951 he voiced his support for a Crime Prevention Week campaign in Los Angeles. Along with local churches and police, he pushed church attendance as a potential solution to the crime problem.[45] During a monthlong 1953 crusade in Saint Louis, newspapers reported that Graham hoped to reduce crime and corruption by 25 to 50 percent in the city through his ministry.[46] Occasionally he even slipped into voicing support for tougher governmental efforts, such as when he told an audience gathered on the steps of the capitol building in Washington, DC, "We must continue to expose crime and irregularities in Government . . . and enact strong legislation to deal with them," or when he noted at a Washington luncheon that Senator Estes Kefauver's investigating committee on organized crime had played a role in the "moral rebirth" of America.[47] New Hampshire senator (and Baptist) Charles W. Tobey would have appreciated Graham's remark, as he lectured gangsters on the need for repentance during the Kefauver hearing. Channeling conversionist sentiment on crime, Tobey read a poem at one racketeering hearing that closed with the lines, "Solution there is none, save in the rule of Christ alone."[48] But for Graham, both of these moments were outliers at this point in his career and may have had more to do with his audience than anything else. Flanked by politicians in both settings, Graham knew he had to voice optimism in the moral potential of the law if he was to curry any favor with Washington's legislative rank and file.

By contrast, Graham was far more focused on the spiritual matters at stake when speaking to "regular" people. In his "My Answer" syndicated newspaper advice column, he was asked the following question: "A terrible crime was committed in our community recently—a tiny girl was brutally violated and killed. How can there be sufficient punishment for this brute?" Graham responded not by blasting the perpetrator or dwelling on the need for punishment but by gesturing toward the deed's sinful qualities that all human beings shared: "I have only horror and disgust for such a crime, but the tragic thing is that all of us are sinners and need God's redeeming grace in Christ. . . . When we think of the terrible sins such as you speak of, we should examine our own hearts and say, 'But for the grace of God that could have been me.'" Ever the evangelist, Graham pivoted to a printed altar call, pointing out that *all* sinners who reject God face punishment and that *everyone* (not just brutish criminals) needed to turn to Christ.[49] Graham's avoidance of naming harsh penalties and his universalizing of the sin problem, even in the face of a deeply troubling crime, indicated a concern that transcended punitive retribution. As with his apocryphal Barabbas story, the spiritual focus verged on insensitivity to the demands of human justice. But, Graham might have responded, that was the whole point: God's ways are not our ways.

This mode of evangelical crime concern and outreach crystallized in *Wiretapper*, a 1955 movie produced by World Wide Pictures, the film arm of the Billy Graham Evangelistic Association. *Wiretapper* was a dramatized retelling of Jim Vaus's criminal past and Christian conversion. Displaying the evangelical willingness to build off crime as an issue of public fascination, various posters for the film marketed it as a crime drama. Intrigued audiences may have been disappointed to find that the film actually contained little action or suspense, even lacking Vaus's threat to a crusade usher. But it was nevertheless, as *Time* magazine called it, "a potent evangelistic tool."[50]

The film begins with Vaus in prison for a crime he committed while serving in the military. After his release, he travels home to Los Angeles, marries his sweetheart, and gradually gets caught up in the illegal activities of a local syndicate. An electronics wizard, Vaus helps gangsters with their wiretapping needs and builds them a machine to cheat on horseracing bets. He finds his marriage and conscience strained by this work, especially after visiting a local Graham crusade (as in many World Wide films, a Graham sermon is the climax of the movie). Vaus gives his heart to God, telling his wife, "Something happened to me tonight in that tent. For the first time in my life I'm willing to face the music, to play it straight. It's a wonderful clean feeling." What is strikingly absent from the film's narrative, however, is the work of law enforcement. As a result of his conversion, Vaus abandons his former mob ties and never faces any legal penalty for his wiretapping. Though he speaks about being saved from his former murderous mobster connections, Vaus could just as easily be talking about avoiding arrest and conviction in one of his statements near the end of the film (a line Vaus regularly repeated in interviews): "The man in the tent tonight showed me a verse in the Bible from the book of Proverbs: when a man's ways please the Lord he makes even his enemies to be at peace with him."[51] Though the "real" Vaus wanted to make restitution for his crimes, the idealized Vaus of cinema encountered a Savior who set the prisoner free from eternal perdition and civil punishment. *Wiretapper* exemplified the new evangelical strategy in terms of its medium and message. The evangelical gospel had relevance to the crime problem, and it could be communicated through the most modern of means: first in national newsprint, and now in Hollywood-style cinema.

This culturally engaged crime messaging reached a fever pitch in 1958 with Graham's widely covered visit to San Quentin prison during his San Francisco crusade. Associated Press reports showed striking photos of

Figure 2.1 Billy Graham preaching at California's San Quentin State Prison, 1958. AP Photo.

Graham preaching to thousands of prisoners (see Figure 2.1), while *Time* magazine and national newspapers noted hundreds of decisions made for Christ at the facility (the *Chicago Tribune* listed 623 conversions, while the *New York Times* counted 627). Excerpts of Graham's sermon, printed in some media accounts, stressed the depths of God's grace: "Regardless of how black your crimes, God will forgive you. . . . Christ stepped forward and said 'I'll serve that sentence.'"[52] Though Graham may have taken for granted the fact that those in his audience were already serving literal prison sentences, the message he preached did not dwell on their crimes except to say that they were forgiven by God.

With Billy Graham as its emblematic media-savvy figure, the evangelical approach to spiritual crime concern gained broader cultural traction. Graham's message was a unique blend of parts of the previous generation's crime consensus. Like both liberals and fundamentalists, he believed that crime was a critical issue of public concern, one that demanded a response from religious leaders. Following public pronouncements of liberal religious authorities, he recognized that criminals were people deserving of care and concern, even if he rejected their social gospel–style approach that focused on environmental drivers of criminality. Like fundamentalists, Graham believed that the individual moral culpability of criminals was the best rendering of the problem, even as he avoided their punitive rhetoric by stressing their spiritual salvation. This represented the broader triangulation of social concern and spiritual focus that new evangelicals had begun to articulate and would be increasingly associated with in the following years. In terms of crime, delinquency, and prison, Graham signaled a desire of postwar evangelicals to wrestle with these issues, and that this struggle could be framed as one of spirit, not flesh and blood.

Ministry to Juvenile Delinquents

While Graham led the way in crystallizing the public conceptual terms of evangelical understandings of crime, others were putting this faith into more concrete action. Building off rising concerns with youth crime, evangelicals in the 1950s and early 1960s embraced direct ministry to juvenile delinquents and gangs, particularly those from urban areas. Though YFC had trumpeted the delinquency cause from its inception in the mid-1940s, the ministry did not make intentional efforts to reach delinquents specifically until the early 1950s. As they moved away from crusade-driven evangelism, YFC leader Bob Cook argued that the ministry needed to do more to tailor its work to youths from the "seamy side of town." YFC named this initiative the Youth Guidance Program, hired a full-time director, and started local outreach ministries to delinquents in Oakland, Los Angeles, and Victoria, British Columbia.[53] YFC was one of a number of youth-centered evangelical ministries that were increasingly conscious of the need to reach urban delinquents. Though the ministries of David Wilkerson, Jim Vaus, and Tom Skinner among gangs in New York started small, each represented a more intensified and intimate version of the simultaneous evangelical concern with crime and sympathy with criminals.

Shortly after Graham's 1957 Madison Square Garden crusade, another preacher made his way to New York City with grand ambitions. David Wilkerson, a slim twenty-six-year-old Assemblies of God minister from a rural Pennsylvania mountain town, had seen an article in *Life* magazine that described a grisly murder that had rocked the city in the summer of 1957.[54] According to the article, several gang members from Upper Manhattan had been accused of killing Michael Farmer, a fifteen-year-old with polio. Though a gruesome crime, the alleged killers were themselves boys, caught up in the violent gang wars that had plagued the city over the past few years. As he read the article, Wilkerson found his stomach churning with disgust at the crime. But then a thought popped in his mind: "Go to New York City and help those boys." He initially resisted the idea. The country preacher knew nothing of the big city, and his growing ministry in Philipsburg, Pennsylvania, had enough demands of its own. But Wilkerson's conscience was afflicted until he yielded to the directive of the still, small voice in his heart. The following day he brought the magazine to his church's Wednesday-night service. Instead of preaching his regular sermon, Wilkerson showed the article to the congregation and told them, "Take a good look at the faces of these boys." At his request, the church took up an offering of seventy-five dollars, enough to cover a car trip to New York and back. Wilkerson's wife, Gwen, was still skeptical. "You really feel this is the Holy Spirit leading you?" she asked him. When her husband responded affirmatively, she finally relented: "Well, be sure to take some good warm socks."[55]

On a mission from God, Wilkerson and his church's youth director drove through the night to New York City. But the enterprising evangelist would soon find his ambitions thwarted. Wilkerson entered the courtroom where the boys were being tried and stepped over the guardrail to tell them of God's love. "Judge Davidson, Your Honor," he said. "Respect me as a minister of the Gospel and let me have one moment, please." The judge, in no mood for theatrics, ordered Wilkerson from the court. Trial reporters, eager for a story, ate up the scene and the next day Wilkerson found an unflattering photo of himself in the New York Daily News. The boys' defense attorney later reported that Wilkerson contacted him about meeting the boys and that, though he was sympathetic to the pastor's interest in "saving the boys' souls," his own concern was "saving their lives"—helping them avoid the death penalty.[56]

Though his initial foray as an evangelist to New York's delinquents had failed, Wilkerson was not deterred. He returned to the city regularly to minister to gang members. He started with street preaching in dangerous areas like the Fort Greene and Bedford-Stuyvesant neighborhoods in Brooklyn, gaining respect early on from street gangs because of his own run-in with the law at the Farmer trial. According to Wilkerson, gang members told him, "You're all right. You're one of us. . . . When we saw two cops dragging you out of the courthouse, that means the cops don't like you. And they don't like us. So you're one of us."[57] He soon moved on to distributing evangelistic tracts and held rallies at a Manhattan boxing arena, where he bused in curious gang members to hear his evangelistic preaching.[58] In 1959 his New York ministry reached a turning point. Wilkerson began to see the need to go beyond more impersonal forms of evangelism and the occasional mission trip. Real ministry would require relocation, so the following year he permanently decamped for the city and set up a brick-and-mortar location in Brooklyn. Besides garnering support from numerous area churches and businessmen, the ministry, now officially dubbed Teen-Age Evangelism (and later called Teen Challenge), became officially linked with the Prison Division of the Assemblies of God's Home Missions Department.[59] Teen Challenge centers soon sprang up in other regions of the country, beginning with a Chicago office in 1961. The ministry initially focused its efforts on outreach to violent street gangs. By 1969, as heroin usage rates continued to surge and broader fears about gangs had begun to subside, it made drug rehabilitation its primary concern.[60] But the early focus of the ministry was the same concern that motivated Wilkerson to travel to New York and interrupt the Farmer trial: concern about the spiritual welfare of delinquent youths caught up in lives of crime.

Wilkerson was not the only evangelical outsider who had moved to New York on mission. After spending a few years on the speaker circuit after his conversion at Graham's 1949 Los Angeles revival and leading a short-lived missionary radio ministry, Jim Vaus moved to New York City in 1958 to work with gangs and troubled youths. Vaus had first begun to think about the possibilities of ministry to delinquents during a prison visit with Oregon secretary of state (and outspoken evangelical) Mark Hatfield. Not long after, a sixteen-year-old inmate at Eastern State Penitentiary in Pennsylvania confronted Vaus during an evangelistic visit: "Mr. Vaus, it was a good talk you gave today. But it would have been better if you had reached us before we got here." Haunted by the inmate's words, Vaus (in a story strikingly similar to that of Wilkerson) finally answered God's call to reach New York's delinquents as he paged through a *Life* magazine exposé on the city's gang violence.[61] He would eventually found Youth Development, Inc. (YDI), headquartered in Harlem.

Wilkerson and Vaus brought their own backgrounds and personalities to bear in their New York ministries. For Wilkerson, a fiery Pentecostal who believed that delinquency and drug use were literally "Satan's fiendish plan to drag today's youth into the pit of hell," his chosen method was a brash willingness to confront unbelievers (and anyone who might stand in his way) with the gospel.[62] This approach got him kicked out of the Farmer trial courtroom, but it served him well in his outreach with gangs, who appreciated his willingness to walk their streets, enter their dens, and engage in heated conversation about the state of their souls. Vaus was more measured. He drew on his electronics background, cleverly using his novel collection of stereos and lightning coils in public demonstrations to pique the interest of Harlem's youths before sharing his testimony.[63] He later built a youth center in East Harlem, where teens could gather for electronics training (for boys), beauty parlor appointments (for girls), a drink at a soda fountain (donated by Billy Graham), and spiritual instruction.[64]

Early on in their ministry efforts, both Wilkerson and Vaus intentionally sought the conversion of major players in New York's youth gangs. During a street evangelism session in Brooklyn not long after the Farmer trial, Wilkerson attracted a large crowd by having a friend blow "Onward Christian Soldiers" loudly on a trumpet. After preaching a sermon on John 3:16, Wilkerson asked to meet leaders of two local gangs, the Chaplains and the Mau Maus. As he spoke privately with the leaders about faith in Christ, some began to weep. "You're coming through, Preacher," said the chief of the Chaplains, a boy nicknamed Buckboard. Others were not convinced. Nicky Cruz, vice president of the Mau Maus, told Wilkerson, "Keep away from me, Preacher, you're not going to make me cry." But after a few more attempts, Wilkerson successfully persuaded Cruz and Israel Narvaez, the Mau Mau president, not only to come to Christ but also to join him in ministry. They acknowledged their spiritual transformation by handing over their weapons to Wilkerson. "I gave Brother Davy a bayonet and he gave me a Bible," Cruz remarked to one curious reporter (see Figure 2.2). Wilkerson began to take Cruz and Narvaez with him on the road for evangelistic crusades as living testimonies of God's work in Brooklyn, an evangelistic technique Vaus also practiced.[65]

As with Graham, the emphasis of urban evangelists like Vaus and Wilkerson was on Christian transformation of lawbreakers, not bringing them to justice. This did not mean that these evangelists did not care about crime or violence, but they viewed the spiritualized gospel as the primary answer to the lawbreaking. The convert Cruz was aware that his newfound life of faith had liberated him not only from a life of crime but also from the threat of punitive criminal justice. After seeing two dozen other gang members he recognized being sent to the reformatory, Cruz noted, "I was pretty lucky, I guess. I had a Bible, and they were chained."[66] Vaus also sought to keep youths out of prison, regularly urging law enforce-

Figure 2.2 Evangelist David Wilkerson reenacting his Bible-for-weapon trade with former gang member Nicky Cruz while Israel Narvaez looks on. Adult & Teen Challenge.

ment and court officials to allow youth offenders to receive parole instead of jail time. Regarding the case of a youth named Richard Morales who had been arrested for possessing drugs, Vaus pleaded with a court officer to keep the boy out of jail, noting his progress in YDI's electronics course and faithful church attendance as hopeful signs: "I do not believe that he would benefit by placement in an institution or any similar controlled environment, but would be best served by a probationary sentence and the skillful guidance of a probation officer."[67] One of Vaus's partners in ministry was Conrad Jensen, deputy inspector for the New York Police Department and head of the Twenty-Third Precinct. A "noted off-duty evangelist," Jensen helped Vaus with outreach to gang members, eventually becoming the associate director of YDI after his retirement from the police force. Vaus would call Jensen if he felt threatened by angry gang leaders. But in keeping with Vaus's desire to prevent youths from getting entangled with the police, Jensen reported that they preferred "a different way" from arrest, such as sitting down to a steak dinner with gang members and talking things through.[68] Jensen authored a series of tracts on crime, delinquency, and policing, some published by the American Tract Society. In the late 1950s and early 1960s, Jensen's vision of crime's cause and solution followed Vaus's: crime was rising and governmental social services oriented to delinquents were failing, but Christ could save lawbreakers. As one of Jensen's tracts concluded, "The answer to juvenile delinquency cannot be found in a program, but in a person— Jesus Christ."[69]

As Vaus's relationship with Jensen suggested, neither Vaus nor Wilkerson forswore discipline as a virtue for delinquents, nor did they villainize law enforcement. Vaus in particular regularly spoke of the combination of "love and discipline" as the solution to teenage crime and partnered with local police (some of whom praised YDI for its crime-reducing capabilities, calling it the "Miracle of the 23rd Precinct").[70] But this discipline was rarely penal in character, and police who worked with Vaus typically spoke of their regard for his ministry's ability to keep teens *out* of prison. Yet a tension between law and gospel could still be felt. Wilkerson wrestled with the problem of wanting to bring delinquents to freedom in Christ but also realizing that many of them had committed serious crimes. This was a "moral problem," he wrote. "It is not a simple question to answer. . . . If a boy confesses to the police too early and is put in jail, isn't there the risk of losing him? On the other hand, he has offended society's law and it will also hold him back spiritually if he harbors guilt. I have come to feel that there is no answer that will cover all cases." Wilkerson told the story of Pedro, a convert who frequented the Brooklyn Teen Challenge center and who felt wracked with guilt for his past crimes. He begged Wilkerson to let him confess to the police to free his conscience. Wilkerson urged him to wait, for "Pedro was so new to his changed life that jail sentence would almost surely set him back. . . . But he would have none of it." Pedro went on to confess a stabbing and two robberies to the police. But the police could not find anyone to press charges, and Pedro was freed into Wilkerson's custody.[71] The story, as Wilkerson narrated it, had a near-miraculous arc. The hoped-for conclusion of Pedro's salvation story was the redemption of his soul and the freedom of his conscience, not the incarceration of his body or the balance of the scales of justice.

This approach sometimes cut against the grain of broader public opinion. An example from Vaus's ministry is illustrative. In 1963 some of the boys who had been attending Vaus's YDI events were arrested by the police for a brutal attack on a social worker, Lou Marsh, who eventually died from his injuries. Because of his familiarity with the neighborhood youth gangs, Vaus was called to the police station to help question the suspects. Vaus asked the police whether he could enter the holding room by himself to talk to the boys in private. There he heard their side of the story: Marsh had confronted them, which started an argument. But, the boys told Vaus, they had not tried to hurt Marsh during the confrontation; he had fallen down *on his own* and smashed his head on the pavement.[72] By contrast, the press reported that the boys had brutally assaulted Marsh, that two boys "held his arms while the other two beat him senseless" (this account went nationwide through United Press International syndication, as well as through a report on Marsh in the *Christian Century*).[73] The *Saturday Evening Post* reported that broader public reactions to the death were calls for "these vicious kids," "animals," and "hoods" to be given "a taste of jail."[74] Most famously, the folk singer Phil Ochs composed a song about Marsh soon after news of the case emerged. The lyrics of "The Ballad of Lou Marsh" read,

> The city is a jungle
> When the law is out of sight
> And death lurks in El Barrio
> With the orphans of the night . . .
> With patience and with reason
> He tried to save their lives
> But they broke his peaceful body
> With their fists and feet and knives.

The more well-known singer Pete Seeger would record a modified version of the song a year later.[75] A radical who would later write anti-Vietnam songs, Ochs had no affinity for law enforcement. But he still played up the quality of the gang members as lawless barbarians.

Vaus saw things differently. Believing the boys' story that they were not responsible for Marsh's death, he drew out somewhere between seven and eight thousand dollars from YDI's coffers to pay for their defense lawyers. This put the ministry in the red for the year, but Vaus believed that without paid counsel the boys would likely be convicted of murder and receive harsh sentences. The attorneys Vaus hired found out that Marsh had a history of seizures and that they were prone to occur under stress. They called doctors as witnesses who testified that a seizure during a heated argument with the boys likely caused Marsh to go rigid, fall straight back, and fracture his head on the pavement. This was almost certainly the cause of his death, the defense argued, for there were no other bruises or signs of injury on Marsh's body. Vaus himself was present every day in court, along with other YDI staff, in support of the boys. He even was subpoenaed by the prosecution, who attempted to discredit him by referencing his criminal past. The boys ultimately were convicted, but for unpremeditated manslaughter (not murder). Instead of receiving long or life sentences, they were paroled into Vaus's care. He took responsibility of keeping track of the boys, helping them find jobs or schooling.[76]

This sympathy for New York's youths, sometimes at great personal cost or in opposition to prevailing popular opinion, characterized the ministries of both Vaus and Wilkerson. Instead of untrustworthy, violent bandits to be feared, juvenile delinquents were perceived by these urban evangelists fundamentally as children of God. Teenage gang members responded in kind. Wilkerson would regularly claim that gang members appreciated his work, but outside news reports often came to the same conclusion. Early in his ministry, one reporter told of a humorous moment when a roving group from the Mau Mau gang approached Wilkerson to help him with a flat tire. An attendant at a nearby gas station spotted the gang and ordered Wilkerson to leave. A Mau Mau retorted, "We'll burn your place down. He's our preacher." While the frightened attendant locked himself in the restroom, the gang changed the tire themselves.[77] Many of New York's teens respected Wilkerson and Vaus for their efforts (even if they perhaps saw the Pennsylvania street preacher and West Coast electronics wizard as a bit odd). For those who converted to Christianity under their influence, there was a profound sense of devotion and, eventually, partnership. One former drug addict and dealer named Benny Torrez described his own entrance into the Teen Challenge treatment program initially as an act of desperation. After having been in prison and floating from one rehab center to the next, Torrez sought out the ministry and encountered Wilkerson at one of the neighborhood evangelistic rallies. "I don't remember what he preached, but what he did, did something for my soul," Torrez said. "He showed me that my problem was sin and that I had sin in my heart, and the only way I can overcome that drug addiction was by going to the altar and asking God to forgive me of my sins. . . . If I accept him as my Savior, then I would be forgiven and my drug addiction would be taken from me completely. . . . That night, the Holy Spirit lifted me up." Beginning that night, Torrez's life started anew. He moved to Teen Challenge's "farm" (a treatment center in rural Pennsylvania), got sober, and after a few months returned to the city to serve as a counselor for other addicts.[78] This was Wilkerson's plan in motion:

the spiritual healing of New York's criminal outcasts, who would, in turn, go out to save others.

Another evangelical convert from New York gang life was Tom Skinner, an African American teen from Harlem. Skinner was born in 1942, the son of a Baptist preacher. An extremely bright boy, Skinner excelled in school, was active in church, and seemed to his parents to be on the straight and narrow. But Skinner hid a secret: his affiliation with the Harlem Lords youth gang and a deep disdain for Christianity. He had joined the Lords as a teenager and, after besting the gang's leader in a knife duel, became the Lords' top man, a position he held for two years.[79] Skinner loved the excitement of gang life, reveling in the brutality and violence. He devised tactics for the Lords in their frequent rumbles with other gangs and had twenty-two notches on his knife, "indicating how many fellows [he] had cut up." He hid his gang affiliation from his parents and church. Though he was adept at maintaining a spiritual and well-mannered facade, "the mob spirit had caused [him] to lose all restraint." He said, "I got to the place where I could break a Coke bottle and put it in a fellow's face and twist it."[80]

Skinner underwent a dramatic conversion in 1956, at age seventeen. While planning a gang fight, he was listening to the radio. The rock-and-roll program was unexpectedly interrupted by a radio preacher, who urged listeners to seek Christ's forgiveness for their sins. Though the preacher was unrefined and reminded Skinner of Sunday school clichés from childhood, the message stuck with him. As the broadcast concluded, Skinner prayed that Jesus would give him a new life. He quit the gang soon after. He miraculously avoided the expected retaliation when, according to Skinner, one vindictive Lords member found his body immobilized by an unseen outside force when he considered knifing Skinner in the back.[81]

Skinner believed he had a calling to reach his neighborhood for Christ. He began preaching in local churches and in 1962 was called by a group of ministers and business leaders to speak for the newly formed Harlem Evangelistic Association. Skinner soon began holding evangelistic meetings in Harlem and abroad, drawing nearly eight thousand attendees to a weeklong crusade at the Apollo Theater a few months later and seventeen thousand at a gathering in British Guiana the following year. The New York Times noted Skinner's rise and his ministry's similarities to that of Billy Graham in its crusade-style form and in Skinner's push for "decisions for Christ." And, like Graham, Skinner zeroed in on the problem of crime and the spiritual solution that Christ offered to sinners caught up in lives of lawlessness.[82] It was a natural pitch for him to make, as it was his own story and one that was intelligible to a growing evangelical movement looking to promote its successes to both co-laborers in the gospel and consumers of Christian products.

The Cross, Switchblade, and Evangelical Public Impact

Apart from the people who benefited from their ministries, Vaus, Wilkerson, and Skinner initially had a small reach. Their ministries started modestly and their budgets were shoestring.[83] Also, as missionaries to troubled youths, their basic methods were hardly cutting edge (particularly those of Wilkerson, who regularly embraced the mantle of the thundering street preacher). But as the 1960s wore on, the methods and aims of these evangelists became more widely known and appreciated, and ultimately would exert influence among evangelicals and in American culture more broadly.

Not long after Wilkerson arrived in New York, he began attracting attention from media outlets. He staged photo ops with gang members for local newspapers, reenacting the scene where he gave Nicky Cruz a Bible in exchange for his weapons.[84] Pentecostal publications began to cover his ministry and gave space to Wilkerson to describe his work and offer his opinions on topics related to delinquency.[85] In late 1961 *Guideposts* magazine published a two-part story on Wilkerson. Founded in 1944 by *Power of Positive Thinking* author and popular Manhattan pastor Norman Vincent Peale, *Guideposts* was a nondenominational publication known for feel-good inspirational stories, not doctrinal rigor. It also had one of the largest circulations of any national publication.[86] Peale's wife, Ruth, had pushed two of the magazine's writers, John and Elizabeth Sherrill, to cover Wilkerson when she heard about his work from a dinner guest. The Sherrills interviewed Wilkerson and began looking into his influence in Brooklyn, and the result was a feature spread across two issues, the first multipart series the magazine had ever run.[87] The story was a sensation, drawing letters from readers all over the nation who were fascinated by the gritty stories of Wilkerson's work in the slums. Sensing an opportunity, the Sherrills took Wilkerson to meet with prominent New York publisher Bernard Geis, who eventually agreed to publish an expanded version of Wilkerson's story as a book.[88]

This book, *The Cross and the Switchblade*, was published in May 1963 and became one of the best-selling religious books of the 1960s and 1970s.

Geis heavily promoted it in national media outlets.[89] Advance sales were strong, with *Publisher's Weekly* reporting that Geis had already ordered a second printing before the book was even released.[90] Part of the book's early success was owed to the fact that W. Clement Stone, a wealthy insurance magnate, positive thinking advocate, and Wilkerson booster, purchased one hundred thousand copies to be distributed for free by Teen Challenge. Stone's purchase saw that every Assemblies of God pastor in the country received a copy.[91] The book went through numerous printings (seven by the end of the first year) and would go on to sell eleven million copies within the first ten years of publication.[92] The book built off what made the initial *Guideposts* story so successful: Wilkerson's country preacher sensibilities, miraculous stories of God's provision, and most of all, gritty accounts of New York gang life. It was, as an ad marketing the book in the *Chicago Tribune* put it, "the inspiring story of a small-town pentecostal preacher who worked true miracles with the gangleaders, molls, and 'incurable' narcotics addicts of New York City's toughest slums."[93] The book's focus on violence, drugs, and illicit sex highlighted the radical nature of God's grace, but it also likely made the story appealing to a broader (in many cases, non-Christian) audience. It was no accident that the book was promoted by Geis, who the same year published *Sex and the Single Girl,* Helen Gurley Brown's controversial best seller that encouraged women to seek sex outside marriage.[94]

Besides providing a thrilling narrative, *The Cross and the Switchblade* cemented Wilkerson's influence and ministry methods in American public life. Before publication of the book, Wilkerson's work had been largely limited to discussions in religious periodicals (other than the embarrassing incident at the Farmer trial). Now he was featured in national news outlets, a product of Geis's publicity machine. As Geis's publicity head later opined, "[Geis] made authors into celebrities and celebrities into authors."[95] Wilkerson would give more credit to God than Geis, but the celebrity effect was the same either way. He went on a promotion tour of his book around the time of its release, including appearances on Art Linkletter's CBS show *House Party* and Jack Barry's interview program.[96] The *Los Angeles Times* cited Wilkerson as an "expert" in a story on teenage drug addiction and featured the city's new Teen Challenge center.[97] *Good Housekeeping* magazine reprinted several condensed chapters from the book in its July 1963 issue, with the front-page headline "How 'Faith in Action' Saved Kids in Trouble." Over sixteen pages, with photos of Nicky Cruz and Brooklyn's hardscrabble streets juxtaposed to a recipe for angel food cake and ads for lingerie and garden hoses, Wilkerson told the "inspiring true story of a small-town preacher who reached the despairing slum children of a big city with the message of God's love."[98] The venue did not domesticate Wilkerson's juicy descriptions of gang life or secularize his Pentecostal fervor (indeed it closed with the repeated refrain, "The Holy Spirit is in charge here"). Instead, it signaled that this was a message that every American household needed to hear. The piece was so popular that the magazine distributed reprints for civic and religious groups.[99]

The Cross and the Switchblade symbolized American evangelicals' arrival into a broader culture that was growing obsessed with juvenile delinquency. Delinquency had become a consumable pop product, from musicals like West Side Story, to dramatic films like Blackboard Jungle and Rebel without a Cause, to novels like The Outsiders. Wilkerson capitalized on this market, producing books on delinquency and drugs at a breakneck pace throughout the rest of the 1960s.[100] Wilkerson's protégé Nicky Cruz penned his own best-selling memoir, Run Baby Run, which was also edited by the Sherrills and the staff at Guideposts and helped launch his own evangelistic career.[101] As interest in delinquency surged in the media, ministers like Vaus, Wilkerson, Skinner, and Cruz began to be seen as evangelical authorities on any number of issues relating to crime. Though he had not abused or sold drugs during his own criminal past, Vaus wrote two books for the evangelical press Zondervan on drug abuse and juvenile crime.[102] He continued his national speaking tours, was featured in publications like Reader's Digest and Ebony, and was interviewed on national television by Merv Griffin, Barbara Walters, and Mike Douglas about his work and general topics like "success, power and crime."[103] Vaus's YDI began attracting significant attention from big-time donors, such as executives at U.S. Steel and Chase Manhattan Bank and former president Dwight D. Eisenhower.[104] Politicians such as Michigan governor George Romney and Oregon governor Mark Hatfield (who had worked with Vaus in the past) visited YDI. Hatfield later paid two more visits and was so impressed that he pushed to have similar programs opened in his home state.[105] In the mid- to late 1960s, Skinner published pamphlets and books through evangelical publishing houses like Baker and Zondervan and began broadcasting sermons on more than thirty radio stations nationwide. Evangelical magazines like Christian Life and Moody Monthly began featuring him as a key authority on urban evangelism and race.[106]

Eventually *The Cross and the Switchblade* was adapted into a feature film, starring actor, singer, and avowed Christian conservative Pat Boone in the role of Wilkerson and Erik Estrada (of later *CHiPs* fame) as Nicky Cruz. It joined a growing list of films that focused on crime and Christian faith, a genre that Vaus's *Wiretapper* had helped to jump-start. Mainline Protestants also participated in the trend. Though mainline leaders were still proceeding along largely progressive lines, their denominations' pop culture products paralleled the emphases of Graham and Wilkerson (a confirmation of both these evangelists' widespread middlebrow Protestant appeal and the haziness of the boundaries between categories like "evangelical" and "mainline" around midcentury).[107]

One prominent example was a film produced by the United Presbyterian Church in the United States in the aftermath of a grisly Philadelphia murder in 1959, entitled *An Epistle from the Koreans*. The film told the story of In-Ho Oh, a Korean student studying at the University of Pennsylvania, who was ambushed one night by a gang of eleven African American youths. They robbed In-Ho of his wallet and beat him severely. He died soon after. The film opens with a dramatization of this violent mugging and follows the story of the arrest, questioning, and trial of several of the boys. Interspersed throughout the true-crime-style narrative are warnings about the delinquency problem facing American society.[108] Religious books and magazines also picked up the story, dwelling on the lurid details of the case. One Mennonite periodical told the story in an article entitled "Blood on the Sidewalk," complete with blood splatters emblazoned across the title page.[109]

But the real focus of the film and related Christian media coverage, as indicated by the film's title, was to showcase the remarkable act of Christian compassion from In-Ho's family back in Korea. Shortly after learning of their son's death, In-Ho's parents and family (who were devout Presbyterians) composed a letter to authorities in Philadelphia, asking that the youths responsible for the crime receive leniency. Though sad about their son, they were also worried about "the unsaved souls and paralyzed human nature of the murderers." The family started a fund for the boys and mailed a check of $500 to help with the boys' rehabilitation. The film framed the Korean family's action as a challenge to the American church to get serious about delinquency and to be "challenged to bring its unique message of forgiveness and redemptive love to everyone." The film was a success for the denomination, shown at five thousand churches across the country.[110]

Fictional films also were produced, movies that paralleled Vaus's and Wilkerson's stories in their sensationalizing of crime and messages of grace and forgiveness for teen ruffians. In the 1966 film *To Forgive a Thief,* Roy Rogers Jr. (son of the famous Western star) played a rebellious delinquent named Dusty who finds himself in constant trouble with the law. He is adopted by a kind family, who attempt to introduce him to positive influences in the form of a surfer preacher named Mike. The family and surfer preacher both share the gospel with Dusty, though he continually resists their evangelistic efforts, believing that "nobody forgives a thief" and that he is headed for hell. Eventually he runs away from home. Mike catches up to him and, pointing to a statue of a cross in a nearby graveyard, tells Dusty about how Jesus loved and forgave the thieves crucified next to him. As the film closes, Dusty asks Jesus to forgive him and Mike tells the gathered family that this was precisely why Christ died: "to forgive a thief." And this forgiveness implicitly meant criminal justice could be circumvented; like *Wiretapper,* the film begins with Dusty in prison but ends with him free. A kindly old judge in the film puts a gloss on this narrative arc, telling Dusty's family, "The courts often hesitate about getting the boys mixed up in religion, but people like yourselves have proven that you have something the boys really need."[111] What was really needed was a message of forgiveness, outside the law. This was the message Graham, Vaus, and Wilkerson had helped to pioneer and popularize, now part of the parlance of American Protestant culture.

Crime Concern and Culture Making

Beneath the surface of the message of forgiveness outside the law, there were three other conceptual contributions evangelicals made to the framing of crime: apologetic formulation, an individualistic anthropology, and the construction of powerful icons of sinfulness. Each signified developments that would persist in evangelicals' understandings of criminality, their ministry to criminals, and their broader influence in American culture.

By seeking to reach criminals with the message of God's love, evangelicals were also acting as missionaries to American culture more broadly. The lives of criminals *mattered* and should be taken seriously by an increasingly dismissive society, but so should the Christian gospel itself. In redeeming criminals, evangelicals could redeem old-time religion. Reaching teens with the gospel, according to Wilkerson, meant helping them understand three things: God loves them, God loves the world, and God loves the world through them.[112] This idea was simple and certainly a claim many Christians had preached countless times before, in various forms. But this message was also an apologetic stratagem for reaching the nation at the particular cultural moment that the immediate postwar era represented. Through ministry to criminals, the gospel evinced staying power in a rapidly modernizing world.

The image of hardened criminals being reached when all other methods had failed was a kind of proof of the power of the gospel itself. Time and time again, Graham, Vaus, and especially Wilkerson made the claim that their methods were not only faithful but *effective*. Teen Challenge, according to Wilkerson, was proved to be the most capable weapon in the fight against illegal drug addiction. This was because drug addiction at its core, as Wilkerson told the *New York Times,* was a "spiritual problem that can be solved only by the power of God."[113] And, Wilkerson and co-ministers argued, the data bore this truth out, pointing to success rates ranging from 60 to 70 percent.[114] These success rates (which in later years were claimed to be as high as 86 percent) were also widely questioned by outsiders, but Teen Challenge's interest in quantifying the ministry's effectiveness indicated a deep concern with the gospel's viability.[115] This concern was regularly framed in terms of the empirical truthfulness of the gospel itself. Frank Reynolds, one of Wilkerson's associates and a Teen Challenge leader, narrated his own work with the ministry as a search to answer the question, as the title of his biography put it, "Is there a God?" The former atheist decided that, given the radical testimonies of gang members who experienced salvation, the answer was "YES!" Reynolds continued, "Not only is there a real, living God, but He has revealed Himself and proven Himself by confirming His Word in real miracles throughout my life!"[116]

Tom Skinner's conversion story followed a similar pattern. Though Skinner wrote of his liberation from violence and gang life, he also narrated this story as an intellectual journey from atheism to Christianity. Skinner portrayed himself in his writing and speaking as a "teenage intellectual," making regular references to his fondness for existentialism, Jean-Paul Sartre, and Bertrand Russell. He framed his journey out of the Harlem Lords as akin to an embrace of rational faith, one that grasped God's existence, the reliability of the Bible, and the love of Jesus. "Every true scientist knows you must never draw conclusions about anything you have never put to the test," Skinner wrote in one evangelistic pamphlet (a reprint of passages from his book *Black and Free*). "As a student of science I was a strong believer in the scientific method. . . . It occurred to me that I had never put God to the test . . . had never given him a chance to work in my life." Skinner walked through standard evangelical proofs on various intellectual challenges to the faith but contended that the most powerful empirical evidence was his own story, the miraculous journey from crime to Christ. "The evidence was that Tom Skinner was a phony and that Jesus Christ died for phonies. . . . No trumpets. No shouts. No visions." This was an intensely logical, empirically driven evangelistic strategy, one that eschewed enthusiasm and religious experience for evidence and intellectual insight.[117]

Apologetic concerns have always been a part of Christian discourse, but their presence was particularly justifiable in the 1960s. God appeared on the outs in a world where the power and prestige of "big science" were on the rise, where godless communism was taking hold, where growing awareness of the Holocaust scandalized notions of theodicy, and where a 1966 cover of *Time* magazine was asking provocatively whether God was dead.[118] But according to evangelicals, God was still alive in America's prisons, slums, and drug dens. After all, criminals, delinquents, and druggies had found him. This reality, as the title of the *Guideposts* piece that brought Wilkerson into the public spotlight declared, was "too strange to be a coincidence."[119]

For insiders and outsiders alike, it was a compelling argument. The situating of the evangelical message of grace within the crime-ridden environs of urban slums showed outsiders that the old-time gospel should be taken seriously as an important resource for addressing America's modern crisis of crime and, indirectly, the theological crises of modernity. A *Washington Post* reviewer of *The Cross and the Switchblade* remarked that Holy Spirit baptism and speaking in tongues "might seem an odd way to change the heart of a dope addict or a tough gang leader. Yet, on second thought, the Rev. Wilkerson may be making a profound observation about what it takes to reach and release people whose experiences have been generally traumatic." Indeed, researchers and social workers could learn from Wilkerson's attention to the emotions of delinquents. Wilkerson's work, as the title of the review put it, "rings true."[120] In a *Woman's Day* article, a student at the liberal Harvard Divinity School wrote of his admiration for the work of Wilkerson, who "has shown even in the most improbable cases that teen-agers can find religion relevant to their lives," from "narcotics addicts, gang fighters, young prostitutes, as well as affluent comfortable teen-agers."[121] Framing the issue in terms of probability was a reference to the hopeless status of delinquents' lives, but it also indicated the power embedded within the evangelical methods for persuading others of the need for personal conversion.

This praise did not go unnoticed by evangelicals. The *Pentecostal Evangel* reprinted excerpts of a positive assessment of Teen Challenge that had appeared in the Jesuit weekly *America*. Kilian McDonnell, the original piece's author and himself a leader of the Catholic charismatic movement, had praised Teen Challenge's success rate and its theological outlook: "There is a Pentecostal jargon, but there is also real substance to the message that is preached. . . . Teen Challenge is effective because it preaches the whole of the Biblical message as the Pentecostals see it." Like most other evangelicals of the day, Pentecostal readers of the *Evangel* would have been skeptical of Catholics' claims to orthodoxy. But if Catholic journalists (called "scientists" by the *Evangel*) were handing out compliments, Pentecostals were happy to take them. The *Evangel* reprinted McDonnell's most glowing praise verbatim: "The preaching at Teen Challenge and in other Pentecostal churches is a reminder that Christian secularity without a consciousness of sin and judgment will degenerate into the vaporizing of a bloodless humanism. The Pentecostal instinct is essentially correct."[122] An outsider's validation of Teen Challenge, over and against secularity no less, was a valuable confirmation of the Pentecostal message.

A second contribution was the diagnosis of crime in the terms of an individualistic anthropology. This flowed from the way evangelicals framed their message about the Christian gospel: individuals were the primary agents of God's salvation, not social structures or institutions. This message had theological roots but also drew from classic populist American self-understandings.[123] Famously individualistic themselves, Americans were used to hearing messages that focused on personal choice and self-driven possibility. For evangelicals considering crime, the individualistic argument went like this: criminals had made conscious choices that put them in their horrible circumstances, and they would have to make a conscious choice to leave. God, in his grace, would welcome prodigals home (and perhaps even run to meet them halfway), but those who chose to sin would, in turn, have to make the first choice. "Salvation doesn't really count until you truly repent!" Wilkerson preached in one sermon. "Repentance can never be anything but your very own act. God will use forces to draw us but will never coerce our wills. . . . Repentance begins with a revelation and an admission of personal guilt. You cannot blame parents or environment or use any pathetic excuses of psychiatrists. You must feel the guilt—admit you are in darkness and that you are condemned and unable to save yourself."[124]

Graham made this approach famous. The climax of his crusades was a moment of *decision,* when individuals asked Jesus into their hearts and walked down the arena aisles to meet with counselors one-on-one. The sociopolitical ethic that complemented this evangelistic approach was what historian Steven Miller has called "evangelical universalism," where the individual soul was seen as "the primary theological and political unit in society." This approach "prioritized relational over legislative solutions."[125] As Graham argued in one op-ed, "Society is made up of individuals. So long as you have a man in society who hates and lies and steals and is deceitful, you have the possibility of racial intolerance. . . . Our great problem today is not social. . . . Our problem is man himself. We've got to change man."[126] Or as Graham put it in a 1957 radio sermon on crime, "We are treating symptoms in this country and very rarely do we check crime at its source. Society is made up of individuals who have all sinned against God and his glory. . . . The world cannot be changed until individuals are changed."[127] The answer to the crime problem, then, was for sinners to ask God to transform their personal nature.

For Vaus, this emphasis had complicated autobiographical resonances that indicated both the individualistic ideal and its potential limits. Vaus's public persona depended on a narrative of dramatic heart change, beginning with his response to Graham's sermon at the 1949 revival. "Behind the headlines was the terrible conflict of a man's soul," his early book *Why I Quit Syndicated Crime* declared. "The answer to what makes a preacher's son become a member of a gangster's mob lies within the heart of every man."[128] A focus on the individual's heart was a helpful gloss for explaining his own journey and likely connected to the audiences who read his work and heard him speak. But Vaus faced challenges as he moved from crusade-style evangelism and writing in the early and mid-1950s to actual ministry in Harlem in the late 1950s and early 1960s. When he preached or wrote to broader audiences, Vaus could streamline and simplify; the gospel was the answer, whatever the problem. In Harlem, however, things could be a bit more complicated. The more time Vaus spent among at-risk youths in the city, the more he realized that their educational, social, and economic needs must be addressed alongside their individual spiritual problems. As his son noted years later, work in Harlem with YDI changed his father. It made him less judgmental, and made him want to care for physical needs, not just spiritual concerns. However, by this point, the frame of the argument was already in place, and the giant crusades and best-selling books of Graham and Wilkerson (the latter of whom, in 1967, left New York City to focus on crusade evangelism) guaranteed that this would be the message most would hear.[129] Indeed, Vaus's ministry would soon be subsumed by Teen Challenge, which continued to focus on the necessity of repentance and the priority of heart change as it expanded across the country and around the world.[130]

Implicit in this idealized vision was a new understanding of *how* social engagement on crime should occur. "Delinquency Ends Where Christ Begins," read the tagline of an ad promoting Vaus's ministry in the magazine *United Evangelical Action*.[131] Simple enough, but the effect (frequently hammered home by evangelicals concerned about crime) was a blistering critique of progressive-style social welfare's potential to help criminals. Unlike many of the social service programs in New York, the evangelical ministries of Vaus and Wilkerson were funded by private individuals, churches, and foundations, not taxes. They were particularly indebted to the generosity of Christian businesspeople, a group who often voiced their disdain for socialistic wealth distribution or governmental intervention in the economy in the name of social welfare.[132] In one interview, George Champion, the board chairman of Chase Manhattan Bank (and chair of Graham's 1957 New York crusade), hailed America's system of free enterprise and urged reduction in governmental domestic spending before pointing to his "favorite charity," Vaus's YDI.[133] Likewise, Wilkerson emphasized constantly that Teen Challenge had a methodology that was different from any governmental approach to delinquency and addiction. "To bring the teen-agers back to a reality we don't take them down the dark alleys of psychotherapy," Wilkerson boasted. "Our social workers are completely untrained in methods of psychology and related fields, and that's the way I want them to be."[134] Supporters of the ministry agreed. Walter Hoving, the chairman of Tiffany & Co. in New York, wrote that he supported Teen Challenge because of the failure of non-Christian attempts to solve America's drug problem: "Only a fraction of a percentage of the addicts have been helped by governmental efforts or by private efforts that approach him by using treatments which appeal to his will power alone to overcome his addiction." Instead, he argued, "an addict must find something stronger than himself, something outside of himself that can help him overcome his craving for narcotics. [Teen Challenge's] method of invoking a complete change in the individual by calling upon the power of God through the Holy Spirit to help him, in my judgment, is the only way."[135]

The final contribution was the construction of new icons of sinfulness, powerful foils to the Christian gospel. The most obvious was crime itself. A paradoxical dynamic was emerging: even as Graham, Wilkerson, Vaus, Skinner, and other postwar evangelists pushed spiritual solutions over penal ones, they nonetheless were making crime and criminals all the more menacing. The ability to narrate the glorious riches of God's forgiveness and grace was only made possible *after* the depravity of the criminal life had been explicated. Vaus's testimony, in person, in print, or on film, was dependent on a robust description of gangster life and tactics. According to one poster advertising the movie *Wiretapper,* "You can get away with *Murder!*" This was "the true-life drama of the man who kept the Gamblers, the Gangsters and the Bookies always one step ahead of the law!" (Figure 2.3). The "inside-story" motif was clearly meant to entertain and draw audiences in, but there was a repeated emphasis in Vaus's public testimony on how threatening gangsters were to America. Wilkerson's broader appeal also depended on his ability to play up the horrors and dangers of city gangs. Readers likely felt assured by the religious dimension of his memoir's narrative, but what really demanded attention was the stark juxtaposition of cross to *switchblade*. Sometimes his gritty focus and warnings about gang activity were overstated enough so as to draw public skepticism. One newspaper challenged Wilkerson's claim during a revival in Elmira, New York, that the small upstate town was a new hotbed of gang activity (Wilkerson claimed eight gangs total). The police, the report claimed, had no knowledge of this underworld. Instead, they said that Wilkerson was mistaking normal groups of young people for organized criminals, making a miscreant mountain out of a molehill.[136]

Evangelicals typically pointed to American cities, a second iconic foil, as backdrops for rampant crime. To hear evangelicals talk about cities was to hear stories of dark dens of delinquency, drugs, racketeering, and prostitution. The effect was that while they were naming the "inner city" as a new evangelical mission field, they were also playing up its essentially sinful and disorderly connotations. Featured as an expert on delinquency in a 1963 issue of the *Los Angeles Times,* Wilkerson rattled off several frightening statistics about the dangerous state of urban America: "I can tell you some 10 to 15 block areas here, where 75% of the teenagers are on drugs. . . . The public has no idea of the extent of this problem or the

Figure 2.3 A promotional poster for the 1955 film *Wiretapper*, based on the story of Jim Vaus. Reproduced from the author's collection.

growth of gangs, mainly with the terrifying purpose of keeping up this habit." A public solution to urban strife, Wilkerson argued, would be something like a "domestic Peace Corps" that would draw fifty thousand young people out of the cities and into forests and camps. "Urban living, for kids," Wilkerson argued, "is unnatural. I think a city boy ought to know how to milk a cow."[137] Vaus and his ministry supporters typically spoke in more measured tones but would have largely concurred. In the early 1960s YDI purchased a tract of land to build a youth camp in Glen Spey, New York.[138] Rural youth camps would be a regular feature of the ministry for the rest of the decade, and the goal was clear: get kids out of the city and into pastoral (and therefore orderly) environs.

One YDI fund-raising brochure indicated the philosophy hovering in the background as it described the problems the organization was trying to tackle. Set against a large photo of a scowling black teen boy on a graffiti-scrawled city street, the brochure read, "Almost 200,000 people live in squalor, deprivation and perpetual hopelessness in a one square mile area of East Harlem in New York. . . . Most of them are Puerto Rican or Negro. The majority have never lived outside the ghetto, never seen a normal middle class home or the grass and trees of an American suburb. Most have never known traditional family life. They are untouched by the influence of Christianity. Their plight is typical of youngsters in the ghettos of every major American city."[139] With statements like this, Wilkerson and Vaus were narrating the situation as they saw it, referencing some of the very real challenges that the people living in Brooklyn and Harlem faced (even as they ignored the long history of Christian presence and church work, particularly by African Americans, in these neighborhoods). But it was not a stretch to imagine how the reception of their ideas would lead other white evangelicals to the conclusion that there was something intrinsically un-Christian about the inner-city existence of people of color, even as it provided a space for the evangelical message to take root anew. This was the beginning of a repeated dynamic that would characterize evangelical urban concern in the second half of the twentieth century. "Cities were stages," anthropologist Omri Elisha has argued, "literally and figuratively—from which the Christian gospel of sin and redemption can be proclaimed to national and global audiences." Elisha continues, "Much like the many foreign and remote locations of the world that typically inspire missionary fantasies, the inner city was represented as an unfamiliar and intimidating space of otherness, except that it was 'in our own backyard.'"[140] This sense of ambiguity about the urban environment would be a driving factor in leading missionaries into the city even as many of their white evangelical brethren, who often had strong ties to cities in the first half of the twentieth century, were increasingly leaving to reside in the suburbs. White evangelicals' growing sense of the "wicked and guilty city" would draw a select number of the faithful into urban engagement even as it led most others to relocate their homes and churches to new environs.[141]

Race was the oft-unnoticed yet crucial variable in this reenvisioning of the city. White evangelicals were framing a response to crime in terms of individual forgiveness at the same time that they were denoting cities (with their growing black populations) as disorderly locales. They rarely acknowledged this racial backdrop directly, instead preferring to understand the crime problem in the most abstract racial terms possible; the boys Wilkerson and Vaus ministered to just happened to be black or brown. Of course, it never was abstract in terms of how criminal justice in American cities actually worked or how their segregation or economic disruption primarily affected people of color. Little was said by white Christians focused on forgiveness about how delinquents' black or brown skin had limited their educational opportunities, prevented their families from accessing decent housing because of racist redlining, led to their isolation from the labor market, and put them at higher risk of arrest.[142]

In his early evangelistic career, Tom Skinner was the most conscious of the ways race framed the crime problem, but his focus on spiritual solutions nonetheless showcased the standard approach and the limits of the new evangelical approach to crime and conversion. "I suffered the injustices of the white power structure just like any kid in the Negro community," he told the New York Times in 1964. "But it has not turned me bitter because I know that it's sin in the heart of the white man that causes the prejudice."[143] The heart, not redlined neighborhoods or segregated school systems, was the fundamental site of both sin's diagnosis and its hopeful solution. Skinner's first book, Black and Free, wrestled with problems of racism, crime, and social concern as they related to evangelical religion and conversion, pointing out the problems that poor black Americans faced in cities across the country and their roots in slavery and Jim Crow. The book's concluding FAQ even noted that black people had good reason to riot given their history of oppression (though, he pointed out, the only ones who did were "the hoodlum element in the Negro community").[144] But the overarching message of the book was that individual conversion of souls was the only true answer, not environmental change. Skinner even went so far as to emphasize the conscious choices that African Americans made when they turned to a life of crime or addiction. In a sermon entitled "The White Man Did It," Skinner actually wondered "how far we can go with this accusation." He pointed to black crime, family breakdown, addiction, and rape as evidence that in fact the core issue was sin in black peoples' hearts. "Rather than attack a race of people and blame them for our dilemma, let us attack the sinful nature of man." As Skinner moved to invite his listeners to accept Christ at the conclusion of the sermon, the choir behind him sang "Just as I Am" as the invitation hymn. That this was the same song Billy Graham used to conclude his crusades was fitting, because it was a similar gospel that was being shared. Skinner concluded, in words that Graham himself could have preached, that "whether their problem was social, economic or educational, Christ was the answer."[145]

The anthropological and theological assumptions built into this vision of human beings making a decision to choose both sin and the life of faith resonated with white evangelicals trying to develop paradigms for ministry to African Americans in cities. It enabled the evangelical magazine *Christian Life* (a publication that catered to white evangelical churches and networks) to entitle an article by Skinner "I Preach the White Man's Religion," even though in the article Skinner did not use the phrase. He had actually declared, in response to black Muslims who accused him of kowtowing to white Christians, "I'm not preaching anybody's religion—I'm preaching God."[146] In a pamphlet from early in his ministry, Skinner declared that his conversion had led him away from not only crime and violence but also prejudice: before coming to Christ, he "was as bigoted as any white racist." Skinner offered white evangelicals a way to view their faith and racism in the most abstract terms possible; racism became a sin that might tempt all people (black and white) rather than a historical and contemporary reality that described specific oppression of black people by whites. In doing so, he confirmed for white evangelicals many of the suspicions they had about the wicked, crime-filled city and reified the confidence that their timeless message of heart change could take hold.[147]

White evangelicals welcomed and amplified this message, believing it to confirm their theological presuppositions about individual conversion and their nonthreatening status in American religion and politics, above the racial fray. Whether Skinner believed this himself at this early stage of his career is not clear, but his ministerial approach fit well in both his framing and the foils he chose. Though he knew racism had contributed to the plight of African Americans in urban slums, the main enemies Skinner faced in his early writing for white periodicals and publishers were black, whether dangerous black gang members or black Muslims and nationalists (who showed up to Skinner's crusade demanding that he be lynched). White evangelicals reading his work could be assured not only that the cities were dangerous, crime-ridden places but also that ghettos, not racism, harbored the most pressing and real danger to black life. Similarly, Skinner's early writing also offered evangelicals proof of the seeming spiritual ineffectiveness of historic black churches that had been present in black neighborhoods (the ones that Wilkerson and Vaus largely ignored in their writing when they characterized ghettos as godless). He spent three chapters in *Black and Free* detailing his problems with mainline black churches, arguing that their corruption and shallow spirituality were a key reason he had originally resisted the Christian message.[148] Instead, for Skinner and the evangelicals who welcomed his message and printed or broadcast it with regularity, the answer was a robust *black* evangelicalism, one that would stress personal conversion and conservative theology. Skinner challenged white evangelicals to acknowledge that their racism in the past had limited their appeal to African Americans, and opened the door for "theological liberal friends . . . like Martin Luther King and Robert Abernathy" to gain a foothold. The way forward was not so much to embrace the civil rights activism of King and others but to expand white evangelicals' ministry in black neighborhoods and to make their mission strategy palatable to potential converts therein. For example, Skinner contended, in order to reach "a typical Negro in the ghetto," evangelical magazines needed to feature black authors and expand beyond the "language of white, middle-class society."[149] The racial problems facing evangelicalism had more to do with mediums of the faith, not the message itself.

The Presbyterian film *Epistle to the Koreans* exemplified the way well-intentioned white Christian conceptions of race permeated their engagement with crime issues. At the same time that the filmmakers isolated the challenge of crime for white American Christians and posited the possibility of forgiveness and sympathy with lawbreakers as a response, they made two other moves: identifying black youths as the criminals and Asian Christians as virtuous exemplars. As historian Hannah Kim has shown, the In-Ho Oh case was a crystallization of the Cold War–era racial politics that permeated Philadelphia and the nation more broadly at the time. Koreans were regularly framed as friends of American democracy and allies in the struggle against communism abroad and, as the film indicated, against delinquency at home. The media (particularly Christian publications) constructed an "idealized imaginary In-Ho" in these terms, positing him and his family as a kind of model minority. Concurrently, as Kim shows, "the African-American attackers became the 'bad minorities' who could not be integrated into mainstream America." This was precisely the position that many local white lay observers of the In-Ho case held, as they wrote letters to Philadelphia newspapers and politicians that lamented what they took to be the poor parenting skills of African Americans and the bad behavior of black migrants from the South (despite the fact that the youths were not from there). At the same time that they deployed these racialized judgments, these writers also urged harsher punishments, including public whippings, longer prison sentences, and the death penalty, as the best response to this crime and juvenile delinquency more generally. Others recommended roving gun squads and forced sterilization of offenders. Black Philadelphians, while they did not ignore the tragedy of the In-Ho case or forswear the need for justice, noticed the racialized subtext being deployed here, with its obvious connections to past assaults on black people in American history. One letter writer warned that the attacks on the suspects were setting the "stage for a lynch atmosphere."[150]

The filmmakers who created *Epistle to the Koreans,* much like Wilkerson, Graham, and Vaus, clearly did not desire a lynch mob. But like the Christians who voiced concerns about lynching in terms of social disorder (and not racial injustice), the film did not attempt to address directly the racial dynamics at play in the murder, the social conditions that produced it, or the white public's troubling response. Instead, the film contended, there was "no reason" for the murder; it was "a brutal senseless act." Or, as one promotional review of the film in the Church of the Brethren magazine *Gospel Messenger* put it, "[The crime] could have happened to anybody. It had nothing to do with race."[151] Indeed, via an imagined scene of white and black civic leaders in conversation, the film suggested that racial problems were decreasing: "Things are changing for black people," contends one African American leader, "and for the better." His white conversation partner suggests that systemic racial issues are to blame for crime, but then moves this progressive rumination into no less of an indictment of black lawlessness: "You can't segregate people and still expect them to behave like saints overnight." Religion is posited as the ultimate solution. Paralleling In-Ho's family's Christian virtues (which the filmmakers describe as "a way of life"), a black boy from the same neighborhood as the killers is shown praying with his family at the dinner table. The film describes how he avoided being swept up in the killing because of his family's religious values.

The In-Ho Oh case also showed the practical limits of forgiveness, in spite of the hopes of Christian commentators and the Presbyterian filmmakers. Though In-Ho's family raised money for the suspected murderers and pleaded for leniency in their sentencing, neither the boys nor their families ever actually received any financial assistance; the act was deemed impractical and "impossible" by Presbyterian administrators. Instead, the money was given to a Philadelphia Boy Scout troop. The youth gang received tough prison terms (with one even getting a death sentence). In response to the murder, Philadelphia's police commissioner ramped up patrols in the city, ordering his officers to uncover gang activity and stop and question suspicious characters.[152] The film and most other Christian renderings of the case ignored or glossed over these complications, preferring instead to see the story as an illustrative parable about the power of forgiveness.

Setting the Terms

The combined effect of these concepts was that evangelicals, as they were entering the public sphere, were helping to set the terms of a broader debate on how crime in postwar America should be understood and addressed. Crime was a national phenomenon (concentrated in cities, yet threatening to spill over into suburbs and small towns), and its effects were tragic and rampant. And yet a solution was possible. The solution was the spiritual balm of the gospel of Jesus Christ for the criminal's wounded soul.

What was often conspicuously missing, and sometimes rejected outright, was an evangelical confidence that tougher criminal justice could solve the crime problem. This fact cuts against the common characterization of postwar evangelicals as passionate advocates for more law and order, harsher punishment for crimes, and the death penalty. There were indeed fundamentalists around this time who framed their understanding of crime in these terms. Harsh punishment (even death) was the demand of God's justice, as the fundamentalist icon Carl McIntire argued. But just as the postwar evangelical movement was consciously moving away from the likes of McIntire (usually framing its critique as a rejection of fundamentalists' "uneasy" cultural isolationism), it was also indicating that strong confidence in harsh punishment was not the best way forward.[153] More important, the movement's adherents believed, it was simply unfaithful. Their message was that every criminal could be washed in the blood of Jesus, the one who bore the punishment for humanity's sins. Evangelicals felt that questions of maintaining the social order or deterring crime through the threat of prison were important, and those doing the work of law enforcement should be respected. But these issues were secondary when there was a gospel to be preached, one that could redeem criminals and noncriminals, who were far more alike in their common fallen state than different.

In the same way, these evangelicals were also rejecting the typical liberal answer to crime, pioneered by the progressives who saw variables like economics, education, and psychology as the best metrics for understanding and addressing crime. Evangelicals believed this "social matrix," as liberal religious representatives had called the necessary framing of the crime problem, removed human moral culpability and, with it, a profound sense of God's grace. This paralleled evangelical frustration with progressive ideology on any number of other issues. For example, progressives pointed to structural reasons for poverty while conservatives (evangelicals typically among them) pointed to the need to recover a sense of personal responsibility. But because it inherently dealt with questions of moral blame, the crime issue crystallized and intensified the debate.

American evangelicals in the early postwar era were both in the world and not of it. They drew on the broad crime concern consensus of the 1920s–1940s in their mutual concern with crime as a defining social issue facing the nation. Lawlessness was truly, as Graham had opined in 1957, "the spirit of our age." But "spirit" here meant more than common concern. It also referenced a numinous reality that transcended temporal solutions, both penal and progressive. Oregon governor Mark Hatfield summed up this point in 1959 in his comments to the United Press about the work of Vaus and YDI: "I didn't believe it until I spent an afternoon on foot in an area where hundreds of policemen and millions of dollars are spent on crime. The transformation is in the very atmosphere. . . . Tax funds and night sticks are not the answer. Love and discipline may be and they cannot be purchased at any price."[154] Ultimately the secular state, in its progressive (tax funds) or punitive (night sticks) forms, did not have the answer to the problem.

Interpretations of evangelicalism that label the movement as synonymous with "tough on crime" conservatism should be revised. But they should not be abandoned. At the end of the 1960s, a massive change in the evangelical approach to the crime issue was indeed on the horizon, a move to law and order. More will be said later about how this movement developed, but for now it is enough to note the need to historicize evangelicals' punitive exploits in criminal justice: it was not always this way, and it was not a foregone conclusion that evangelicals would travel this path.

However, there were certainly seeds planted by the evangelicals who preached to criminals and ministered to gangs that helped set the stage for evangelical law and order. These seeds were the "icons of sinfulness" of crime itself and the racialized inner city. Each would serve as a target for a later generation of evangelicals who were equally concerned with lawlessness but who utilized a sharper set of tools to address the problem. Consider Wilkerson's own rhetoric as an emblematic example. Though he had proclaimed Christ as the spiritual solution for addiction (over and against secular treatment programs and imprisonment), he also grew to see drugs as a *social* problem that threatened to move beyond the inner city into the suburbs.[155] And social dangers required social solutions, which is why Wilkerson increasingly spoke of the need to criminalize drug usage later in the 1960s, even as he maintained that progressive-style measures were insufficient. "I consider marijuana the most dangerous drug used today," he wrote in one feature article entitled "Should Marijuana Be Legalized." He continued, "90 percent of all drug addicts we have ever treated began with marijuana and then graduated to something harder." Besides urging youths to avoid weed, he also taught them how to recognize it and, importantly, report those smoking it to the police. "If you think this is asking too much, just ask yourself: 'How would I like it if that stick of pot was offered to my younger brother or sister?'"[156] The push to recognize the necessity of legal prohibition and law enforcement, and the castigation of other social efforts to reduce drug addiction, made Wilkerson's ministry an ideal partner for a later generation of conservative politicians. By the 1980s, Nancy Reagan would visit Teen Challenge centers as part of her broader antidrug push and President Ronald Reagan would declare, "I speak from more than 20 years of knowledge of the organization when I tell you that the Teen Challenge program works. It's effective—it's literally changing the lives of young Americans from every walk of life. The government can't do it alone no matter how hard it tries."[157] Despite a lack of confidence in governmental solutions and state control, Reagan would nonetheless exert a great deal of effort in fighting drugs with expanded law enforcement, tougher prison sentences, and the rhetoric of an all-out "war on drugs." Wilkerson's vision and ministry were complementary partners.

Even as they planted seeds that would lead to a more punitive approach to crime, the evangelicals profiled here also helped to birth another movement: evangelical ministry in America's expanding prison system. In the latter half of the twentieth century, evangelical work inside American prisons would grow immensely, as ministries were founded, evangelistic literature printed, and volunteers recruited. Most observers place the beginning of evangelical prison ministry in the mid-1970s, as figures like Charles Colson took interest in reaching inmates for Christ. But as we have seen, evangelicals were concerned with criminals long before. Later prison ministers were innovators in their own right, but as they framed their gospel message as an antidote to crime and sometimes an alternative to harsh punishment, they were drawing on important precedents from an earlier generation.

Besides revising typical understandings of how evangelicals related to crime, this chapter nuances another common understanding of evangelical social concern. Crime concern was an ideal ministerial context for the voicing of what has been called the "personal influence strategy."[158] Simply put, this strategy understands positive social change as happening through individual conversion; if enough people become Christians and adopt Christian moral norms, then society will change for the better and racism, oppression, greed, and violence will cease.[159] In conversations on poverty, race, and other issues, white evangelicals have endured critique for the individualistic perspective this strategy entails. Implicit here is a lack of recognition of any systemic evils or top-down solutions (hence the argument proffered by many white evangelicals that segregation was a problem best solved not by government involvement but by changing the hearts of racists). The personal influence view was present among evangelicals on a variety of other social issues, particularly among criminals and delinquents: convert criminals and they won't commit crimes any longer. Criticism about the efficacy and appropriateness of this formula emerged along the lines one might expect: this strategy blinded evangelicals to the systemic realities at play, such as the massive racial disparities in the prosecution of criminal justice and the economic well-being of black neighborhoods.

This lack of consciousness of systemic social ills was evident in Wilkerson's journey to New York for the first time. Drawn to the city by the Michael Farmer trial, Wilkerson wanted to "go to New York City and help those boys" by preaching the gospel to them. But what Wilkerson missed was the broader context of the Farmer killing itself, the ways that racial segregation had made the crime itself possible and framed public opinion about the trial. The killing was not a random murder but rather the result of long-simmering racial tensions between African American and Hispanic minorities and the surrounding Irish, Jewish, and Greek neighborhoods. The black and Hispanic group of boys who killed Farmer had identified him as part of a rival Irish gang that had recently chased them from a local swimming pool. Angry over this informal practice of segregation, the gang attacked Farmer when he unwittingly wandered into a park where they were congregating. The dispute over what races were allowed in a pool was emblematic of the deep racial tensions that marked mid-century New York and the nation more broadly.[160] As someone who saw the Farmer crime in totally spiritual terms, Wilkerson missed this broader racialized context. As someone who continued to frame delinquency and drugs in spiritual terms, he would continue to underplay or even ignore the power of other causal factors, whether racism, poverty, or mental health issues.

Nevertheless, the personal influence strategy had power as a method of evangelical engagement with criminals. For one, it allowed for *personal* encounters and relationships with a population otherwise reduced to faceless statistics in the bureaucratic apparatus of state power, both progressive and punitive. Evangelical personal influence may have been flawed as a strategy for ridding America of crime or the systemic social realities that cause it, but it was a tangible way for criminals to be rehumanized in a society that was prone to forget them. This was the positive side of Wilkerson's New York mission. When recounting his unheeding entrance into the Farmer trial to meet with the suspected murderers, Wilkerson later noted that the prevailing opinion of those in the courtroom was not only that the boys were guilty but that they deserved death. "They ought to get the chair, all of them," said the man sitting next to Wilkerson. "That's the way to handle them. Can't be too careful. God, I hate those boys!" Wilkerson, without missing a beat, retorted, "God seems to be the only one who doesn't."[161] Not long after, when Wilkerson was first visiting with some other gang members, he confessed the same conviction. "I don't know why God brought me to this town," Wilkerson told a gang member named Willie. "But let me tell you one thing. *He* is on your side. That I can promise you."[162]

The fact that Wilkerson often ignored systemic or therapeutic analyses of crime in favor of a personal response indicated that evangelicals concerned about crime had their blind spots. This blindness was problematic on its own, and it would have even more tragic consequences in later years as the gears of the machine of mass incarceration began to turn. But this same personal response, though limited, was a genuine effort to try to make sense of and offer a compassionate response to instances of human depravity and brokenness. Evangelicals like Graham, Vaus, and Wilkerson were certain that God was on *their* side, a belief that verged on overconfidence. But they also believed God was on the side of criminals. For those who wanted forgiveness, this could be a blessed assurance.

3

RELIGION IS A REAL WEAPON

Henry Schwarzschild needed help. The head of the Capital Punishment Project of the American Civil Liberties Union, Schwarzschild was a key leader in the battle against the death penalty in America, and he was trying to find partners to join his cause. The stakes were high. The death penalty had been the subject of fierce debate in American life long before the Supreme Court struck it down as "cruel and unusual punishment" and for its racially discriminatory application in 1972's *Furman v. Georgia.* Now a recent case, 1976's *Gregg v. Georgia,* had reinstated executions, provided they met certain conditions. Schwarzschild intuited that the debate about capital punishment had sacred currency in America, as advocates and opponents regularly quoted scriptures and appealed to religious teachings to justify their various positions about the taking of human life by the state. To help mobilize support for the anti–death penalty cause, he began inviting various religious groups to join the National Coalition against the Death Penalty, an organization founded to rally public opinion against the new ruling. Based on the positions of numerous American Christian denominations (and a few Jewish groups), Schwarzschild had reason to be optimistic. The United Methodist Church, United Church of Christ, United Presbyterian Church, Christian Church (Disciples of Christ), Quakers, Unitarian Universalists, American Baptists, Reformed Church in America, American Jewish Committee, Protestant Episcopal Church, Lutheran Church in America, National Council of Churches, and various Catholic groups all had passed resolutions condemning capital punishment. Their reasons included the fallibility of human justice, the disproportionate number of poor people and African Americans on death row, and, for the Christian denominations, the peace witness of Jesus Christ. This was a massive consensus, and Schwarzschild had already persuaded several of these religious groups to join his newly founded coalition.[1]

Now he had hope that another ally could be added to the fold: the National Association of Evangelicals (NAE), an organization founded in 1942 as a conservative alternative to the liberal Federal Council of Churches. The NAE was the closest thing to an organizational representative that American evangelicals had in 1976, the year Schwarzschild wrote Floyd Robertson, the NAE's secretary of public affairs.[2] He inquired about the possibility of the organization making a formal pronouncement against capital punishment and affiliating with the cause that so many other religious denominations had joined.[3] The reply he received from Robertson was cordial in tone, and Robertson did not embarrass Schwarzschild for incorrectly addressing him as "Mr. Robinson." But it was nonetheless a firm no: "We cannot agree that your objective is either in the best interest of our society of justice or the criminals which you seek to help." Robertson then took several paragraphs to spell out the rationale, quoting first from a recent NAE resolution that argued "from a biblical perspective" that the elimination of capital punishment devalued human life and therefore that it should be retained for premeditated capital crimes. He then cited a recent editorial from the official NAE magazine. With reference to penal substitution atonement theory, he contended that "God does not forgive sin without appropriate penalties." Just as Jesus had to pay the "supreme penalty" so that humanity's sins could be forgiven, governments must seek "just retribution" for all violations. Indeed, capital punishment was actually in the best interests of the criminal: "A man is much more apt to think seriously if he knows he's going to die next Tuesday than if he merely expects to die sometime in the future."[4]

Schwarzschild's reply was biting: "I thank you for your letter . . . for taking the trouble to write so extensive a rationale for the passionate avowal for the National Association of Evangelicals of the social and spiritual usefulness of legal killing." He charged the NAE with poor readings of scripture and a distorted equation of sin and crime. The idea that conversion could be encouraged by setting an execution date particularly incensed Schwarzschild. He closed with a burning reference to his own Jewish religious heritage: that such horrific ideas existed within the Christian tradition made him all the more grateful to God for preserving the existence of Jews. What frustrated Schwarzschild was that the NAE's argument was framed "entirely in terms of civil justice and social effect" (not scriptural injunction, as Robertson had claimed), and the good news of the Christian gospel here was enmeshed with the human taking of life. It was "truly appalling," in Schwarzschild's estimation, that one could believe it desirable and possible to "terrorize and kill others into a love of God." In order to showcase what he believed was an illuminating exchange, one that showed the foolhardy logic of the pro–death penalty camp, Schwarzschild sent the series of letters to the liberal Protestant magazine *Christianity and Crisis,* which published them a few months later. It was not clear whether Robertson approved of the publication of his personal correspondence, but either way, he was given no opportunity to offer a printed rejoinder to Schwarzschild's critiques.[5]

This exchange was emblematic of broader trends in the postwar evangelical approach to matters of crime, law, and justice, which coalesced in the 1960s and formalized in the 1970s. The first shift was indicated in Schwarzschild's puzzlement: Was the NAE not representative of a gospel (*evangel,* literally "good news") of God's grace and forgiveness? Schwarzschild was frustrated that evangelicals equated crime with sin, but this was not the core issue, for the equivalence in years past had pushed evangelicals to preach a message of God's forgiveness to delinquents and criminals. This evangelical gospel had often been framed as purely one of spiritual renewal, with the penalty for sin satisfied by Jesus's salvific death. The real question now was what harsher criminal penalties have to do with that of divine justice. Increasingly from the mid-1960s on, the evangelical answer was *everything.* More law and order, not the spiritual redemption of criminals, became the primary evangelical answer to lawlessness.

Schwarzschild's framing of the denominational landscape indicated the second trend. A number of religious denominations (many with deep historical roots in American public life) had trumpeted the need to abolish capital punishment, yet here was an upstart organization pushing the opposite position. But it was the relatively new NAE that was tracking not only with the prevailing legal opinion but also with broader popular sentiment: Americans at this time were largely supportive of capital punishment, with a 1977 Harris survey reporting 67 percent of Americans in favor, up from 59 percent in 1973 and 47 percent in 1965.[6] Schwarzschild thought his publication of the letters in *Christianity and Crisis* would serve as an exposé of the twisted logic of the evangelical position. What he perhaps did not consider was that more Americans would have sympathized with Robertson's conclusions than with his own. Robertson, as the policy head of an organization attempting to increase evangelical influence in American public life, could not have asked for better free advertising.

Postwar evangelicals helped make crime something to fear even as fear of crime helped make postwar evangelicalism. Evangelicals moved in a more punitive direction, and they capitalized on crime and punishment to boost their public presence. To be sure, they were not inventing the problem: crime rates began rising steadily in the early 1960s. But it was not clear how America would respond. Evangelicals at this time helped to name crime as a particular kind of threat and made a punitive response desirable. And their evolution and capitalization on crime would have serious consequences in terms of the growth and influence both of America's carceral state and of evangelicalism itself. Crucially, this anticrime consciousness sharpened as evangelicals grew more moderate on other public issues, such as race and civil rights. The linkage of postwar evangelicalism and law and order is therefore best understood less as a story of total backlash and more as one of consolidation, the shoring up of broad alliances and the framing of the issue in terms of consensus and popularity.

Evangelical crime concern shifted in three ways from the late 1950s to the mid-1970s. First, increasingly anxious evangelicals internalized crime fears and developed positions that pointed to law and order's moderate, "neutral" quality. Second, as they pursued broader cultural influence and respectability, evangelicals developed intellectual and theological justifications for tougher criminal justice within publications such as *Christianity Today*. Finally, they fully embraced a law-and-order position through their engagement in broader debates about Supreme Court cases, urban unrest, and mainline Protestant denominational culture wars.

Going Public

The image of criminals coming to Christ was a powerful one, but the focus on spiritual, individual conversion had its limits if evangelicals were going to exert influence in American political life. Evangelists such as Billy Graham and David Wilkerson had framed law enforcement as an inadequate attack on the "symptoms" of the sin problem, but the reception of their message and shifts in evangelical political consciousness helped boost evangelicalism's affinity with temporal law and order.

These evangelists spoke into a religious culture that was obsessed with sin, what one historian has called the defining feature of postwar Protestant theology. Though the postwar era was marked by positive thinking and *Leave It to Beaver* optimism, it was also an "age of anxiety," a culture of existential struggle that emerged in the hearts of Americans concerned with nuclear threats, racism, and economic uncertainty.[7]

Anxiety about crime was no different. And the effects of the age of anxiety could be seen through leading evangelicals' functional priority of sin over gospel in their discussion of the crime issue. Though he had prescribed the healing balm of individual salvation as a response to crime, Graham's frontloading of his sermons with horrifying anecdotes and dramatic statistics about the crime crisis guaranteed that at least part of their homiletic effect would be to play into broader anxiety about lawlessness. For the lone penitent lawbreaker who heard these sermons (like the wiretapper Jim Vaus), God's pardon was indeed good news. But for the masses of nonlawbreakers who heard his sermons, the effect was different. Most of the attendees of Graham crusades were *not* criminals (or even non-Christians), and though the gospel of forgiveness for crimes was less relevant, the overarching concern about America's lawless streets was not.[8]

The seeds of these evangelists' crime-inflected messages, the icons of sinfulness of crime and urban disorder that they regularly referenced, did not fall on rocky soil. Their devotees expected and appreciated this kind of message. Newspaperman and crusade volunteer Morgan Blake wrote about the expectations for Graham's 1950 Atlanta events in precisely these terms. "What are the people praying for?" Blake asked, before turning to a short list of spiritual and temporal hopes of the crusade. The first of the latter concerns was international, "the godless communists in the world." But the bulk of the piece focused on the domestic concern of "the far-flung criminal underworld in this land." Prostitution, gambling, racketeering—"this criminal underworld is even more menacing at present to the preservation of law and order and our democratic form of government than the Communists." These concerns, Blake said, inspired many at Graham's revivals to pray that those "on the threshold of criminal lives" would find their hearts softened.[9]

The appeal of Graham's anticrime message was potent enough to lead Roy Lundquist, a retired Sears analyst living in Wheaton, Illinois, to conduct his own study of the effect of Graham crusades on urban crime rates. Evangelicals at the time often calculated crime rates in the wake of an evangelistic crusade, but Lundquist offered a particularly detailed study of the linkage.[10] Using FBI statistics, he examined the shifts in crime rates from 1961 to 1965 in several American cities before and after Graham crusades. He calculated that many of the cities experienced favorable reductions in crime rates directly following a crusade. Persuaded that this was evidence of the crusades' power, he offered his brightly colored charts to the Billy Graham Evangelistic Association. The association was unwilling to publicize the research, which may have been owing to Lundquist's status as a lay researcher or the fact that postcrusade crime rates actually went *up* in a few cities. Nevertheless, Lundquist's project showed how crime's place in Graham's gospel equation had filtered down into the anxious popular imagination.[11]

A second development that reframed the evangelical conception of crime was the movement's gradual acceptance of the power of civil authority for promoting social holiness, specifically racial equality. The context for this development was the civil rights struggle of the 1950s and 1960s. A product of the rural South, Billy Graham saw nothing wrong with racial segregation in his early life and ministry. However, in 1953, after a few years of waffling on the issue, he began to reconsider this view and soon desegregated his crusades. He increasingly spoke about racism as a sin in magazine articles, welcomed African Americans to his crusade planning team, rebuffed ardently racist White Citizens' Councils that blasted his integrated events, and invited Martin Luther King Jr. to offer a prayer at the 1957 Madison Square Garden crusade. But Graham was no radical. He downplayed the importance of secular protest or civil rights laws in favor of spiritual solutions. As he wrote in *Life* magazine in 1956, "The Christian layman must speak out against the social ills of our times, but he must be careful to speak with the voice of the biblical prophets and apostles and not in the spirit of secular and socializing views."[12] The best way to change society was for sinners to come to Christ. More than legislation, Jim Crow needed prayer and conversion.[13]

This belief dovetailed with his proclamations at the time concerning solutions to the crime problem. Gradually Graham began to acknowledge the need for civil rights legislation (though not as a replacement for spiritual renewal). This development was as pragmatic as it was principled. The tide was turning in broader American culture in terms of sympathy for southern African Americans' plight, and court decisions such as *Brown v. Board of Education* in 1954 had made integration the legal default for the nation's schools and public spaces. By 1958, Graham was arguing that segregationists needed to abide by this new law of the land (though he was not totally consistent on this point until the 1960s). But this argument differed from that offered by civil rights leaders like King. It was a more moderated appeal, a "politics of decency" that decried racism *and* zealous protests for social justice.[14] In terms of Graham's relationship to the crime issue, the effect of this approach would be decisive.

The launching point of Graham's politics of decency was the late 1950s, when he appeared in southern locales that had been rocked by racial upheaval. In 1958 he visited Clinton, Tennessee, where segregationists had bombed the local public school in response to the *Brown* integration order. Graham's sermon to the gathered, racially mixed crowd sounded familiar pietistic notes: "[Christians] must not allow integration or segregation to become our gospel. . . . Love and understanding cannot be forced by bayonets. . . . We must respect the law, but keep in mind that it is powerless to change the human heart."[15] One year later, Graham sounded similar tones in Little Rock, Arkansas, where, according to the Billy Graham Evangelistic Association, fifty thousand people met "not as integrationists or segregationists, but as Christians." "If people lived like Christ and believed in him," he preached, in his only sermonic reference to the city's racial tensions, "there would be no problem in Little Rock."[16]

Graham's approach seemingly demonstrated a focus on a spiritual solution to racial tensions, over against reliance on policy solutions or identification with a particular political stance on civil rights. But the local newspapers reporting on Graham's work in Clinton and Little Rock pointed to an altogether different effect: "Evangelist Calls for Love, Law and Order," read one headline, while one paper's political cartoonist linked Graham's crusade with the statement, "Triumph of Law and Order." For a revival campaign that seemingly placed so little confidence in worldly political causes or legal authority, the "law-and-order" gloss was striking. It paralleled the rhetoric of Little Rock ministers at the time (sixteen ministers had condemned the resistance to desegregation with reference to the need for law and order) and referenced the fact that Graham's rallies had proceeded without social disruption and were characterized by, as historian Steven Miller has put it, "obedience to constitutional authority, but not support for any specific reform of protest agenda."[17] This marked Graham's first sustained association with the concept of law and order, a phrase that would mark anticrime concern for years to come.

At the time, the term seemed most applicable to the white segregationists who were violently resisting *Brown,* as Graham argued that they needed to "obey the law" and allow for the integration of public spaces. Indeed, this had been precisely how other pro-integration clergy had adopted the law-and-order mantle around the same time in the wake of violence against blacks (an analogue to past antilynching activism).[18] But as the legal successes of the civil rights movement mounted, the call for law and order turned into a critique of demonstrations and protests for equality, particularly the civil disobedience strategies that King and other activists utilized to great effect to push for racial justice beyond *Brown*. The fact that the Clinton and Little Rock crusades were integrated was seen as a win over segregationists *and* a challenge to black protesters, who were increasingly deemed disruptive by white moderates like Graham.[19] The effect of civil rights gains was that the law was now seen as morally neutral, color blind, and the guarantor of security for all people. This was good news for a society where the law had, for so long, obviously *not* been neutral or color blind. But it had unintended long-term effects in terms of criminal justice issues beyond white violence against black people.

Though Graham would trumpet the need for individual salvation for the rest of his ministry throughout the twentieth century, from this point on, he demonstrated a sense that law and order, the quelling of social disruption and lawlessness, could somehow be linked with the evangelical gospel. He was not the only Christian voice proclaiming crime concern in the immediate postwar era, but as one of the most admired and popular people in America, he was making this particular approach mainstream.[20] He had staked out bipartisan, "moderate" terrain with his neutral law-and-order appeals. The stage was set for other evangelicals to take up this cause and deepen its intellectual roots and political applications.

Law, Order, and the Evangelical Mind

Around the same time that Graham began shifting the cause of law and order beyond individual conversion, another iconic American was making a complementary appeal. J. Edgar Hoover had been making much of the crime issue for years after his installation as director of the Bureau of Investigation (the forerunner to the FBI) in 1924. In the late 1950s he found a new forum in which to sound his warnings. In 1958 he penned an op-ed about American lawlessness, focusing on the problem of youth crime, "a most potent danger to law and order." But this was no standard newspaper piece. Hoover wrote these words in an article for the new evangelical publication *Christianity Today* (*CT*), and the tone of the piece showcased deep familiarity with the religious concerns of his audience: "In this year of 1958, when the world is so rent by divisive forces, America stands in great need of spiritual guidance. . . . Ministers of America are truly on the front lines of the battle for freedom. On their shoulders, in large measure, depends the future of our nation."[21] Hoover (and his ghost-writers) had recently been trumpeting a similar message in their broader promotion of the need for national moral and spiritual redemption in the midst of the Cold War. He urged Americans in his book *Masters of Deceit* to fight communism by spending "a little time each day . . . studying the Bible and the basic documents of American history. . . . All we need is faith, real faith."[22] Other Christian magazines regularly cited Hoover as an authority.[23] But *CT* had secured Hoover's own literary contribution. Head editor Carl F. H. Henry was no doubt thrilled, placing the piece at the very front of the issue. He also followed it with his own addendum. There he noted the law enforcement leader's influence and reprinted other remarks Hoover had given on violent films' negative influences on youths and the inability of liberalism to combat lawlessness and communism. Hoover's presence in the pages of *CT,* a bookish publication at the time, represented evangelicals' growing intellectual affinity for the law-and-order cause.

The Hoover piece and its accompanying comments from Henry were all standard *CT* fare, as they revealed a desire for cultural influence, interest in contemporary issues, and skepticism of liberal solutions. The magazine had been launched in 1956 with precisely these concerns in mind. Taking its cues from the ideals undergirding the new evangelicalism, *CT* articulated its statement of purpose in its founding issue by pointing to the foils of liberalism and fundamentalism. The former had "failed to meet the moral and spiritual needs of the people," while the latter had botched the winsome application of "biblical revelation to the contemporary social crisis."[24] Positioning itself between these two extremes, editors at *CT* understood their mission as bringing traditional Christian faith to bear on the complex issues of public life, ignoring neither what they deemed was the timeless message of the gospel nor the call for Christians to enter and transform society. Or, in the words of Graham (who provided the original vision for the magazine and served as a contributing editor) decades later, *CT* was to be a publication "that would give theological respectability to evangelicals."[25] Hoover and his FBI colleagues saw the potential with the partnership as well. Though Hoover himself often spoke on religious topics (such as detailing the biblical justifications for the death penalty in an FBI law enforcement bulletin), *CT* provided him an opportunity to reach a new religious audience.[26] One internal FBI memo commended the research that a crime records division agent had performed for Hoover for three of the *CT* articles, noting, "We are receiving very favorable publicity and comment from the clerical field."[27]

Though discussing the crime question was only one of the ways that the neo-evangelicals at *CT* brought Protestant orthodoxy to bear on modern social questions, America's lead law enforcement official was probably the most famous writer (other than Graham) to grace the pages of the magazine in its early years, writing fifteen pieces from the magazine's inception to the early 1970s in addition to being cited in many more.[28] *CT* editor (and Billy Graham's father-in-law) L. Nelson Bell reported to oilman J. Howard Pew, the magazine's lead booster, that the Hoover association had resulted in "a tremendous amount of publicity." Newspapers across the country had reprinted Hoover's pieces (including one Italian magazine that requested use of the entire series) and, Bell proudly noted, "in each case *Christianity Today* has been given credit."[29] Evangelical readers, such as the president of Wheaton College, hailed Hoover's *CT* presence in appreciative letters to the director.[30] Many of Hoover's articles were about the dangers of communism, but he usually found ways to tie problems of lawlessness to the broader Red Scare and related "subversive forces," all of which were products of an increasingly godless society: "Materialism has fathered both crime and communism."[31] For Hoover, the collapse of America's religious foundations through atheistic communist influence had resulted in the loss of a national moral compass, which explained the turn to lawlessness. "A world without moral disciplines," he explained, in a 1962 *CT* op-ed, "must degenerate into a world without legal disciplines. . . . We are witnessing this degeneration on a national scale as atheistic materialism expresses itself in lawless terrorism on city streets and rural byways."[32]

Other authors writing for *CT* in its early years also talked about the threat of crime. Some pieces were simply pointed laments with tough punitive prescriptions. In 1958 Bell editorialized about youth lawlessness and proposed faith in Christ as the only true solution, while also blaming licentious media, bad parenting, and the "forgotten art" of "a good sound thrashing."[33] A year later the magazine devoted an entire issue to juvenile delinquency. Compared with Bell and Hoover's jeremiads, most authors in this issue adopted a moderate tone. But all exhibited the same general approach: identify crime as a relevant social issue, dismiss typical liberal approaches to the problem, and name faith in Christ as the ultimate solution. "Delinquency prevention begins in the hearts and minds of fathers and mothers before their children are born," argued one author, a New York City juvenile delinquency expert. "It begins the day parents dedicate their lives to Christ. . . . It is the only answer."[34]

At times, CT's regular proposal of Christian conversion as the answer to every social issue appeared trite, such as when the magazine argued in the midst of civil rights protests that "what the Negro needs now is not more laws—indispensable as these may be—but more room in the white man's heart."[35] But a particular kind of theological apparatus was developing underneath the way CT talked about crime, one that would distinguish the publication's stance from that of other Christians who also pointed to Christ as the "only answer" but showed less interest in bolstering the law enforcement capacities of the state. In the lead editorial for one 1958 issue, the magazine's editors contended that the answer to the "flagrant sin erupting all about us" (which included union leader Jimmy Hoffa's misdeeds, obscene literature, Sabbath secularization, and juvenile delinquency, "our major social problem") was not only "earnest prayers of God's people and the proclamation of Jesus Christ and him crucified" but "the preaching of the Law. . . . The preaching of the Gospel, defined in the narrow sense of the Atonement alone, is not sufficient." The law had functioned as Martin Luther's "schoolmaster," leading him to see the depths of his own sin. Now it could serve a similar purpose of conviction if it were to be "woven into the crown of thorns and pressed into the brow of the nation." It is not clear to what extent the editors would have distinguished between the jurisdictions of "Law" in the traditional theological sense and the "law" of America's municipal, state, and federal codes (indeed, the piece began by capitalizing the term but switched to lowercase about halfway through). But by frontloading the piece with reference to Hoffa, obscenity concerns, disregard of the Sabbath, and youth delinquency (all subjects of legal debate in American public life) *and* by modifying the standard "Christ alone" prescription, the editors made the connection clear enough: God's redemption of America was dependent on some kind of temporal triumph over lawlessness.[36]

One year later, another lead editorial on juvenile delinquency cast the shift in theological terms that had political resonances. The root of the problem, the piece argued, was an "antinomianism" that had seeped into evangelical Christian culture. Literally meaning "anti-law," "antinomianism" was a term used to describe freewheeling hippie behavior, but it also held important resonances in Christian history.[37] Most famously, the Boston rabble-rouser Anne Hutchinson had borne the label in the 1630s after she was accused (and eventually exiled) by New England's puritan clergy of preaching a covenant of works rather than grace in their insistence on righteous living. Though they did not hold the same authority to chasten heretics, the editors of *CT* nonetheless desired to stake a claim against the modern-day Hutchinsons, the liberal social reformers and uncultivated leaders of youth rally "singspirations" who had failed to call church and culture to full moral account.[38] As they surveyed their lawless land, *CT*'s editors grew more willing to modify, if not dismiss altogether, the notion that more laws were useless.

In publishing commentary like this, editor Carl Henry, a highly educated theologian, would not have seen *CT* as veering into works-righteousness territory. After all, he still believed that the law (whether civil or Mosaic) was fundamentally temporal and that lasting salvation was found only in Christ. Elsewhere in his lectures and writings, Henry unpacked the political theology that made sense of the law-first focus in *CT*. God ordained government to preserve justice in a fallen world, he argued, so as to protect human beings' God-given rights. Keepers of the civil law were to be praised. "The Christian movement therefore has a vital stake not only in justice and law, but also in the legal profession as such," he told a gathered audience at Fuller Theological Seminary. "To encourage keen young Christians to pursue law as a profession and to serve ultimately as judges is no less important than encouraging them to enter the ministry or fields of medicine and science." A Baptist with strong Reformed leanings, Henry hailed Calvinism in particular, for it "has produced not only great theologians but great jurists." If the Christian church was to remain fully engaged in modern society, it would need to cultivate "professional interest in jurisprudence."[39] Henry even argued that successful propagation of the gospel could be said to depend on the state's maintenance of the law. While the state had a divinely ordained role in restraining evil, Henry was far less optimistic about its ability to promote good. Progressive social programming had failed in this regard, downplaying justice at the same time it "benevolently bent toward people's socio-economic wants." The state should focus on what was *due* to wrongdoers rather than trying to create a "utopia." Though the church was to be concerned with promoting love and compassion, a Christian understanding of political life was marked not by benevolence but by a concern for the restraint of evil.[40]

Not all evangelical thinkers affirmed Henry's views, and at times *CT* itself reflected the various tensions present in public debate about criminal justice issues, particularly the theological grounding of the law-and-order perspective and the proper understanding of punishment. However, the magazine eventually made it clear where it stood, and what direction it wanted the new evangelical movement to go. In January 1959 the magazine printed a summary of a dispute between Oxford literary don C. S. Lewis and criminologist Norval Morris on crime and punishment. This debate, which had originally occurred in an Australian law journal, saw Lewis arguing against the "Humanitarian theory" that "removes from Punishment the concept of Dessert." Morris defended the standard progressive line, that therapeutic intervention was a proper task of criminal justice. *CT* did not come down one way or the other in this particular case, though the chronicler of the debate praised the thoughtful "public disputation . . . conducted in the best academic tradition."[41] Later that year, the magazine published a hearty defense of capital punishment by Presbyterian leader Jacob J. Vellenga. Letters poured in, most of them contesting Vellenga's position and arguing against the death penalty. Sensing that they needed to give voice to such a vociferous perspective, *CT*'s editors agreed that they should run the two best dissents, one from the Mennonite theologian John Howard Yoder, the other from ethicist Charles S. Milligan, a professor at the Methodist Iliff School of Theology. However, Henry did not want to give these dissenters the last word. He wrote his former philosophy professor and *CT* contributing editor Gordon Clark, telling him, "I feel like we must give some expression to another side, and then meet it effectively." He asked Clark to write a "companion piece," one that would "take hold of the arguments in the essays, indicate where they lead, and come at the issue of capital punishment in greater depth." Given the weight of the topic, Henry was reluctant to charge just anyone with such a challenging task. But, he told his former teacher, "I can't get away from the impression that you're the man."[42]

The result was an entire edition of the magazine focused on the issue of the death penalty. Both Yoder and Milligan stressed the biblical case against capital punishment. "These observations are not humanistic theories or vague utopian philosophies," Yoder argued. "They are realities to which God's Word speaks." However, tempering Yoder's and Milligan's critique was Clark's addendum, which argued that "the opponents of capital punishment offer no theory of civil government, they seriously misinterpret the Bible, and they are in conflict with principles of Christian ethics." Indeed, Clark surmised, "in the present depraved condition of the United States, we might even wisely execute adulterers and pornographers."

Clark's formal association with *CT* did not indicate that his was the magazine's *official* position on the topic. But Henry's work behind the scenes and a note in the issue indicating that Clark would serve as a kind of arbiter on whether Yoder's and Milligan's pieces properly appealed to the Bible indicated that Clark's was the perspective he wanted to frame as the last word. An editorial (with no author listed but likely written by Henry or Bell) near the end of the same issue drove this point home. This piece argued not with reference to biblical or theological justifications but by citing the arguments of legal authorities Roscoe G. Sappenfield and Judge Marcus Kavanagh. The piece noted the death penalty's effect in deterring crimes but argued that capital punishment's propriety was ultimately found in the retributive requirements of justice. Like those who reject eternal punishment of sinners, "modern social conscience suffers from an undervaluation of the righteousness of God and of the wickedness of wrongdoing." Violation of the law, whether divine or human, demanded a punitive response.[43]

Henry's hailing of keepers of the civil law and the parallel editorial maneuvering of *CT* sprang from a distinctly Reformed mode of the neo-evangelical intellectual consciousness. It was no accident that Henry praised the Calvinist tradition of jurisprudence (John Calvin himself had originally been trained as a lawyer) or that perspectives such as that of the Anabaptist Yoder emerged as a minority report to Vellenga's and Clark's (both of whom were Presbyterians). In the sixteenth century Calvin had distinguished his own thinking on church and state with modifications to Martin Luther's strict separation between God's "two kingdoms" of temporal law and spiritual gospel. Calvin developed a "third" use of the law, one that was more optimistic about the possibility of spiritual benefits that the law could grant to Christians. The state and church were not the same entities in Calvin's Geneva, but this did not mean that magistrates could not force citizens to adhere to a particular religious confession.[44] In drawing heavily on Calvin's political theology, *CT* helped ensure that the neo-evangelical intellectual movement would have a particular affinity with Reformed theology. Outsiders like Yoder (as well as those from Wesleyan traditions) shared many of the same general interests and sought to include themselves in this emerging movement. At times *CT*'s editors were happy to have them on board, though they generally tried to fill editorial roles with "Reformed or Presbyterian" types. "I agree with you that, insofar as possible, we must follow a strictly Calvinistic policy," wrote Bell to Clark. "However, this must be subordinated to some extent in the hope of reaching as many Methodists and Lutherans as possible." Outsiders like Yoder could chip in occasionally on the crime issue, but the visions of pacifist Anabaptism or Wesleyan social holiness (which generally included proactive governmental interventions on behalf of the poor, not simply state defense) were more difficult to channel into a full-fledged political engagement strategy in terms of the coercive and violent functions of the state. Though the magazine continued to advocate for an interdenominational brand of evangelicalism, Reformed thinking and application largely won the day for the foreseeable future on the crime issue. "Non-Reformed evangelicals," as historian Molly Worthen notes, "had no choice but to adapt.... The credo of the *Christianity Today* crowd was becoming evangelicalism's public theology."[45]

As the leading journalistic organ for the new evangelicalism, *CT*'s frequent editorials on crime and criminal justice in the late 1950s formalized culturally savvy conservative Protestants' concern with the issue and indicated a new path. If popular evangelists like Graham and Wilkerson had pushed evangelicalism's concern with crime into mainstream American popular culture with their sermons and books, *CT* was providing the intellectual backbone with its theological glosses on punishment and its prominent endorsement of law enforcement authorities such as Hoover. *CT* was also proving that evangelicals could go beyond simple conversion as the primary frame through which to understand the crime problem.

A famous case that captured the nation's attention exemplified this development. Caryl Chessman had been sentenced to death for a series of brutal kidnappings and sexual assaults in 1948. Over the following decade, however, many Americans warmed to the prospect that Chessman had reformed and should not be executed (or, at the very least, had been subjected to illegal police interrogation by force). This was a bipartisan cause, with unlikely bedfellows such as Eleanor Roosevelt, William F. Buckley, Marlon Brando, and the editors at the *Christian Century* all arguing that Chessman should live.[46] Joining this eclectic group begging for mercy was none other than Billy Graham.[47] But the editors of *CT* broke from their founder on the matter, lamenting the repeated deferments of Chessman's death by California's governor and the calls of Christians for clemency. By contrast, *CT*'s editors (joining with conservative southern Presbyterians, who were also against clemency) argued that the "Biblical precept of retributive justice" demanded putting sentimentality aside. They got their wish. Chessman was executed in California's gas chamber, despite the fact that a stay of execution was ordered (coming in just minutes late because a clerk had dialed the wrong number).[48] Not long after the execution, *CT*'s editors wrote that the broader debate about Chessman's execution summed up the "post-Christian" age. The lesson, they argued, was "that these United States can no longer afford the luxury of protracted criminal justice."[49] Again, they would get their wish. As evangelical Christianity moved to exert further influence in public life in the 1960s, a foundation was laid for important changes in how the nation understood crime and moved to address it with forceful policy.

Countering Revolution

CT's break with Graham on Chessman's clemency case indicated that there was tension in the evangelical ranks about the prospects of punitive politics. But as the 1960s wore on, most evangelicals (including Graham) would resolve the tension by fully associating with the law-and-order cause. The context of the evangelical consolidation around the crime issue in favor of a harsher response was the broader cultural and political milieu of the early and mid-1960s. Here, evangelical Christians were thriving numerically, but also embattled.[50] The civil rights struggle, the sexual revolution, the counterculture, and Great Society social programs all were causes of concern for many evangelical Christian laity and leaders, who tended to have conservative social and political views. However, these challenges also galvanized evangelicals, leading them to organize politically and opening up opportunities to form alliances with other concerned Americans. This was just as true for issues of crime and punishment as it was for concerns about sex, drugs, and rock and roll. Evangelical leaders and laity gradually formalized a new crime consciousness over the course of three catalyzing disputes in the 1960s: debates about the verdicts of Earl Warren's Supreme Court, response to riots that enveloped American cities, and the fracturing of Protestant denominations.

The civil rights cause scored victories beyond *Brown* with the Civil Rights Act of 1964 and the Voting Rights Act of 1965. But though racial equality was cautiously welcomed by most mainstream evangelical leaders, the demonstrations and civil disobedience that had made legislative accomplishments possible received their scrutiny. Even as it praised their motives, *CT* lamented the "basic sinfulness of the 'Freedom Riders' riots," equating civil rights demonstrators' tactics with "mob pressures" that exhibit "a distrust of democracy."[51] Editorials in other evangelical publications made similar claims, assailing the demonstration of "hundreds of yelling children" as "a violation of human rights" and praising the "restraint exercised by many of the police who were charged with enforcing law and order . . . in the face of mob demonstrations."[52] Encouraged by the increased association of his gospel with the moderate qualities of "law and order," Billy Graham joined with J. Edgar Hoover, a frequent critic of civil rights protests, to express concerns about "subversives" in the movement.[53] Though he had integrated his crusades and was sympathetic with certain civil rights goals, Graham avoided demonstrations like the 1963 March on Washington. Indeed, a few days after Martin Luther King Jr. delivered his "I Have a Dream" speech, Graham preached to a gathered crowd at his crusade in Los Angeles that "the racial problem in America is getting worse and dangerous, and will not be settled in the streets." He critiqued clergy "who have made the race issue their gospel" as well as those who would argue that juvenile delinquency is a result of poverty. He also noted, "There are almost enough people here tonight to have a march on Washington. And if they keep throwing the Bible out of the schools, we might do just that."[54]

The "they" Graham referred to was the institution that white evangelicals were increasingly seeing as a threat to orderly Christian civilization, one far greater than segregation: the United States Supreme Court. After its ruling in *Engel v. Vitale* in 1962 (which struck down state-sponsored prayer in public schools) and *Abington School District v. Schempp* in 1963 (which declared school-sponsored required Bible reading as unconstitutional), evangelicals worried that the court, under the leadership of Chief Justice Earl Warren, was leading the nation down the road to secularism. Though many evangelicals had avoided the religious coalition supporting the civil rights movement because it seemed too "political" or "worldly," debates about the Warren court drew evangelicals into the American political fray, many for the first time.[55]

Besides perceived assaults on school prayer and Bible reading, also problematic for evangelicals was the Warren court's expansion of the rights of suspected and convicted criminals around the same time. Most famously, *Miranda v. Arizona* (1966) protected criminal suspects from self-incrimination by requiring police to notify arrestees that they had the right to remain silent, the right to know that any statement they made could be used against them, and the right to have an attorney present during police questioning.[56] One *CT* editorial bemoaned criminals' release through decisions such as these. "A confessed rapist walks out of a Washington jail on a technicality," the piece lamented, likely a reference to the recent *Mallory v. United States* ruling. In this case the court unanimously ruled that Andrew Mallory's confession of rape after a seven-hour interrogation by federal officers violated the rights of the accused, since Mallory had not been informed of his rights to counsel or silence, and because officers did not officially arraign Mallory until *after* he confessed.[57] The decision, in *CT*'s estimation, was nothing more than "legal hocus-pocus," and it was hampering police efforts and endangering public safety. The piece also assailed a Supreme Court ruling that restricted federal wiretapping (*Benanti v. United States*), contending that it "is denying to our scientific age one of the useful methods of crime detection." Echoing common conservative critiques of the court's civil rights rulings, the piece contended that these rulings were "based on social concepts rather than law.... [The Supreme Court] should not be a debating ground where the personal opinions of its members compete with the law." It concluded with a call to readers to "an aroused public opinion.... If this requires action then let us have it."[58]

For the National Association of Evangelicals, "action" on these troubling Supreme Court rulings meant educating church leaders on the crime issue and introducing them to the rough and tumble of American political life. The NAE began hosting seminars in Washington, DC, in the 1960s, making good on the neo-evangelical call to Christian civic engagement. These seminars, dubbed Christian Responsibility in Public Affairs and later called the Washington Leadership Briefing, allowed evangelical pastors and laypeople to meet with congressional leaders, tour government buildings, and hear briefings from political movers and shakers.[59] Crime concern was a feature of these seminars, with law enforcement officials offering their perspective to attendees through talks such as "Law Enforcement and the Role of Churches in Preventing Crime." The 1966 meeting targeted the Supreme Court more directly. Attendees heard from the Washington police chief about how *Mallory* and similar rulings had hamstrung police efforts and ennobled criminals. Illinois Republican congressman John B. Anderson suggested to the gathering that the answer might lie in a constitutional amendment, which could have "a therapeutic affect [*sic*] on the U.S. Supreme Court."[60] In engaging crime and the court at gatherings like this, evangelicals had their finger on the pulse of the nation. As one scholar has put it, "No issue seemed to animate as much [national] discussion as the Court and the problem of crime."[61] The explicitly religious questions of prayer and Bible reading in public schools might not have garnered evangelicals much favor with the rest of the country, but the crime issue afforded them a great deal of common ground.

The effects of this national consciousness motivated both major presidential candidates of the 1964 election, Republican Barry Goldwater and Democrat Lyndon Johnson, to trumpet the crime issue. However, what form a federal response to crime would take remained an open question. It was also not yet completely clear how evangelicals would align. Goldwater made more overt law-and-order appeals in his campaign, often framing these concerns as a critique of the "lawless" civil rights movement. Johnson talked about crime in more measured tones, linking the issue to social uplift more generally and criticizing Goldwater as a candidate who "bemoans violence in the streets but votes against the war on poverty."[62] Johnson ultimately won the 1964 election in a landslide, a testament to his broader appeal with a national electorate that was suspicious of Goldwater's hardline conservatism.[63] The Goldwater campaign's propensity for bungling its messaging (with its overtures to Christian conservatives and segregationists alike) was a factor too, as evidenced by its role in the creation of a promotional film entitled *Choice*. The film juxtaposed lawless streets, scantily clad women, and images of African American protesters to images of white schoolchildren reciting the pledge of allegiance, small-town churches, and John Wayne, all in an attempt to link the former to Johnson and progressives' role in moral breakdown and the latter to Goldwater's rock-ribbed conservatism. The film also portrayed white police confronting unidentified black people, with no word as to whether they were civil rights demonstrators or common criminals. Through these images the film made, as historian Michael Flamm has written, "numerous and obvious" racial insinuations. The film also cited scripture, drawing a parallel between the parable of the rich fool in Luke 12 and America's current complacency: both said they would "eat, drink, and make good cheer," but judgment was at hand. Goldwater would eventually pull the film before its planned airing on network television (though it had already shown on several local stations), calling it a racist provocation. But the damage had been done, as his campaign had already been linked to the inflammatory film in the media.[64]

Though many evangelicals (particularly in the South and Sunbelt) supported Goldwater, Billy Graham remained in Johnson's camp because of their personal friendship (though Goldwater's limited national appeal may have been a factor as well).[65] Nevertheless, Johnson knew his administration had a mandate on crime, and he made the issue a key part of his Great Society policy campaign.

In July 1965, via executive order, Johnson established the Commission on Law Enforcement and Administration of Justice, known as the Katzenbach Commission, after its chair, Attorney General Nicholas Katzenbach. The commission's makeup was middle-of-the-road, even "bland," as one commentator called it, a bipartisan mix of leaders from politics, business, and law enforcement.[66] One member was former Minnesota judge and governor Luther Youngdahl. A centrist Republican and devout Lutheran who regularly spoke about his faith at Graham crusades and Youth for Christ events, Youngdahl exemplified a moderated evangelical approach to the crime issue.[67] Though his early career was marked by his aggressive pursuit of gambling, bootlegging, and prostitution rackets in Minnesota, Youngdahl eventually became well known for his liberal civil liberties rulings.[68] By the mid-1960s Youngdahl's public tone on crime was balanced. Crime could be reduced not through harsher punishment but by "exterminating its roots—the roots of slums, overcrowded schools, denial of job opportunities because of race and color of skin." Convicted criminals should be punished, but they should generally be pushed toward alternatives to incarceration, such as probation and halfway houses.[69] The Katzenbach Commission's recommendations were in line with Youngdahl's approach and the broadly liberal mantle that characterized the Johnson administration: "Widespread crime implies a widespread failure by society as a whole." To solve this failure, work was needed "to eliminate slums and ghettos, to improve education, to provide jobs."[70]

Youngdahl's presence on Johnson's crime commission was not enough, however, to placate evangelicals who understood the roots of crime differently. After some initial measured praise of Johnson for including crime in part of his broader Great Society campaign against social ills, CT criticized the commission for recommending liberalization of certain laws and its ignorance of the agency of individuals in favor of "external controls." The problems owing to the "lack of a more significant respect for moral standards" might have been mitigated, CT argued, if the commission had clergy representation.[71] Indeed, one member of the commission itself seemed to agree. In an addendum issued alongside the commission's findings, the Pennsylvania Democratic attorney (and devout Roman Catholic) Genevieve Blatt lamented the lack of reference to "man's alienation from his God" as "a crime-inducing factor." In America's war against crime, "religion is a real weapon." Blatt said, "In my personal opinion, it is the best weapon. And it should be used." Evangelicals happily trumpeted Blatt's minority report, a remarkable development considering their lingering suspicion of Catholics' place in American public life. Indeed, on the same page that *United Evangelical Action* listed an ad for a Pennsylvania "soul-winning mission" to Roman Catholics (who were "lost without love, trapped by traditions, paralyzed by popery"), the magazine dedicated a column to reprinting the Catholic Blatt's critique. One Indiana Evangelical United Brethren church devoted its regular newspaper space to praising her analysis, albeit with more of a "born again" emphasis. In his regular column for the evangelical Sunday-school publication *Christian Times,* Illinois congressman John Anderson lamented that the commission (excepting Blatt) had failed "to explicitly recognize godlessness as the basic cause of crime."[72]

The fact that Graham did not endorse Goldwater and that the evangelical Youngdahl could find a place on Johnson's crime commission indicated that broader evangelical alignment with punitive politics was not a foregone conclusion. But everything changed in the mid- to late 1960s, as large urban uprisings enveloped parts of several American cities. One of the most famous occurred in the African American Los Angeles neighborhood of Watts, where racial tension had been simmering for years and accusations of police brutality were common. Large-scale unrest broke out in August 1965 after a white police officer stopped a black man for drunk driving. Black residents of the neighborhood began vandalizing white-owned businesses and harassing police, with more than thirty-five thousand residents eventually joining the fray. Los Angeles police and National Guard soldiers mobilized to quell the violence. The aftermath of the uprising was the destruction of entire city blocks, three thousand arrests, and thirty-four dead.[73]

While civil rights advocates named the riots as the logical conclusion of the racism and impoverished conditions that black Americans faced, conservative voices used the riots to blame civil rights leaders and double down on the need for a swift, harsh governmental response. From the floor of Congress, South Carolina congressman Albert Watson, a segregationist and Baptist deacon, condemned the rioters, urged tough punishment and support of police, and blamed "professional troublemakers" such as "Martin King." Watson refused to use King's full name so as not to, in his words, "desecrate the memory of that great religious leader, Martin Luther."[74] These alignments were not unexpected in theory, but what was beginning to change was that many more Americans were gravitating to the punitive side.[75] Among them was Billy Graham, who, over the course of the riots, became the chief religious exponent and symbolic reference to this end. He named communists, "leftist" influence, and civil rights demonstrations as the culprits for the unrest.[76] "We need salvation from lawlessness," he preached on August 15, 1965, in Montreat, North Carolina (the Watts riots did not subside until the next day). "There is an organized attempt in America to down-grade the policeman. . . . There is a breakdown of law. . . . Our city streets have been turned into jungles of terror, mugging, rape, and death." He then immediately pivoted to the civil rights movement. America has made a valiant effort to solve its racial problems, he argued, but in the case of racial justice, "laws and legislation are not enough." Thus far, this was largely familiar messaging. But then, a shift: "Congress should immediately drop all other legislation and devise new laws to deal with riots and violence such as we have witnessed in Los Angeles."[77] The evangelist who had previously proclaimed personal conversion as the ideal response to crime had himself had a change of heart: laws were indeed necessary in order to address the rampant, widespread disorder, the "dress rehearsal for revolution," on America's streets. "In this dangerous situation we need tough new laws," he preached, "as well as a great spiritual awakening in America." Graham's push for laws to address social disorder immediately had an impact. His comments to this effect were cited by others who blasted the civil rights movement's alleged influence in the riots and who wanted to see more tough justice. One California legislator cited Graham as an authority in his critique of the "subversives" behind Watts, while the *Chicago Tribune* saw fit to put Graham's image on a tough-minded column, though the evangelist was only quoted briefly in the piece.[78]

Evangelical leaders spoke out on Watts with similar punitive appeals, some of which targeted the civil rights movement more directly. Others simply avoided any discussion of the complaints of African Americans, choosing instead to frame the riot as simply a matter of lawbreaking and cultural breakdown. A pastor at an Assemblies of God church not far from Watts preached a sermon in the midst of the uprising (printed soon after in the *Pentecostal Evangel*) that connected riots to the disintegration of family values, disloyalty to America, and disregard of the nation's laws.[79] Samuel H. Sutherland, the president of the Bible Institute of Los Angeles, attacked the "mobsters" rioting in Watts and critics of law enforcement who "wail" about police brutality. The roots of their derangement, Sutherland argued, lay in the "anarchistic" view of civil rights leaders who in-

Figure 3.1 Assemblies of God youth rally on the capitol steps in Sacramento, California, in 1967. Characterized as a rally for "law and order" by newspapers covering the event, youths heard from Governor Ronald Reagan's appointments secretary, who told the gathering that the governor "is 100 per cent behind law and order on campuses as everywhere else." Center for Sacramento History, Sacramento Bee Collection, November 25, 1967, p. A-6, Church Youth Rally.

sisted they had no obligation to obey unjust laws. Here Sutherland was almost certainly referencing Martin Luther King Jr.'s "Letter from Birmingham City Jail." For Sutherland, the Watts crisis had demonstrated how protesters, civil rights leaders, and liberals had shirked their duty to the nation and the "principle of law and order" found in the Bible. Sutherland, who a year before had privately praised the institute student newspaper editor's defenses of segregation and anti–civil rights opinions as "extremely wholesome," believed evangelicals were now the remaining faithful remnant holding chaos at bay.[80]

The Billy Graham Evangelistic Association organized an intensive evangelistic campaign in Watts (to "hold out spiritual direction to the people of Watts in solving their difficulties"), but Graham's choice of surveying the neighborhood via helicopter while clothed in a bulletproof vest was in keeping with his growing belief that the welfare of flesh and blood was at stake, not simply spiritual forces.[81] He was in good company, as the immediate and long-term governmental response to situations like Watts also stressed militarized security. Sixteen thousand federal troops were marshaled to the neighborhood, arriving in helicopters and tanks. After the smoke cleared in Watts and other areas affected by riots, a strong law enforcement presence remained, with ramped-up practices of surveillance and policing. The Watts response presaged the aggressive mode of policing that would characterize America's crime war in future decades.[82]

Riots such as those in Watts also moved the Johnson administration to redefine its understanding of the sources of black criminality. Whereas Martin Luther King Jr. and civil rights activists saw the riots as proceeding primarily from generations of racism and poverty, other observers argued that urban crime stemmed from the breakdown of the black family unit. Daniel Patrick Moynihan, an aide to Johnson, had written a report in March 1965 entitled *The Negro Family: The Case for National Action* that made such a claim.[83] Absentee fathers and overbearing mothers in black families were to blame for the criminal chaos enveloping black communities. In the wake of Watts, Moynihan's report became the go-to reference point for national politicians and press attempting to contextualize the violence.[84]

While Moynihan's analysis was important in shaping elites' understandings of urban crime unrest, evangelicals were diffusing a complementary perspective into broader American culture. Though crime was equated with sin and individuals were ultimately culpable for their choices, lawbreaking still had complex causes. For evangelicals, these causes were primarily to be found in the breakdown of families, the effects of licentious media, and the broader absence of Christian influence in American life. Waxing on the problem of juvenile delinquency, a military academy chaplain posed a question to *CT* readers: "Can the immorality of the teenager be divorced from the moral climate in which he or she is raised?" No, he argued. "Teen-agers live not in a vacuum but in a context. They adapt to and adopt the dominant patterns of the nurturing society at the level of their ability and interest. No child is an entity, 'an island entire of itself.'" The "threefold guilt" for juvenile delinquency therefore lay in the deficiencies of the American home, school, and church; mothers and fathers have abdicated their parental responsibilities, schools have settled for "mediocrity in instruction," and churches have positioned themselves as little more than social agencies with "no direct and relevant summons to an eternal service."[85] In a critique of the 1968 report from the National Advisory Commission on Civil Disorders (known popularly as the Kerner Commission), which had concluded that white racism was to blame for rioting, *CT* contended that a better answer "is not so much prejudice as avarice. The inordinate desire for 'more, more, more.'" *CT* characterized rioting African Americans who looted stores as analogous to white housewives who took jobs to earn extra money instead of homemaking— both were acts of greed, and therefore "blame must be shared by Negro and white." Urban disorder and the violation of traditional gender norms may have seemed totally different, but both were linked by a common "social problem," a selfishness "common to all races."[86]

This was evangelicals' version of the progressive philosophy: social ills could be attributed to diverse contributing factors beyond individual choice, but these ills were linked to the loss of conservative religious and philosophical virtues. It reflected a different emphasis from progressive explanations of poverty and racism as the decisive factors in driving crime. And as *CT*'s reference to the shared vices of black and white Americans in its critique of the Kerner Commission indicated, it also allowed evangelicals to use a softer touch on matters of race. Avowed segregationists, especially fundamentalists from the South, had named crime, riots, and poverty rates as indicative of African Americans' inherent inferiority and the "scriptural" justification of segregation. "The Negro," one fundamentalist editorial argued in 1968, "is incapable ... of attaining the white man's cultural level."[87] By contrast, moderate evangelicals' stress on environmental concerns like the breakdown of traditional family discipline gave them a different frame of reference, that of a cultural decline that was not inevitable but no less real. Black and white people alike *were* capable of being law-abiding citizens, but they could be led into temptation in the chaos of the permissive 1960s. If African Americans were lawless, neither white racism nor their inherent inferiority was to blame. Rather, they had fallen under the spell of various sinful spirits of the age, such as alcohol, the "social problem" of greed, the "growing permissiveness" that tempted all Americans, and, most prominently, the "breakdown of American family life." For evangelicals, all of these social factors eclipsed poverty and racism as explanations of unrest in black communities.[88]

This social vision would later push evangelicals into political engagement on other issues more directly related to "family values," but here it was still linked directly to crime and delinquency concerns.[89] "It is time for the citizens of our nation to support our law enforcement agencies and encourage proper punishment of offenders," wrote one like-minded evangelical pastor in an article for *Evangelical Beacon* entitled "The Home and National Order/Disorder." "At the same time," the pastor continued, "let us begin a crusade at home. Let the discipline be just and severe enough so that the child will respect the parent's word."[90] Driving these issues' connection home, the NAE lamented that President Johnson had ignored its request to "provide help and encouragement to those fighting obscenity" while also pointing out that the president's 1965 address to Congress on crime lacked any reference to illicit literature.[91]

Congressman John Anderson, an outspoken evangelical, criticized Johnson in similar tones from the House floor in the wake of the riots in Newark, New Jersey. In a speech supporting anti-riot legislation, Anderson claimed that while the president was focused to a fault on social programs, "I find not a single syllable of protest against what we have seen in Newark and in other cities." He acknowledged that black Americans faced significant challenges and that "much remains to be done to aid the Negroes of this country," while also rejecting the notion that the anti-rioting bill was an attempt to silence "those who are engaged in legitimate civil rights activities." Instead, Anderson offered an Old Testament justification for the legislation and the concurrent responsibilities of black Americans who had previously endured the yoke of slavery and Jim Crow. "Let me remind you that 3,000 years ago there was another nation of people . . . which had been in bondage literally for four centuries." The connection of blacks' plight to that of Israel was not a new idea, as antislavery advocates had regularly made this analogy. But Anderson zeroed in on a particular aspect of the story: God's offering of the Ten Commandments after Israel's liberation from Egypt. Israel "agreed to yield themselves to the restraint of law and order." And they did so, Anderson pointed out, before they entered the promised land, when they still were hungry, thirsty, and in poverty. But "they knew that if they were going to endure as a nation and as a society . . . they knew that liberty is something that could exist only under law." The lesson for Anderson was clear. In passing anti-rioting legislation, "we will be merely giving expression to that idea."[92] Black Americans may have experienced racial oppression, but they nevertheless were expected to be obedient citizens. Just as Anderson did not pursue the analogue of white America to Pharaoh's Egypt, he did not explore the racial dimensions of urban decline, police brutality, and segregation. These were the realities that many black people pointed to as the necessary context for the uprising, the America that had failed them. For Anderson and other white evangelicals, blame lay in the black communities themselves.

As evangelicals spoke out on the rioting, liberals like President Johnson tried to mobilize religious appeals and constituencies in a progressive-style attack on urban unrest. However, *who* Johnson chose to appeal to indicated a misunderstanding of who was increasingly driving the public conversation on crime in American politics and Christianity. On July 27, 1967, just days after Anderson's public critique, Johnson proclaimed a National Day of Prayer and Reconciliation in response to the riots. "We dedicate ourselves once more to the rule of law, in whose absence anarchy is loosed and tragedy is born," the statement read. "We pray to Almighty God, the Author of our liberty, for hearts free from hate, so that our Nation can be free from bitterness."[93] In his accompanying comments, Johnson distinguished between the work of civil rights protesters and that of rioters: "The looting, arson, plunder and pillage which have occurred are not part of a civil rights protest."[94] Johnson also made similar appeals directly to Christian leaders. In a March 1968 meeting with Baptist leaders in the White House Rose Garden (organized by the Christian Life Commission of the Southern Baptist Convention [SBC]), Johnson argued that the answer to social problems such as crime was a renewed sense of communal responsibility. However, he noted, in an apparent nod to the frequent "heart change" refrain among evangelicals in the SBC and elsewhere, legislation could only do so much: "The roots of public policy must lie in private morality."[95]

Johnson's coordination with SBC leadership reflected a broader complementarity on the crime issue among leaders of Protestant denominations and liberal politicians. Though the SBC's Bible Belt–centered history connoted the preaching of a traditional old-time gospel, those who controlled many of the denomination's seminaries and agencies took moderate stances on a number of social issues, such as abortion.[96] A day after Johnson met with SBC leaders, Johnson's attorney general, Ramsey Clark, spoke to the conference, calling for more church involvement in crime prevention and support for law enforcement, but also in criminal rehabilitation. During Q&A, the audience applauded Clark when he stated his opposition to the death penalty.[97] Foy Valentine, head of the Christian Life Commission, had previously made similar moderated statements. Though he admitted that black radicals probably had a role in triggering urban riots, he argued that the true cause of urban unrest was the tragic state of poor, segregated African American neighborhoods.[98] Valentine and other SBC agency heads elsewhere made overt pro–civil rights appeals and urged their fellow Baptists to consider the riots as rooted in economic and racial injustice.[99]

In making statements that generally tracked with Johnson's understanding of the relationship of crime and rioting to systemic social problems, SBC leaders reflected the approach of their counterparts at more liberal Protestant organizations and denominations. These leaders had successfully mobilized on civil rights over the past decade and a half, defining the issue of racial justice, as the president of the United Church of Christ put it to delegates at the General Synod meeting of 1963, as "the over-riding moral issue" of the time.[100] The influence of mainline organizations such as the National Council of Churches reached the height of influence on this issue in 1963–1964 with their mobilization of laity in letter-writing campaigns in support of the 1964 Civil Rights Act. When faced with questions about crises of urban law and order at their denominational meetings in the late 1960s, mainline leaders spoke in tones sympathetic to the plight of African Americans. The Right Rev. Ned Cole Jr. told an Episcopal mission conference, "Blacks feel that they have not been helped by the law. . . . I'm not in favor of burning, but this is the only way they can call attention to their lot."[101] A few months later, the Episcopal bishops of the United States unanimously adopted a position paper that stated that "law and order" must never be separated from "justice" and "the necessity for a more just society."[102] Black pastor Harold L. Hunt preached at a United Church of Christ synod in 1967 in Cincinnati, "You will not have law and order until there is justice." The riots in black neighborhoods, he argued, were better understood as rebellions: "These people were rebelling against a system that is insensitive to their needs."[103]

Mainline leaders had a loud voice with which to shepherd their churches on law-and-order matters, but many in their flocks were wary. Part of this was a result of past successes. The mainline movement lost steam after their initial work in lobbying for civil rights, as later efforts were hindered by a lack of concrete legislative objectives in the struggle for racial justice. Similarly, moderate and liberal Protestant leaders also lost social capital because of shifting tides of public opinion around issues of law and order in the grass roots of their own denominations.[104] Not long after SBC leaders applauded Ramsey Clark's anti–death penalty stand, the national SBC newspaper reported that the majority of the denomination's local pastors were pro–death penalty (10 percent higher than the American public more broadly).[105] SBC pastors and Sunday-school teachers were also reported to be overwhelmingly in favor of conservative Supreme Court justices, primarily because of law-and-order concerns.[106] While the Christian Life Commission consistently pointed to the enmeshment of crime issues with racial and economic injustice, polling showed that crime as a *singular* issue was a top concern of Southern Baptist laypeople (notably separate from race, which was also in the top three, along with war) and that most people surveyed knew little about the work or stances of the commission.[107] The views of the SBC rank and file looked more like those of conservative Baptist pastor and former segregationist W. A. Criswell, who urged the nation to commit itself to law and order in the wake of Robert Kennedy's assassination and urban uprisings, the same day he declared his church integrated.[108]

Among Presbyterians, conservatives pointed to the divergence among denominational leaders and laity on crime issues as symptomatic of the theological divide over doctrinal issues regarding evangelization and scripture. The *Presbyterian Journal* (originally founded by L. Nelson Bell as the *Southern Presbyterian Journal* to be a counterpoint to the liberalizing Presbyterian Church in the United States) was fixated on crime issues. It pointed to crime as a key example of conservative-liberal divides in the denomination and the mainline more broadly. In well over a hundred articles during the course of the 1960s, the magazine argued for the death penalty, lamented that national church organizations were trying to promote "forgiveness" and leniency to criminals, and commended politicians for hardline stances. Some editorials did double duty, such as the one that praised North Carolina for killing an anti–death penalty bill while simultaneously bashing the National Council of Churches and liberal Presbyterian leaders: "Happily state legislatures are acting more responsibly than many churchmen."[109] The *Concerned Presbyterian,* a conservative paper also created over worry about the liberal direction of the denomination, likewise argued that liberalized crime approaches were not only immoral but also evidence of the detachment of church leaders from the pulse of the faithful and the American public at large. One 1968 piece pointed to recent Gallup polling that showed that the majority of Americans believed religion's impact to be waning and that one of the top four reasons was "growing crime, immorality and violence." The implication was clear: "Most of the major denominations must bear their full share of responsibility. . . . Church leaders have encouraged crime by condoning the violation of laws . . . [and] they have encouraged violence by taking the position that violence is necessary when other means fail."[110] One laywoman characterized out-of-touch denominational leaders and lawlessness in similar terms in a letter to the editor of the *Cumberland Presbyterian* periodical. Though the Cumberland Presbyterian denomination departed from other Presbyterian traditions in its more Arminian views of free will, the internal debates regarding crime were the same. "We would like to read less about the controversial National Council of Churches," she wrote, "as many of us feel that in some degree this organization has been a cause of the breakdown of law and order in our country." Instead of a social gospel, the nation needed sermons on "personal salvation" and "law and order." If denominational leaders did not awaken to the fact that numerous laypeople believed "Christian morals and law and order go hand in hand," then "the breach between clergy and laity may become so wide that it will be difficult to heal."[111]

The fabric holding many Protestant denominations together was beginning to tear. This tear would eventually produce a split in Presbyterianism. Though tensions had been brewing for some time in Presbyterian denominations over numerous issues (from the ordination of women to debates over ecumenism), the "most notorious" crisis in the United Presbyterian Church in the United States of America was the financial support from a group of denominational officials for the legal defense of black radical Angela Davis in 1971.[112] Davis, a University of California, Los Angeles, philosophy professor, had been arrested as an accomplice in the murder of a judge during a hostage-taking by Black Panthers in Marin County, California. Davis was not involved personally, but a weapon used in the crime was registered in her name, and she was eventually placed on the FBI's Most Wanted list. In 1971 the denomination's Council on Church and Race donated $10,000 to her defense fund.[113] Progressives were attuned to the symbolism given the state of race and criminal justice in the nation: "Angela Davis may very well be guilty," one New York pastor argued. "We're not guaranteeing innocence; we want American blacks to be guaranteed justice."[114] Conservatives were outraged. Over ten thousand letters poured into the denomination, opposing the Davis grant at a seventy-to-one ratio, and traditionalist churches blasted Davis and the Presbyterian progressives who supported her, contending that this was the final straw and that denominational realignment was the only option.[115] Davis, who would go on to become one of the leading critics of the carceral state, became a religious emblem, crystallizing liberal and conservative concerns about crime, race, black protest, and the proper role of the state. She was, as one observer put it in 1975, "the most influential person in the [United Presbyterian Church] since 1971. . . . And she isn't a member."[116] This dispute capped off the larger tensions within Presbyterianism, and the result was the creation of a new evangelical denomination, the National Presbyterian Church, which soon changed its name to the Presbyterian Church in America. The church was formed in 1973 by conservatives in the southern Presbyterian Church in the United States who used the Davis episode to strengthen their rationale for leaving the denomination as it prepared for reunion with the more progressive United Presbyterian Church. "Thank God," concluded one editorial (the tenth entry in a recurring series on crime that the *Presbyterian Journal* ran in the early 1970s), "there is a Presbyterian Church now lifting its head in the land whose testimony concerning both sin and salvation will be Biblical!"[117] The Presbyterian Church in America's founding was a victory for conservative theology and for law and order.

Division occurred elsewhere as well, from a conservative resurgence in the SBC (where conservatives took over the denomination's executive offices, boards, and seminaries), to a broader exodus of many conservative laity from other denominations that did not formally fracture but nonetheless lost members to evangelical congregations. While moderate leaders of the SBC often argued into the 1970s that their denomination was distinct from the emerging evangelical coalition, they missed the fact that their conservative brethren were increasingly attaching themselves to evangelicalism's associated cultural, theological, and political markers (and eventually the term "evangelical" itself).[118] Protestant denominational splits at this time have often been narrated as theological disputes over issues such as biblical inerrancy, or divides over standard "culture war" issues such as feminism, abortion, or homosexuality. But debates about crime were also a key factor, one that contributed to the alienation of liberal leadership from more conservative laity.

The burgeoning evangelical movement capitalized on these intense rifts and shifts over crime, law, and civil rights. Conservative Presbyterians mobilized the term "evangelical" to describe their position on crime as distinct from that of liberal church councils: "The evangelical Christian realizes ... that where grace does *not* abound the law *must* abound. For unregenerate humanity, restraints, police power, and punishment—the law fairly, impartially and firmly administered—are necessary for justice and for social tranquility."[119] Prominent editor and educator James DeForest Murch assailed "liberal educators in church-related colleges and denominational staff executives" who were falling prey to an oversentimentalized view of the nation's law and courts.[120]

The death penalty proved to be particularly powerful glue for conservative Protestants, and sometimes it was hard to see much light between neo-evangelicals and fundamentalists on the issue. In 1965 G. Archer Weniger, a popular Oakland, California, Baptist pastor with southern loyalties, published a long defense of capital punishment in the *Sword of the Lord,* an influential fundamentalist periodical. Titled "God Commands Death Penalty for Murder," Weniger's piece read less as a theological treatise and more as a roll call of conservative Protestant pastors, intellectuals, and organizations that supported capital punishment. Among them were the usual fundamentalist suspects Carl McIntire and John R. Rice (founder of the *Sword*). But also cited were Carl Henry (praising the execution of Caryl Chessman) and pro–death penalty pieces from the more moderate organs *CT, Eternity,* and the NAE's *Action.* For Weniger, this wide array of sources was powerful evidence to confound any liberal who might try to paint the pro–death penalty position as beyond the pale of Christian morality.[121]

At other times, fundamentalists showcased the divide with their more moderate evangelical brethren, though the vision of tough justice remained complementary. In 1973 McIntire launched an initiative anticipating America's bicentennial, called Revival '76. This revival would reclaim the "Law of God" as an answer to Philadelphia's crime problem and serve as a challenge to moderate evangelicals who had embraced the spirit of ecumenical cooperation with mainline Protestants and Catholics in a national evangelistic effort called Key '73.[122] The impetus for Revival '76 was the murder of a Taiwanese student, Yi Lyi Chuang, who had attended Faith Theological Seminary in Philadelphia, which McIntire had helped to found. "Key '73? No! Revival '76? Yes!" trumpeted McIntire's promotional materials, which called for the conversion of criminals to Jesus, fulminated against ecumenical toleration, and urged the "return of capital punishment." McIntire led a march of two hundred people on Independence Hall, his followers carrying signs with slogans such as "Lord Send Revival" and "Capital Punishment."[123]

Disagreement on ecumenical matters aside, these were slogans evangelicals of all stripes could affirm. In an editorial titled "What Do Churches Really Think about Capital Punishment?," *CT* characterized anti–death penalty statements from Protestant denominations not only as unbiblical but also as "not fairly reflecting the views . . . of American Christians."[124] The death penalty would continue to unite conservative Protestants throughout the 1970s and beyond. It also offered a way for conservatives to distance themselves from liberals in their denominations, who were increasingly finding themselves in the minority in terms of American popular opinion on the practice. American support for capital punishment would continue to grow, from 67 percent in 1976 to 79 percent in 1988.[125]

Perhaps no one was more excited to trumpet evangelicals' affinity with law and order at the expense of liberal Protestants than L. Nelson Bell. In his *CT* column, Bell regularly blasted church denominations that offer "support of individuals and movements that are challenging constitutional procedures and encouraging a spirit of rebellion and anarchy." Civil disobedience created the riotous conditions ravaging America, and yet this "moral cancer" of lawlessness garnered "the approval of most of the major denominations." He begged future denominational meetings to "take stock of what has been loosed upon the land" and to consider the fact that "our most distinguished jurists and law-makers have deplored the actions of various church courts in condoning civil disobedience."[126] These critiques were appeals to populism (leaders were "not fairly reflecting the views"), but also to respectability (seen in the nod to "distinguished" experts). The latter move was especially important. As mainline denominations fractured, the new evangelical movement was framing itself as a reputable religious option that stood over and against liberal Protestant leaders. They not only believed in traditional Christian truth, but they also took seriously the expert opinion of those who made and enforced the law. There was, in more ways than one, a new sheriff in town.

As if to drive the contrast between liberal Protestantism and the emerging evangelical movement home, the NAE released its own crime resolutions in 1966 and 1968 that linked crime with other dangerous forces threatening to envelop the nation. "The Christian community recognizes that law and order are essential principles in the divine economy," the 1966 resolution stated. The NAE named crime as a "revolutionary" force, tying it to other evangelical political bugaboos, such as civil rights and Vietnam War protesters, and contending that there was "no more ominous sign of crisis" in the country than the fact that "law and order are breaking down on a national scale." The answer was closed legal loopholes and the promotion of "strong and effective law enforcement." Passed by delegates representing around forty conservative Protestant denominations and organizations, the 1968 statement made a very brief nod to the need for offender rehabilitation. But gone were the days when the sinful yet sympathetic stories of individual criminals (such as Jim Vaus) were highlighted. The sympathetic figures now were the police, who "often stood helplessly by while acts of vandalism and looting took place before their eyes." Officers faced inconsiderate courts and indiscriminate charges of police brutality, the 1968 statement contended, before targeting the "civil and religious leaders who have shown themselves seemingly more concerned for the criminal than the victim of his crimes." Presumably the NAE meant the likes of liberal Protestants and the Warren court, but the description could have easily referenced their evangelical brethren Vaus or Wilkerson, who ministered to criminals in such a way only a decade earlier.

Another shift this resolution indicated was that the NAE saw crime as a means through which to solidify evangelicals' status as America's civil religious authorities. The 1966 statement expressed concerns that paralleled standard neo-evangelical concerns with liberalism and fundamentalism. Like the liberal theology that had damaged faithful biblical witness, the "un-American mood which has invaded our society . . . demonstrates itself as godless, revolutionary and disloyal to the government." Like fundamentalists, in the case of "loyal Americans," the problem was not their beliefs but their ineffective application: "For too long loyal Americans have sat back and watched with dismay the erosion and disintegration of many of our divinely-bestowed freedoms. . . . We have remained undemonstrative, thereby confusing Christian self-control with indifference. . . . Because of our silence and lack of involvement we have deprived the new generation of a vision and cause to live for."[127] The NAE's official statements, portions of which would be reprinted in denominational publications, signaled that the cultural architecture for a new religious consensus on crime was in place. Now, there was work to be done.

4

GOD'S LAW AND ORDER

In March 1991, an African American man named Rodney King was brutally beaten on the side of a road by three white Los Angeles police officers, who had originally pursued him for speeding. Eighteen other officers stood by and watched. The beating was caught on camera and eventually beamed worldwide after a television station obtained the tape. The initial broadcast, and announcement of the not-guilty verdicts for the officers a year later, ignited immense and destructive protests across the city. Many Los Angeles residents, particularly those from communities of color, saw the video of King's beating as simply a televised confirmation of what they already knew: the Los Angeles Police Department (LAPD) had a long history of racism and brutality toward people of color, not to mention the disproportionately high number of black and brown Californians who languished in the state's overcrowded jails and prisons. As one head of a local NAACP chapter put it, "This is not an isolated incident!"[1]

One prominent Los Angeles leader had a different interpretation. Robert Vernon, the assistant chief of police at the LAPD, described his understanding of the case and the subsequent social disorder in a book entitled *L.A. Justice,* published by the evangelical family values organization Focus on the Family. As the cover's promotional verbiage put it, the book offered "the inside story" and "lessons from the firestorm." Though Vernon acknowledged that the King beating was horrifying, he believed critics were wrong to focus on issues of police racism and brutality. Instead, readers should put "the alleged conduct into perspective" by realizing the LAPD was not filled with racist and brutal cops. He believed that, in fact, the LAPD enjoyed a great deal of support from African American residents; the angry voices were mainly outside "sharks" who played the race card as they unfairly lambasted the police. Neither were the riots the "voice of the unheard," a refrain from activists and progressive politicians that targeted root causes and echoed civil rights advocates like Martin Luther King Jr. during similar 1960s uprisings. Instead, for Vernon the true emblems of moral decline were street gangs (he believed the riots were in part the result of their "preplanned" criminal conspiracy), while the root causes of riots were not poverty and racism but rather materialism, hedonism, loss of self-discipline, and the arrogance of liberal elites. The breakdown of the family itself was "the most urgent root cause," the site in which these other cultural problems played out. When Vernon wasn't blaming the riots on loss of family values or the machinations of gangs and liberals, he pointed to the ways some members of the LAPD had failed in their response. Much of the book read like a self-exoneration of Vernon's handling of the riots, with one chapter titled "The Plan That Wasn't Carried Out," which provided an explanation of the proper organizational response to a riot that his associates ignored.[2]

Though Vernon's book was published in 1993, the perspective he gave voice to had been crafted long before, during the 1960s and 1970s. It was the culmination of the ways evangelicals had injected themselves in the politics of crime, punishment, and policing in California and the nation more broadly. Evangelicals like Vernon increasingly showcased a great deal of power in executing justice on the national, state, and local levels. They were conscious of the ways critics (including some of their own brethren) framed law and order as racist. They therefore crafted alternative explanations, such as the racially neutral nature of the law, African American support for police, the breakdown of traditional family values, and the needs of crime victims and crime-ridden communities.

This last point was crucial. The reliability of crime rates from the 1960s on has been debated at length, with some critics arguing that FBI statistics are suspect. But though some skepticism is warranted, as legal scholar James Forman Jr. has argued, "there is no doubt that crime increased dramatically." Street crime rose, the rate quadrupling between 1959 and 1971. Between 1963 and 1974, murder rates doubled and robbery rates tripled.[3] Though they may have overstated its importance, missed how crime was linked to other social issues, or codified unrest in racialized terms, evangelicals were right in their understanding that America's streets were growing more dangerous. Other Americans sensed the danger as well, which opened the door for these conservative yet engaged Protestants to make their mark on American society by leading on the issue. The crime issue was helping to make the term "evangelical" politically intelligible, a marker of conservative Protestant concern at the grass roots that could be fashioned into a powerful new political tool to fortify America's systems of discipline and punishment (and following the national political party realignment of the mid-1960s, this evangelical power was increasingly concentrated in the Republican Party). However, crime never exists in a political (or religious) vacuum. Policy makers, law enforcement officials, and the evangelicals they courted had choices about how exactly to best understand and respond to lawbreaking. Here we will look at the particular ways they chose (and chose not) to mobilize in the 1960s and 1970s.

Evangelical crime concern would be a powerful asset as presidents, members of congress, governors, and police enacted their vision to make America's streets and neighborhoods safer. They enacted a wide array of anticrime legislation, sentencing policies, and policing strategies that would make the United States the worldwide leader in imprisonment. Evangelicals were instrumental in cultivating support for politicians and policies that led to prison growth, and they provided energetic new support for law enforcement. They did this by linking their movement's political aspirations to increasingly mainstream concerns about public safety and disorder. Evangelicals led in the development of tougher crime legislation and played a key role in the election of Richard Nixon. Some African American Christians challenged evangelical law and order for its racialized character, but evangelicals made peace with crime fighting by appealing to the justice system's "color-blind" qualities. Their influence trickled down to the state and local levels, most prominently in the politics and policing of Ronald Reagan's California.

Lockdown

No one recognized the political potential of the emerging evangelical bloc better than the 1968 Republican candidate for president, Richard Nixon, who made law and order a trademark of his campaign and outreach to conservative Protestant voters. Though Barry Goldwater's similar rhetoric had alienated many voters in 1964, the effects of urban rioting and a rising crime rate broadened this appeal. Nearing the end of his term, Lyndon Johnson saw the writing on the wall: if crime legislation was to receive any of his influence, he would have to work with a Congress that was increasingly sensitive to the nerves that Nixon had touched. In 1967 Johnson had proposed the Safe Streets Act, which provided funding for law enforcement professionalization and modernization, as well as crime prevention through social services. This was legislation in the mold of the 1965 Katzenbach Commission, which had recommended more funding for police even as it argued that "warring on poverty, inadequate housing and unemployment, is warring on crime."[4] But in the months after its proposal, the Safe Streets Act evolved into something altogether different. Republicans and southern Democrats dropped the bill's focus on social programs (such as rehabilitation efforts for juvenile delinquents) in favor of bolstering law enforcement's power and reach through state block grants.

Foreshadowing the emerging southern coalition that would galvanize Republican control of the South and propel Nixon to victory, southern Democrats shaped punitive parts of the legislation and broke with their party's opposition to amendments that downplayed poverty concerns in favor of tough justice. Senator John L. McClellan was a Democrat from Arkansas and former prosecutor who had made a name for himself in leading the federal charge against labor union racketeering and organized crime during the late 1950s. McClellan defended segregation under the states' rights banner and regularly opposed the civil rights movement in Congress, assailing activists' tactics as mob rule and linking them to urban rioting. He was also a committed Southern Baptist. Seeing Johnson's openness to signing crime legislation as an opportunity, McClellan worked to advance provisions that would expand law enforcement's surveillance powers and challenge the Warren court's *Miranda* ruling on the rights of suspects.[5] In the midst of debate about the Safe Streets Act, McClellan introduced a letter into the *Congressional Record* from a concerned citizen that was a classic articulation of Christian law-and-order tropes. Jesus might forgive crimes, it read, but the state had a divine responsibility to deal harshly with lawbreakers. Though the Supreme Court had "made a mocking travesty of Moral Law, Justice, and Order," McClellan and other politicians could chart a new course by supporting tough new laws.[6] Evangelicals, in turn, would cite or feature McClellan in various anticrime and pro–capital punishment publications.[7] Though his stand against the civil rights movement had failed, McClellan showcased how southern politicians could still exert profound influence in shaping domestic policy in the wake of the defeat of their opposition to civil rights legislation. He was emblematic of what Vesla M. Weaver has called "frontlash," the legislative solidification of anticrime efforts as an issue where losers (in this case southern opponents to civil rights) became new winners in the political arena.[8]

Another key voice in pushing the revamp of the Safe Streets Act, albeit with a different framework in terms of race and civil rights, was Representative John Anderson of Illinois. Anderson represented the northern, moderate evangelical departure from the segregationist crime politics of southern leaders like McClellan. He was a Republican congressman who had previously spoken at National Association of Evangelicals gatherings on crime and in 1964 had been named the organization's "Layman of the Year."[9] Anderson wore his evangelical pedigree on his sleeve. As a young boy he had accepted Christ at a revival tent meeting. He practiced law in his hometown of Rockford, Illinois, before eventually winning elections as state's attorney and congressional representative in the US House. His early career in Congress established him as a diehard conservative in his voting record, and he made a name for himself in 1961 when he proposed a constitutional amendment that recognized America's status under "the authority and law of Jesus Christ" and empowered Congress to "provide a suitable oath or affirmation for citizens whose religious scruples prevent them from giving unqualified allegiance to the constitution, as herein amended." The amendment was controversial for its clear violation of the separation of church and state, and died in committee. Not long after the amendment fiasco, Anderson began to temper his hardline conservatism, most noticeably in the area of civil rights. On April 9, 1968 (just days after Martin Luther King Jr.'s assassination, which sparked riots nationwide), Anderson cast the tiebreaking vote in the House Rules Committee to allow consideration of a bill that prohibited racial discrimination in housing. With the riots, King's death, and a growing recognition of America's tragic legacy of racial discrimination all weighing on his conscience, Anderson broke with his fellow GOP lawmakers (who argued that the bill violated property rights) and his constituents (whose letters to his office indicated enormous opposition to the bill). His vote in support of the bill led civil rights leaders to hail him as a hero, and Anderson later called it "the great turning point in [his] life."[10] He explained to *Moody Monthly*, in a cover story interview, that the vote was rooted in his growing conviction that "all men are created of one blood and in the divine image just as the Bible teaches. . . . As Christ was our Mediator . . . we as Christians can be agents of reconciliation and mediate between blacks and whites" (see Figure 4.1).[11]

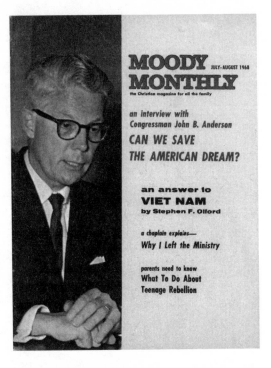

Figure 4.1 Illinois congressman John B. Anderson, an outspoken evangelical, on the cover of *Moody Monthly*. In this interview, Anderson warned Christians that America was "descending into a pit of lawlessness and disorder" and named new anticrime legislation and reverence for law as necessary, alongside civil rights measures and racial reconciliation. *Moody Monthly*, July–August 1968. Moody Publishers.

Anderson's conversion on civil rights was not unlike that of other evangelical public figures at the time, such as Billy Graham, who had come to recognize the injustices African Americans faced. Anderson was also influenced by his Christian constituents (many of them from mainline Protestant churches) and evangelical media outlets that had taken cautiously pro–civil rights stands, such as *Christianity Today*.[12] Anderson even wrote to *Christianity Today* to say that its editorials were helpful for him as he "reassessed" his own position on the issue.[13] They no doubt gave him needed gumption, as many white constituents were aghast at his evolution on civil rights, or what one voter called the "broken promises" to "decent white people" in favor of "negro mobs."[14]

But if the changes of heart on civil rights were analogous, so was the doubling down on crime fighting. Constituent letters detailing crime fears outpaced those of civil rights concerns, such as that of a group of gas station owners who wrote Anderson en masse in 1970 to ask that robbery of service stations be made a federal crime.[15] Crime could also serve as a common-ground issue, a way to appease ardent constituent critics on the civil rights bill who framed their letters in terms of frustrations about lawlessness.[16] Anderson's desire to stake a claim on both crime and civil rights was hinted at in his passionate speech in support of the housing bill, where he simultaneously blasted perpetrators of the riots that had erupted in the aftermath of King's assassination: "In voting for this bill I seek to reward and encourage the millions of decent, hard-working, loyal, Black Americans who do not riot and burn. I seek to give them the hope that the dream of owning a home in the suburbs or a decent apartment in the city will not be denied the man who was born black. . . . I do not condone the rioting. Rather, I say, punish the violators of our laws. Let all men, black and white, understand that the religion of liberty is based on a reverence and respect for the law."[17] In the same *Moody Monthly* interview where he articulated a theological defense of civil rights legislation, Anderson lamented that America was "descending into a pit of lawlessness and disorder." Anticrime legislation, "better paid and better trained police authorities," and a renewed reverence for the law by Christians were needed to address the problem.[18] Racial and criminal justice were linked.

Two months later Anderson got his chance to prove his commitment to legislative defense of the "religion of liberty" when he became a key voice in the punitive modifications to Johnson's Safe Streets Act. As debate between House and Senate leadership took place over which version of this bill should move forward (under McClellan's influence, the Senate's bill had added provisions to make government wiretapping easier, to restrict handgun sales, and to weaken Supreme Court rulings regarding criminal confessions), Anderson urged his colleagues to accept the Senate version, and quickly. Public pressure was mounting on House members to do something about the crime issue, particularly in the wake of Robert Kennedy's assassination a few days earlier. The bill, he argued, offered a "very clear signal" that "we are making a national commitment to a war on crime even as we have to the war on poverty. . . . I think it is going to serve to reassure our Nation." Anderson presented his argument to fellow House members with a biblical flourish: "The Scriptures remind us that to everything there is a season, and a time to every purpose. I suggest that the time is now and not at some uncertain date in the future that we indicate our purpose to enact this crime control bill into law."[19] Anderson believed any deliberation on the bill in negotiations between the congressional bodies would water the bill down or even kill it. He rebutted Democratic representative Emanuel Celler's critiques that the Senate bill "tosses away fundamental rights of the accused" and was heightening tension between Congress and the Supreme Court: "The confrontation will be between the American people and the Congress if we fail to pass a strong bill. . . . The public will rise up in disgust if we don't pass this bill." Anderson was persuasive, and liberals broke with Celler to oppose further deliberation.[20]

The next obstacle was Johnson's veto threat. Anderson telegrammed the White House to press Johnson to help "decent Americans who so fervently cry for protection from the criminal predators who would turn America completely into a lawless jungle." Johnson was not enthusiastic about certain provisions in the bill, such as those regarding wiretapping, but relented because it contained "more good than bad." The "good" was the large federal law enforcement grant to states, $100 million in 1969 and $300 million the year after. Though Johnson had originally wanted more federal oversight of the grants, states' rights advocates (primarily Republicans and southern Democrats) had pressed the block grant approach, which allowed the money to be spent as states saw fit. One such advocate was Senator Everett Dirksen, the Republican minority leader from Illinois. Dirksen's political path paralleled that of Anderson, as he had likewise lobbied for religious constitutional modifications (in the form of a school prayer amendment) and was instrumental in making deals to pass civil rights legislation, bucking the will of many in his party.[21] On crime, however, Dirksen wanted control in the hands of states, not large cities or the federal government. State governors tended to be ideologically conservative, and if funds went to cities, then liberal Democrats or African Americans would likely administer them.[22] Johnson begrudgingly agreed. "I sign the bill because it responds to one of the most urgent problems in America today," the president remarked, "the problem of fighting crime in the local neighborhood and on the city street."[23]

If they had considered the impact of Johnson's support more carefully, evangelicals might have had less of a negative reaction to the direction of the Democratic administration in terms of crime control and been more willing to consider Johnson's vice president Hubert Humphrey's bid against Nixon. But evangelicals' negative perception of the Great Society's economic programs, their discomfort with Johnson's Civil Rights Act of 1964, and Johnson's seemingly light touch in terms of criminal justice (despite his willingness to sign the Safe Streets Act) was enough to drive them to Nixon's side. Though Billy Graham's 1956 *Hour of Decision* sermon had offered a strong "No!" to "more laws, heavier sentences, streamlined administration," Graham disparaged Johnson's approach to crime in radio sermons leading up to the 1968 election. Congress had tried to give police more authority to catch criminals in crime-wracked Washington, DC, Graham noted, but Johnson had vetoed the bill. Months later he noted the nation's loss of law and order and the fact that today "law means less than at any time in American history. Our crime is the greatest in the world. . . . We need new tough laws against subversive elements and those harming police. . . . Supreme Court decisions have disregarded the right of the people to be secure." The problem "may be a greater emergency than the war in Vietnam." Quoting J. Edgar Hoover, Graham said, "The people will stomach no more, the choice is ours. . . . With the election year coming up, American people want law, order, and security."[24]

These exact lines from Graham's sermon were mobilized by southern Democratic congressmen from Alabama and South Carolina, who read them aloud on the floor of the House during debates about amendments to the Safe Streets Act that would provide localities more control over law enforcement. But Graham's real gift was to Nixon, the presidential hopeful who wished to charm southern Democrats to the Republican side.[25] And the setup for Nixon, the self-proclaimed "law-and-order candidate," could not have been more perfect. Nixon had privately told Graham in 1966, "I could not agree more with your comments with regard to the current wave of lawlessness which is sweeping the country." By 1968 Nixon had enlisted Graham in his campaign as, in Steven Miller's words, a "public and private cheerleader," and the evangelist's alliance with the candidate (despite no formal endorsement) helped deliver southern, white, and formerly Democratic voters as part of the California Republican candidate's "southern strategy." Graham's Bible Belt bona fides did not hurt, but the law-and-order issue was crucial to a region still smoldering from the civil rights struggle.[26]

After Nixon's defeat of Humphrey, Graham was a continual source of support for the new president, his policies, and his cultivation of the "silent majority" of white, suburban voters who supported him. As in the campaign, the crime issue was key. Though he did not mention any other political issues, Graham began his prayer at Nixon's inauguration by naming the consequences of an "increasingly materialistic and permissive and society" that ignores God's law: "We have sown to the wind and are now reaping a whirlwind of crime, division, and rebellion." This lamentation complemented materials distributed by Nixon's inauguration committee that included a Bible verse from 1 Peter, a command to "be subject for the Lord's sake to every human institution, whether it be to the emperor as supreme, or to governors as sent by him to punish those who do wrong and to praise those who do right."[27] The verse, Graham's lament, and his subsequent exhortation for the nation to "turn by simple faith to the One who said, 'Ye must be born again,'" showcased the power of evangelical ideas and the political hopes evangelicals had for the new president.[28]

Though many of the actual programmatic details of Nixon's crime war mimicked Johnson's, the policy effect of Nixon's victory was that crime concern became philosophically detached from national antipoverty efforts. Nixon's attorney general summarized this change when he remarked that the Department of Justice "is an institution for law enforcement—not social improvement."[29] The result was that Nixon focused federal efforts not on crime prevention but on punishment: the administration moved to increase prison sentences for crimes and led a drive to build new prisons. Under the influence of scholars like James Q. Wilson, Nixon's prison administrator dispensed with the ideal of rehabilitation as the function of prisons, replacing it with deterrence and retribution.[30]

While most evangelicals were likely not intimately familiar with all the details of Nixon's crime war, their influence had helped make it possible. They had been instrumental in making crime an issue of national concern, defining the terms of the debate, and delivering support to the Republican candidate Nixon. At a police appreciation breakfast at a Christian Business Men's Committee meeting in Minnesota, speakers repeatedly declared their gratitude to law enforcement in tones that echoed Nixon's campaign sloganeering (and past conservative Protestant criticisms of their progressive brethren and politicians). The New York Police Department officer-turned-evangelist Conrad Jensen emphasized to the gathered crowd of 235 that though liberal clergymen cause police "more trouble" than any other group and Lyndon Johnson's Katzenbach Commission failed to mention God, the "silent majority" wants "law and order." This echoed themes from a book on crime and policing that Jensen wrote in 1964 for the American Tract Society, in the midst of growing evangelical capitalization on fears about courts, crime, and disorder, that argued for capital punishment and critiqued "generous and forgiving" juries. The book showed Jensen speaking of police work as separate from that of evangelization: one could address the delinquency problem as a "professing Christian or as a professional policeman. Speaking as a Christian . . . Christ was the answer," but for a police officer, the answer was "more cops and bigger jails." The president of the committee that hosted Jensen praised his words to the group and concurred with his approach: "It's wonderful to see you uphold God's law and order. We are really proud of you."[31]

Though the new president had been accused of race-baiting in his courting the electorate on the crime issue, many evangelicals believed that crime fighting was a moral issue that transcended race. For them, criminal justice was part and parcel of the flourishing of American society. Some evangelicals were less than adept at making this point, as in a piece published in the *Presbyterian Journal* in 1969 by a "concerned mother" who repeatedly *praised* "police brutality" because of its positive social effects on young people. Better for teens to face police misconduct than the brutality of crime or drugs. Neither the author nor the *Journal*'s editors acknowledged the obvious racial dimensions of debates about police misconduct that framed the issue in the late 1960s.[32] Points like this were more common among outright fundamentalists like Billy James Hargis, who could barely conceal his disdain not only for common criminals but also for the "lawbreakers" who advocated for "so-called 'civil rights.'" Claims of police brutality, according to the segregationist Hargis, were the product of a communist conspiracy aimed at "discrediting the police" in service of subversion.[33]

A 1970 book by John Anderson, published by the evangelical press Zondervan, was more careful. It was emblematic of centrist evangelical ruminations on crime, which frequently framed the issue in terms of moderate politics and the common good (such as Richard Wolff's *Riots in the Streets,* a book Anderson praised, and *Facing Today's Problems,* published by Scripture Press and containing chapters both on "crime and violence" and on "racism").[34] In his book, published just two years after his housing and crime bill efforts, Anderson wrote of his own Christian faith with reference to American politics. He narrated his own recognition of problems of racial injustice in America.[35] He lambasted overspending on military and pushed for more investment in poverty-stricken inner cities even as he argued that Republican ideals of fiscal restraint and decentralization of governmental power were key to America's well-being.[36] Anderson argued that the GOP needed to be inclusive, rejecting the pull of "sectional interest and prejudice." "Our challenge," he noted, "is to make the Republican Party safe for diversity." Similarly, evangelicals "should remove the blinders of indifference and use [their] peripheral vision to see the need for Christian influence in solving our social and political problems.... Christians, who are bidden to be the salt of the earth, have an inescapable responsibility to assert their influence in this area of human affairs."[37]

He was confident of a bright future with Nixon at the helm, who he repeatedly implied was a positive result of these impulses.

Anderson dedicated an entire chapter in his book to "crime, violence, and the law." He pushed back against the charge that Nixonian law and order was racially coded: "The man who had been robbed, the woman who had been assaulted, the family whose home had been burglarized—these people were hardly being racist when they cited their experiences as proof that there had been a breakdown of law and order." Crime had civic significance, in that it threatened to "turn our citizens into fearful strangers suspicious of each other, and make of our nation the very kind of closed and repressive society which our Founding Fathers were so determined to prevent." Though he referenced the need for tackling social contributions to crime like poverty, racial discrimination, and the media's glorification of violence, Anderson praised Nixon's conception of the problem as a "war" and the fact that the otherwise fiscally conservative president had requested a doubling of federal aid to local law enforcement, to $1.3 billion.[38] These remarks paralleled his comments from the House floor that same year, where he pushed for extension of the Law Enforcement Assistance Administration's block grants by arguing that "we must face the fact that a successful war on crime can not be financed on a bargain basis."[39] Anderson concluded his book chapter with a spiritual exhortation: "We have not seen the end of crime and violence, for we live in times marked by conflict, turbulence, and fear. But with God's help, and with faith in the principles that have brought us safely through other storms, the rising tides of crime and violence can be checked and the religion of liberty prevail."[40]

Anderson believed that crime could be defeated "with God's help." One thing was clear: the federal government, while powerful, could only do so much. Federal prisons only accounted for a small percentage of carceral facilities nationwide, and the success of initiatives like the Safe Streets Act depended on individual states' use of block grants for law enforcement. States and municipalities had a great deal of power to exert in the making of their crime policy and in determining the priorities of their police. As the effects of the religious law-and-order crusade filtered down into states, cities, and suburbs, evangelicals began to start pushing crime concern on local levels in ways that would have profound effects in creating American mass incarceration over the long term. In order for this localized effort to succeed, though, as Anderson put it, the cause needed to be made safe for racial diversity.

Race and Color-Blind Justice

Skin color has long been the complex backdrop to American concerns about crime, especially during Jim Crow. Over the course of the 1960s, the specter of crime became further defined in racialized terms even in the midst of civil rights gains, in part because of the assumptions already pervading white culture regarding the presumed inherent criminality of black men, as well as rising crime rates and riots in majority-black neighborhoods. White evangelicals bought into both of these frames of reference. But as indicated in the work of Anderson, this was a complicated story; many white evangelicals believed that the cause of racial justice *demanded* they take the problem of crime in black neighborhoods seriously. In some cases, they joined with certain black Christian leaders who were making similar arguments for crime control. At other times, they projected this belief onto inner-city neighborhoods. And even when black evangelicals managed to voice their concerns about the racial problems of law and order, white evangelicals found that these concerns could be pushed aside or, in some cases, channeled in punitive directions under the "color-blind" label."

At a 1970 gathering known as Urbana, thousands of young evangelicals from across the nation gathered to reenergize their faith and mobilize for mission to the world. Though previous years of Urbana had largely featured white speakers and worship leaders, this year was different. Attendees were met by the soul-music sounds of Soul Liberation, an Afro-coiffed band that wore African-style outfits and peppered their lyrics with Black Power–type slogans. Then, Tom Skinner took the stage. For the first few years of his evangelistic career, the former Harlem gang member had carefully articulated his own racially and socially conscious view of the gospel while also emphasizing individual conversion, not politics, as the answer to America's social problems. But as he spoke at Urbana, the man who had previously been known as "Harlem's Billy Graham" adopted the mantle of American prophet, not pastor.[41] Skinner had recently begun associating with an emerging progressive evangelical movement, a small but vocal number of Christians who contended for economic justice, civil rights, and peace while retaining evangelicalism's core theological distinctives. This movement also contested punitive politics, with the small, progressive, evangelical magazine *Freedom Now* dedicating an entire issue to the problems of law and order in 1968.[42] Skinner began his Urbana message with a genealogy of race and religion in America, exploring the troubling history of slavery and segregation and the toleration or endorsement of Christians of these injustices. During slavery and segregation, he preached, "the evangelical, Bible-believing, fundamental, orthodox, conservative church in this country was strangely silent." When Christians have evangelized black people, it has usually been done with the goal of social control: "We will preach the gospel to those folks so they won't riot . . . so that we can keep the lid on the garbage pail." He then pivoted to the other side of this gospel of pacification, the swaths of evangelicals who have "joined the hoot and cry for 'law and order.'" What they actually mean by law and order, Skinner declared, is "all the order for us and all the law for them. . . . The police in the black community become nothing more than the occupational force present in the black community for the purpose of maintaining the interests of white society." Instead of focusing on the corrupt politicians or slumlords who ravage black neighborhoods, evangelicals support the policies that lock up poor black teenagers. This matter went beyond political preference, for it was fundamentally an issue that was keeping black people from believing in Christ: "There is no possible way you can talk about preaching the gospel if you do not want to deal with the issues that bind people" (see Figure 4.2).[43]

Like an Old Testament prophet, Skinner spoke uncomfortable words that challenged the religious mainstream. Though he had been hailed by Billy Graham for his leadership on racial and social issues, Skinner publicly challenged Graham's understanding of race in America even as he noted that the white evangelist had good intentions. The problem, Skinner argued, was Graham's recent framing of American law enforcement as a divine instrument of God's will. "From my background in Harlem I grew up not trusting policemen," Skinner maintained. "They never came to my rescue when I needed them. . . . You can imagine its effect on the black community at large."[44] His Urbana address marked a public shift in Skinner's approach to ministry, one that had begun in the aftermath of the Newark race riots of 1968. Whereas before he had sounded bold conversionist tones even as he delicately guided white evangelicals to consider problems of racism and inequality, now Skinner unleashed a message that sought to upset the political and racial status quo. The issue for him was less the question of individual conversion and more racial and social justice.[45] As if to signify this shift, Skinner now rejected the comparison with evangelicalism's elder statesman even as he blasted the nation more broadly. "No, I do not consider myself a black Billy Graham," Skinner contended a year after Urbana. "I'm trying not to give the impression that

Figure 4.2 Tom Skinner speaking at the 1970 Urbana Conference. Billy Graham Center Archives.

I'm trying to save the system through my preaching. I'm not convinced that the American system is salvageable."[46]

But like the Hebrew prophets' warnings, Skinner's words often went unheeded or were rejected altogether. Not long after Urbana, Skinner fell out of favor. Like many on the evangelical left, he was too theologically conservative for movements like the New Left or black nationalists (whom he often disparaged) but also too politically radical for mainstream evangelicals. His radio program was dropped by the Moody Bible Institute, and Clyde Taylor, director of the National Association of Evangelicals, told the *New York Times* that "we feel he's a little too pepped" on race issues.[47] When Skinner endorsed George McGovern in his 1972 presidential bid against Nixon and appeared with him in a campaign event at Wheaton, he and the hopeful candidate (who would go on to lose the election by a landslide) were met with boos. His divorce from his wife soon after did not help matters, giving white evangelical leaders the pretense they needed to distance Skinner and his toxic politics formally from their organizations.[48] All of this was occurring as Skinner continued to double down on his anti–law and order messaging and soften past indictments of African American urban life. In a 1974 book, he argued for recognition of the problems of racism and brutality by white police officers as catalysts for riots, and expressed concern that some people read his past work (and books by Nicky Cruz and David Wilkerson) as if every block in Harlem were "infested with hoodlums killing people every two minutes."[49]

With Skinner's eclipse, conservative to moderate white evangelicals needed a new partner more in line with their approach, one who could speak tough words about crime and punishment but avoid the racial connotations. They found it in black Baptist pastor E. V. Hill. Born in Texas in 1933, Hill had a hardscrabble early life before advancing in civil rights and black political causes in the 1950s. In 1961 he took a job at Mount Zion Missionary Baptist in South Central Los Angeles. Though he had supported the civil rights movement and had denounced Nixon in 1962 (then a California gubernatorial candidate) for disrespectfully addressing him as "Sonny" during a rally, he soon began voicing frustrations with Johnson's Great Society programs and joined with Billy Graham in the evangelist's tour of Watts in the aftermath of the riots.[50] Following the riots, Hill served as a vocal supporter of conservative Los Angeles mayor Sam Yorty. Eventually Hill served as his adviser on numerous city initiatives and commissions.[51] Hill began blasting progressive responses to rioting and crime, calling Lyndon Johnson's policies that stressed social uplift "Operation Frustration" for their inefficiencies and ineffectiveness. Indeed, he later noted to a journalist, it was the aggravation with Johnson's "Operation Frustration" that led Watts to explode (he did not mention the original catalyzing moment of frustration with police, which also had a deep history in the neighborhood).[52] This was the ally white evangelicals had been looking for. As one sympathetic white Christian biographer wrote of Hill in excited tones, "Except for the grace of God, Hill might have turned out to be an angry black militant." Instead, "to make matters worse from the liberals' point of view, Hill makes no bones about supporting the police." As one white Wheaton College student noted after a summer working on Hill's staff, "He's pro-America, pro-police, pro-law-and-order." As if noticing the possible tension he had introduced in his description of Hill in terms of his black neighborhood and congregation, the student remarked, "And yet they keep coming—every age, every profession, every color."[53] This was the color-blind, disciplined gospel in action.

For whites wanting to ramp up law and order, such as Yorty or Graham, the presence of supportive black leaders like Hill was crucial.[54] Hoover's FBI had pioneered this approach in the mid-1960s, enlisting conservative black minister Elder Lightfoot Solomon Michaux in its attempt to discredit Martin Luther King Jr. as a communist.[55] Though Graham believed he advocated a racially neutral gospel, preaching in a message entitled "Rioting and Righteousness" that sin is "not a poverty problem . . . not a race problem," he knew he needed black allies.[56] In the aftermath of urban unrest, the presence of black leaders like Hill enabled whites to maintain fervent law-and-order rhetoric and elide possible charges of overt race-baiting. In the same sermon where Graham called for tougher laws in the wake of Watts, he made sure to mention that he was "certain that the responsible Negro leaders are equally as disturbed as the rest of America at the things that are happening." Though "an entire race should not be blamed for what a relatively few irresponsible people are doing," Graham nevertheless asked King and other civil rights leaders to declare a moratorium on protests until things settled down. He was careful to frame this request in such a way so as to avoid charges of racism. Besides arguing that extremists "on both left and right" ought to be curbed, he mentioned that he looked forward to traveling to Los Angeles soon with Ralph Bell, a black evangelist on his staff, to examine the situation firsthand.[57] Though many black leaders had decried Nixon's law-and-order rhetoric in 1968 (calling it an appeal to "white backlash people"), Hill put aside his earlier frustrations with Nixon and provided an important endorsement of his candidacy in the 1972 presidential campaign, one in which Nixon doubled down on his law-and-order messaging.[58] Hill appeared regularly at Nixon rallies and was a key figure in mobilizing the candidate's "Black Silent Majority," a small but symbolically significant group of largely middle-class African American preachers who lent their support to the candidate's conservative cause.[59]

Hill endured critique from liberal black religious leaders for alliances like these, but in terms of the crime issue, he could rightfully reject the "Uncle Tom" label. African American civic and religious leaders led anti-crime coalitions like Hill's in cities nationwide. Though they were more likely than conservative whites to argue for the need for systemic social reforms in the broader fight against lawlessness (such as better education, jobs, and the end of discriminatory practices like redlining), those leading these efforts still would push for harsher criminal penalties and increased policing. In New York, the Rev. Oberia Dempsey (originally of Harlem's Abyssinian Baptist Church) led other black clergy in allying with Governor Nelson Rockefeller to sign harsh antidrug policies into law (an alliance the *Presbyterian Journal* trumpeted as a contrast with the "permissive" white liberal Protestant approach).[60] In majority-black Washington,

DC, local pastors regularly partnered with the city council and activists to push harsher penalties for drugs, violent crimes, and gun possession, causes that African American neighborhoods in the city themselves supported overwhelmingly through ballot initiatives.[61] "Local Leaders Plan Crime War" read the headline of one *Los Angeles Sentinel* article that chronicled a meeting of more than 125 black and white civic and religious leaders on the issue. The publisher of the *Sentinel,* a black newspaper, had convened the meeting. Hill was present, as were pastors from other black churches (including some, like Second Baptist's Thomas Kilgore, who had been active in the civil rights movement). At the meeting, a white attorney spoke up and said that the city's rich and poor people all want "the same thing. We've got to come up with tougher penalties for people who commit crimes." The black pastor of the First African Methodist Episcopal Church concurred, critiquing local police for not patrolling black neighborhoods nearly enough.[62]

Though they shared a similar concern with crime and often displayed the same disciplinary response, black and white Christian leaders nonetheless were operating from different reference points, both geographically and conceptually. Black pastors in cities saw firsthand how the introduction of heroin and increased violence were destroying the neighborhoods surrounding their churches, and sometimes harming the churches themselves. In Harlem two hundred churches halted their Sunday-night services because of fear of rising drug-fueled crime. Dempsey subsequently begged the Department of Justice to enforce law in "this raped, ravished and scourged city. . . . We demand freedom to come and go without fear of being assaulted, mugged, brutalized by the drug crazed dope addicts, victims of the organized crime syndicate." Dempsey had tried to ward off drug abuse through rehabilitation initiatives, but it was not enough.[63] Crime was personal, and more law and order may not have been the ideal response, but desperate times called for desperate measures. White evangelicals, by contrast, did not face nearly the same threats of crime in the suburbs for which they increasingly decamped in the 1950s and 1960s. For Hill and others, the heat of the fires of Watts could literally be felt; Hill's own church was just four blocks from the center of the uprising.[64] For Graham, they were more of a metaphor for a sinful and disorderly nation. It was no accident that in the same breath that Graham and other white evangelicals blasted criminals, they also warned of their conceptual connections to godless communists and unruly, libertine student protesters. Black pastors' worries were more exigent than existential. Their own parishioners faced robbery, assault, and addiction, and something had to be done to put a stop to it.

Nevertheless, the crime concerns of black pastors would prove to be a helpful addition to the law-and-order consensus of white politicians and the evangelicals who supported them. Though some black Christian leaders voiced skepticism of the execution of the law-and-order paradigm (or outright hostility to it, in the case of Tom Skinner), white politicians and evangelicals were able to leverage black support of their anticrime rhetoric and proposals where it counted: avoidance of the charge of race-baiting and promotion of the status of anticrime efforts as "color blind" and even a help to inner-city black communities.

The case of black evangelist Howard O. Jones was emblematic. Billy Graham appointed Jones to his staff in 1957, the first African American he had named to his inner ministerial circle. Often the only black person on the crusade platform, Jones regularly endured dirty looks from white audiences (and was denied entry to a whites-only hotel on a crusade trip abroad). Graham saw Jones as a key figure in both his evangelistic appeal to African Americans and the distancing of his ministry from overt racists and segregationists, a move Jones himself termed "radical."[65]

Though more conservative than Skinner, Jones could still speak in similarly pointed terms about the problems black Americans faced even after desegregation. Jones had himself suffered a horrific assault as a young man by a group of drunken whites as police stood by and did nothing to stop it (even threatening to shoot Jones's father if he interfered). He wrote about this episode in a book published by the evangelical Moody Press in 1968.[66] Elsewhere, in his book *White Questions to a Black Christian*, Jones argued that America's police forces needed to "undergo a major cleanup," removing the police who "use their badges, guns, and clubs as a means of displaying their racism and bigotry." He attacked the "double standard" of American courts, which dispensed justice unequally, with black people being speedily tried and imprisoned while whites regularly avoided arrest and conviction: "The law is often pushed aside or changed to favor and protect the white lawbreakers."

The answer for Jones was clearly not more racialized law and order. But the way he framed his complaints about American criminal justice revealed a hope that law and order could be redeemed if it gained a fully color-blind status. He decried the work of black radicals like Angela Davis, who saw incarcerated black people as political prisoners and called for the total abolition of prisons. Jones had confidence that, reformed of their past racial sins, prisons were able to function in a race-neutral manner: "The truth is that today our prisons are filled with various races of people. . . . Their imprisonment is punishment all guilty criminals deserve." He similarly characterized courts: "We must remove injustice from the courts, and enforce the law fairly in all cases," he wrote. "Individuals who break the law should bear the full penalty." The problem was not the tough prosecution of crime itself but the disparate manner in which it was prosecuted. "The majority of black Americans want law and order," Jones wrote. There is a need to "restore dignity and respect for the role of the law enforcement office."[67] Jones did not specify what these ideas could look like in practice, but his continuing association with Graham and other mainstream white evangelicals who condemned overt racism while calling for tougher criminal justice indicated that there could be common ground. Evangelical publishing houses like Moody Press and Zondervan, both of which catered to white evangelical audiences, were more than happy to print Jones's ruminations. He was one of the few black authors on their publishing lists, but he charted crucial territory for them. He offered a black evangelical perspective that pushed against overt racial discrimination but that also removed contemporary policing practices from consideration. The practical outworking of this color-blind, moderated vision would be further realized in the late 1960s and 1970s, particularly in the state that exemplified a new frontier of politically savvy evangelical public engagement: California.

Golden State Discipline

Ronald Reagan knew something had to change. The former film actor was worried about the direction of California in terms of the moral character of the populace and an overspending, inefficient government. This was why he was considering a run for governor in 1966. But the problems were not limited to the state. He sensed that conservative politics needed to evolve as well in order to appeal to a diverse populace. His Hollywood charm could only do so much to make dry conservative critiques of budgets and bureaucracy compelling to a broader public. If his campaign for governor was to succeed, he needed a new vision to energize the electorate.

This vision came from William Steuart McBirnie, a minister at the independent United Community Church of Glendale, California, and founder of the California Graduate School of Theology. Embracing fundamentalist doctrine but eschewing its isolationism, McBirnie had been active in California conservative politics for several years. In 1965 he met with Reagan to brainstorm about a potential gubernatorial run. Their conversation at Reagan's home was difficult. Other advisers at the meeting were pressing Reagan to develop a driving concept for his campaign, but it was not yet clear what that should be. On McBirnie's way home from the gathering, however, inspiration struck. In a letter to Reagan ("Ronnie," as he called him) soon after, McBirnie suggested a name for a "more positive direction which you might try out in a speech," one akin to the names of other visionary programs like the New Deal and Great Society. "Why not try," he proposed, "the Creative Society." This would be "more than a slogan," based on the idea that California's problems could be solved by its own talented citizens, "without the growth of bureaucracy." He then offered five examples, three of which related to business, science, and education. But the other two, including the example McBirnie led with, dealt with criminal justice. "The legal profession could, if invited to participate creatively, clean out the snarls and log jams in the courts." Similarly, "the penal system could be overhauled, if the sociologists, psychologists, and others were invited to think new thoughts and if they were encouraged by a state administration which would change laws so as to create a new atmosphere of freedom to deal with old, tough problems." All of these examples of the Creative Society vision were built on the ideals of self-help, individualism, and common sense. Unlike "the so-called Great Society," this vision would also transcend ideological lines, the "tired old stereotypes of Right Wing vs Left Wing." Perhaps most important, McBirnie concluded, the vision could have "national repercussions."[68]

Reagan took the minister's suggestions to heart, building on them in his famous "Creative Society" speech at the University of Southern California in April 1966. He argued for reimplementation of the "original dream which became this nation . . . that you and I have the capacity for self-government." The attempt to solve social problems through centralized governmental efforts, most prominently seen in Johnson's Great Society, not only did not work but also abdicated freedom. Instead, a "Creative Society" would streamline government and unleash the "rich human resources of California," the state's business, scientific, educational, and charitable organizations: "The Creative Society must return authority to the local communities." Until this point, Reagan's speech was largely vague in terms of specific issues, focusing mostly on the grand conservative vision. But then, paralleling McBirnie's emphases, he launched into the particular social problems the state faced. Like McBirnie, he also began with criminal justice: "A skyrocketing crime rate has given California almost double its proportionate share of crime—crimes of violence—simply because the state, as a result of certain judicial decisions, denies local governments the right to pass ordinances for the protection of the people." Instead, "government must call upon the best minds in the field of human relations and law and penology for a creative study of our penal and our parole systems." Later in the speech, Reagan offered another possible solution to crime with reference to small, privately run youth-outreach efforts. A boys' ranch in Texas (likely a reference to Cal Farley's Christian ranch in Amarillo, which Reagan had visited a few years before) and a California B'nai B'rith lodge—exemplifications of "a little time and a little human compassion"—not only helped young men but also saved taxpayers thousands of dollars compared with government juvenile detention. Both institutions were not only privately run but religious.[69]

This was a logical response to the religious framing of the crime issue occurring on a national level at the time. And after all, it was a minister who had inspired Reagan's Creative Society vision, with crime concern as a major point. Later in the campaign, Reagan doubled down on this messaging, urging support for a "law and morality week" that had been organized by a group of Christians and Jews in the state. He quoted Abraham Lincoln in a press release: "Let reverence for the laws be breathed by every American mother to the lisping babe that prattles on her lap[;] . . . let it be preached from the pulpits, proclaimed in legislative halls and enforced in courts of justice."[70] The best response to the Watts crisis, he argued, was found not in the government's top-down response to the problem but in the business and church communities' work in "proving the value of individual initiative."[71] The emerging networks of California evangelicals, many of whom were transplants from the Bible Belt, would be receptive to this message.[72]

This vision not only helped Reagan appeal to Golden State evangelicals but ultimately drove his outreach to other voters. Capitalizing on rising crime, the public's fresh memory of Watts, and Democratic incumbent Ed "Pat" Brown's failure to deal effectively with unruly student protesters at Berkeley, Reagan pledged throughout the campaign to fight crime and disorder.[73] He knew his audience. Polling at the beginning of the general election showed that crime was the top issue among California voters, with "racial problems" coming in second.[74] Reagan won the governor's race handily, by a margin of one million votes.[75]

Reagan had run his campaign in rhetorical opposition to the progressive specters of Lyndon Johnson and an overextended governmental bureaucracy, but that did not mean California was going to refuse the millions of dollars it received through the block grants of Johnson's 1968 Safe Streets Act. Already evincing a sense of the national electorate's sensibilities, Reagan argued that crime, not Vietnam, would also be the defining issue of the 1968 presidential campaign, and he knew that Republican success in the future would depend on strengthening governmental power in service of law and order.[76] Crime was, Reagan told the state legislature in 1969, "America's most important internal problem."[77] To help execute his criminal justice plan, Reagan appointed Herbert Ellingwood as his legal affairs secretary. Ellingwood was a former district attorney in Alameda County and lobbyist for California's law enforcement and state bar. Reagan adviser Ed Meese, a longtime friend of Ellingwood, recommended him because of his experience in criminal law and in legislation development.[78] Along with Meese, Ellingwood worked on numerous projects related to the justice system, such as judicial appointments (providing Reagan the names of suitable candidates), corrections, trial court reform, campus disturbances, and disbursement of block grant funds for law enforcement. Ellingwood was also a committed evangelical. He was active in the Assemblies of God and was outspoken about the connections of his personal faith to his professional work, and the import of Christianity to the betterment of society.[79] "Every Christian should be involved in social action," he wrote in one Pentecostal publication in 1968. Anticipating rebuke from "fundamentalist circles" who would "raise a red flag" at this contention, he acknowledged evangelism's priority. He then turned his sights to critiquing social gospelers and those who misunderstand the correct methods of Christian social action. Those who practice civil disobedience violate God's commandment in Romans 13 for souls to "be subject to the higher powers." Civil disobedience therefore is "unChristian." By contrast, "the traditional methods of social action will accomplish our goals." He spoke of his work with youths as an example. Ellingwood served as a lay leader for Teen Challenge and had used his legal background to help incorporate a halfway house.[80] Elsewhere he spoke of the church as a hospital for "all kinds of people . . . drug addicts, alcoholics, criminals, bad people and good people. . . . There is a great deal of compassion." And yet, Ellingwood continued, "at the same time there is a strong belief in individual responsibility."[81]

It was this latter sentiment that framed Ellingwood's implementation of criminal justice policy under Reagan's governorship. The governor's attitude toward criminal justice, Ellingwood claimed, was "aimed at developing individual and corporate responsibility, [and he was] more of a prosecutor than a regent." Ellingwood worked on several policies to that effect. He worked to toughen anti-rioting laws. "One broken window will not be tolerated. . . . The leaders of the pack of senseless hoodlums must be singled out and dealt with severely," he jotted in his legal affairs notes as he sketched out plans to move riot incitement from misdemeanor to felony status.[82] He helped develop policy that subverted the exclusionary rule (which stated that evidence gathered through police misconduct could not be admitted in a trial) on the basis that the rule only served for "enhancing a criminal's career." Individual accountability demanded that criminals be held responsible for their actions and that this evidence be admitted. Police who acted against policy could be disciplined separately from the trial.[83] This effort particularly incensed the ACLU and Democratic state senator George Moscone, who argued that the elimination of the rule "legalizes police lawlessness." Of Ellingwood's involvement, Moscone noted angrily, "Give Herb a chance to put someone in jail, and he'll do it. And you can tell him I said that."[84] For those convicted of crimes, mandatory penalties were administered, which required that certain crimes receive an absolute minimum sentence. This idea, which would later become known as "mandatory minimums," was characterized by Ellingwood as originally being popularized by Governor Reagan's administration before moving to other states. These penalties were administered primarily for drug crimes, which Reagan viewed as "the principal social problem of the State of California," and weapons violations.[85] Mandatory minimums were increasingly seen as a form of "color-blind" and egalitarian criminal justice, an attempt to eliminate disparities in sentencing among black, white, poor, and wealthy defendants. Though much later they would be criticized for their harsh application, they initially were welcomed by figures all over the political spectrum for their seeming fairness. A brilliant piece of political maneuvering, mandatory minimums could effectively appeal to hardliners who wanted tough penalties and those concerned with the rampant inequality in America's justice system.[86]

The Reagan administration's focus on individual responsibility led to a reframing of the crime problem in California in terms of "victims' rights."

Though victims' rights would become a recurring theme of 1980s criminal justice policy making, Ellingwood noted that Reagan was the first governor to frame crime in this way.[87] Victims' rights was another way to cast the anticrime cause in neutral terms and broaden its appeal; the disproportionate number of victims of crime in black neighborhoods saw this framing gain particular traction therein, with black and white joint sponsorship of events like California's Forgotten Victim's Week (an event that E. V. Hill participated in).[88] One of Reagan's trusted men here was Vernon Grose, a former aerospace engineer and vice president of the Tustin Institute of Technology. Grose served on committees like the California Council on Criminal Justice and the Governor's Select Committee on Law Enforcement Problems.[89] He was charged with the responsibility of developing policy concerning victims' rights, particularly in terms of trial court practices.[90] Grose was also an outspoken evangelical, well known for his lobbying for the inclusion of creationism in California's public school curriculum.[91] Though lacking a formal legal or law enforcement background, Grose brought his unique training as an expert in systems engineering to his committee work in the true spirit of Reagan's Creative Society, where private citizens drove governmental approaches to problems. Grose would work on criminal justice issues for the remainder of the 1970s, arguing that America's "Judeo-Christian" values necessitated a streamlined courtroom environment where criminals did not escape on technicalities or endless appeals.[92]

The call for victims' rights provided one way for Reagan and his allies to appeal to a broad audience and sidestep difficult questions about the effect of policing on communities of color. White evangelicals who supported Reagan and who championed the law-and-order cause also knew that black anticrime efforts could be a powerful rhetorical asset. As Ellingwood sketched out his tough anti-rioting policy proposals in response to Vietnam War–era college campus protests, he put obtaining "minority support" on his to-do list.[93] Not long after helping devise Reagan's Creative Society plan, McBirnie published a booklet entitled *The Attack on Your Local Police* that sounded familiar warnings on the breakdown of law and order and the loss of public respect for law enforcement. He cited law enforcement officials and L. Nelson Bell to warn about rising lawlessness and the possibility of communist infiltration among civil disobedience advocates. He concluded the booklet by pointing out how bipartisan the crime concern was and, more importantly, how it transcended racial divisions. Like Howard Jones, he acknowledged that policing in the past may have been racist: legitimate cases of police brutality were prevalent "twenty years ago," but the past few years had seen such progress "in the discretion, honor, and discipline of the city police forces that brutal practices are now rare." McBirnie also knew that he was opening himself up to charges of race-baiting when he quoted a policeman who complained, "If I make an arrest in the minority groups, I know I'll be hauled before the [civilian review] Board to explain why."[94] He was aware of skeptics of his own background and political involvement; opponents of Reagan regularly accused him of cavorting with the ultra-right-wing John Birch Society.[95] McBirnie therefore referenced a *New Republic* piece that argued for modernized police forces, a recovery of liberal concern with the issue, and a renewed sensibility that police were "representative of *all* the people in the communities—not just whites." McBirnie jumped on this latter point. "We must heed the voice of the true and responsible minority," he wrote, citing the work of the black Los Angeles Citizens Committee for Better Police Protection: "This minority group asked for *more* not *fewer* police." McBirnie believed that besides allowing him to elude charges of race-baiting, the presence of this neighborhood group allowed him to offer a clear critique of black civil rights protesters and dismiss their concerns and tactics as lacking broad appeal. Earlier in the booklet, McBirnie castigated Martin Luther King Jr. for his civil disobedience. He reported that, by contrast, most of the minority community supported the police and wanted to see "more officers of any race on hand to help curb lawlessness."[96] Racial equality here was being framed not in terms of civil rights gains but with reference to the legitimacy of black and white police officers' presence in black neighborhoods.

A booklet emblazoned with the governor's office seal (though notably not produced at taxpayer expense) offered visuals that corresponded with the state's new punitive, religious, and color-blind aspirations. Part of a series of Creative Studies reports, the booklet was entitled *To Keep Our People Safe and Free* and showcased the Reagan administration's law-and-order philosophy and successes through written copy interspersed with large photographs. The booklet was a call for the "average citizen" to accept "personal responsibility" in the struggle for law and order. It noted biblical warrant for this approach: "The Good Samaritan did not just seek the nearest emergency center, he ministered to the victim himself—he became involved, because he cared enough to act." Some booklet photos displayed police at work, while others offered a glimpse of California's apparently lawless past via shots of police patrolling a burning street in

Watts and pinning protesters to the ground. The header of the final section of the booklet posed a spiritual query: "What has happened to the soul of America?" A spirit of lawlessness had invaded "our homes, our schools, our churches, our courts and our governments." But, the booklet concluded, "the time has come to state that the law will be upheld—and mean it." This was something the state would work toward, but it needed help from citizens. Perhaps most of all, it needed prayer. The second-to-last page of the booklet closed with a photo of a white family at the dinner table, hands folded and heads bowed. The booklet's back cover showcased a much different setting: a city street. There, two kindly white patrolmen stood among a group of black children, clasping their hands. Reverential prayer and racially sensitive policing—a creative foundation for a more peaceful and safe California (see Figures 4.3 and 4.4).[97]

With federal funding from the Safe Streets Act, California developed the most powerful planning effort of any state in the national war on crime.[98] Not long after entering office, Reagan signed legislation that bolstered statutes on burglary, robbery, rape, and violent crime.[99] He also oversaw police modernization efforts, such as the improvement of law enforcement communication systems.[100] Because of an intransigent Democratic state legislature, many of Reagan's other criminal justice policies were not implemented during his terms as governor. But these proposals would prove visionary. Beginning in 1975, under the leadership of Democratic governor Jerry Brown (the son of Reagan's earlier opponent), the state passed a series of laws that prioritized punishment over rehabilitation, increased the use of mandatory minimum sentences, and revoked parole (or made it more burdensome).[101]

Police presence grew across the state. Among them were evangelicals who were willing to bring their faith to bear in the work of law enforcement. In 1971, two enterprising officers in Long Beach founded the Fellowship of Christian Policemen (later known as the Fellowship of Christian Peace Officers, or FCPO). Over the next few years, the FCPO would expand throughout California, eventually forming one hundred chapters nationwide over the next twelve years. The FCPO was nondenominational but drew support from evangelical pastors like J. Vernon McGee and had a statement of faith that contained boilerplate evangelical language.[102] In true evangelical fashion, the FCPO's goal was to spread the gospel among departments and to help officers and the public see that policing and Christianity were compatible, that one could be a tough cop and "still love and serve Christ."[103] Dennis Kraus, an officer from the San Bernardino

159

Figures 4.3 and 4.4 Images from *To Keep Our People Safe and Free*, a Creative Studies report on crime from the office of California governor Ronald Reagan. State of California Governor's Office.

chapter (which claimed around seventy members by 1979), found confirmation of his divine calling through his time in the organization. Before joining, Kraus fretted that his work was incompatible with his faith, because of Jesus's command to "turn the other cheek." But, he concluded, citing Romans 13, "I have found I have an obligation to the Lord as a Christian to perform the duty as an officer. . . . God put the government in power, the laws on the books and officers on their jobs. Enforcing the laws of the land are [sic] enforcing God's law."[104] Blending past evangelistic tropes with crime-fighting prowess, police who were members of FCPO and similar organizations also spoke of the benefits their faith had for those they arrested. One deputy in the El Monte Police Department's Christian Fellowship carried a Bible with him and had a "God Squad" sticker on his clipboard. Though he was cautious about sharing his faith on the job with those he apprehended, he noted he still had "plenty of opportunity." The El Monte chief and sheriff defended the deputy's evangelism, contending that religion could be a valuable tool for officers and that they had received no complaints about church-state violations. The state deputy attorney general voiced some concern but eventually concluded that the religious message being propounded was allowable since it was being offered to citizens by police as a community resource. For California's outspoken Christian police, constitutional questions were secondary. As one officer put it, the real concern should be for the lawbreakers who ignored God's commands: "If you don't want to be afraid, keep the laws. . . . The policeman is sent by God to help you. But if you are doing something wrong of course, you should be afraid, for he will have you punished. He is sent by God for that very purpose."[105]

A scene in 1971 encapsulated some of the positive possibilities of Christian policing. Sergeant Gary Barrett, a Van Nuys policeman, had initially fielded a call from a drug-addled, mentally unstable man named Frank Hoffman, who was holding someone at gunpoint in a recording studio and threatening to kill him unless his demands were met. After some negotiations via phone, Barrett eventually went to the scene of hostage crisis, got on his knees outside the door to the building, and began to sing hymns like "Amazing Grace" with Hoffman through the mail slot. As they prayed the Lord's Prayer and Psalm 23 together, Hoffman unloaded his gun and dropped the bullets through the slot. Police then rushed into the studio and cuffed Hoffman. For his heroic efforts, which defused the near-lethal situation, Barrett was awarded the Medal of Valor, the city's highest honor. Not long after, evangelicals memorialized the event in various pop cultural

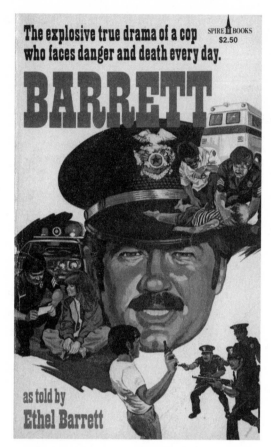

Figure 4.5 Front cover of the book *Barrett,* which told the true-life story and Christian testimony of Los Angeles Police Department sergeant Gary Barrett. The back cover called Barrett "a man, a cop, a Christian." Copyright © 1978 by Ethel Barrett. Used by permission of Revell, a division of Baker Publishing Group.

products. A book about the "street cop who cared" was published (see Figure 4.5), and Barrett went on to star in his very own autobiographical 1976 film, entitled *Barrett,* about the event and his career as a Christian lawman.[106]

Though in the film, as the original hostage situation, Barrett manages to peacefully (though no less heroically) deescalate a dangerous situation with prayer, much of the rest of the film was an apologetic for more forceful modes of police work and the idea that Christians might serve faithfully in the role of law enforcement. A "conversion" that takes place in the film is not of Barrett, or even a criminal, but of a fellow officer whom Barrett originally chides for failing to execute his policing duties. The officer explains the difficulty he had in drawing his gun: "I believe in the Bible and it tells me that I've got to turn the other cheek and love my brother. I can't deal with injuring somebody or killing someone in the line of duty. . . . I don't know if I should be a policeman or not." Barrett challenges his logic by pointing to the violent example of Jesus driving out the moneychangers in the temple, assuring him, "I think he probably used that force which is necessary." Barrett's own life demonstrated that one could be a cop and "a Christian too." This was the message that the California FCPO championed as well, and the organization hosted screenings of the film at churches (including one in 1977 that attracted 1,315 people).[107]

Barrett may have had his own movie, but there were other influential evangelical police officers who exerted deep influence in California's law enforcement and Christian communities. LAPD deputy chief James G. Fisk, a longtime elder at the prominent Hollywood Presbyterian Church, regularly spoke at churches and evangelical gatherings. Fisk saw his work as an opportunity to "live out [his] faith," and he embraced his role as the department's community relations coordinator (which included serving as a liaison to the city's African American community). Fisk sometimes spoke in patronizing or simplistic ways about faith, civil rights, and the plight of Los Angeles's black residents, telling a group of 125 magazine editors at the Evangelical Press Association that what was needed in Watts after the riots were white-led evangelical churches. Black residents do not respect black ministers, he contended, and white evangelicals could help develop black Christian leaders by "giv[ing] them the gospel straight, without apology."[108] But overall Fisk was an important ally for civil rights activists in the city. He dialogued with the NAACP and elsewhere spoke in challenging tones to his fellow white evangelicals about their tradition's racial prejudices, urging them to listen to minority voices. In 1969 leaders of minority neighborhoods championed Fisk as the next LAPD chief and expressed their disappointment when he was passed over, despite repeatedly scoring the highest on the department's exam.[109]

Another evangelical policeman was Robert Vernon, then a deputy chief in the LAPD who had served as an officer since 1954. Later, at the peak of his career, he would serve as the department's assistant chief of police (where he penned the evangelical treatment of the Rodney King uprising in 1993).[110] In the late 1960s and 1970s Vernon was ascending in his influence. He was on the board of the Bible Institute of Los Angeles and regularly wrote and spoke in Southern California venues. He attended the fast-growing Grace Community Church, pastored by John MacArthur (who would soon become one of the most popular preachers in the nation) and penned a Christian memoir in 1977 entitled *L.A. Cop: Peacemaker in Blue*. Though jokingly known among some fellow officers as "the Rev. Bob" and "Chief Billy Graham," Vernon was intensely serious about the impact of his faith on his profession: "I honestly believe God has put me here. . . . This is the Lord's work."[111] He appeared as an expert on crime, youths, and urban issues at evangelical gatherings. At one National Association of Evangelicals event, Vernon conveyed the stakes of the drug and crime problem in Los Angeles as he sketched out his justification for the increased use of a tank and military-style technology in the LAPD: "We are at war."[112] Vernon saw policing as a humanitarian intervention, echoing the "victims' rights" orientation that Ellingwood and Reagan advocated. Murder, rape, robbery—Vernon's "victim orientation" took these crimes seriously and animated his desire for a "righteous bust."[113]

However, Vernon understood that police officers, if they were to have a lasting impact and reflect Christian love, could not use force indiscriminately or rely on violence for lasting change. "I began planning strategies," he wrote in his memoir, "which would put criminals behind bars with as little bloodshed as possible."[114] Vernon therefore innovated a "team policing" program in Los Angeles as a way to improve law enforcement's standing in areas they patrolled, promote better relations with civilians, and, as the *Los Angeles Times* put it in a profile of Vernon's program, "bring the community in on the policing function."[115] Vernon piloted team policing (with the acronym TEAM, or Team Experiment in Area Mobilization) in Venice, California, which was initially funded by a grant from the Law Enforcement Assistance Administration.[116] He had sketched out his plan for team policing in a master's thesis at Pepperdine University (itself a recently founded Church of Christ school with conservative political ties).[117] In places the thesis read like a social scientific rendering of Reagan's Creative Society in its argument for community-police partnerships versus a centralized law enforcement apparatus.[118] In the spirit of community "nonpunitive" policing strategies that had been introduced in Los Angeles a decade earlier in minority neighborhoods, TEAM officers recruited civilian volunteers as liaisons and held regular "kaffee klatch" and student engagement meetings to promote conversations with residents in their homes and schools.[119] The Venice police substation was rebranded as a "community center." Vernon believed the strategy gave officers a deeper sense of responsibility to their patrol areas and could improve residents' relationships with officers. The *Times* reported the approach had cut crime in half and improved police-community relations and was expanding to other areas because of its success.[120] "Hate Is Giving Way to Amity" read one *Times* headline.[121]

But innovations like these had detractors. The targeted areas were often minority neighborhoods, and officers typically white.[122] James Fisk's community relations work was undermined by the fact that his superiors offered him little manpower and pushed him to obtain intelligence on civil rights activists. When Fisk did secure officers to assist him, he found that most did not live in the neighborhoods they policed and harbored views of residents as inherently criminal.[123] Echoing complaints about Vernon's insensitivity to a black neighborhood's problems with police harassment from a few years earlier, a columnist for a local African American newspaper criticized Vernon's strategy and the presence of police in black neighborhoods more generally. He wrote about one interracial meeting where, despite black residents' desire to speak with Vernon about issues of police brutality, all the deputy chief wanted to talk about was his new policing strategy. The columnist concluded, "One seriously questions his ability to perceive the problems felt by blacks and other minorities outside the context of a basic police manual."[124] More broadly this reform, like many others that the LAPD implemented around this time, had its limits. As historian Max Felker-Kantor has argued, community policing reforms were, overall, focused more on changing perceptions of law enforcement, not their operation.[125] Another study of the TEAM implementation found that "responsiveness to citizen demands is being sacrificed to the objective of crime control" and was "more of a matter of controlling crime than of changing priorities." Team policing was an attempt to lessen the likelihood of aggressive police encounters, and there is evidence that it succeeded in some cases. But the actual result was less about increasing civilian oversight of police and more about expanding police power in neighborhoods. With its "proactive" style of engagement, team policing broadened the overall law enforcement footprint in community life.[126] It placed police at the heart of neighborhood affairs that might have been better handled by other services and mobilized residents as law enforcement's eyes and ears.[127]

As a result of California's new cultural, political, and religious consensus on crime fighting and the accompanying changes in policy and law enforcement strategy, the state's prison populations began to grow. Though there were some dips in the 1970s, by the 1980s the rate was moving steadily upward, from 86 sentenced prisoners per 100,000 residents in 1978 (21,325 total) to 161 in 1984 (43,197 total) and 314 by 1990 (97,309 total).[128] By 1991 California was being called "the largest prison building program in the history of the world."[129] The fundamental reason for this change was a perception by politicians that the public now wanted to get tough on crime, a product of Reagan's reframing of the political norms on crime in the state.[130] Evangelicals were not the only ones who had pushed Reagan in this direction or who executed his vision, but their influence had been substantial. With a theological gloss that spoke volumes about how evangelical understandings of social engagement had shifted with the crime issue, Ellingwood wrote about this development during Brown's tenure in a piece on crime for an evangelical magazine. Deviating from the conversionist standard that had previously characterized Graham and other evangelicals, Ellingwood wrote, "It's not enough to say, 'Sin is the cause of crime and Jesus is the answer.'" Instead he praised a recent criminal justice change in his state, the abolishment of indeterminate sentencing, and the institution of mandatory, fixed penalties. "In California," he argued, "*punishment* is again legitimate."[131] In 1980 Ellingwood reported to readers of *Christian Life* that, while Reagan had supported drug rehabilitation programs like Teen Challenge to keep youths out of prison, his criminal justice policy "has more than doubled the percentage of felons sent to prison in California." For Ellingwood this was powerful evidence that Reagan had evangelical interests at heart as he pursued the presidency.[132]

To be sure, crime was not the only issue that evangelicals in California were interested in. For example, they organized during Brown's tenure to support a ballot initiative to ban gays from public school employment.[133] But "family values" at this time intersected regularly with worries about crime and discipline, all built into the Creative Society framework. As Reagan put it in one speech, "Law and order must begin at home and it must begin with the individual."[134] Family values were a frequent concern of Vernon, who published a book entitled *The Married Man* that offered tips for Christian fathers on child-rearing and marriage in ways that intersected with police vocabulary and concepts. A man's authority in the home paralleled police authority on the streets.[135] Just as he hoped for better relations between officers and civilians, Vernon offered tips for husbands wanting to communicate more effectively and lovingly with their wives and kids, even as they attained and exercised godly discipline. Vernon regularly spoke on these topics at local events and was quoted in

Larry Christenson's best-selling *The Christian Family* as an authority on youth discipline ("Neither parents nor the courts are doing youngsters any favors by being too lenient").[136] These were the concerns that would animate his analysis of the King beating and uprising twenty years later.

Family values became a national evangelical touchstone through the work of University of Southern California psychologist James Dobson, who founded the highly influential Focus on the Family organization in 1977, originally basing the offices in Pomona, California. Dobson's landmark 1970 work *Dare to Discipline,* which would sell millions of copies and go through numerous printings, was written as a response to "widespread drug usage, immorality, civil disobedience, vandalism, and violence." In a manner strikingly similar to how evangelicals had blasted progressives who framed crime in environmental terms, Dobson assailed so-called parenting experts who stressed "patience and tolerance, ruling out the need for discipline" because "love is enough." Dobson argued instead for a recovery of spanking, though fundamentally as an act of love. Throughout the book, Dobson framed his arguments with reference to broader concerns about social disorder and crime: there were discussions of the leniency of juvenile courts, quotations from criminologists, critiques of the allegedly antidisciplinary ACLU and "tired old judges," and the linkage of student riots to loss of disciplinary standards. He dismissed crime's connection to poverty ("The crime rate will continue to escalate as long as the odds favor the criminal so definitely") and dedicated an entire chapter to drug abuse (cleverly titled "Discipline Gone to Pot"), written with input from the LAPD. This was, as the title indicated, a book not so much about family values but about *discipline,* a theme that would have resonated with the evangelical parents who had been hearing about crime and lawlessness in sermons, religious magazines, and political appeals for years.[137] It certainly resonated with the Nixon White House, as a copy of the book was placed in its library in 1972.[138] Family values concerns would capture the hearts of evangelicals and conservative Americans for the remainder of the century (with Dobson at the helm). But these were rooted in challenges to the authority of the state and police as much as they were in challenges to the authority of parents. Law and order had helped to take evangelicalism public. Now, it was coming back home.

5

A SERMON IN YOUR CELL

Bill Lutker was frustrated. The Southern Baptist leader of a small evangelistic organization in Oklahoma, Lutker dedicated some of his time to ministry in local jails. He found few fellow believers who shared this interest. In reply to a 1957 enquiry from a Southern Baptist administrator about recent prison evangelistic efforts in the denomination, Lutker spoke bluntly about the problematic situation. A good Baptist, he referenced scripture in his complaint, quoting Matthew 25 to note that though " 'I was in prison and ye visited me' has been in our position all that time . . . until now we have done very little in this field." He reported a recent success in winning three people to Christ at a local jail, but felt alone in this work. Jailed men there had told him they had no other resource: "You are the first one in here." Pushing the Southern Baptist Convention administrator to respond, Lutker concluded his letter with an exasperated, capitalized flourish: "There is need for someone in a position like yours to give the challenge and the direction . . . YET NONE RISE TO THE OPPORTUNITY." Other letters to the same administrator, while less aggravated, indicated similar issues. Though there was some interest in prison ministry, the work that did exist was disorganized and lacking broader support and recognition. Prison ministers had no inmate-focused curricula, encountered difficulty gaining permission to get inside facilities, and faced a general lack of interest from fellow believers in providing even part-time financial backing.[1]

Less than two decades later, the landscape had changed. A front-page article in a 1976 issue of the *Los Angeles Times* declared in its headline that a nationwide "prison revival" was in full force. The article was reprinted in other newspapers across the country. The piece listed famous converts that this revival ("most of it of the evangelical Christian variety") had claimed, from members of Charles Manson's clan to the Black Panther Eldridge Cleaver. The *Times'* lead authority was a prison ministry leader named Ray Hoekstra, who made the bold assertion that "there is far more Christian action in prisons today than in the entire 200-year history of the American prison systems." Other prison ministers, chaplains, and administrators corroborated the claim. The piece discussed the new ministry of Charles Colson, a former Nixon operative and new Christian convert, who had recently begun gathering men from various federal prisons to attend two-week seminars in Washington, DC. It also mentioned several other figures, such as former NFL star Bill Glass, evangelists from Hoekstra's publishing network, and small county jail ministers.[2] The article, published in what commentators were calling the "year of the evangelical," was a powerful acknowledgment that evangelicalism's arrival in prisons was part and parcel of their arrival on the American cultural scene.[3]

Even if Hoekstra was being hyperbolic, the *Times'* report rightly pointed to some important shifts that had occurred. A national evangelical prison ministry directory published a few years later confirmed it. It listed the founding dates of 317 active prison ministries "committed to sound Biblical principles." Only 4 ministries had nineteenth-century origins (one of which was the Salvation Army Correctional Services), while 15 were started between 1900 and 1959. Twenty-six ministries were started in the 1960s. In the 1970s, 140 ministries were started, most of them in the second half of the decade.[4]

Between Lutker's complaint and the *Times'* article, a new evangelical prison ministry movement emerged. This was a domestic missionary crusade, and attending to its characteristics through the lens of mission history illumines its power and distinctiveness. First, it was evangelistic, focused intently on conversion. Evangelicals largely assumed that the masses of people inside America's prisons were ignorant of the gospel. In many evangelical prison ministers' minds, state-funded chaplaincy, with its generally liberal theological disposition, clinical emphases, and stress on facilitating religious diversity, was not a truly faithful Christian response. This transition mirrored the shift in American foreign missions that had occurred just a few decades earlier, as evangelicals interested in preaching the gospel internationally eclipsed mainline movements that had deemphasized proselytization for social concern. Second, this missionary movement was entrepreneurial and grassroots. It existed largely because of the work of unordained laypeople unconnected to denominational infrastructure or large organizations (at least initially). Third, and most important, this movement found itself caught up in tensions that American missionary movements have often struggled with on their various errands, tensions that the *Times* piece and other accounts of the new prison revival largely ignored: How should traditionally minded preachers of the gospel relate to other Christians who had very different visions of missionary work, particularly those with more liberal sensibilities? Do missionary loyalties lie with colonizing forces, or with the "natives" they sought to reach (who usually bore the brunt of colonization)?[5]

These missionary challenges formed another series of recurring questions that evangelical prison ministers moved to answer, some more successfully than others: First, should prison ministers align themselves with the burgeoning forces of law and order and the harsh and growing prison system it had produced, or with the prisoners caught up in it? Second, should the "established religion" of prisons (state chaplaincy) be challenged, accommodated, or embraced? There was no universal answer to these questions. Some evangelicals who ventured into prisons made their support of the growing carceral state known, while others questioned prisons' punitive nature and the cultural consensus that underlay it. Some showed appreciation for state-funded chaplaincy; others scorned it. Many sought compromises. They acknowledged problems with prisons and the increasingly punitive culture that underlay them while also pointing to the necessity, or even providential blessing, of confinement for lawbreakers. This idea, that one does not become truly free without first enduring captivity, was as powerful as it was problematic.

A diverse and influential cast of characters ventured into prisons and triangulated various evangelical concerns in the 1960s–1970s. The evangelical prison work at midcentury, the kind that ministers like Lutker practiced, indicated an alternative to the state chaplaincy paradigm but was limited in size and scope. A new fleet of evangelical prison ministers eventually arrived who likewise focused intently on inmate conversion but brought with them heightened aspirations for innovation and influence. They embraced strategies and trends that increasingly characterized evangelical ministry from midcentury on, such as the adoption of small-group ecclesiology, creative use of radio and print media, and stress on masculine virtues and fatherly fellowship. The culmination of all of these trends was a full-fledged evangelical prison ministry culture that, by the mid-

1970s, was noticed by national media and helped spawn countless other like-minded efforts. But several tensions within this burgeoning missionary movement remained, each of which indicated its complicated place in prisons and American culture more broadly.

Old-Time Prison Religion

Thrice weekly at Cook County Jail in Chicago, a red wagon bounced down the cellblock, filled with toiletry items to be passed out to indigent inmates. Pulling the wagon was the African American Baptist laywoman Consuella York. She was a striking sight, her tiny five-foot-two-inch frame cloaked in a black cassock, with a clerical collar and silver cross chain around her neck. Like many women ministers among prisoners in the late nineteenth and early twentieth centuries, she went by the title "Mother." Emblazoned on the side of York's wagon, in bright white lettering, were exhortations: "Look up! See God! Help is on the way. I love you." These words and the wagon that bore them were emblematic of her ministerial approach: deep concern for inmates combined with an old-fashioned, almost quaint, evangelistic method.[6] This was a far cry from the new "scientific" state chaplaincy model, and while it shared similar conceptual emphases, it also obviously differed in scope from the work of York's more famous evangelistic contemporaries, such as Billy Graham.

Evangelistic work in prisons did not disappear with advent of the state chaplaincy model in the years around World War II, but it did become less popular, despite the occasional visit from celebrities like Graham. When this work did occur, it typically took the form of small, informal missionary efforts. The Assemblies of God, which showcased an interest in prison work from its founding in 1914, was one exception. The denomination employed a national prison chaplain and its publications regularly promoted prison mission trips and literature distribution. Yet Assemblies prison work, though it foreshadowed future trends, still was highly localized.[7]

York offers an example of the most common form of evangelical prison ministry that *did* occur around midcentury. She displayed certain qualities of Holiness evangelists from fifty years earlier, but her work was thrown in sharp relief in the midst of the new dominant chaplaincy paradigm. York began evangelistic work at Cook County Jail in 1952, during her final year at the Chicago Baptist Institute. York had heard from Mother

Elizabeth Oglesby of a need for ministers at the jail and accompanied her to the facility to observe. While praying in the jail, York was moved by the sight of men looking back at her through the bars. She felt the Lord speaking to her: "Supposing one of those were your sons fifteen years from now. How would you feel?" From that moment on York felt a maternal connection to prisoners and a strong desire to reach them with the message of salvation.[8]

Several aspects of York's work are illustrative. First, she was *not* from the mainstream Protestant clergy culture of the day, in either its liberal or its conservative form. As a woman, York faced opposition to her sense of calling to ministry as she attended the Chicago Baptist Institute. Though she strongly believed she had a call from the Lord to preach, she regularly had to answer to skeptical denominational officials for challenging the male ministerial status quo. She took a position as an associate minister at a small Chicago church, but the hostility remained. Unlike in the parish pulpit, York found that her gender did not limit her ministry inside the jail. Only rarely did someone challenge her because of it, and the few who did were no match for her sharp wit. "Mother York," one prisoner scolded, "I don't think a woman should preach." She replied, "I don't think a man should sin." To others she stressed her pastoral calling with a reminder of their current status: "If some of you men would get up and do as you were [supposed to] . . . He wouldn't have to call so many of us [women]." A similar indicator of her status outside the clerical mainstream was that, for all of her efforts, she received no compensation. When one reporter asked York whether she had 501(c) tax-exempt status, she replied, "No, I've never even heard of it before." She later did gain tax-exempt status, but her ministry remained a low-budget affair, with all proceeds going to provide needed toiletries to inmates.[9]

Second, York was consistent in her presence at the jail. Some Christians might make an occasional trip to the jail for a Sunday sermon or Bible study, but York showed up on a regular basis.[10] When an inmate would express indifference to her preaching, York would tell them, "You stick around long enough . . . you'll come around to my way of thinking. . . . This is not a study course for me. It's a way of life. So you may as well adjust yourself. . . . I'm going to be your celly [cellmate] whether you like it or not, and I will return." Unlike volunteers who showed up occasionally (some of whom ignored the seriousness of prison work, or who, in her words, just wanted to "tell some of those prisoners off"), York's work was a calling (see Figure 5.1).[11]

Figure 5.1 Rev. Consuella York leads men incarcerated at Chicago's Cook County Jail in prayer in 1981. AP Photo/Charles Knoblock.

But it was a vocation different from that of a state-certified prison chaplain. Not taking a salary or fiddling with clinical pastoral education endorsements meant that York could preach a blunt message of conversion unhindered by the need for religious sensitivity or therapeutic concern. This did not mean she was tactless or unaccommodating to non-Christians. For example, she sought out pork-free snack items to offer to Muslim prisoners. But she also was quick to tell these same inmates her own negative estimation of their faith: "If you [go to the] holy city of Mecca now and to the Mosque of Omar, and you look in there, they'll show you where the bones of Mohammed . . . the ashes [are]. . . . All the other places you go, to China, they'll tell you about Confucius, and he's dead. . . . But you go to Jerusalem, and they say 'He's not here. He's risen as He said. . . . The Christ we serve is alive. All your leaders are dead, and mine is alive." It was a message as inspired as it was illiberal.[12]

York was similarly straightforward regarding her sense of prisoners' sinful condition. She welcomed improvement of jail facilities and expansion of educational programs. Yet environmental and therapeutic upgrades had their limits. "Christ has to come in and change the heart of every individual," she said. "If there is no heart change, all this other stuff won't mean nothing." Particularly when faced with criminals who had hurt others, there was simply no other way than that of repentance and conversion. "I try to make them see," York said, "you've got to be sorry. . . . Suppose somebody did that to your mother or to your sister, or to your wife, your daughter. How'd you feel? . . . Remember, you done that to somebody's wife, some-body else's mother or sister. . . . If you be sorry about it and tell the Lord you're sorry about what you have done, then the Lord can, He will forgive you." This was a forceful message of conviction, but York was simultaneously compassionate. She knew Christ had her jailed flock in mind when he said, "I haven't come to call the righteous, but sinners, to repentance" (Matthew 9:13). As she would tell downcast prisoners who felt unloved because of their deeds, Christ died among thieves on the cross. He was, as Isaiah prophesied, "numbered with the transgressors" in an act of solidarity. "He understands well what's happening to you."[13]

A Prison Revival

York exemplified important attributes in evangelical prison work that became standardized and popularized by the mid-1970s. This later generation of evangelical leaders and organizations would further themes of conversionism and lay leadership while adding unique twists that tacked along with developments in evangelicalism more broadly. The result was a ministry paradigm that persists to the present and remains ubiquitous in correctional institutions today. As Tanya Erzen has observed regarding the contemporary scene, "Conservative Protestants have the monopoly on prison ministry."[14] This approach was formalized and innovated in the 1960s and 1970s with the arrival of four other leaders: Elton Trueblood, Bill Simmer, Bill Glass, and Ray Hoekstra. Trueblood's Yokefellows ministry pioneered lay-led small groups in prisons. Simmer's contribution was a privately funded, unapologetically conversionist prison chaplaincy model. Glass's influence was in the masculinization of prison ministry work. His ministry stressed athleticism as its attraction and ideals of fatherhood and fraternity. Hoekstra's contribution was not so much a message but a method: he pioneered literature distribution, blanketing America's growing prisons and an interested public with prison-themed evangelical books and magazines. Though different, all four figures and their respective ministries had common emphases that other emerging evangelical prison ministries also channeled: they charted new territory in terms of religious social organization, they connected prison concern to an increasingly curious public, they helped to define the terms of the ideal inmate conversion, and they proffered an important argument about the insufficiency of secular methods of rehabilitation and the practical necessity of inmate conversion as a solution to America's prison, criminal, and racial woes. They also helped to make evangelistic prison ministry popular, drawing others into the work for the first time. Small evangelical "mom and pop" ministries very similar to York's would become all the more common in the years ahead (and York herself would begin receiving a great deal of media attention in the 1980s).[15] American prisons have not been the same since.

Elton Trueblood and Yokefellows

Elton Trueblood was an unexpected source for grand transformations, precisely because he prized smallness. He served as a chaplain at Harvard and Stanford (and was a tenured professor at the latter) but later decamped for the tiny Earlham College in eastern Indiana in 1946 because he favored its size. He said he found Stanford's "bigness" distracting, writing about this decision in a popular *Reader's Digest* article entitled "Why I Chose a Small College."[16] A Quaker with an undergraduate degree from Harvard and a PhD in philosophy from Johns Hopkins, Trueblood exhibited Unitarian tendencies in his early life before connecting with more evangelical strains in Quakerism later on. He eventually became highly regarded in more bookish evangelical circles.[17] His fondness for smallness and simplicity often concealed his elite credentials and ambitions. He noted later in life that he had aspired to be something like an "American C. S. Lewis."[18]

In the same way that he saw virtues in the modest status of Earlham, Trueblood believed in the power of the grass roots for the life of the church. While acting as dean of the chapel at Harvard, he told students gathered one Sunday in 1935 of the need for "abolition of the laity." For Trueblood it was obvious God never intended for ministry to be handled by professional clergy while laypeople sat idly by. "Christianity withers when it's a spectator sport," he later told *Christianity Today*. "A layman in medicine is one who cannot practice. The same with law. But there is no place in the Christian Faith for those who cannot or will not practice. There are no passengers on the ship of Christ. All are members of the crew."[19] In this he was a classic Quaker: all people had the sacred "inner light" inside them, and with it personal access to the will of God. But his application was in line with emerging evangelical trends. Sensing that the postwar era would be a "post-denominational age," Trueblood pushed for the empowerment of everyday, untrained lay Christians for the "purpose of renewal." Laity could be mobilized in "cell groups," especially at colleges, building communities of spiritual encouragement and support. The image that Trueblood gravitated toward to explain this ministry was that of the cattle yoke: drawing on Jesus's words in Matthew 11, "Take my yoke upon you," Trueblood believed he saw "Christ's clearest call to commitment. . . . Being yoked with Christ may mean a great deal more, but at least it means being a participant rather than a spectator." He settled on the term "Yokefellow" to describe lay Christians who work together to further the faith without any formal theological training, formalizing the organization Yokefellows International in 1952. The first Yokefellow supporters primarily had professional backgrounds in business and law. "Not one of them earned his living by being professionally religious," Trueblood boasted. He later noted the similarities between this movement and the "Christian worker" movement of revivalist Dwight L. Moody a century earlier, who mobilized corporate leaders in pursuit of the Lord's business and utilized the term "yokefellow" in his own day.[20]

The Yokefellow ministry grew, gaining crucial financial backing from sources like the Lilly Endowment. A new horizon opened up in 1955, when Trueblood addressed a conference of prison chaplains in Washington, DC, on his small group renewal movement model. He recounted later that he "spoke on the power of the small group of people who have a common discipline and who share both their problems and their faith with one another." Two chaplains took Trueblood's exhortations to heart and established Yokefellow groups in prisons in Tacoma, Washington, and Lewisburg, Pennsylvania. The model spread to other prisons, and before long the movement formalized as Yokefellow Prison Ministry.[21]

Over the next two decades, Yokefellow Prison Ministry expanded into prisons in other states. By the 1970s one newspaper columnist in Asheville, North Carolina, was calling it "the most widespread prison ministry in the country."[22] A chaplain estimated in 1977 that there were more than four hundred Yokefellows groups working in prisons in thirty-five states.[23] The Yokefellows organizations formed in Pennsylvania (in 1968) and North Carolina (in 1970) would go on to be two of the largest: by the 1980s the Pennsylvania Yokefellows would have some sort of presence in every federal and state prison in the commonwealth, with more than one thousand inmates participating.[24]

Small groups of around twelve people (usually ten inmates and two noninmates) would meet weekly in these gatherings to pray, read scripture, and talk about the skills needed for living in and outside prison.[25] There was typically no hard programmatic structure to the discussions. Instead, they functioned similarly to the cell groups that were starting to proliferate in evangelical churches nationwide at the time, as sites of friendship, positive conversation, and spiritual accountability. "Coming to the meetings has meant a great deal to me," one seventeen-year-old inmate told a North Carolina newspaper. "Since getting involved with the Yokefellow group I have begun to go to church every Sunday and think differently about my life." Another inmate from the same prison, who was about to complete his sentence, spoke in similar terms: "I feel better prepared to face the outside world, because these Yokefellow people have shown me that I am not alone and that I do have friends."[26]

Yokefellows was intentionally nondenominational, drawing volunteers from a variety of churches and Christian traditions. It also was less officially interested in inmate conversion and spiritual concerns than other evangelical ministry efforts, though observers did note that volunteers who participated hoped to "spread the gospel."[27] Indeed, lay control meant that local Yokefellows groups had a great deal of power in shaping the agenda of meetings, so gatherings sometimes would turn into full-blown revivals. A group of inmates who dubbed themselves "the McNeil Brothers" and a local ministry chairman called a Yokefellows retreat a "Holy Ghost victory" after six inmates from McNeil Island prison were baptized and others made deeper commitments to Jesus. "They call themselves 'The McNeil Brothers,'" the announcement explained, "because they are born again members of the family of God."[28]

Yokefellows' lay-driven and ecumenical character reflected a hybrid of two trends in the social organization of American religion. Though precise quantitative data on small groups from this period time are hard to come by, one later study suggests that conservative Protestants were disproportionately more involved in small groups compared with Roman Catholics and mainline Protestants when the groups were based in churches. When they were unaffiliated with churches (and focused on addictions, community causes, general self-help, or other nonspiritual issues), small groups were more likely to attract Catholic, mainline Protestants and infrequent churchgoers.[29] Yokefellow Prison Ministry combined both emphases. First, it was evangelically oriented. "When it began," Trueblood said of his movement in 1977, "it represented an early form of the

New Evangelicalism."[30] But it was also focused enough on the spiritual well-being of prisoners more generally that it could appeal to a wide variety of participants and, most crucially, prison chaplains. Yokefellows was not at all antagonistic toward chaplains, who regularly supervised their in-prison meetings and spoke highly of the ministry to newspapers and at conferences. But the ministry indicated that an alternative to the chaplaincy paradigm was possible. Yokefellows showed that Christians need not be paid or clinically and theologically trained in any formal sense. It was in this way a bridge movement for evangelicals, a nonthreatening alternative to state-funded chaplaincy. And it exemplified a broader trend: the engagement of nonspecialists in prison work. Yokefellows gave people who otherwise would never have interacted with prisoners a chance to get to know them and their concerns. The context was low pressure and for inmates might only have been a short respite from the daily stresses of prison life. But for participants coming in from outside churches who found themselves newly sensitized to the plight of prisoners, the experience could be life changing.

Bill Simmer and Good News Prison Ministry

The independent minister Consuella York and the lay-driven Yokefellows movement indicated that there were other possible prison ministry paradigms that did not depend on state employment or clinical certification by the mainline religious establishment. But tough and ambitious though she was, the reach of York and other solitary, independent evangelists was limited. Likewise, Yokefellows was growing, but their presence in prisons was intermittent, at most a few hours a week. There was space for innovation, on which a former air force intelligence officer named Bill Simmer capitalized. An Iowan born in 1928, Simmer experienced conversion at a Baptist church revival in Virginia in 1953. Not long after, he left a successful business career behind to attend Washington Bible College in Washington, DC. Inspired by his professors, Simmer began ministering in the nearby Fairfax County jail, and eventually enlisted several other students.[31]

Simmer brought his business acumen to bear in organizing his jail ministry in three ways. First, he was ambitious, and he wanted to expand.[32] Not content with a small ministry at one institution, he had a desire to move to new locales and introduce others to prison work. He knew many Christian ministries folded because they were too dependent on one leader.[33]

Second, he wanted professionalism. Simmer felt there was a general lack of commitment in prison ministry, with most churches avoiding prisons as a site for ministry, and the volunteers who *did* go showing up haphazardly.[34] He knew that if a new prison ministry effort were to succeed, it would also need to be properly funded. Though he appreciated the self-directed fund-raising of foreign missionaries (and had nearly become one himself), he thought that the method of raising one's own support was too unpredictable. Prisons were institutions built on regimentation and regularity, and Simmer believed wardens would not appreciate prison missionaries taking time off for fund-raising furloughs. He wanted an organization that could pay chaplains a salary and raise funds on their behalf.

Third, Simmer was an entrepreneur, one who knew that economies needed innovation and disruption. He wanted to challenge what he believed was a staid quality of prison chaplaincy, which had stability through state funding but, with that, a host of other problems. He believed that state chaplaincy generally attracted the "dregs" of those in ministry, people who had not made it as pastors or who had personal failures (such as divorce) that got them kicked out of their churches. Just as problematic, Simmer thought, state chaplaincy allowed for non-Christian ministers (such as Muslims) or even women (whom he believed the Bible prohibited from preaching). With state chaplains, he said, "we are ministering side by side with people who we learned in seminary are just cults. . . . If you are accepting government money, you have no choice in these matters."[35]

Simmer's answer was Good News Jail and Prison Ministry, which he founded in 1961. Simmer was the first full-time chaplain for Good News, working at Fairfax County Jail. The work was a combination of evangelism, discipleship, and pastoral care: engaging in impromptu preaching on the cellblock, leading Bible studies, and holding counseling sessions with depressed inmates. For Simmer, it was exhilarating. "Here was real Christianity," he later said, "pitting the word of God against the system of the world. . . . If there was a place where Satan dwells on earth it would be our jails and prison cells, and yet here I see the gospel effectively getting the attention of men and changing their lives . . . when mankind had given up." Though focused on evangelism, Simmer and the others who joined him as paid chaplains sometimes worked to better inmates' in-prison lives. Good News started libraries and educational programs in various facilities, and Simmer later launched the first inmate work-release program in the state of Virginia.[36]

In 1976 Good News had twenty-one chaplains in prisons on the East Coast, with a $1 million budget.[37] It expanded westward soon after. Simmer and his chaplains proudly broadcast each of Good News' distinctives as the ministry grew. Good News chaplain Rick Bartosik, a graduate of Chicago's Moody Bible Institute and the evangelical Trinity College in nearby Deerfield, told a Honolulu reporter of his clear evangelical motivations for migrating to Hawaii to minister at two prisons there: "I'm not here as a do-gooder. I'm here to communicate the love of Jesus Christ, to communicate the gospel." Simmer echoed Bartosik. The way to address the "real spiritual vacuum" of prisons, he told the Honolulu reporter, was to provide "what a good, growing, thriving evangelical church offers its members on the outside."[38]

Good News indicated a new professional model for evangelicals who wanted to minister to inmates. It was emblematic not only of a shift in Christian prison work but also of the latest in a long trend of innovation and rupture with the professional religious status quo in evangelical history more broadly. In the evangelical awakenings of the 1740s, spellbinding preachers like George Whitefield had led laity out of their churches and into fields for revivals, opening up a new religious marketplace where an upmarket degree from Yale or Princeton meant little. Similar breaks characterized the movement from then on, from early nineteenth-century camp meetings that moved worship out of churches and into the woods, to later Holiness "come outer" and fundamentalist challenges to established mainline denominations, to postwar evangelicals' use of mass media and stadium preaching to reach seekers who would never have otherwise darkened the door of a church.[39]

Parallel with the emergence of a new prison ministry paradigm, evangelicals in the second half of the twentieth century were making similar moves in other realms of outreach and social engagement. These evangelical efforts were part of the postwar "restructuring of American religion," in which religious special-interest groups increasingly challenged denominational dominance in American public life. Whether in foreign aid, higher education, or prisons, evangelicals channeled new energy and dissatisfaction with what they saw as increasingly liberal theology and moribund organizational structures in the Protestant mainline. The broader source of this common expansion, as Robert Wuthnow has argued, was the expansion of state power. From the New Deal into the 1960s, government influence expanded in nearly every major sector of American life.[40] In higher education, for example, the GI Bill dramatically increased the number of college students, with governmental grant funding for public universities following suit. Nondenominational and evangelical college student ministries such as Campus Crusade capitalized on growth in American higher education while also distinguishing themselves from campus ministries run by mainline Protestants.[41] The construction of suburbs (zoned by the state) meant there was quite literally new geographic territory for religious groups to explore. New, casual "megachurches" sprouted in these locales, taking on architectural, cultural, and organizational forms that stood in stark contrast to the tall-steepled, mainline "First" churches downtown in America's cities.[42] Broader anxieties about communism and the place of the United States on the international scene led evangelicals to build their own global relief agencies, such as World Vision, which operated outside the mission arms of Protestant denominations.[43]

The same was true of prisons. In the postwar era of law and order, the American state was expanding in its most core function: the ability to use coercive force for the maintenance of social order. The state had aligned with the Protestant mainline in the form of sponsored chaplains, but there was more territory for religious entrepreneurs to exploit. Simmer intuited this and structured Good News as a direct challenge to the state chaplaincy paradigm. He did so with the argument that connected state chaplains with the worst parts of the prison system. In arguing for Good News' necessity, Simmer said that he wanted a chaplain who was "not paid by Caesar."[44] He believed that inmates would prefer a chaplain who was not funded by the very entity that was holding them captive. With a privately funded chaplain, "inmates know that this is not the 'government's man' and that they can trust him."[45] In sum, Simmer wanted to build a ministry that would have the regularity, professionalism, and institutional access of state chaplaincy, but without the various theological troubles, image problems, and inflexibility of the state-sponsored system. By the early 1980s, Good News employed 30 chaplains nationwide (and this number had jumped to 370 worldwide by 2012).[46] But the broader impact was the charting of new conceptual terrain that later groups of evangelicals would incorporate as more entered the contested religious turf of the prison system.

Bill Glass

Bill Glass was in prison because he had hit people. But he was no felon. He was a former defensive end for the Detroit Lions and Cleveland Browns, having played more than a decade of professional football in the NFL. When he wasn't laying bone-crushing broadsides on opposing quarterbacks during football season, he studied theology at Southwestern Theological Seminary (a Southern Baptist school in Fort Worth, Texas), receiving a degree in 1963. Soon after, he began holding Billy Graham–style evangelistic crusades during off-seasons, often coordinating informally with the Billy Graham Evangelistic Association to speak in cities that the elder evangelist had declined to visit.[47] When Glass's football career came to a close in 1969, he founded the Bill Glass Evangelistic Association and began work as a full-time evangelist.[48] In 1972 he held a crusade at the Marion State Prison, Ohio. He had initially dreaded the event because of a bad experience in prison ministry during college and the fact that his association was already overburdened and in debt.[49] But the event was a success, and Glass and his associates began planning other prison events alongside their standard city crusades, announcing in 1973 that he planned to visit three prisons a year every year.[50]

Prison crusades were logistically complex and expensive, but a generous gift from the owner of the Cleveland Browns helped keep Glass's prison ministry afloat in its first few years and ultimately served as a sign to Glass that he could ramp up this effort.[51] Glass kept his three-prisons-a-year promise until 1975, when the ministry held eight prison crusades (and seven nonprison crusades). The rate was similar the next year, and the ministry added more in later years as it transitioned to a full-time prison focus.[52]

Each weekend prison crusade followed a standardized format. Various athletes from professional sports teams put on clinics and demonstrations during the day on the prison yard, and in the evening services were held, with speakers offering their testimonies. The speakers included a mix of celebrities, athletes, former inmates, and Glass himself. For example, the Marion, Ohio, crusade had athletic clinics led by players from the Chicago Bulls and New York Yankees, as well as karate and weight-lifting demonstrations.[53] Many of the athletes were or would soon become household names. Later, in the 1980s, a budding University of North Carolina–Chapel Hill basketball star named Michael Jordan would volunteer at a Glass crusade, only narrowly avoiding serious injury when a karate demonstration he volunteered to help with went awry.[54] Numerous volunteer counselors (sixty in the case of Marion) would help provide a more personal touch, walking the prison yard and venturing into the cellblocks to chat with inmates and share the gospel.[55]

The key to Glass's appeal as an evangelist was his status as a former football star. Football-shaped promotional stickers from the early days of his ministry were emblazoned with photos of Glass in shoulder pads and slogans like "Get in the Game for CHRIST."[56] He made a name for himself as a speaker in the Fellowship of Christian Athletes, or FCA. Fellowship of Christian Athletes events often featured sports clinics, where youths could rub shoulders with famous athletes and glean tips for catching, throwing, and tackling.[57] Glass borrowed the sports clinic idea from FCA and brought it into his city crusades and eventually his prison events. During the prison crusades, inmates could watch basketball stars like Jim King and Clifford Ray shoot three-pointers, or take turns catching passes from quarterback Roger Staubach.[58] According to one ministry worker, the most popular athletes Glass brought were weight lifters, no doubt because of the astounding feats of strength they performed in front of crowds of inmates. Paul Anderson, an Olympic gold medalist who claimed the title of "World's Strongest Man," bent nails and lifted tables on which volunteers would sit. Other lifters challenged inmates to squat competitions, drove nails into boards with their bare hands, and encouraged inmates to punch and jump on their rock-hard stomachs.[59]

Glass believed athletes' star power and physical prowess could persuade otherwise suspicious or indifferent inmates to show up to his crusades. He explained his approach with reference to the success of his Marion crusade in a retrospective column entitled "Recreation in Prison Evangelism" for a Southern Baptist magazine. "Inmates enjoyed all forms of sports," he wrote, "and they were thrilled to be able to meet and talk with some of the top athletes of the country." More than this, "prisoners are usually impressed by physical strength. Every one of the men I had with me was big and tough, or at least an eminently successful athlete, so the program went surprisingly well."[60] The Glass newsletter quoted one inmate's positive assessment in similar terms: "We didn't want nobody preaching at us. We wanted to see the karate guy and listen to Bill Glass talk about football. After that night we just wanted to hear more about God" (see Figure 5.2).[61]

Sports and athleticism were not simply sideshows, or even mediums for Glass's evangelism. They were a key part of the message itself. The power lifters who pumped iron and inmates alike were always quick to connect demonstrations of their physical prowess with spiritual transformation. In the words of one volunteer, the testimony of a weight lifter "silences the critics who believe Christianity is for wimps and sissies."[62] In

Figure 5.2 Prison minister and former NFL star Bill Glass speaks to inmates at Goree Prison in Huntsville, Texas, in 1999 as part of his ministry's Weekend of Champions event. Copyright © Todd Bigelow Photography.

his first prison crusade, while preaching to inmates gathered on the institution's baseball diamond, Glass gave a presentation of the gospel in keeping with the setting. "First base in life is salvation. . . . [Jesus] can forgive you just like he did me. You can have a whole new start in life. . . . But then you're on to second base. Second base is relationship to other people. . . . You must have Christian friends. On from there to the third base, which is service. . . . Really happy people are the ones who have discovered the joy of service." By this point in his talk, Glass later noted, "they were really listening to me. I had their total attention." He then moved to the sermonic climax. "But what's home plate? It's heaven!" He gestured toward the counselors standing nearby. "If you'd like to find a way that you can have all your sins forgiven and have eternal life, hang around. These guys will be glad to talk to you about it."[63] This sports-inflected message was appealing not only for its communication of the gospel but also for its perceived pro-social qualities. One law enforcement official wrote Glass to ask him to hold a crusade in a local prison, noting, "It is our very firm conviction that the active involvement of professional athletes in our recreational/rehabilitative program would propel inmates toward observing the rules of good sportsmanship and a consequent greater respect for the rights and property of others." Bringing in "celebrated and respected athletes" and offering sports activities "would serve as proof to inmates that 'society' is concerned with their welfare!"[64]

Sports and Christianity have long been entwined in American history, particularly within evangelicalism. Though early American Christians often worried about athletics' corrupting influence (in part because of its association with gambling and the brutality of sports like boxing), by the mid-nineteenth century Christian leaders began to speak of the virtues of a "muscular Christianity": manliness, morality, health, and patriotism.[65] The Young Men's Christian Association (YMCA) emerged, with its stress on the complementarity of physical and spiritual fitness. Though theological conservatives and liberals alike found common cause with the YMCA's approach in its early days, by the early twentieth century, fundamentalists began shifting some of the terms of the debate, particularly as the YMCA became a bastion for social gospel–style progressivism. Billy Sunday exploited his status as a former baseball star in the 1880s in his hellfire preaching, but the key term here was "former." Though he regularly argued for a highly masculine version of the faith, the fundamentalist Sunday assailed baseball for its un-Christian qualities and only embraced his past insofar as it was a means to an end. "Baseball and Christian work," one study of Sunday has put it, were "mutually exclusive endeavors." Culturally accommodating neo-evangelicals in the late 1940s and 1950s were friendlier to the cause of athletic faith, showcasing Christian athletes in their evangelistic events. At the same time that he was broadcasting the miraculous testimony of the converted criminal Jim Vaus in his crusades, Billy Graham was also giving track stars like Gil Dodds a platform to speak about running life's race for Christ.[66]

While he was indebted to this evangelical tradition (having been one of Graham's athletic platform guests in the 1960s), Glass represented a new and intensified phase of muscular faith. He was resolutely conversionist and had little interest in offering a social gospel–style gloss on the proper integration of physical and spiritual well-being. Unlike Sunday, Glass embraced sports beyond its basic pragmatic value and showed that good athletes could not only be good Christians but also serve as ideal spiritual examples. But unlike Graham, Glass showed that an athlete could lead the charge and that athletics itself could be the centerpiece of an evangelistic crusade. As he wrote in one of his first books concerning the time he flew to speak at a Christian youth rally the day after winning the NFL championship, "A world's championship football game and proclamation of the good news of Jesus Christ were almost simultaneous events."[67] Sensing the skepticism about sports within straight-laced evangelical culture, Glass told the *Los Angeles Times* in 1972 that his organization was "not a hyper-right, super-conservative organization politically, but we do defend sports—and Christianity—at points where it's been unfairly attacked."[68]

Glass's intensifying prison interests from the mid-1970s on indicated that he saw prison ministry and muscular faith as another kind of simultaneous concern. This was also not an entirely new development. One of the very first celebrities of muscular Christianity, former boxer Orville Gardner, was famous for his evangelism in prisons in the mid-nineteenth century.[69] In his own prison work, however, Glass innovated. His message gradually took on other valences beyond sheer athletic power, as manly fellowship and loving fatherhood became the chief ends to which his athletic evangelism was pointed. When Billy Sunday preached his fiery messages in the early twentieth century, he zeroed in on the need for a hard-nosed and aggressive Christian faith with literal fighting words: "I'd like to put my fist on the nose of the man who hasn't got grit enough to be a Christian."[70] By contrast, Glass reveled in highly relational and emotional language that prized intimacy between men, especially sons and fathers. The answer to innumerable social problems, according to Glass, was the recovery of "the Blessing," an assurance of unconditional love, value, and belonging.[71] The blessing ideally should come from a father, but it could also come from other trusted authority figures, mentors, or coaches. These were people who could be, in Glass's words, "substitute fathers" and who could speak words of encouragement like "I love you, you're terrific, and you're mine." At its best, a blessing entailed strong verbal and physical affirmation. Glass spoke of the power of his own father's blessing in precisely these terms: "My earliest recollections are that my father would sit on my bedside and rub my back and tell me what a fine boy I was, and almost every night, he would kiss me on the mouth. He was a pro baseball player, a very manly man. But he had no problem expressing his love and blessing to me and to my brother and sister."[72]

Only later in his ministry did Glass devote sustained attention to detailing the specifics of fatherly blessing, like in his 2005 book *Champions for Life*. But as his coauthor wrote in the introduction of this book, "'the Blessing' speech . . . has been the heart of his ministry for about thirty years." And as Glass has said, "'the blessing' was there from the very beginning."[73] In his prison ministry, Glass sought to help inmates understand their own incarceration in these terms, as fractured fatherly relationships were the prime cause of criminality. "Several years ago," Glass wrote, "I was walking down death row in Parchman, Mississippi. Forty-four men were on death row at the time, and I asked every man the same question, 'How do you and your dad get along?' Forty-four out of forty-four men said they had a poor relationship with their fathers."[74] The way forward, then, was for men to acknowledge their relational brokenness and to seek to connect to a new "father" figure. They could begin with their Heavenly Father, but loving relationships with other inmates and ministry volunteers who could bless them would be welcome as well.

Fatherhood and fellowship were concepts that marked muscular Christian culture in America from the 1970s on. It reached a climax with the advent of the Promise Keepers, a parachurch organization with similar athletic origins and emphasis. Founded by University of Colorado football coach Bill McCartney, Promise Keepers pushed men to keep their hearts pure, remain faithful to their wives, and seek reconciliation with one another (often across racial lines). According to sociologist John Bartkowski, Promise Keepers triangulated a combination of "instrumentalist" and "expressive" forms of masculinity. Instrumentalist masculinity drew from essentialist notions of masculinity that stressed aggression and strength, while expressive masculinity referenced the possibility of intimacy among men. More provocatively, Bartkowski argues that Promise Keepers emphasizes sports so much because of the danger inherent to the expressive style: evangelical men might appear gay with all of the intimacy talk, so sports are referenced to alleviate any conscious or subconscious anxiety.[75] Glass no doubt would have seen his stress on sports in a less Freudian manner. But at least in terms of the combination of expressive and instrumentalist styles, Glass's prison ministry was operating with the same basic concepts a full decade before Promise Keepers brought them to national prominence. It was not hard to see why this approach was so appealing. After all, the most powerful of muscles, when well trained, could also offer the most intimate embrace.

Though it shared certain theological commitments with evangelical prison ministers from previous generations, Glass's brand of prison religion departed in its masculine character. Earlier in the twentieth century, women had been some of the most prominent prison ministers, even as they labored among men. They had claimed their right as women to preach the gospel and reach criminals with the message of Christianity. In Glass's ministry, men made up the vast majority of the ministry's staff, pool of counselors, and speaker corps. But more important, the very message of the ministry itself was a masculine gospel of athleticism, fatherhood, and manly fellowship. In 1900 the paradigmatic evangelical prison minister was a woman who went by "mother." Now, it was a masculine endeavor, a legion of "fathers" entering prisons to offer inmates the blessings that they so desperately needed.

The foregrounding of fatherhood was in keeping with the broader gendered nature of prisons that had existed since the late nineteenth century. It was then that women, often at the behest of Christian reformers, began to be separated from men into their own prisons and subjected to a highly domestic model of correction that accorded with their idealized existence in a separate, feminine sphere on the outside.[76] Glass's later emphasis on reclaiming true masculine identity not only helped to reinforce gendered norms of carceral spaces, but by pushing evangelicals to orient their efforts around the needs of men, it implicitly reified their idealization of women (including women prisoners) as helpmeets. As Tanya Erzen has shown in her study of contemporary women's prison ministries, when they weren't glossing over the needs of women altogether, fatherhood-focused prison ministry initiatives placed female prisoners in a tough spot: "The focus is to promote a standard of married heterosexual families and transformed fathers, rather than discovering ways to make the more common and arduous process of mothering from the inside feasible."[77] Women could be objects of evangelical ministry, but they would exist as the submissive foils to faithful fathers, whether human or heavenly.

By bringing his particular form of muscular Christianity into prisons, Glass was helping create a new form of prison religion. And like other evangelical prison ministers, he was doing so outside the given chaplain-led, diversity-sensitive religious norms of prisons. Glass was suspicious of chaplains who he deemed as insufficiently evangelistic, and he often felt there was a real "liberal bias" among them.[78] Though Glass regularly worked closely with chaplains to secure access to prisons (and regularly received and reported their praise), he also consciously resisted parts of this culture in order to bolster his ministry's appeal.[79] In front of inmates, Glass avoided appearing too close to the prison warden or anything that resembled what he called "the Establishment." He wanted Christianity to grow organically in prisons, without too much top-down administrative influence or programmatic overhead.[80] He intentionally held his events outside prison chapels. Chapels, Glass and his associates believed, were places that many inmates avoided, and "those are usually the inmates we are the most concerned about reaching."[81] Anything that seemed too "churchy" at the outset was likely to fail, and "it was much easier to get the non-Christians to baseball fields than to the chapel." The final night of a crusade would often take place in the chapel, but that was only after an entire weekend of bonding over sports, shared meals, and close conversations with counselors.[82] Glass's approach was exemplified by one interaction he related in his 1976 book *Free at Last*. There, he told of a crusade counselor who managed to corner the prison's psychologist in hope of bringing him to Christ. The psychologist apparently "had a church background," Glass wrote, "but did not have a vital relationship with Jesus Christ." Glass witnessed the interaction and could not have been more pleased. "Isn't that something, Waddy?" he whispered to fellow evangelist Watson "Waddy" Spoelstra. "[He] has the guts to tackle a psychologist with the simple gospel plan." Waddy agreed: "Yes, look. He's gonna put the Four Spiritual Laws on him now." Glass and Waddy were both thrilled when their counselor friend reported that the psychologist had indeed come to Jesus.[83] An organic, gutsy, and conversionist Christianity, one that sometimes put the religious status quo in its crosshairs—this was the kind of prison faith Glass hoped for.

Chaplain Ray and International Prison Ministry

Later in life Glass boasted that he had been in more prisons than "any man that's ever lived."[84] He no doubt had good reasons to believe this, but he had a serious challenger in Ray Hoekstra (about whom the *Los Angeles Times* made a similar claim in 1979).[85] Born in 1913 in Joliet, Illinois, Hoekstra grew up in the shadow of the famed Joliet penitentiary, which he later said "trigger[ed] [his] initial concern with crime and punishment and their relationship to God and repentance."[86] Though his parents were part of the Dutch Reformed Church (and later became Seventh-day Adventists), Hoekstra initially had little interest in religion. He left home as a young man and drifted around California before "giving [his] life to God" during a service at the Anchor Rescue Mission in San Jose. He was ordained soon after, accepting a call as pastor of an independent church in Indianapolis. On a visit to New York, he stopped by Sing Sing prison at the request of a friend and found himself moved by what he saw: "The visit to Sing Sing reinforced my belief that the Lord was calling me to a special ministry for prisoners."[87] He began making ministry to inmates and former inmates a part of his pastoral routine before fully entering prison work full time.

By the early 1970s, Hoekstra (who by now had embraced the title "Chaplain Ray") had found his ministry niche. Despite his title and his regular visits to prisons, Chaplain Ray was not a chaplain in the official sense, though he regularly worked closely with state-sponsored institutional chaplains. Instead, his signature contribution was his blanketing of prisons with evangelistic literature and radio messages, under the auspices of International Prison Ministry (IPM), founded in 1972. At the end of the 1970s, according to one account, IPM was sending five hundred thousand books and bibles to prisoners each year, broadcasting on one hundred radio stations in thirty-eight different states, and publishing a prisoner magazine with a circulation of 150,000.[88]

Though Yokefellows, Simmer, and Glass were finding their way into prisons, these institutions still were difficult for outsiders to access. This was not only because of barriers and security clearances but also because of the fact that prisons were often built in far-flung rural areas. Chaplain Ray's efforts marked a different kind of evangelical entry into prisons, one in keeping with the long-standing history of evangelical engagement in American public life through the media. In the early twentieth century, conservative Protestants like Aimee Semple McPherson had been on the forefront of radio broadcasting.[89] In the 1930s and 1940s radio became a ring in which conservative and liberal Protestants did battle, not simply over doctrine but also over the limited times available for broadcast. Conservatives were increasingly marginalized by national broadcasting companies' alliances with mainline Protestant groups such as the Federal Council of Churches, which lobbied for nonsectarian religious programming "of the widest appeal." This meant "vague spiritual messages" instead of the blunter, sectarian sermons of conservatives.[90]

Broadcasters' ideal religious radio programming resembled the ideal religion of the state chaplain-led prison ministry that was emerging around the same time. One commentator on religious radio in 1938 could have just as well been talking about prison religion when he wrote, "Quite naturally, radio corporations and sponsors do not want disturbers on their programs. . . . They favor conciliators, pacifiers, minimizers of differences between sect and sect, not delvers into fundamental dogma, but sippers and samplers, tasters, purveyors of sweetness and light."[91] Self-funded programs like Walter Maier's *Lutheran Hour* and Charles Fuller's *Old-Fashioned Revival Hour* enjoyed the largest audiences in religious radio, but when network stations gave any time to conservative Protestants, they were typically limited to an early Sunday-morning slot.[92] Over the next few decades, some evangelicals worked to mitigate this loss of access, founding the National Religious Broadcasters Association (which became the "official radio arm" of the National Association of Evangelicals in 1947) to "foster and encourage the broadcasting of religious programs" that aligned with their theological outlook.[93]

Chaplain Ray carefully negotiated both radio worlds. As with prisons, if he wanted to have an impact he would need to be flexible. From the 1950s on, he would purchase time on local affiliates of the ABC and Mutual broadcasting companies.[94] He also broadcast on dedicated Christian (though no less commercial) stations, such as New York City's WWDJ, where he was featured daily in the 8:45 a.m. slot, just before Jimmy Swaggart's *Campmeeting Hour* at 9:00.[95] In 1971 his promotional materials listed a presence on around forty medium to large city stations.[96] Chaplain Ray was still invested enough in the success of Christian radio that he served as president of the southwest chapter of the evangelical National Religious Broadcasters.[97]

Chaplain Ray's radio programs, which ran an hour or more in length (but often broadcast in shorter segments), were a combination of sermons and interviews—all prison themed. Interspersed between conversations and sermons were performances of gospel songs by inmate choirs (such as the men's choir from San Quentin prison) and the reading of letters from listeners (most of whom were inmates themselves).[98] Interviews showcased stories of inmate conversion. Other programs focused on Christians involved in prison ministry, or who had personal experience with being incarcerated. On one program Chaplain Ray featured Corrie ten Boom, a survivor of German concentration camps during World War II. A Dutch Christian, ten Boom was well known in evangelical circles for her stories of hiding Jews from Nazis and surviving the horrors of the death camps once she was captured and charged with sedition. She published several books, most prominently *The Hiding Place,* which was eventually made into a feature film. Chaplain Ray had met ten Boom at the Lausanne Conference on World Evangelism in Switzerland in 1974 and persuaded her to do an interview for his prison-themed program. She connected her own stories of brutal imprisonment (often in solitary confinement) in a Nazi concentration camp with that of her American incarcerated radio audience. She told inmates that just as God was with her in "the hiding place" of solitary, he could be with them in whatever difficult circumstances they might find themselves. However bleak things might be behind bars, prisoners who accepted Christ had an eternal hope: "On judgment day, Jesus is your lawyer, your advocate. . . . We have nothing to fear."[99]

Though he remained a regular radio fixture, Chaplain Ray joined with the broader evangelical move to book publishing that had occurred in the second half of the twentieth century.[100] He adapted some of his radio interviews into small paperbacks, which became the bulk of his book production. Most of the paperbacks told of famous criminals, or people who had committed particularly heinous crimes, coming to Christ. For example, *Disciple in Prison* (first published in 1975) tells the story of Robert A. Johnson, a man imprisoned for the murder of his children. While awaiting trial, Johnson dedicated his life to the Lord in a jail cell. When the judge reduced his charges to second-degree murder (down from first degree, which would have likely given Johnson the death penalty), he praised God for delivering him. Deliverance imbued Johnson with a sense of spiritual purpose that he was in prison to minister to others. The remainder of the book follows Johnson through prison life, focusing on his regular practices of prayer, evangelism, and Christian fellowship. This new life rescued Johnson from his guilt and from the travails of prison existence: "Being a prisoner, caged in a little cell of stone and steel, can be a dreadful life if that is all one has; but being a prisoner with Jesus living within takes away the dread and replaces it with hope."[101]

Other Chaplain Ray paperbacks and radio programs followed a similar pattern: horrific crimes and criminal pasts, followed by an abrupt conversion to Christianity, and concluding with stories of "Jesus living within." Chaplain Ray's messages were clearly intended for the inmates who would tune in on their prison-issued radios or page through his latest book sent as a gift, and many of his interviews featured tips from lifers on how to manage the challenges of prison life. Unsurprisingly, this advice typically tracked back to Jesus, and sometimes in very simple terms. When Chaplain Ray asked Robert Johnson what he would tell someone coming into prison for the first time, Johnson replied, "I feel that if a man could get the Spirit of Jesus . . . he could put his time aside and forget about it." To be sure, there would be challenges, "but the Spirit that lives within me and the love that's in my heart and the feeling of contentment and peace help cast these disagreements aside."[102] Whether with guests like Corrie ten Boom offering encouraging words or Chaplain Ray preaching that Jesus has solidarity with prisoners ("He was one of us"), the hope was that inmates could, in turn, feel welcomed by Jesus Christ no matter what they had done.[103]

Impact

It is difficult to document the reactions of prisoners to these pioneering evangelical ministry efforts. No doubt many inmates simply wanted a break in the monotony of prison life and attended Yokefellows small groups for the benefit of casual conversation or went to Glass's events just for the spectacle of athletes performing feats of strength (which accorded with Trueblood's and Glass's intentions). It is also impossible to verify the "genuine" quality of the conversions that prison evangelists claimed, which often were reported as being very high. Other inmates, as we will see, chafed at the prison ministry surge because of its overspiritualized quality. But the occasional archived inmate letter indicates a level of deep appreciation for these ministries. An inmate named Don, from McNeil Island prison in Washington State, wrote to Bill Glass soon after the ministry's visit there. He introduced himself as "the Texan who shook your hand" and said, "I was sincere in my thanks to you then and now." Don explained that he was in prison for bank robbery and, with so much time apart from his wife and children, he was absolutely miserable. He "cried constantly" until he eventually found himself in the prison chapel, where he begged God for help: "I prayed like I have never done before. I asked God to help me and my family." God answered, Don wrote, "by sending you and the men with you." He reported that Glass's talk at McNeil and the work of crusade volunteers all "helped [him] immeasurably." For a man "looking for a way to salvage [his] life," Glass's talk "seemed to relate specifically" to him.[104]

Likewise, Chaplain Ray's ministry to inmates was widespread and, for some, quite welcome. In 1972 IPM reported receiving around 150 letters every day from inmates (and that it answered every one in some form).[105] Inmate letters read on his radio program or published in Chaplain Ray books and magazines, though preselected, also give some sense of the power of the ministry. "Chaplain Ray," one inmate named Charles wrote, "I am writing to you in deepest sincerity. I am in a Florida prison doing five years. . . . I am deeply moved by all your material that I have read." Another inmate in Colorado told Chaplain Ray, "A lot of people here read

Figure 5.3 Volunteers associated with Bill Glass's prison ministry pray with inmates at Coffield Prison near Palestine, Texas, in 1999. Copyright © Todd Bigelow Photography.

your books. . . . It's good to know people still believe in you, even though you're in jail."[106]

The relationship of prisoners to Consuella York was emblematic of the positive response that an independent prison minister could have. She was beloved throughout her career as a minister at Cook County Jail, with prisoners mailing her artwork and messages of appreciation. She became a symbol for solidarity with prisoners, so much so that inmates from Menard Correctional Center, where likely many of the former inhabitants of the jail ended up, mailed her a card after her son died that contained numerous messages of sympathy. Many of the prisoners were on death row, including John Wayne Gacy, who signed the card. A prisoner named George told her, "You have always been a blessing and a mighty witness in my life. I miss you and hope to see you again." A Muslim inmate offered her the "peace and blessing of Allah," an indication that, despite York's exclusivist gospel message, she had admirers beyond the Christian fold.[107]

Whatever their immediate impact among inmates, evangelical ministries also exerted a profound influence in drawing other Christians into prison ministry and concern for inmates more generally. For every ten prisoners that Yokefellows groups reached, two or more laypeople from local churches were getting involved in prison ministry, many of them entering prisons for the first time. Simmer's Good News Jail and Prison Ministry was staffed by professional chaplains, but it depended on private donations and connections to local churches.[108] Though the selling point of Bill Glass's crusades was the presence of athletes, each prison event relied on a small army of volunteer counselors. For those who could not serve as an in-prison crusade counselor, Glass's ministry worked to encourage laypeople to build relationships with inmates through mail. Their Friend of a Prisoner program was an initiative that connected inmates who had accepted Christ at Glass crusades to volunteers on the outside who agreed to write them every thirty days and pray for them daily.[109]

Exposure to prisoners via ministry could push evangelical laypeople to more humanitarian positions, a reference point for recognizing the shortsightedness of law and order. In 1976 a woman named Mrs. R. W. Childs wrote to the editor of the *Presbyterian Journal* to contest another reader's complaints about the "coddling" of prisoners. This earlier complaint praised the *Journal*'s recent punitive pieces on crime. But Childs had a different perspective to share. She had been corresponding with an inmate for two years and recently returned from a visit to a maximum-security prison with fourteen other church members. "We'll never be the same again," she wrote. Instead of focusing on punishing the guilty "as the *only* deterrent to crime," Childs pointed to job training and evangelism as more practical and faithful alternatives. She urged Christians to consider their common humanity with inmates: "We have all sinned and fallen short."[110] In the context of the *Journal,* her sympathetic entreaties stood out. Her evangelistic experiences had given her the motivation and credibility to challenge the punitive status quo.

Chaplain Ray in particular saw public outreach as a crucial part of his ministry. He encouraged broader Christian concern with prisoners and offered guidance for churches interested in prison ministry. In an early issue of his *Prison Evangelism* magazine, Chaplain Ray noted that his goal was to reach both prisoners and public.[111] He aimed to convince these "freeworld" readers and listeners that prisoners deserved their care and concern.[112] Ever the evangelical preacher, Chaplain Ray could lay guilt and conviction on skeptics, blasting those who believed criminals to be outside the reach of the gospel.[113] He also regularly sketched for interested listeners and readers what the model prison ministry should look like. Christians were not to support the provision of generalized religious services in prisons or be content as long as inmates seemed spiritually validated by the state chaplain; they were to work to save inmates' souls. One chapter of a Chaplain Ray book indicated this dual approach of compassion for prisoners and gospel fervor. He told the story of Harry Howard, the Protestant chaplain at the famed San Quentin prison in Northern California. He praised Howard for doing what no other chaplain would do, in two senses. Howard was willing to go directly to inmates' cells, practicing face-to-face ministry in a place deemed dangerous by most other chaplains. And even though he was a state employee, Howard also tried to convert inmates to Christianity. He did this, Chaplain Ray noted, even though he was supposed to be "neutral."[114] His message for potential prison coworkers was that their work should be characterized by an unapologetic sense of concern for inmates' humanity *and* their souls, over and against those who deemed inmates as beyond hope and those who believed in a more liberal brand of ministry.

The absence of formalized professional requirements and clinical training, combined with introduction through prison ministry networks and promotions by ministries like Bill Glass's, Yokefellows, IPM, and Good News, proved to be precisely what brought so many other evangelicals into the prison ministry movement. In 1976, one Honolulu newspaper profiled the new chaplain, Don Clevenger, at the nearby state prison. Clevenger had been introduced to prison work through his experience as a volunteer counselor at a Glass crusade and follow-up discipleship events at the facility. "Many of us [volunteers] had never been in a prison," Clevenger noted, but the experience deeply affected him. "You cannot come into a place like this and talk to a man for nine or 10 weeks without becoming closely related to him in a very personal way." Though he was not ordained and lacked formal theological training, he started subbing in as volunteer chaplain when the state chaplain resigned. He got in touch with Bill Simmer and Good News, who provided him advice and materials. Simmer eventually came to visit Clevenger, who formed a Good News Mission–Hawaii council with other prison ministers, many of whom also had originally volunteered with Glass. The lower barrier to entry opened access, but it also made for more difficult work. Clevenger worked for free, dedicating at least twenty to thirty hours a week to inmates. He felt guilty that he couldn't do more: "I feel like I'm dropping the ball when I'm not here."[115]

Clevenger's story was emblematic of surging evangelical interest in taking up the challenge of prison ministry in the 1970s, often as a response to being introduced to prison work by leaders like Glass and Chaplain Ray, or through networks that Yokefellows and Good News helped facilitate. "The thing we did for prison ministry," Glass later said, "was that we popularized it. We made it something people wanted to do."[116]

Many evangelicals started their own lay-driven ministries and connected with one another through conferences and associations. Duane Pederson, a minister popular in evangelical circles for his work with California hippies (he had reportedly coined the term "Jesus People") and inmates alike, assembled a gathering of prison ministers in 1978 for a Congress of Prison Ministries. More than sixty organizations were represented, with two hundred people registered, many likely there to hear Corrie ten Boom speak (registered attendees were reportedly guaranteed a photo op with her).[117] The congress, according to Pederson, helped provide a sense of common purpose for evangelicals who, until this point, thought they were the only ones laboring in prisons. "We didn't know there were any groups out doing anything," Pederson said he had one participant tell him. "We thought were the only ones!" Pederson told the gathering in his opening address that he was encouraged to see other Christians across the country getting engaged in prison work. He noted the diversity of theological beliefs of the participants, but it was clear that this would be an evangelical affair when he then said, "We have one goal: to proclaim the message of Jesus Christ, a freeing message, a message of new life." The loud utterances of "amen" that could be heard coming from the audience in reply indicated that the gathered ministries from across the country had a unified purpose as co-laborers in the gospel.[118]

Other organizations that connected smaller prison ministries, most of them evangelical, would sprout up in the following years, such as the Association of Christian Prison Workers (which ten Boom helped found in the late 1970s with Pederson) and the Coalition of Prison Evangelists.[119] The coalition was founded in 1984 by Frank and Cheryl Costantino (Frank, a former inmate, had been the subject of a Chaplain Ray paperback). It counted around three hundred ministries as members by the late 1980s.[120] Other new ministry organizations started in the late 1970s that remain influential players in prison work today. Kairos Prison Ministry was one unique product of this period. Beginning as a Roman Catholic–influenced *cursillo* program in 1976, it eventually rebranded in 1979 as the nondenominational Kairos Prison Ministry (which in 2017 had more than thirty thousand volunteers in thirty-seven states).[121] Though Kairos volunteers avoided explicit association with "revivalist" forms of faith, it adapted the "prison ministry" paradigm and name that was now being made intelligible by evangelicals: distinct from state chaplains, lay driven, interdenominational, and dependent on local churches.[122]

Most famous was the prison work of Charles "Chuck" Colson. A former Nixon administration "hatchet man," Colson was a close adviser to the president who helped shape much of the administration's political strategy. Some said that Colson, known as a ruthless political operative, was the kind of man who would walk over his own grandmother if it meant getting Nixon reelected.[123] However, Colson's political career collapsed when news of Watergate broke. Though he was not directly involved, he confessed to crimes that came to light as a result of the investigations. He was sentenced to one to three years in federal prison. Before his trial, Colson converted to Christianity. While reared Episcopal, he later admitted he never thought much of religion during his early life and professional career. However, the combination of his lowly estate, the calming presence of several evangelical friends, and the convicting words of C. S. Lewis all conspired to claim him for Jesus. He eventually took his new faith with him into federal prison, where he served seven months.

Colson's newfound faith and a testing prison experience led him to start his own prison ministry organization, Prison Fellowship, less than two years after his release. His interest in this ministry was rooted in his own experience of the loneliness and difficulty of prison life. But as he worked to establish Prison Fellowship, he was indebted to prison ministry strategies and networks built by others who had been working in prisons years earlier. For example, immediately after Colson decided to devote his life to prison ministry, he served as a special guest speaker at a Bill Glass crusade in Washington State. Much to his chagrin, Colson served as a karate expert's volunteer in a sword skills demonstration at the event, where he had a potato resting on his neck chopped in half. "Quite a debut for our ministry, wasn't it?" he told his friend Fred Rhodes on the drive home. "I didn't think I'd be sticking my neck out quite so soon."[124] Bill Simmer actually visited Colson when he was incarcerated, and Good News allowed Prison Fellowship to utilize one of its halfway houses to board inmates for one of its seminar events in the ministry's early days.[125] Colson addressed the twenty-fourth annual Yokefellows national conference in 1977. Though he was clearly the most famous speaker on the program (outshining even Elton Trueblood, who introduced Colson to the crowd),

Colson needed association with this time-tested, respectable gathering of prison ministers in order to convince a skeptical public of his own heart change and his commitment to prison work. He was grateful for the connection. Trueblood announced that Colson had given a $500 gift to help cover conference expenses.[126]

More important than these personal connections were the conceptual innovations of evangelical prison ministry that shaped Prison Fellowship's emphases in its early days and into its eventual evolution into the world's largest prison ministry. Colson, a recent convert with no theological training, believed that prison ministry was a vocational calling for him and for other laypeople. To be sure, Colson was smart. He dedicated himself to learning about both prisons and theology, devouring academic works on Christianity and criminology alike. But in his conversion he had internalized the idea that formally trained chaplains had no monopoly on prison work. Colson also worked from the outset of his career to frame prison ministry in terms of small-group "fellowship." Fellowships were characterized by inmates (mostly men) devoting themselves to one another, speaking about their struggles and hopes, all with the ultimate goal of becoming more devoted parents for their own children. The combined effect was a ministry that sought to connect inmates to ministry outside the prison system, apart from state-funded chaplaincy and the progressive penology that informed the correctional environment. Instead, inmates would find spiritual rehabilitation through Prison Fellowship–funded chaplains and programs and, ultimately, through fellowship with each other.[127] Inmates' families were also seen as potential sites of radical transformation, a perception that culminated in popular programs like the Angel Tree Christmas gift program for the children of prisoners. Lastly, Prison Fellowship would become a global brand through savvy marketing and widespread media exposure. Colson's own successful memoirs *Born Again* and *Life Sentence* would be the first of several books he wrote linking his own spiritual autobiography to that of prison concern.

Prison Fellowship therefore was a product of an evangelical prison ministry culture made possible by the lay-driven, small-group emphasis of Yokefellows; the private chaplaincy of Good News; the intimate masculine brotherhood and family focus of Glass; and the media savvy of Chaplain Ray. Colson and Prison Fellowship have received the most scholarly and popular attention of any prison ministry effort—evangelical or otherwise.[128] This attention is justified. Not long after its founding, Prison Fellowship began exerting tremendous influence both in prison work and in publicizing evangelical engagement with inmates more broadly. However, Prison Fellowship and Colson were only part of the story of evangelical prison ministry. Focusing solely on Prison Fellowship or labeling Colson as evangelical prison ministry's mastermind misses other important characters and organizations that were influential in their own ways. Even as Prison Fellowship soared further into the public limelight in the 1980s, other, smaller prison ministry efforts remained. Wheaton College's 1986 prison ministry guide showed a Prison Fellowship presence in a number of states across the country.[129] But the vast majority of ministries were independent efforts unaffiliated with Prison Fellowship, even as they drew on the common evangelical prison ministry culture that shaped Colson's ministry and their own.

Prison ministry had become such a powerful marker of evangelical social engagement in the late 1970s that other growing evangelical ministries adopted it. Campus Crusade for Christ, a ministry to students at American colleges and universities, started P.S. Ministries in 1974. Campus Crusade staff member Larry Benton helmed the endeavor. Benton had gotten interested in prison work after he and his wife, Beverly, developed a relationship with a prisoner who had previously broken into their house, assaulted Beverly, and stolen their car. After offering the man forgiveness, the Bentons eventually led him to Christ through consistent letter writing over the course of three years. The "P.S." initials in the ministry's name reportedly stood for "personal Savior, prodigal son, personal solution, powerful solution and programmed solution." If the branding was a bit confusing, P.S. ministerial goals were familiar: establishment of "para-chaplains" in state and federal prisons and engagement of volunteer ministers for work in smaller county and city institutions.[130]

Prison ministry emerged in other quarters of evangelicalism as well. Jim and Tammy Faye Bakker's PTL ministry network, which had started in 1974, was becoming well known (and rich) through its television programming (PTL stood for Praise the Lord or People That Love). In the early 1980s, PTL started various service ministries, such as counseling, food distribution centers for the needy, and a home for unwed mothers. PTL also started a prison ministry. According to historian John Wigger, Tammy regularly visited prisons in the late 1970s, paying particular attention to the needs of women inmates. Inmates appreciated her because she spoke "without condescension or judgment." Though regularly lampooned in American pop culture for her folksy demeanor and the gobs of makeup she wore on television, Tammy had a genuine connection with prisoners. As Wigger writes, "It was perhaps the only audience in front of which Tammy felt sure that she was not being judged for her lack of polish and sophistication."[131]

PTL television programming was widely available in prisons (more than one thousand carried the channel, Jim Bakker claimed). In order to facilitate broadcasts, PTL offered to provide prisons with satellite equipment if they did not already have it. Just as they appreciated Tammy's preaching, some inmates were grateful for the offering. "A sermon in your cell, when you are there alone with your thoughts, can do a lot of good," one inmate told a Louisville, Kentucky, reporter writing on the arrival of PTL programming at a nearby facility. Bakker claimed that the cell sermons his ministry beamed out had helped convert thirty-seven thousand inmates.[132] Prone to hyperbole, he was probably exaggerating. But it was true that PTL had a significant prison presence across the country, with more than thirty PTL-affiliated prison ministry offices in several states by 1984.[133] The prison ministry appeal became personal for Jim Bakker after his own five-year prison stint for financial improprieties a few years later (he had defrauded investors in PTL's vacation timeshare business). Though he never jumped into the work full time, he reportedly considered prison ministry part of his public reemergence after his release.[134]

Unresolved Tensions

In 1972 Billy Graham appeared on Phil Donahue's daytime television talk show in a broadcast from a women's prison in Marysville, Ohio. Most of the program consisted of Graham answering questions from prisoners and guest callers. Donahue and Graham joked about the irony of the clean-cut evangelist's presence in a prison (with Graham drawing raucous laughter after he said the only time he had been imprisoned was when his wife, Ruth, had locked him in the bathroom at their house—he had to clarify later that it was accidental). Graham tried his best to show how much he cared about prisoners, and how Jesus did too. Graham also expressed his own concern for the prisoners' well-being and his desire to learn more about prison issues. He made sure to mention his own affinity with matters of crime and punishment; he reported that his ministry received five hundred letters a week from prisoners and that he had visited prisons on every continent.

But some of Graham's words fell flat or proved controversial. Though winsome, Graham insisted on the theological exclusivity of the Christian gospel. This may have played well among his home crowd at crusade venues, but it was controversial at Marysville. Inmates and callers interrogated Graham on topics like the doctrine of hell, world religions, whether Jesus would return to earth, and the occult. Inmates even asked Graham about his astrological sign, and he admitted that he was "November" ("Scorpio," Donahue clarified). Inmates also pushed Graham repeatedly on problems in American criminal justice, including capital punishment and their own prison's poor conditions. Though Graham had mentioned early on in the program that Marysville didn't even look like a prison, but more "like a beautiful campus at a university," inmates offered a different perspective. They complained to Graham about the harshness of the prison administration, police brutality, their own loss of humanity in the face of the prison's bureaucratic procedures, and the fact that wealthy people never seemed to wind up incarcerated. Graham diplomatically declined to speak to specific problems or controversial issues, mentioning instead, in generic terms, the need for prison reform. He attempted to resolve the tension in the room by universalizing the dilemma in terms of the Christian gospel. "There's a sense," he said, "in which all of us—the whole human race—is in a prison." In response to a prisoner who asked Graham what inviting Jesus into one's heart could possibly mean for the women undergoing the prison's horrible medical treatment, Graham gestured toward the peace with God that he had observed among wounded soldiers in Korea: "You can have peace with God here, and then live the Christian life with a smile on your face and share your joy and your happiness. . . . Because everybody here is suffering [in] one form or another." Everyone faced trials (literally or figuratively), and trusting in God was the only true solution.[135]

Race also framed part of the backdrop to Graham's visit. Marysville's population was over 50 percent black, and though Graham did not mention this fact, he made sure to present the gospel with reference to race, albeit with a color-blind gloss.[136] "A lot of people have gotten this idea that Jesus was a white man. That's not true at all. He wasn't as black as some people. He wasn't as white. But he probably had a brown skin color. He belongs to all the races and all the people."[137] Jesus did not belong solely to whites, but neither did he belong exclusively to blacks. "There are many white people [who] think they're the chosen. Many black people think they're the chosen. We're all God's children—people. The whole human race."[138] This was the color-blind gospel in action: emphasizing Christian racial equality in the face of dramatic racial disparity, without acknowledging the ways systemic issues framed the problem. Graham's other mention of race came in news reports following his visit. The Associated Press report of the event included a revealing line from Graham: "There was this beautiful black girl, and she never got a chance to say anything. But I did hear her say quietly . . . 'I'm here because I deserve to be here.' That touched me."[139] Graham showed concern for black inmates, but he took it as a given that their presence in the prison was necessary.

There were three unresolved tensions in the burgeoning prison ministry movement, each encapsulated by aspects of Graham's televised prison visit. First was the complicated relationship of the evangelical gospel to other religions and faith expressions. The second was related to idealizing and validating inmate conversions, particularly those of people of color. Third was the question of whether law and order, with its racialized connotations and manifestations, was complementary with or contradictory to evangelistic concern for inmates' souls. In the same way that Graham had been placed in a difficult spot during the prison broadcast, American foreign missionaries had regularly faced "no-win" situations as they negotiated the competing demands of evangelism, national identity, and social concern.[140] Evangelical prison ministers likewise found themselves in difficult spots, pulled among competing ministerial ideals and constituencies and the religious demands of law and gospel.

Chaplaincy and Other Faiths

The 1976 *Los Angeles Times* cover story that heralded a national "prison revival" lumped a few nonevangelical and non-Christian groups into the ministry surge, such as the Metropolitan Community Church (a ministry to the San Francisco gay community), the Church of Scientology, and a Muslim prisoner movement. It also quoted several prison chaplains, some of whom seemed quite amenable to the new presence of evangelicals in prisons despite the clear differences in the scope and goals of their ministries. By the mid-1970s some evangelicals found themselves able to negotiate adoption of the "neutral" chaplaincy model (with its accommodation of religious diversity). Other evangelicals spoke of state chaplaincy in highly critical tones, setting up showdowns.

The emerging evangelical prison interest occasionally manifested itself in the form of professional, state-sponsored prison chaplaincy. Some evangelicals seemed increasingly willing to play by the rules of institutions, provided they could frame their work in ways that did not infringe on their consciences and that made sense to fellow believers. This was particularly true for denominations that sought to serve as endorsing agencies for evangelical chaplains. The Assemblies of God sponsored its first federal prison chaplain in 1971, and by 1978 there were forty Assemblies chaplains working nationwide.[141] Paul Markstrom, the head of the denomination's institutional chaplaincy program, was instrumental not only in helping interested Assemblies clergy and laity get involved in prison ministry but also in interpreting the professional chaplaincy role to potential Pentecostal skeptics.[142] The official Assemblies of God chaplaincy manual presented progressive penology and psychotherapeutic instructions not unlike what would have been found in a great deal of clinical pastoral education training materials of the day. This may have been alarming for Pentecostals, who often utilized supernatural categories in diagnosing and solving personal problems. But Markstrom penned a cautionary preface to assuage such concerns: "Certain areas and ideas presented in these papers may raise some questions. . . . This treatise is not submitted as portraying final truths but is placed before you to assist in better understanding the dynamics of criminology and penology . . . with its weaknesses and strengths." Markstrom characterized those who had developed the chaplaincy manual as "honest and sincere" men, despite the fact that "the full supernatural power of God with its accompanying redemptive resources is not understood or brought into play." He concluded the preface with an exhortation to his fellow Pentecostals: "As ambassadors of the most high God, let us always bring into focus the vast intrinsic resources of the Spirit-filled clergyman."[143] Pentecostals could be in the world of clinical chaplaincy, if not always of it.

At other times, however, evangelicals expressed deep animus toward state-sponsored chaplaincy. The frustrations Simmer and other evangelicals had expressed with state chaplaincy (frustrations that had pushed them into ministry in the first place) started to boil over, particularly when prison administrators had to choose which religious representatives would exert authority in their facilities.

A Good News chaplain named Dale Pace published a book in 1976 entitled *A Christian's Guide to Effective Jail and Prison Ministries*. It was released by the Fleming H. Revell Company, which published Charles Colson's *Born Again* and Francis Schaeffer's *How Should We Then Live* that same year. Pace drew on materials from Good News' chaplaincy courses, and Bill Simmer reviewed early drafts of the manuscript.[144] He argued in his introduction that the "Church's interest in ministry to prisoners is somewhat parallel to its interest in missions." And as with foreign missions, this evangelistic zeal had sadly faded: "The Church has done little more than provide for prisoners the religious services sought by the state." But based on recent evangelical activity, Pace was optimistic. A renewal of the "great missionary outreach" was possible, if only Christians would gain a biblical sense of urgency. "'The harvest truly is plenteous, but the laborers are few.' . . . There exists no more appropriate application for these words than to those sheep without shepherds in our nation's jails and prisons."[145] Pace implied here that inmates had been without a shepherd for some time, and he made this sentiment all the more clear in his critiques of the progressive chaplaincy model throughout the book. Regarding the management of religious diversity, Pace wrote, "No godly chaplain is going to add to inmate confusion by assisting the spread of error and false teaching among the inmate population." Regarding clinical approaches like clinical pastoral education, Pace said that there was instead a "counseling privilege that dwarfs all others": "soul winning." Pace excoriated the American Protestant Correctional Chaplains Association for its liberal tendencies and offered the new Association of Evangelical Institutional Chaplains, Good News, and Chaplain Ray's IPM as more faithful alternatives.[146]

Pace's book was the closest thing to a textbook that the budding evangelical prison ministry movement had at the time. State chaplains did not receive it well. A 1978 article by Philip B. Taft Jr., "Whatever Happened to That Old-Time Prison Chaplain," in *Corrections* magazine discussed the conflict. Many chaplains who were trying to be "ecumenical" in their accommodation of various faith groups and use their clinical training to help inmates adjust psychologically, Taft noted, found their work challenged by upstart "dissident Christian sects." Taft highlighted the frustrations of "clinically-trained liberals" (such as the American Protestant Correctional Chaplains Association president) with Colson's Prison Fellowship chaplains, some of whom had been appointed by officials in a Memphis prison without certification by clinical chaplaincy accrediting bodies. He then turned to Good News, a "fiercely evangelical" group, and Pace's book. Taft said that "mainline" chaplains despised the book: "It did us a disservice," complained one federal chaplain, while another said that "Pace and his people are closed-minded bigots. Most CPE [clinical pastoral education] people don't like him." Colson, Pace, and "other independent non-denominational groups," Taft reported one chaplain as saying, were "ding-a-ling evangelicals."[147]

Taft's piece concluded with profiles of three different chaplains, two who had adopted the clinical, nonproselytizing model (one even preferring the term "social worker"), and one (a Pentecostal) who rejected the title of clinician. For Taft, neither approach seemed all that impressive: evangelicals were too illiberal in their views of God, while "therapy oriented chaplains" "seldom mention Him." Taft gave no clear proposal of his own except to offer a few comments about nineteenth-century penitentiaries, sites where chaplains held places of prominence and were key to the operation of the facility.[148] His longing for a simpler time missed the often dreadful and equally contested history of prison work a century earlier. But he was right in naming the current problem. Prisons were state-controlled spaces with neutral aspirations that housed people of many different faiths, but they were located in a society where evangelical religion was highly influential.

Contested Conversions and Color Blindness

One problem that prison administrators and critics of prison ministry often discussed was "jailhouse religion," the worry that prisoners feign religious conversion and practice to get in the good graces of administrators, guards, and ministers. Evangelicals were offering a new and exciting religious product, but whether prisoners were buying it in good faith was another matter. The 1976 *Los Angeles Times* piece mentioned one prosecutor who claimed that jailhouse conversions were a deceptive front. The other problem evangelicals faced was how to interface with the increasing public awareness of the growing numbers of black people incarcerated in American prisons. Evangelicals in prison ministry spoke to both of these developments, sometimes with peculiar results.

Evangelicals made arguments to convince others of the genuine nature of their model by deploying powerful conversion stories as proof that their methods were sound. These stories tended to come from ministers who had more interest in cultivating a public media presence, not so much from organizations (such as Yokefellows) that spent less time broadcasting their work. For example, Chaplain Ray's paperbacks usually focused on prisoners who had committed remarkable crimes or achieved high levels of notoriety (see Figure 5.4). Besides the murderous Manson gang members and Robert Johnson, there was Jack "Murph the Surf" Murphy (a famous jewel thief known for stealing the priceless Star of India gemstone from the New York Museum of Natural History), mobsters and Mafia associates like Frank Costantino and Gene Neill, and "Public Enemy No. 1"

Figure 5.4 Advertisement from May 1977 for Chaplain Ray's popular book *God's Prison Gang*. Used by permission, *Eternity Magazine*, published by the Alliance of Confessing Evangelicals.

Floyd Hamilton of the Bonnie and Clyde gang. Chaplain Ray used these stories as proofs: besides appealing to broader audiences, they proved beyond a shadow of a doubt that the gospel *worked* in prison. Christ could transform the vilest offenders and could therefore be trusted by prison administrators, other interested inmates, and the public more broadly. It was a strategy that had been used countless times before in Christian evangelism, beginning with the previously persecutory Saint Paul's self-referential proof of the power of the gospel: "Christ Jesus came into the world to save sinners—of whom I am the worst" (1 Timothy 1:15, New International Version). Prisoners noticed. One article in an inmate journal mentioned that the only reading materials one could reliably find in solitary confinement were bibles and Chaplain Ray's "gangster to God" paperbacks. The response to the paperbacks for this author was to read their stories of "criminal exploits" and then "trash the book at the first mention of salvation."[149] The books' value here was found in their stories of sin, not redemption.

This approach had another effect: the definition of "crime" as an abstract concept in terms of professional gangsters, murder, and high-level offenses. This approach fit with the broader pattern of how American media narrated crime in the 1970s: focusing on high-profile criminals (like serial killers) or devoting disproportionate attention to particularly heinous offenses.[150] This was just as true of Hollywood as it was of the nightly news: upon its release in 1972, the mobster drama *The Godfather* was enormously successful, and movie studios upped their production of gangster films for years to come.[151] But the other effect was that, if crime could be made intelligible by defining it as sin, it also needed to be intelligible in terms of moral culpability. This was the advantage of big-time crime as well: it allowed Chaplain Ray to frame crime in terms of conscious moral choice. Chaplain Ray opened his foreword to Frank Costantino's 1979 book *Holes in Time* with the line, "Frank was a professional criminal. He deliberately decided to be a thief and a robber."[152] Framing Costantino's work in terms of deliberate intention and professionalism was a convenient foil to how evangelicals like Chaplain Ray envisioned the gospel taking hold in prison. Converting to Christ would involve leaving one vocation for another through the same kind of conscious choice that led one to crime in the first place. Conscious choice, whether in entering a life of crime or the life of faith, was a helpful sentiment for law enforcement and prison officials who were increasingly justifying their system's punitive existence with reference to individual responsibility.[153]

What was often missing or underplayed in evangelical conversion narratives like Chaplain Ray's were the less remarkable ways that a great number of people also ended up in the criminal justice system, such as low-level theft or drug offenses. To be sure, more minor crimes and drug use showed up in Chaplain Ray's stories and testimonies, but they were typically in reference to the "gateways" that introduced ne'er-do-wells to the broader criminal underworld. There was no paperback on a teen who shoplifted once and yet found his life turned upside down through arrest and conviction. Neither was there much attention to systemic factors that led to crime, such as the loss of inner-city jobs that opened up drug markets as forms of economic opportunity (the exception being Chaplain Ray's argument that the freewheeling 1960s helped foster a godless, immoral culture that bred disrespect for the law).[154] There was also little conscious attention to race. Though black inmates regularly wrote Chaplain Ray and were featured in his magazine in short columns, the converts he dedicated his paperbacks and feature stories to were mostly white. The whiteness of Chaplain Ray's court of criminals was not unusual when compared with the overwhelming whiteness of American evangelical publishing and public ministry at the time. However, the black prisoner population in the American prison system had been growing at a steady pace, more than doubling from the mid-1920s to 1986 (by that year, 44 percent of all state and federal prison admissions were black).[155] The ideal convert, in Chaplain Ray's telling, was one who understood the moral weight of his or her crimes and was unburdened by economic or racially discriminatory factors. It was a person who focused moral blame on himself or herself, not society, and made a conscious decision to follow Jesus.[156]

Bill Glass framed prisoner conversion narratives in a similar manner. He regularly spoke of the positive benefits that emerged from inmates' turning to Christ in ways that minimized racial injustice or the complicated problems inmates faced while behind bars, even as his ministry recognized inmates' humanity and need for friendship. Glass did not believe that American prisons were too harsh, nor did he think that the nation incarcerated too many people.[157] In his telling, prisoners often came across as childlike. They needed entertainment and stimulation in order to pay attention (hence the need for athletic and celebrity events) and were emotionally needy.[158] One black inmate whom Glass highlighted in one of his books, nicknamed "Lefty Dog," had eyes that "flashed with defiance" as he "ranted about all the injustices he suffered." When Lefty Dog accused Glass's team of being tools of the state and of white oppression, a counselor retorted that they were actually privately funded and that they had black volunteers who also worked with them. Eventually Lefty Dog came around, striking up a relationship with the counselors and asking them to write him. He "was no longer a left out dog," as his nickname indicated. Instead, he was "Frank . . . a man [who] had a name to prove his worth." He was now "appreciative and open. Rather than our biggest opponent, he was now a friend." With this new friendship and new name, Frank had left two other things behind: his anger and his blame of an oppressive and racist society and prison system. Strikingly, Frank/Lefty Dog did not convert to Christianity, but he had come to realize another important truth: that "love and respect" were the solution to inmate woes, not critical questioning of the prison itself or its racial dynamics.[159] For Glass, that was good enough.

The implication was that problems in American criminal justice were not the result of systemic racial issues related to poverty or overpolicing, but interpersonal and emotional challenges arising from men's abdication of their manhood and of openness to friendship. To be sure, Glass and his co-laborers were aware of America's racial tensions. But they moved, quickly, to "reconciliation" as the marker of Christian influence in American criminal justice. The title of Glass's first prison ministry book, *Free at Last*, indicated his hope that men could find spiritual and emotional liberation. Indeed, though he never mentioned Martin Luther King Jr. or the civil rights leader's use of the phrase "free at last" at the climax of his "I Have a Dream" speech, Glass and his co-laborers had internalized a form of King's vision. They hoped to fight racial prejudice and create a color-blind Christian community behind bars. "Jesus loved us so much," one of Glass's ministry leaders said to one inmate, "that he just takes the color away and makes us color blind."[160] The problem was that this color blindness also helped to blind evangelicals to the more subtle racial dynamics still at play as the criminal justice system was beginning to transform into a "new Jim Crow," with a growing number of black men caught in its grasp.[161]

These tensions were evident in evangelical prison ministers' references to Attica Correctional Facility in the 1970s and 1980s. Attica, a prison in upstate New York, was famous for a 1971 prisoners' uprising in response to the terrible conditions at the facility. Attica's prisoner population, as Heather Ann Thompson has chronicled, was "overwhelmingly young, urban, under-educated, and African American or Puerto Rican" and was regularly subjected to cruel treatment. Though serious offenders were incarcerated at Attica, there were also low-level lawbreakers serving sentences.[162] On September 9, 1971, prisoners took hostages and made demands for improved conditions, and amnesty for the uprising itself. But law enforcement attempted to retake the prison by force. The retaking, which was hastily planned and utilized violent, shoot-first tactics, was bloody. Many hostages and inmates were killed, with some prisoners shot by guards *after* the retaking had been completed. The full mismanagement of the state's negotiations by figures such as Governor Nelson Rockefeller and a later cover-up of many of the horrific details of the retaking have only recently come to light.[163]

Many evangelicals clearly had a heart for the prisoners who faced brutal conditions like the ones that had prompted the Attica riot.[164] On his radio program, Chaplain Ray hosted Attica chaplain Jeff Carter, who spoke in humanizing terms about Attica inmates and criticized the punitive impulse that ignored prisoner suffering (Carter was black and had been appointed to Attica a few years after the uprising).[165] But elsewhere Chaplain Ray used the specter of Attica as a backdrop for his gangster-style conversionism. In a television special entitled *God's Prison Gang*, produced with CBS star Art Linkletter, Chaplain Ray assembled prominent "Public Enemies" to Attica for taped speeches and interviews.[166] Each interviewee had a unique rap sheet and an inspiring conversion story.

George Meyer was Al Capone's chauffer, Floyd Hamilton was a bank robber associated with the Bonnie and Clyde gang, and Jerry Graham was listed as "the robber king" of California. An interview with Tex Watson, one of the infamous Manson murderers, was also included. Ted Jefferson was the only African American featured, and was simply referred to as "one bad dude." Jefferson received the least screen time of all the inmates featured. Each told how he had come to Christ in dramatic ways, and all (sometimes at the prompting of Chaplain Ray) stressed their emotional change of heart. Though they had been cold-hearted and numb criminals before, they could now cry and feel emotion. The gangster-to-Christ narrative in *God's Prison Gang* was popular and effective. News releases played up the infamous origins of the interviewees as they promoted local viewings. Churches hosted screenings, while inmates and law enforcement officials wrote IPM to praise the special and ask for more materials from the ministry.[167] Chaplain Ray received an Angel Award at a banquet hosted by the Religion in Media committee at the Hollywood Palladium.[168]

The television special was successful because it was a streamlined story, one that spoke confidently of the evangelical message's transformative power for the hearts and minds of lawbreakers. But it was difficult to know how to interpret the backdrop of Attica in light of this message. What about the low-level offenders housed there? What about inmates who had endured regular beatings by prison guards, inhumane living conditions, or botched medical treatment? Christ had liberated gangster George Meyer's guilty conscience, but what did he have to say to Elliot "L. D." Barkley, a twenty-one-year-old who was in Attica simply for driving without a license (and thereby violating his parole), who had been shot in the back during the Attica retaking?[169] *God's Prison Gang* did touch on some of the horrors of Attica, but it made only a brief mention of the material changes needed to prevent future prison rebellions by treating incarcerated people more humanely. Instead, the real solution to inmates' plight was spiritual rehabilitation through Christ.

Likewise, instead of dwelling on these complicated cases or the unequal racial dynamics they suggested, Bill Glass's answer was to point out how successful the evangelical message could be in defusing future prisoner protests. In *Free at Last,* Glass quoted one journalist and ministry volunteer who noted that he "covered riots where blacks and whites were at each other's throats, killing and harming one another. . . . As I looked about the room [at the crusade], I noticed blacks and whites together, bound in true love because of Christ. . . . To me, this will stand out above everything else, for I've seen only bitterness and hatred while covering stories of riots."[170] Glass seized on this sentiment, what he saw as the color-blind, calming potential of his ministry. Reporting on a violent prison in Kansas, Glass wrote to his supporters in a newsletter that his own crusades were ready "to fight a three-day battle to bring things under control." However, this would not be the revolutionary strategy of the inmates who had taken over Attica or the racial justice and prisoners' rights activists who cheered them on: "Not the Attica-styled thing, but a way that is much more effective—through Christ!"[171]

A Captive Audience?

Streamlined conversion narratives focused on high-profile criminals allowed evangelical prison ministers in the 1970s to frame their work in the most positive terms possible and sidestep complicated questions related to injustices at places like Attica. This was not because all these evangelical prison ministers loved punitive politics. Instead, they wanted to appeal to inmates, administrators, and the broader public. But it was a message easily adopted by Christian law enforcement officials who had a vested interest in fighting crime. For these Christians, evangelical prison ministry was a perfect complement to law and order.

Evangelical prison ministries were exemplars of the Creative Society that Ronald Reagan had heralded in his 1966 California gubernatorial campaign, and that political conservatives idealized in the 1970s and after. Here were private citizens working their way into a public space formerly controlled by the state, bringing to bear their unique, largely nonprofessional perspectives on a social problem. This accorded with William Steuart McBirnie and Reagan's vision that "the penal system could be overhauled, if the sociologists, psychologists, and others were invited to think new thoughts and . . . create a new atmosphere of freedom to deal with old, tough problems."[172] But the issue was that advocates of this very Creative Society (such as Reagan) had presided over the state's *expansion* by extending law enforcement's reach in fighting crime and punishing lawbreakers. Some prison ministers missed this dynamic altogether, while others saw it less as an irony and more as a complementary state of affairs.

Herbert Ellingwood had made a name for himself as a prosecutor and as legal affairs secretary under Governor Reagan. He was a strong advocate for the toughened, streamlined criminal justice platform that Reagan appealed to in his governorship, and later in his presidency. At a 1972 event sponsored by the National Association of Evangelicals, Ellingwood gave a speech titled "Making Faith Work—across Two Worlds." "Two worlds" was a reference to Congressman John Anderson's book *Between Two Worlds* (Anderson was also present at the event). Ellingwood aimed to build on Anderson's work and outline his own understanding of how he negotiated spiritual and political callings as an evangelical. Early in his talk, Ellingwood gave an example: prison ministry. He told the story of a woman in the local jail whom he had witnessed to. Though from a troubled background, she ultimately came to Christ. Through work like this, Ellingwood went on, "God is at work in the prison system." Indeed, the American prison system is "a beautiful picture, spiritually, as far as potential is concerned." He believed this was fully the result of evangelical prison ministry. Chaplains, by contrast, "haven't done too much about it." The impact was a prison revival among "some of our worst guys . . . because people are involved on a one to one basis . . . showing the importance of personal salvation." Ellingwood told more stories. He spoke of "a famous murderer," George Otis Smith, who had been led to Christ by someone in Ellingwood's Sunday-school class. He talked about taking singer Pat Boone into a maximum-security prison to witness. He summed up his prison ministry discussion by telling the National Association of Evangelicals faithful about prison ministry's huge potential in terms of maximizing spread of the gospel. "This is a captive audience," he concluded, "but it's one that ought to be exploited."[173]

Ellingwood seemed to be attempting a joke. But the sentiment was nevertheless accurate: forced confinement was not incidental to prison ministry, but welcome. It was not a context to be overcome, but an advantage to be, as he put it, exploited. At the 1978 Congress of Prison Ministries, Duane Pederson invited Ellingwood to offer some introductory remarks. Ellingwood noted he was speaking on behalf of the attorney general, who he hoped would be "our next governor" (referring to Republican Evelle J. Younger, who was then running against incumbent Democrat Jerry Brown). Speaking to the gathered prison ministers, Ellingwood remarked, "The programs that we're involved in here are the programs that governors want to see promoted. . . . So I'll say on behalf of the state welcome. . . . I hope that at all times that we can help you promote this particular cause." Then, with a sly send-off, he closed: "If you ever have any problems, call me, in the attorney general's office and then in the governor's office."[174] The fact that Ellingwood was even present at this gathering was significant, but his remarks on behalf of California's lead law enforcement office indicated just how excited those leading American criminal justice were about the movement.

Some law enforcement officials went further, using prison ministry as a foil for progressive correctional models. A 1977 film entitled *Set Free* told the story of evangelical revival in San Quentin prison. The film largely tracked with the broader narrative laid out by Glass, Chaplain Ray, and other evangelical ministers. San Quentin chaplain Harry Howard (who regularly appeared in Chaplain Ray materials) told how the revival, helped along by prison ministry, had reduced violence at the prison, and several inmates interviewed confirmed the radical spiritual change at the facility and how God had led them out of sinful lives of drugs, black nationalism, and crime. Ellingwood was featured in the video, as were other law enforcement officials, such as Los Angeles deputy chief Robert Vernon and FBI official Don Jones. The common point they made was that American prisons were in crisis. This was not because prisons were too harsh or because too many poor people of color were caught up in the justice system. The problem, Jones argued, was that "rehabilitation doesn't work." Instead, he elaborated, as he sat underneath the large FBI seal hanging over his office desk, "I am convinced that the only answer for a man's problems, the only thing that makes him go straight, is a personal knowledge and faith in Jesus Christ." Vernon offered similar thoughts, contending that it was impossible to change behavior "unless you change the man committing that behavior . . . from the inside out." Following Ellingwood's, Jones's, and Vernon's comments in the film were shots of inmates reading bibles at San Quentin, testifying about their radical conversions (at least one of which was the subject of a Chaplain Ray feature), and saying the Sinner's Prayer together.[175]

The simultaneous assault on the behavioral modification of rehabilitation and the championing of the transforming power of the gospel was very similar to the "Jesus alone" perspective that had been offered by Billy Graham, Jim Vaus, and David Wilkerson years earlier. But here, the context of the argument was different. Those who needed heart change were incarcerated, already subject to state control. Toward the end of *Set Free*, an ex-inmate prison minister looks into the camera and says, "I couldn't depend on my government and my state, or my city government to give me another chance. The only way was Christ in my whole life." For Ellingwood and other law enforcement leaders, and the filmmakers who juxtaposed the inmates' comments to excoriations of the progressive correctional models, this was a perfect concluding example of the power of the gospel over the progressive correctional ideal. But it ignored the fact that state control itself was never in doubt, only noting that it so often proceeded with a progressive gloss and without a divine referent.

That was why there was little mention at this point of total, urgent reform (much less abolition) of prisons by evangelicals and the law enforcement leaders who championed them. There was little said about the total disruption of prisons' cold, bureaucratic grip, even as many evangelicals spoke of their desire to disrupt these facilities' religious status quo. Instead, the image of inmates at prayer and reading scripture was the ideal vision: inmates' hearts and minds were being changed, even as they remained subjects of the state. Souls were "set free," but not bodies. Ray Rogers, an ex-inmate who now worked as a prison evangelist, confirmed this sentiment in a sermon to inmates on the San Quentin yard at the end of *Set Free*. He spoke forcefully to the gathered men of God's forgiveness of sin: "He will abundantly pardon." But then, as if sensing the potential slippage he had introduced with his language choice, he speedily resolved it. "You want a pardon? You want a pardon? Come to the Lord Jesus Christ. Don't ask him to get out! Don't ask him to bring your old lady back! Ask him for a new brain! Ask him for a new life!" The door to new life in Christ was open, even as prison doors remained locked shut.

Prisoners noticed. One inmate named Carl Robins, who was serving a life sentence for drug possession, penned a column for the *Houston Chronicle* that offered "an 'inside' view of prison ministries." He said the Texas prisoners he knew had "mixed emotions" about the ministries. Many were frustrated that the ministries offered little practical help and instead "want only to 'lead them to heaven.'" One inmate Robins quoted, a robber serving twenty-five years, was blunt: "What about the prisoner's earthly needs? Is he wrong for wanting freedom? For wanting to hold on to his wife and kids? For wanting a job and a decent place to live?" Most inmates were not worried so much about the illiberal nature of proselytizing or the threat that evangelicals posed to the state chaplaincy paradigm. They simply wished these prison missionaries would find a way to "translate love into practical assistance . . . helping a prisoner get out of prison and return to his family."[176] Inmates knew prison could not be romanticized as a kind of spiritual retreat center. Ministries who allied themselves with the carceral state too closely risked a high degree of distrust.

On his radio broadcasts, Chaplain Ray occasionally displayed an understanding of the problem inherent to framing prison ministry in this way. He saw it as a challenge as old as Christianity itself: the dual (and sometimes competing) demands of justice and mercy. God's forgiveness may have been unending, but Christians from Saint Paul onward believed that the state had some sort of divine mandate to restrain and punish evil-doers. Chaplain Ray knew for certain that the answer was not to be found in progressive posturing. "Liberal speculators will tell you that poverty, society, environment, [or] genes are the cause of crime," he said in one radio broadcast, "but this is wrong." By contrast, he proclaimed, "The gospel is the only real rehabilitation program that will work." Just as important, "our God is a God of law and order and of justice. The gospel is not some namby-pamby attitude towards crime. Law and order demands justice." But then, a pivot. Law and order did demand justice, "but Jesus pays our debt." Jesus has stepped in to meet the requirements of justice on the cross and thereby made mercy possible. Christians therefore have an obligation to act mercifully toward criminals. When they do not care for criminals, they are ignoring the second part of God's dual command in Micah 6:8 to "do justly, *and* to love mercy."[177]

Chaplain Ray believed that a way to make sense of these biblical demands of justice and mercy was to focus on restitution. He pointed to the enormous distance between the biblical ideal of punishment and the current state of affairs. "Vast expensive prisons are a relatively late invention of mankind," he noted in one radio broadcast. By contrast, "in the biblical epoch, there was no need for large prisons." He quoted texts like Exodus 22:1, which indicates that the penalty for stealing livestock was repayment four- or fivefold in return. Restitution was a form of "forgotten justice," but its recovery could eliminate the necessity of new prisons being constructed while taking the plight of victims of crime seriously. A person who sat in prison had little hope of rehabilitation and was likely to return to the life of crime, while their victim suffered financial or emotional loss. "There's no justice in this kind of punitive, expensive, fruitless, crime breeding system," Chaplain Ray concluded. The answer was clear. "If we'll turn back to the simple basics of the Bible and wherever possible, substitute restitution for retribution, then we'll have simple biblical justice and the benefits will be more and more rehabilitation."[178]

Chaplain Ray called himself a law-and-order conservative but emphasized that at the same time he was "compassionate." He heralded the work of law enforcement, but the evangelical prison ministry paradigm gave him a way to reframe this push in terms of mercy. To listen to Chaplain Ray try to reconcile these commitments could be frustrating; on his radio broadcasts he often seemed to be unsure of how exactly to negotiate the demands of justice and mercy, frequently catching and correcting himself when he starting leaning too far one way or the other. While hosting the Dallas county sheriff on his radio show, Chaplain Ray critiqued the people "who cling to the old redneck ideas that we should lock up people and throw away the key." Yet he spoke glowingly of the sheriff's work in arresting criminals and leading them to Christ in jail. The sheriff had recently allowed Chaplain Ray and other evangelicals into his jail and was excited about the pacifying potential of the gospel. He told Chaplain Ray that "if you can keep the inmates reading the Bible, then they aren't going to be causing any more trouble." Chaplain Ray was sensitive to the hazards posed by blunt language like this and would have probably preferred not to have had the sheriff unintentionally channeling Karl Marx's theory of religion as an opiate for the masses on his show. But he was otherwise thrilled, telling the sheriff, "You are setting an example at the Dallas jail for how we should treat prisoners." Perhaps hoping for some resolution to the law-versus-gospel conundrum, Chaplain Ray asked the sheriff whether he believed prisoners should be punished or whether we should simply seek their conversion. The sheriff sidestepped the question, instead saying that he hoped program listeners would contact him with their own thoughts.[179]

Chaplain Ray occasionally spoke with force about the promise in a restitution model as a way to resolve this tension, such as in a 1983 book he published on "biblical restitution" that posited the model as an alternative to the warehousing of prisoners. It also offered instruction for Christians on how they might lobby for the model in their own states.[180] But this book was the exception; most of Chaplain Ray's actual work was focused not on policy change but on evangelism. Prison ministry had given him some sense that there was another way beyond both the progressive and punitive paradigms. But without a consistent vision for how to relate justice and mercy, the tension remained. It would be up to other evangelicals to develop a more robust response.

6

THERE ARE BETTER WAYS

"Please God, Help me." Charles "Chuck" Colson scribbled on a yellow legal
pad from inside the dingy dormitory at the federal prison camp located
at Maxwell Air Force Base near Montgomery, Alabama. "I read the
37th Psalm & Daily Bread for today but I can't control myself. . . . I can't
escape from my own mind and the depression is nearly overwhelming."
Colson, who had been incarcerated for his role in various Nixon administration illegalities, was feeling profound despair. He had converted to
Christianity right before entering prison, but behind bars he wrestled with
the spiritualized piety that designated him free in Christ. He knew that
being "born again" in theory should set his mind above earthly concerns:
"I suppose if I am true to Christ . . . what is done to me . . . shouldn't
matter." But his own experience in prison seemed to be driving him away
from the Lord. Incarceration was not a redemptive blessing.[1]

Colson also journaled about the difficulties of prison life he and other
prisoners endured. Inmates at Maxwell felt "bitter and destroyed," given
their rat- and roach-infested housing, forced labor for little to no pay, and
regular mistreatment by staff. He blasted the bureaucratic morass, with
its nonsensical rules. Some prisoners had found a crate of unused flight
jackets that the air force had disposed of, and grew excited about the possibility of having some warmer clothes during the chilly winter months.
But the prison, which only provided substandard, worn-out jackets, refused to allow them to wear the higher-quality air force clothing because
it did not match the required brown inmate uniform. The warm jackets
sat unused. As a result, Colson and fellow inmates had to track down
brown dye, sometimes having visitors sneak it in covertly, and color the
jackets on their own. More frustrating than capricious rules about clothing
was the harsh, unpredictable sentencing. Long sentences (often disproportionate to the crimes committed) and unclear expectations for parole,

Colson jotted down in his notes, "eroded men's souls." As he reflected on the flight jacket fiasco and his frustration with prison regulations, Colson concluded that "idiocy [is] so present. . . . Damn system denies *any* rights to Prisoners and subjects him to real risks." That Maxwell was a minimum-security facility with more privileges than many other American prisons did not matter much to Colson. "It is all capital punishment of the soul; simply a question of degree, whether man's flesh is destroyed in electric chair or one year is taken away."[2]

Colson grew close to some of his fellow prisoners. He participated in a Bible study and prayer group, a parallel to his elite "fellowship" back in Washington, DC. A lawyer by training, Colson helped some inmates with legal matters, despite warnings from prison administrators not to practice law in prison. Other times he assisted with simpler tasks, such as the drafting of a letter to a judge for an illiterate inmate. The fact that prisoners had so few resources and that illiterate inmates could not even read their own charges, much less argue against them, was infuriating to Colson. As he left Maxwell after a seven-month sentence, he told his new friends that he would not forget them.[3]

Colson stayed true to this promise. The fellowship he experienced at Maxwell with other inmates helped to spur him on to prison ministry. He would soon become the most popular figure in the evangelical prison ministry movement as the founder and leader of Prison Fellowship. Prison Fellowship's ministry work was significant in its own right, notable especially for its professionalism and ambitions. Though initially small, it quickly moved on from shoestring status. By the early 1980s Prison Fellowship was operating with a multimillion-dollar budget, twelve thousand active monthly volunteers, and a large nationwide staff.[4] But Colson's most groundbreaking effort was where Prison Fellowship departed from the path other prison ministries had pioneered: the direct engagement of issues of prison and criminal justice reform.[5] Colson never forgot the suffering of prison life. Though he was convinced that the work of saving souls was paramount, he came to believe God could also use him to alleviate the bodily suffering of prisoners, something he himself had experienced.

Colson approached prison and criminal justice reform with similar conceptual frameworks as past evangelical advocates for both inmate ministry and law and order, but with different results. He combined skepticism of state bureaucracy, an individualistic anthropology, and a personal influence model of social change into a potent critique of the burgeoning carceral state. The result was an early entry in what later was called "compassionate conservatism," an approach that tried to adopt the anti-statist, individualistic, faith-based ideals of the conservative movement, shore up flaws in application, and direct them toward humanitarian ends.[6] There was no better target for a conservative looking to do good than the nation's prison system, the "most thoroughly implemented government social program of our time."[7] Other evangelicals, particularly those aligned with the burgeoning Christian right, continued to advance arguments in favor of toughening American criminal justice, but they increasingly had to reckon with Colson. Since Colson's approach to reform depended on conservative arguments and alliances, however, he also had to reckon with them. The result was that Colson gradually built trust with other evangelicals who may have otherwise looked askance at the reform agenda. But his general comfort with Reagan-era conservatism meant that Colson's vision always risked being marginalized or co-opted for more punitive causes by those who had not experienced prison life firsthand. He came to represent, for better or worse, the bendable social conscience of American evangelicalism.

Colson and his various ministry efforts adopted a reformist evangelical approach to crime, punishment, and imprisonment in the late 1970s and early 1980s. Though this approach departed from the spiritualized practice of prison ministry pioneered over the past decade, it was still grounded in Colson's personal experiences of prison evangelism. It was also firmly conservative in character, a rebuttal of what Colson saw as a progressive, rehabilitative prison regime. Colson's cause ran into challenges in the mid-1980s. Other evangelicals continued to push for law and order, and his reform work floundered at times in the face of broader social pressures and internal tensions. From the mid-1980s on, his reform cause regularly had to regroup, make peace with competitors, and work out compromise models, such as restorative justice. Advocating compromise had a dual legacy. Colson's movement was regularly co-opted by other evangelicals and politicians seeking compassionate cover for law-and-order politics in the 1990s, and he sometimes gravitated toward more punitive forms of justice himself. But he also maintained strategic influence and persisted as a trusted presence in the halls of power. By the 2000s Colson had become one of the most influential evangelicals in Washington, outpacing activists for more traditional culture war causes through his careful political maneuvering and relationship building.[8]

Conserving Justice

Colson's prison reform work grew out of his ministry experience. He adopted a consciously conservative philosophy regarding matters of reform, drawing on complementary criminological theories and theologies to fashion his critique of American prisons. He carefully built alliances with other evangelicals and public figures as he developed his philosophy and lobbying efforts.

Colson's ventures into reform work did not happen immediately after his conversion. His evangelistic ministry was the most immediate product of his incarceration experience. But as he traveled to prisons across the country in his early ministry, Colson thought about new possibilities. For the first few years of his work after Prison Fellowship's founding, he was reluctant to voice publicly any strong criticisms of American prisons. If reform was mentioned, it was usually as an outgrowth of the long-standing evangelical personal conversion social strategy: convicts coming to Christ would ultimately solve the crime problem and eliminate the need for prisons.[9] The reluctance to voice negative appraisals was partly a result of his tenuous relationship with prison administrators. In his best-selling memoir *Born Again* (published in 1976, the same year Prison Fellowship began work), Colson wrote briefly about the poor conditions at the Atlanta County Jail. This was a facility he never spent time in personally but that had housed fellow inmates he lived with at Maxwell, who told him harrowing tales about their experiences. Not long after publication of the book, officials at the Atlanta jail accused Colson of libel and threatened to sue for defamation. His ministry had only just begun and its long-term success was now in question. Colson was forced to go on an apology tour of the facility, though he later said he thought the jail had deceptively covered up its inhumane conditions only *after* he had made the accusations public.[10]

Colson's evangelistic focus was also a reflection of his new involvement in conversion-centered and conservative evangelical culture. After observing and interviewing Colson at a Washington prayer breakfast in 1976, journalist Garry Wills called him "a bit shuffling and apologetic over his reform efforts, since much of the evangelical movement opposed the social gospel." When Wills mentioned Catholic peace activist Philip Berrigan as a possible comparison during the interview, Colson made sure to note his opposition to politically active ministers. Wills noted the starkness of the shift in the former Nixon aide's persona. Here was "a supremely political man now renouncing politics."[11]

The longer Colson spent working in prisons, however, the less he shuffled. In April 1978 Colson and Prison Fellowship staff bounced around new ideas, such as hiring two or three staff members to research prison reform and stay in touch with legislators.[12] A few months later Colson was speaking at an evangelistic event for Prison Fellowship at a federal penitentiary in Atlanta (a separate facility from the county jail where he had previously had trouble). This prison, which housed two thousand inmates, had seen an enormous amount of violence as of late, with regular murders, fires, and assaults. Though Colson and his fellow ministry volunteers welcomed this challenge, they knew the success of their event was in question, for two reasons. First, it was blazing hot, and the prison lacked any air conditioning. Second, and more challenging, Colson had been told that the inmates would be skeptical of overtly preachy religious talk or mentions of Jesus Christ. Instead, some of Colson's inmate advisers suggested before the event, "Maybe you could talk about prison reform, Chuck. Everybody is for that." Colson reluctantly agreed. But while standing before the eight hundred inmates gathered to hear him speak, Colson had a change of heart. In the heat of the moment, he folded up the notes he had sketched on prison reform and put them in his coat pocket. He then told the men gathered before him that they could find new life in Jesus Christ.

As Colson narrated this story in his follow-up book to *Born Again,* entitled *Life Sentence,* it seemed as if he had forsworn reformist advocacy. After all, inmates accepted Christ in droves at the event and afterward thanked Colson profusely for his spiritual exhortation. But as he departed the facility, Colson looked at the faces of the inmates who had welcomed him and realized they were not only converts but his "Brothers." His eyes turned also to the five-story wall of cages where the men would be herded after he left. "What a torture," he thought. "These men come back from the spiritual high of this meeting and then live in this hell. But this, too, will change. I know it will. When Christians see what this is all about, they will do something, I know." This was, Colson wrote, narrating his own sense of call, a "life sentence" to mobilize fellow believers on the outside to help meet prisoners' needs across the nation.[13] After his visit Colson spoke about the situation in Atlanta to reporters. Adopting the mantle of spokesman for the prisoners there, he talked about the inhumane conditions,

Figure 6.1 Charles Colson greeting inmates during a prison ministry event. Prison Fellowship.

chiefly overcrowding, which Colson claimed was responsible for the violence.[14]

For the rest of 1978, Colson began including comments about prison problems in his speeches to evangelical groups, detailing his opposition to oppressive aspects of American criminal justice. He spoke to four thousand members of the Church of the Nazarene about the need for Christians to get involved in prisons and his frustrations with the challenges inmates had with reentry into society ("They can't vote, they can't get a driver's license and they can't be bonded for employment"). He mentioned that a Virginia state official had proposed restoring his citizenship rights, but Colson refused to accept the offer until there was a system-wide change for all inmates.[15]

Up to this point, Colson largely had spoken about the need for prison reform as a personal cause, but beginning in 1979 he led Prison Fellowship to adopt the task as its own. In its annual report, Colson summarized the tragic state of American criminal justice. Prisons were overcrowded, but the only solution lawmakers had offered was to simply build more. This was the wrong approach, Colson argued. Besides costing taxpayers billions, building prisons did nothing to address "the additional cost in human lives, both to non-violent offenders who would be ruined by unnecessary incarceration, and to the society which imprisons them." He urged Prison Fellowship supporters to "weigh our criminal justice practices against the commands of scripture" and look to alternative methods, such as halfway houses and alcohol treatment programs. A year later, Prison Fellowship published its first mission statement, which listed three goals: building up Christ's church in prisons, connecting local churches to prison ministry, and working for "a more just and effective criminal justice system."[16]

Colson's calls for reform were rooted in his growing sense of injustices that prisoners faced, but they also were a result of his realization that he could frame the cause in terms that, at best, transcended political divisions or, at least, appealed to the generally conservative political leanings of fellow evangelicals. Part of this appeal was pragmatic, as evidenced in Prison Fellowship's mission statement. Not only would Prison Fellowship's reform proposals advocate for "more just" ends, they would push for practical, "effective" goals. Reform would "control crime, save tax funds, and aid victims."[17] This also was why, standing outside the Atlanta federal prison, Colson had critiqued the horrible conditions but avoided a direct challenge to conservative Georgia politicians or the prison's warden. From his time in political life, Colson knew he should not alienate sympathetic authorities and allies with needless boat-rocking.[18]

In 1979 Colson spoke at the annual meeting of the Southern Baptist Convention (SBC) in Houston. At the time, the SBC gathering was ground zero for denominational conflicts over biblical inerrancy and politics. Speaking like a missionary at home on furlough, Colson urged the gathered crowd of fifteen thousand to pray for prison evangelism. He garnered applause in his talk when he urged Baptists to resist the "moral rot and sickness" of television and a "sentimental" Christianity that did not demand repentance.[19] Evangelism, anti-Hollywood sentiment, and guilt inducement for sin—this was messaging in line with the conservative piety of the SBC faithful. But then Colson made his way to the offstage pressroom with a different message in mind: opposition to capital punishment. He noted before reporters that many Baptists at the convention would disagree with him, so he offered what he hoped would be a compelling rationale. "As a lifelong conservative, I have always been reluctant to give the state the power to take human life." He had clearly thought about the issue, citing statistics that indicated the death penalty's failure to deter crime and his own experience with death-row inmates who claimed innocence. Then, he issued the ultimate Baptist broadsides, mobilizing biblical authority, conversionist rationale, and suspicion of the state's pretensions to divine claims. "In my reading of the New Testament," Colson argued, "I cannot accept the practice of capital punishment if I am to live by the commandments of Jesus." The death penalty eclipsed the possibility of conversion, because "once you execute that man, it's too late." He asserted, "I don't think the state should play God."[20] It was not clear whether Colson was changing any minds at the SBC, but he knew his audience. More moderate members who were anti–death penalty (such as seminary professors or denominational leaders) could agree with that conclusion, while more conservative laity could find something to appreciate in his argumentation and the evangelical persona he had maintained.

From the outset of his public ministry, Colson's conservative political philosophy was on display. As he narrated his own indictment in *Born Again,* he noted that he "knew now what it was like for one person to stand virtually alone against the vast powers of government." His life preceding conversion was characterized by sin and a lack understanding of the conservative tradition, despite having worked his whole adult life in Republican politics: "How calloused I'd been all those past years about the importance of one individual's rights." He spoke about the challenges that prisoners faced as if he were detailing a small-business owner's suffering under governmental overregulation: individuals were being constrained by inefficient bureaucracies, unable to live up to their full potential.[21]

Colson also believed that the individual facing down the vast powers of government was a self-determined, rational actor who could make his or her own moral choices. Not long after he began his ministry work, he began reading the work of psychiatrist Samuel Yochelson and psychologist Stanton Samenow, who had together written a three-volume work entitled *The Criminal Personality.* These authors concluded that "hard core" criminals exhibited "rational choice" in their development. Cutting against the grain of a great deal of recent criminological theory, they focused on "how much a criminal is a victimizer, rather than a victim—a molder of his environment, rather than a mere product of that mold." Indeed, they pointed out that many of their subjects were economically secure and employed, "but crime remains." They discounted therapeutic measures designed to rehabilitate criminals through outward verbal self-discovery, such as psychoanalysis. Instead, they argued, change had to come by actually altering criminals' internal thinking and motivations. Since a criminal had deluded himself into thinking that he was "basically decent," what was needed was for him to face "just how rotten a person he was." To focus on the environment was to ignore the fundamental issue of the "inner man."[22]

Academic reviewers were skeptical. One review concluded that the work's case studies lacked theoretical value and that "it must be doubted seriously whether Volume I will find its way into many such classrooms."[23] Its disputed academic import was of little consequence, though, when Colson began to promote the theories widely. He made a few modifications along the way. Yochelson and Samenow remained agnostic about the ultimate cause of crime, *why* criminals made the choices they did. Colson had an answer: sin, the spiritual sickness that ailed all people and distorted their desires. Christ had solved this problem through his death and resurrection, and Christian conversion (being "born again") was the proper response. In the same way that Yochelson and Samenow argued that their treatment regimen was meant to "capitalize on and intensify whatever self-disgust is present," Colson knew he had to begin with sin as well. This was a classic Protestant move: preach the law (which no one could live up to), allow sinners to feel their inevitable guilt, and then offer the gospel. Yochelson and Samenow had proposed "habilitation" as the name for their clinical intervention in changing criminal thinking (as opposed to outer rehabilitative efforts).[24] Colson had a different term: "discipleship," the process of living into one's conversion through practices of Christian prayer, scripture reading, and accountability. For him, the Washington fellowship was the habilitative project that had awakened him from his own spiritual ignorance. Applied in prisons, in a "prison fellowship," he believed the results could be the same.

Colson's staff was briefing him on the work of Yochelson and Samenow as early as 1977, and from then on he cited them as inspirations for both his ministry and his reform efforts.[25] Regarding reform, Colson referenced them to contend that state response to offenders had to acknowledge their moral choices and allow for the possibility of their transformation. Colson believed that the awful conditions in modern correctional facilities meant that neither of these results was attainable. Overcrowding caused violence and gang activity, lack of paid prison labor encouraged laziness, and harsh punishment of nonviolent offenses bred resentment.[26]

Colson found theological inspiration for his reform views in the work of Jacques Ellul and C. S. Lewis. Ellul, a French legal and political philosopher who regularly wrote on Christianity, gave Colson conceptual tools to understand the brokenness of large human institutions. Colson channeled Ellul's anarchic tendencies into a conservative critique of the state's power over individual freedom, families, and voluntary associations, as well as its eclipse of their reliance on God.[27] Colson had learned the basics of the faith through Lewis's *Mere Christianity*, so he sought out what the trustworthy Oxford don had to say about punishment. He read Lewis's 1953 piece "The Humanitarian Theory of Punishment," where the scholar argued against the rehabilitative (humanitarian) paradigm and for retributive theory. In the hands of an earlier generation of evangelicals (such as those at *Christianity Today*, where the piece had been covered in 1959), Lewis's articulation of the importance of "the concept of Desert" was seen as a justification for punitive measures. Colson, however, zeroed in on Lewis's description of the horrors of the progressive rehabilitative paradigm: "It may be said . . . they are not punishing, not inflicting, only healing. But do not let us be deceived by a name . . . to be re-made after some pattern of 'normality' hatched in a Viennese laboratory to which I never professed allegiance. . . ." What advocates for rehabilitation saw as "kindnesses" were experienced by offenders as "abominable cruelties," the "humane pretensions which have served to usher in every cruelty of the revolutionary period in which we live."[28] Colson believed this to be an apt description of what modern prisons were doing: ineptly trying to treat criminal behavior as if it were an illness and naming correctional practices as rehabilitative, which in turn caused observers to overlook the practices' machinelike impersonality or, even worse, their injustices.

Colson used Lewis's analytical frame as he described his visit to Purdy Women's Prison in 1980 in an internal Prison Fellowship memo. What struck him was not so much the poor conditions (the prison was nice, as prisons went) but its sterility. "It was straight out of *1984*," he wrote, "a modern, clean efficient institution, yet somehow I had the feeling that I was in a laboratory, not in a prison." The banal character of the "crisp, cold, efficient social workers" and other administrators of the "bureaucratic machine" (including the chaplain) in the prison unsettled him: "The head woman . . . looked fully capable of marching people into gas chambers." His meeting with the inmates gave him a similar impression. They seemed to be in a "mechanical" stupor. "Whatever goes on in this prison totally destroys the emotions of the residents. I suspect that's part of the therapy, part of the treatment." Colson then reflected on what this meant for his ministry's relationship in the broader criminological currents of the day. Here was the rehabilitative paradigm at its pinnacle but, citing Lewis, it was little more than a "test tube . . . the ultimate expression of totalitarianism in our society, cloaked as it is in the appearance of humanness."[29] Rehabilitation was oppression.

Colson's conservatism was a potent blend of traditionalism, with its focus on the cultivation of (Christian) virtue, and libertarianism, with its skepticism of the state. This combination reflected the integration of these themes in American conservatism more broadly in the years after World War II, usually with anticommunism as the major foil. Generally, Colson utilized the libertarian strain for critiques and the traditional one for his constructive proposals, though he leaned into one or the other as it suited his purposes. This approach followed the principled pragmatism of other prominent postwar conservatives, such as William F. Buckley.[30]

Trusting him as a fellow conservative, Buckley found Colson compelling. In the 1960s Buckley had trumpeted the law-and-order cause, labeling criminals as evil and lobbying for fewer restraints on policing.[31] But in 1982 he hosted Colson on his *Firing Line* television show and wrote approvingly of him in the *Washington Post* a few days later. He praised not only his ministry but also his work "persuading the American public for God's sake to listen to reason" on reform: prison populations were growing too fast, a humanitarian and fiscal disaster, and half of inmates were not even convicted of a violent crime. Colson's cause, as Buckley put it with his trademark literary flourish, was "profoundly conceived, existentially appealing, splendid in ambition." He was elated that these ideas were coming not from a progressive activist but from a Christian conservative.[32]

These were conservative arguments, but some progressives concerned about prisons appreciated them. Many had likewise come to see the failures of the rehabilitative paradigm themselves. As socialist academic Robert Martinson famously argued in 1974 in his consideration of correctional efficacy, nothing worked: "the rehabilitative efforts that have been reported so far have no appreciable effect on recidivism."[33] Colson welcomed complementary views like this and structured his reform efforts to operate separately from Prison Fellowship's evangelistic ministry, so as to not alienate outsiders. "It's very important," he wrote to Prison Fellowship employees, "that we broaden its appeal so that it will reach mainliners, other activists and big hunks of the evangelical church. . . . It's the results that I care about in the long haul, not the credit to the organization."[34] Al Bronstein, the head of the ACLU's prison reform project, was quoted in a front-page *Washington Post* piece on Colson's advocacy: "He's doing great things. Everything he's saying about prisons and [bad] conditions and alternatives to incarceration is almost exactly what we're saying. . . . Colson is reaching a conservative audience that we can't reach."[35]

Colson's staff started pushing the National Association of Evangelicals to consider prison reform as a lobbying issue.[36] Colson began writing occasionally for *Christianity Today* in the late 1970s and became a regular columnist in 1985.[37] Likely in part because of Colson's influence, the magazine evinced a shift on criminal justice issues, allowing for much more sympathy toward criminals than had existed a generation earlier.[38] More important, however, was Colson's regular presence in major newspapers, on television, and at Christian conferences and events. Just as Colson had helped publicize the "born again" catchphrase as a marker of public evangelical faith in the mid-1970s, he was beginning to construct a new form of conservative evangelical social engagement at the outset of the 1980s, transforming the evangelical conscience on a challenging public issue.

Colson quickly gained awareness of precedents for this approach. At the behest of his assistant Michael Cromartie, a former volunteer with the progressive evangelical magazine *Sojourners,* he acquainted himself with nineteenth-century evangelical reform work in prisons. Cromartie sent Colson an excerpt of Norris Magnuson's *Salvation in the Slums,* a work on the history of late nineteenth-century Salvation Army and Holiness work with the poor and prisoners.[39] Colson was enthusiastic, forwarding it to several Prison Fellowship staff members. "The attached article is MUST reading and rereading for each of us," he wrote. "There are remarkable historical parallels with our ministry."[40] Colson knew that nineteenth-century evangelical prison reform projects had regularly failed. But he was confident that, under his leadership and with a renewed focus on Christ, this time the result could be different.[41]

Colson was nothing if not confident, but he had good reason to be. He was reaching the public in ways that other Christians with prison reform aspirations had failed. Progressive evangelicals' outreach on criminal justice provides a point of contrast, from the critiques of law-and-order race-baiting by activists like Tom Skinner, to the public speeches made by none other than the most prominent evangelical politician in the country, Jimmy Carter. As the Southern Baptist peanut farmer turned governor considered a run for president, he spoke out on the need for criminal justice reform. His most famous speech on the topic was delivered in 1974, known also for its citation of Bob Dylan and Reinhold Niebuhr and because gonzo journalist Hunter S. Thompson praised it. Carter's speech sounded populist tones on the negative effects prisons had on the poor, which bolstered his status as a progressive icon and helped to lift him above presumed Democratic presidential nominee Edward Kennedy.[42] But as with much of Carter's later political career, his justice reform push failed to connect to conservatives and did not move the needle much for evangelicals who might have been sympathetic to the issue. Colson, by contrast, framed his advocacy in a manner that likely would have left Thompson unimpressed but that fellow conservatives could find compelling.

Political Consequences

A great deal of Colson's early work on prison reform was simply promoting the issue to anyone who would listen. But he gradually moved into lobbying work on concrete matters of prison administration and policy. He began by forming a bipartisan task force to offer him recommendations. At the suggestion of the task force and the president of the Christian Legal Society, Colson hired a young evangelical attorney named Daniel Van Ness to serve as special counsel on criminal justice in 1981.[43]

One of Colson's first efforts was in Washington State. Though he had been troubled by his visit to the Purdy Women's Prison, his primary target was the state's prisons for men. More than any other state he had visited, Colson saw the conditions in its prisons as horrifying, even "demonic," for their overcrowding, use of solitary confinement, and filthy living quarters. "The Washington State system," he instructed his staff, "is one we need to assault."[44]

The men's prison at Walla Walla was the biggest challenge. In October 1979 Colson visited the facility. A guard had been killed only months before, prisoners were on lockdown as a result (in their cells twenty-three hours a day), and Colson was nervous. Upon entry into the facility, he saw how poorly administrators had handled prisoner concerns. Once in front of the inmates who gathered to hear him speak, Colson launched into his standard evangelistic spiel. Unlike in other contexts, however, the Walla Walla inmates responded unenthusiastically, offering cold stares. As he departed the prison, he told two inmates, "We'll do everything to help you guys." He assigned two Prison Fellowship staff members to the facility to begin running a fellowship seminar and reconciling rival gangs inside the prison. Within a few weeks a staffer had led some men to Christ, and things began to simmer down.

As Colson recounted this story a few years later, it seemed at this point to have a similar arc as the ministry narrations of evangelists like Bill

Glass: a prison has problems, a prison minister enters, and unruly inmates are settled. But all was not well. Despite Prison Fellowship's best efforts, the horrors of Walla Walla remained. Some inmates protested by slashing their wrists, blood pooling in the cellblocks. A Prison Fellowship minister looked on in shock at the sight and then moved to quell the chanting of other inmates, who were threatening further violence. "Don't blow this thing," he told them, before promising that Colson would speak to the state legislature about the problems. From Colson's perspective, the gospel may have been preached and souls won for Christ, but more work was needed.

Colson had cultivated contacts in the state's political class, including Bob Utter, the chief justice of the state supreme court. Colson went to the legislature and met with both the Democratic and Republican caucuses about the problem. The immediate result was a House resolution pledging to address conditions at Walla Walla. Over the next few years Colson and his staff continued to lobby state leaders about the prison, with varying degrees of success. He rejoiced when a ruling came down from a US district court that practices at Walla Walla constituted "cruel and unusual punishment," but was saddened months later when he returned to the facility and found that horrible conditions remained, particularly among inmates housed in solitary. Inmates had demanded that the warden, who ignored their complaints, be removed. Colson visited the inmates housed in solitary and saw why. The warden had refused to do anything about the human waste and rotting food strewn all over the unit, declining even to enter the solitary unit. Though Colson typically avoided direct confrontation with prison administrators, he was incensed. He held a press conference the next day where he detailed the conditions. The warden was soon transferred from the facility. Progress was slow, but under the leadership of Judge Utter (who took chairmanship of a prison reform committee) and other Christians whom Colson had lobbied to get involved, conditions at the prison began to improve.[45]

An anecdote that Colson shared as he later narrated events at Walla Walla was emblematic of the conceptual shift he had introduced into the evangelical prison ministry paradigm. He told the story of a Walla Walla inmate named Fred LeFever, who had recently come up for parole after his imprisonment for robbery. LeFever had joined a prison ministry while incarcerated and reconciled with his victims. During his parole hearing, he confessed to other robberies, despite the good chance that he would have avoided a guilty verdict. As a Christian, he said, "I knew I had to come clean. . . . Even if you should decide that I should be further punished, I will go back to prison and serve Jesus Christ in there." But instead of returning him to prison, the judge ordered his release, requiring LeFever only to pay restitution to the victims (a sentencing formula that Colson and Utter had been pushing in the state since Walla Walla). The gathered family members, friends, and Prison Fellowship staff rejoiced, bursting into the doxology inside the courtroom.[46] For Colson, the work at Walla Walla was indistinguishable from his evangelistic work. "There was simply no way that we, as conscientious Christian ministers, could decline [prisoners'] requests. And so we found ourselves, without having planned it that way at all, in the prison reform business, not instead of our prison ministry but as a natural inescapable outgrowth of it."[47]

Colson believed this cause could move beyond the state level. In 1982 he ventured to Washington, DC, to testify before the House Judiciary Committee on revisions to the federal criminal code. In a potent display of political showmanship, Colson packed the audience of around fifty people, many of whom were inmates and their families currently in Washington attending a Prison Fellowship seminar. Colson went on to discuss how his ministry had led him to concern with poor prison conditions and unjust sentencing practices. He explained the high moral stakes of the hearing: "In the United States today we incarcerate more people as a percentage of population than any other nation on the face of the Earth except the Soviet Union and South Africa, and we have the highest crime rate." He then asked the committee to go even further on the code reforms they were considering, to address the barbaric system of American punishment that was "100 years behind the times." Colson made sure to stress that crime was a moral issue and that punishment was still necessary, particularly for violent crimes. He also acknowledged the tempting pull of law-and-order politics for elected officials. But, he pleaded, "there are better ways." He urged the committee to add provisions in the code that required judges to only use prisons for incapacitation of violent offenders, to allow sentence reductions for good behavior, and to reform the sentencing and parole process so as to "get the men out of prison as soon as possible."[48]

Colson pulled no punches when demonstrating his evangelical credentials. He spoke in overtly religious terms about his own conversion and call to ministry: "I sit here today because I have committed my life to Jesus Christ, and this what I believe God called me to do." But he made sure to note that his evangelistic work was only the beginning of his calling:

"I can't go to a prison and just preach to guys living in conditions that are subhuman. I care about them just as Jesus cared as much about feeding people as preaching to them."[49]

Through his calls for prison reform and his activism on the issue, Colson had developed a resolution to the tension his brethren had introduced over the past twenty years as evangelicals called both for more law and order and for heightened ministry to prisoners. He made prison reform a "safe" issue by framing it in terms that made sense to politically conservative instincts and by tying humanitarian impulses and political consequences directly to Christian conversion. In 1983 Colson wrote approvingly in *Christianity Today* of a Christian judge who had recently bucked the harsh trends of the criminal justice bureaucracy. This judge had declared mandatory minimums unconstitutional while attempting to give leniency to a convict who turned his life around and converted to Christianity.[50] Colson's praise of the judge was striking. Mandatory minimums had been advocated fifteen years earlier by evangelicals like Herbert Ellingwood, but here was Colson using the same conservative line of reasoning to push against them: mandatory minimums were actually representative of state overreach. More importantly, however, Colson knew that the criminal in question had undergone a change of heart, a *conversion*. This was the goal that earlier evangelical prison ministers had isolated and promoted, but often restrained in terms of political import.

Thorns in the Flesh

Colson was not the only politically savvy evangelical seeking to influence politicians and the public on criminal justice issues in the early 1980s. The new "Christian right," exemplified by figures such as Pat Robertson and Jerry Falwell and organizations such as the Moral Majority (founded by Falwell in 1979), had their own plans for mobilization on the issue.

The "Christian right" is regularly used as an umbrella term for a variety of conservative evangelical personalities, organizations, and movements in the second half of the twentieth century. Daniel Williams's definition of the "second stage" of Christian right development at this historical moment is helpful. Beginning in the late 1960s, conservative Protestants began making inroads into the Republican Party, not on a Cold War platform as in the 1940s and 1950s, but as a reaction to the threats of feminism, abortion, pornography, and gay rights.[51] The Christian right increasingly drew the battle lines of the culture war around issues of crime and punishment as it began its struggle against the onslaught of liberalism more broadly. The most persistent mobilization of the Christian right around crime and punishment was rhetorical: a continuation of the trope of law and order. Law and order was something that had been lost; America's moral foundations were crumbling as a result of the rising tides of secularism, feminism, and humanism. Though this mobilization on crime was similar in tone to past calls for law and order, at the turn of the 1980s it exhibited some important differences. The focus was less on rioting and the perception of widespread disorder in the streets and more on the dangers of drugs and the impact of crime on victims.

In the eyes of the Christian right, the effects of liberalizing social shifts were twofold: first, an unfortunate *rise* in public expectation for the state apparatus to exert influence in areas of life best left up to more traditional institutions of local governance, the family, and the church, and second, an equally worrisome trend of state *withdrawal* in the enforcement of the moral laws of America. Simply put, the government spent too much time interfering in matters that it should have stayed out of (such as school prayer or the market) and not enough time catching criminals. Along with divorce, abortion, and pornography, Jerry Falwell listed rising crime (particularly drug dealing) as a sign of America's moral decline in a 1982 newspaper op-ed. "Crime is epidemic," he complained, and "criminals are better protected by the law than the people on whom they prey." Falwell warned that he and other concerned Americans would not remain silent on these issues, and he listed Martin Luther King Jr., the Berrigan brothers, and William Sloan Coffin as examples of outspoken activists who likewise melded religion and politics (thereby undercutting progressives worried about church/state enmeshment). Falwell pledged that the Moral Majority would take up the cause of justice and moral realignment by registering voters and mobilizing local campaigns on various issues of Christian concern.[52]

Concern about crime was not the only, or even the most important, issue that Falwell and the Moral Majority mobilized on. But it was nevertheless a reference point in their public appeals. Concern about drugs framed some of their rhetoric. One Moral Majority marketing brochure listed ten matters of concern, including abortion, support for Israel, and family values. The fourth concern listed was "the illegal drug traffic," and the brochure noted that "through education, legislation, and other means, we want to do our part to save our youth from death on the installment plan."[53]

The Moral Majority's lobbying efforts on criminal justice policy focused less on drugs and more on crimes related to violence and sex. Throughout the late 1970s to the mid-1980s, Congress frequently debated how to revise and update the US criminal code. This was a bipartisan discussion, with people from each side, such as Congressmen Strom Thurmond (a southern Republican) and Edward Kennedy (a New England Democrat), agreeing that revision was necessary. The Moral Majority and liberal groups like the ACLU also saw revision as essential, but their specific crime policy recommendations diverged. For example, in 1981–1982 the Moral Majority criticized proposed code changes that replaced life sentences for murder and rape with twenty-five-year sentences without possibility of parole. At the very same House subcommittee hearing on the criminal code where Colson had testified, Moral Majority vice president Ronald Godwin appeared to make his own case. He told the subcommittee, "We are experiencing a violent crime wave that is sweeping America. . . . We call for a restoration of existing maximum penalties and insist that all existing death penalties be carried forward." Godwin framed his appeal in populist terms. He testified that he received around fifteen thousand pieces of mail daily, many of them written by people concerned about violent crime. Americans of all stripes (particularly African Americans) wanted tougher laws, and Godwin asserted that members of congress should likewise "check their mailboxes" to hear the voices of their fearful constituents. He claimed that ministers regularly told him "people no longer want to go to church on Sunday night . . . because they are afraid to leave their homes after dark." When Representative John Conyers voiced concerns about Godwin's understanding of the harm of long sentences, Godwin doubled down: "I just simply know this, that while the person is in jail he can't rape my wife or my daughter and he can't perpetuate a violent crime upon society. . . . I believe it is genuinely the primary concern of most people."[54]

Though Godwin's testimony was criticized by both liberals and conservatives for derailing carefully crafted legislation that made concessions to various constituencies, it nevertheless produced results. Because of Moral Majority lobbying, two senators withdrew their sponsorship of the proposed revisions that would have taken this particular crime bill in a less punitive direction.[55] Later, seven amendments were added by Republicans on the Senate Judiciary Committee to "relate to the concerns expressed by the Moral Majority." They generally were focused on crimes of a sexual nature, such as the doubling of prison terms (from six to twelve years) without parole for obscenity and sexual exploitation involving minors. Even though the Moral Majority was pleased with these additions, it nonetheless opposed the bill, which eventually died for lack of broad support.[56] Though the Moral Majority had only been on the political scene for a few years, in leading a populist charge to kill the code revision bill, it had shown its ability to exert power in a manner similar to that of other influential interest groups, such as labor unions and civil liberties advocates.[57]

Perhaps more important than their work on the federal level was the Moral Majority's influence in state and local politics, particularly judicial elections. The chairman of the Ohio Moral Majority branch announced in 1981 that his organization would be targeting "lenient" judges in the upcoming election by mailing out a scorecard of judicial candidates' records on issues of note: "I feel that we can curb crime by causing the people involved to get sentences that would cause them to recognize teeth in our laws." The prosecutor in populous Hamilton County responded to the chairman's proclamation by announcing his support for the effort, saying he would help make judges' records available. "I believe in what the Moral Majority stands for," he said, "the precepts of God and their desire to see that justice is administered in our courts. . . . Finally, we've got somebody who is speaking out about too much leniency in the courts. . . . People are entitled to know which judges go easy on defendants."[58] Other political aspirants saw the value of playing off of Moral Majority concerns about crime as well. At a Florida election rally hosted by the Moral Majority, one local candidate mentioned law and order alongside more well-known Christian right tropes like pro-life politics and taking America back for God. According to the local paper covering the event, "His talk of 'law and order' brought a few bursts from the crowd when he promised to 'vigorously enforce' drug laws in Pinellas County."[59]

The Christian right's mobilization of law and order acquired another new valence in the 1980s: victims' rights. The crime victims' movement arose in the 1950s and 1960s, a product of progressive organizers in the United States and Europe who linked victims' concerns with the broader economic and political aims of the welfare state. In other Western nations that had a strong welfare apparatus, the victims' movements remained closely linked to the provision of social services. But the comparative weakness of the welfare state in the United States meant that victims' concerns eventually grew detached from progressive politics and instead were channeled into the retributive political consensus that coalesced in the late 1960s and 1970s (such as in Reagan's California).[60] By the 1980s it had become the lingua franca of various anticrime constituencies, the Christian right included.

President Reagan sought out guides to help craft his administration's approach to securing victims' rights, assembling a team of legal and criminological experts for a Task Force on Victims of Crime in 1982. He also invited a preacher: Pat Robertson, the president of the Christian Broadcasting Network and host of *The 700 Club* television program. Both the network and the program were leading forums for evangelical news and entertainment. Robertson was originally ordained as a Southern Baptist but exhibited charismatic sensibilities more typically associated with Pentecostals. Before his ordination, Robertson had attended Yale Law School. After failing the bar exam, he entered ministry, but his legal interests remained. He regularly interfaced with key figures in Reagan's legal circle, naming Herbert Ellingwood to the board of trustees of CBN University (later Regent University) and hosting Ed Meese (a key leader in Reagan's gubernatorial administration and later his attorney general as president) on *The 700 Club*. The legal ideology that Robertson, Ellingwood, and Meese shared (that later made its way into the Regent Law School curriculum) was a stress on God's "objective legal order that man is bound to obey."[61]

Robertson was delighted to be named to the task force. It was a sign that Reagan, who had sometimes been at odds with the religious right since assuming the presidency, was willing to accept evangelical influence on a key public issue.[62] "We live in a society that has gone to extremes at times to protect the rights of defendants, those accused of crimes, while often neglecting the rights of those victimized," Robertson said in his announcement of his acceptance of Reagan's invitation. "We hope to arrive at some practical proposals . . . that will lessen the physical, financial, and emotional toll now imposed on crime victims in our land."[63]

The task force's final report was a combination of troubling descriptions of crime victims' struggles and a series of recommendations for federal and state action. The report opened with a detailed story of a violent rape and the various challenges the victim faced in getting help, working with law enforcement, and pushing for prosecution of her assailant. At each stage, the report argued, the victim was forced to endure new trauma. Some of the report's recommendations addressed problems in this process, such as suggesting that victims need not testify in person.[64] Other parts focused on criminal justice directly, such as the recommendations for abolition of the exclusionary rule, the abolition of parole, and the limitation of judicial discretion in sentencing in order to limit unfair or "token" punishment that would do injustice to past victims or endanger future ones.[65] These recommendations for a tougher approach to crime, regular appeals from conservatives in the 1960s and 1970s, were now linked to the rights and welfare of victims.

Robertson highlighted this linkage. In a Department of Justice–sponsored interview several years later, he commented on the importance of the task force in connecting the well-being of victims with punitive justice. He spoke of challenges that rape victims faced in seeking justice, the "indignities" that caused "re-victimization." But as a result of the report, in his home state of Virginia, "something happened." Though there was still much work to be done, there had been serious progress. "We abolished parole here in the state of Virginia and I know that violent crime has gone down. We've got an exile program for anybody that's found guilty of using a firearm in the commission of a felony. I think that the idea that not only are we helping victims, we're getting tough on criminals and that's the flip side of this report."[66]

The report included specific directives for religious communities in its "Recommendations for the Ministry" section. The section's commentary began with a nod to the recent surge in religious concern for prisoners, as well as a note of distress that crime victims had been overlooked as a result: "All too often, representatives from the religious community come to court only to give comfort, support, and assistance to the accused. This is indeed a noble endeavor. . . . [But] there is as great a need for a ministry to victims as there is for a ministry to prisoners." One of the report's featured quotes from a crime victim made the same point, though more bluntly: "We were left alone to bury our daughter. . . . People don't know what to do or say so they stay away. Even the religious stayed away. To this day they visit the killer and his family weekly, but for the victim's family there doesn't seem to be any time." The need was obvious: clergy and laity should get involved in victim support and counseling and should foster a broader awareness that "every congregation will have members who are victimized."[67]

Conservative Protestant activism on crime and victims' rights occurred on the local level as well. In Philadelphia, around four hundred people (representing one hundred churches) gathered for the first meeting of Concerned Citizens against Crime at the local civic center in 1984. Under a giant banner that read, "CITIZENS VS CRIME," the Philadelphia Boys Choir performed, while local religious leaders, the police commissioner, and the assistant district attorney exhorted the gathered crowd to work as "your brother's keeper" through crime prevention. Fundamentalist icon Carl McIntire also was in attendance. Reflecting religious anticrime alliances of years past, this was a multiracial, if largely conservative, affair. The event was organized by Rev. B. Sam Hart, a prominent black pastor. For Hart, the crime victims' cause was personal; his son and daughter-in-law had been murdered in their home only months earlier. Combatting serious crimes like these would not happen through social programs or education. Instead, the answer was the change of human hearts through divine power, as well as constraint by the state. "The answer lies, principally, in being able to change a man. And this is something only God can do. This is something the church and state can work together on, hand-in-hand, to effect the spiritual side." Hart therefore spoke of his evangelistic organization's support of neighborhood-watch-style programs and partnerships with local police.[68]

The highlight of the event was the reading of a letter from President Reagan, who had previously named Hart to his civil rights commission in 1982 (though the minister resigned over criticisms of his traditional stance on homosexuality). Reagan praised the Philadelphia group's work, linking it with similar "watch programs" across the nation. "What we are really witnessing is a reaffirmation of American values," he wrote. "A sense of community and fellowship, individual responsibility, caring for family and friends, and a respect for the law."[69]

The 1980s Christian right was controversial and often ineffective in much of its direct political advocacy, with Reagan's selection of Sandra Day O'Connor (whom Christian pro-life groups opposed) as his first Supreme Court nominee being the most obvious example. But on crime, it was thoroughly in the mainstream and touching a nerve. Worries about crime, drugs, and victims' rights aligned it closely with other interest groups and engendered sympathy from people who might have otherwise looked askance at Falwell's fundamentalism. These included members of women's rights groups that increasingly joined with law-and-order coalitions in support of tougher anti–rape and sexual assault laws.[70] One member of Mothers Against Drunk Driving (a victims' rights group founded in 1980 that lobbied for more than 2,500 anti–drunk driving, victims' rights, and underage drinking laws) registered her approval of the

Moral Majority in a letter to her newspaper in 1981.[71] Though she no longer attended church, she argued, "I think more of the churches should get involved and help Jerry Falwell and the Moral Majority try to get some law and order and decency back in our country like we used to have. Jerry Falwell and the Moral Majority are the only ones who have tried to do anything in this line."[72]

Pat Robertson understood this broad appeal. He reflected on the work of the crime victims' task force in a retrospective Department of Justice interview. "I think the question was there was a cry in the society for some remedy. It was a perceived need all across the board. That's why the recommendations of this task force have found virtually universal acceptance. There's been almost no criticism of these recommendations because they touched a nerve right down to the community and I do think they've been implemented." When Robertson ran for the Republican presidential nomination in 1988, he referred to his experience on the task force to indicate his credentials as a "national policy leader."[73] He did not win the nomination, but that credential was a memento of the Christian right's influence in bolstering the anticrime cause in terms of victims' rights, terms that many other Americans readily accepted.

This competing evangelical crime cause and the populist sentiments it drew on posed big problems for Colson's reform movement. Skillful politicians picked up on this intrareligious tension. In Mississippi Colson had advocated in 1982 for alternatives to incarceration for nonviolent offenders.[74] Though he garnered support from the Democratic governor, the effort ultimately failed in the state senate. Critics had successfully marked the bills as "soft on crime" (even though they were far more modest than the original suggestions promoted by Colson). State senator Robert Crook, who opposed the reform measures, hinted that Colson was an untrustworthy carpetbagger who threatened public safety.[75] This was all standard law-and-order-style populist politicking. But Crook went further, one-upping Colson's Christian bona fides with his own diagnosis of the crime problem. The "two reasons people do not commit serious crimes," he contended, were "(1) A personal moral code based on Christian teachings and (2) Fear of swift and certain punishment as an effective deterrent to crime."[76] The message in the thick of the Bible Belt was as clear as it had been in the halls of Congress with Godwin: Colson did not have a monopoly on Christian messaging on criminal justice, and he had a long way to go if he was to convert skeptics to his cause.

Restoring Justice

Colson and other evangelicals advocating for prisoners realized that they had to take the more punitive Christian right coalition and its mobilization of victims' rights seriously if they were to gain influence and change policy. The contrast between Godwin's and Colson's congressional testimonies was clear. Dan Van Ness, Colson's associate, who had been present at the hearing, told *Christianity Today* in response, "We have to check our instinct to raise prison sentences, because it's a false impulse. It makes us look like we're getting tough, but it really doesn't accomplish anything."[77] But the question remained as to how Colson and his allies would manage the conflict over the long term, whether through direct confrontation or by building consensus with conservative Christian constituencies and Republicans and Democrats more generally. They chose the latter option, organizing two key efforts to further their religious and political influence. Along the way, they would integrate the victims' rights cause into their broader reform framework. The first effort was an ambitious campaign to pass national legislation. The second was the development of restorative justice, an alternative model to the criminal justice status quo.

Colson had a complicated relationship with the Christian right, chiefly Jerry Falwell. As Falwell entered the public eye, Colson expressed frustration with the Moral Majority leader's approach to political engagement. The problem was less about the issues Falwell mobilized on and more about the methods and his ideological foundations. Colson was privately troubled by Falwell's willingness to equate conservative politics with Christian theology, calling Falwell's equation of the two "awful" in internal memos to Prison Fellowship staff in 1980.[78] But Colson was also friendly to Falwell, calling him "brother." They each went to bat for the other professionally.[79] Falwell urged a news organization covering crime to devote attention to Colson's work, while Colson praised Falwell's adoption ministry to unwed mothers in Prison Fellowship newsletters.[80] It was a genuine, if sometimes tenuous, friendship. More than that, Colson knew he could not alienate Falwell and his allies if he was to maintain broad appeal among evangelicals.

Colson carefully fostered a relationship with Falwell, going to great lengths to quell Falwell's outrage whenever their relationship seemed to be on the rocks over political differences.[81] This paid dividends in terms of achieving sympathy for the criminal justice reform cause, seen chiefly through the impact that Colson had on Moral Majority staff member and Falwell aide Cal Thomas. When Colson wrote to the Moral Majority to protest Ron Godwin's criminal code testimony, Thomas responded considerately, saying the point "is well taken." Colson pushed the Moral Majority to consider how alternatives might be found for nonviolent offenders, and Thomas admitted he thought this idea was compelling and said he "would lobby Jerry" on it.[82] Colson was thrilled about the possibility of "converting" Falwell, telling Dan Van Ness, "This is an opportunity to turn the Moral Majority around. This would be one of the most significant things we could accomplish this year."[83]

Colson's cultivation of the Christian right's goodwill was necessary given his next big project: making a bold move on national policy, beyond state-level reforms and testimony before subcommittees. Colson had lunch with Senators Sam Nunn and William Armstrong. He convinced both of them of the humanitarian and fiscal benefits of promoting sentencing alternatives for nonviolent offenders, such as community service, instead of incarceration. The bipartisan alliance of Nunn, a Democrat from Georgia, and Armstrong, a Republican from Colorado, would ensure that the proposal would have widespread appeal. The senators invited Van Ness to help them draft the legislation.[84] On July 20, 1983, the senators introduced Senate Bill 1644, the Sentencing Improvement Act of 1983. The bill recapitulated the logic of Colson's advocacy from the past few years: reduce incarceration rates and prison overcrowding by requiring courts to use fines, probation, or community service for nonviolent offenders. And as if nodding toward skeptics, the bill also referenced and built on the success of the victims' rights movement: victims should receive restitution through payment or an arrangement of an alternative sentence. It also declared that imprisonment was totally appropriate for violent offenses or for offenders who presented a substantial danger.[85]

Colson and Van Ness mobilized broad support for the bill. They distributed a fact sheet on the legislation to Christian groups and published requests for support in their ministry newsletter.[86] Though the National Association of Evangelicals and *Christianity Today* had helped lead the evangelical charge for law and order in past decades, they joined Colson's coalition and endorsed the bill. Other progressive Christian groups joined as well.[87] Crucially, Colson also counted the Moral Majority among the supporters of the measure (the organization was likely attracted to the bill because of its emphasis on restitution for victims).[88] Armstrong and

Nunn did not mention Colson or evangelical advocacy in their floor speeches, but they did not have to when they had one of the most vocally evangelical senators on their side: Mark Hatfield. The Oregon senator delivered his own speech supporting the measure, one that repeated concern for criminals and suspicions of punitive solutions from earlier in his career.[89]

However, the bill soon ran into problems. A challenge was the presence of another major piece of criminal justice legislation, the Comprehensive Crime Control Act, a collection of bills that represented the long-hoped-for criminal code revisions that numerous members of Congress supported (the same general legislative thrust that Godwin and Colson had testified on in 1981).[90] Armstrong and Nunn argued in their floor speeches that their bill was compatible with the objectives of this other legislation, part of which included some harsher sentencing procedures for certain offenses. But there was concern among Reagan's Justice Department staff that the sentencing provisions would be a distraction. Lacking a presence on the judiciary committee, Armstrong and Nunn could not force the issue. Attempts to even add the bill in the broader legislative package as an amendment also failed. The only available option Armstrong and Nunn had remaining was to put a "sense of the Senate" resolution derived from S. 1644 into the legislation, a symbolic move with no legal force. The resolution carried with it an expiration date of two years.[91]

Hatfield was angry about the result and publicly reamed the Justice Department in response. "I am very disappointed . . . due to the fact that the Justice Department has stonewalled any effort to come up with a meaningful alternative program to sentencing." The Justice Department, he noted, had been complaining constantly about prison facilities, but its rejection of the Nunn-Armstrong measure showed that this was empty rhetoric. The "meaningless" resolution was "not a half a loaf, it is barely a crumb." Then Hatfield pivoted to the heart of the matter: the harmful punitive potential of the Comprehensive Crime Control Act if sentencing reform were not included. "Perhaps this body should pause and consider whether this highly touted anticrime bill will have the impact upon crime that it alleges." The country was facing a crime problem, he acknowledged, but tough "doubled or tripled" sentences would not deter crime. Instead, "people will be going to prison for longer periods of time . . . and our overcrowded prisons will become more so," a fiscal problem and a catalyst for heightened recidivism. "We have dodged the issue long enough and have smothered it in anticrime rhetoric long enough. Our approach to corrections is an unabashed failure."[92]

Colson was similarly irate. He dashed off a column to Prison Fellowship supporters in the ministry's monthly newsletter where he reported and explained the letdown. Ever the conservative, Colson explained the failure not as a result of a law-and-order surge or even the intransigence of the Reagan administration (he cited Attorney General William French Smith's warnings about relying too much on prisons) but as a result of the overweening power of big government: "Entrenched bureaucracies can be formidable barriers to the popular will." He argued that prosecutors in the Justice Department had opposed the measure in hopes they could maintain the "threat of prison to coerce defendants into plea bargaining." At the conclusion of the letter, he listed the contact information of Congress and the White House so that Prison Fellowship supporters could voice their support for future reform efforts. He was hopeful that a new chapter might be written with "the Christian conscience aroused—God's people sharing His passion for justice and breaking down entrenched prejudice."[93]

Colson's missive was heartfelt, but perplexing in places. If the bill was the product of such massive cultural and religious consensus, how could it fail? If Attorney General Smith was theoretically supportive of such measures, why had his Justice Department torpedoed the measure? The answer lay just as much in the even deeper cultural consensus that crime remained a threat and that it should be dealt with primarily through punitive measures. As Dan Van Ness put it a few years later, the act was "relatively simple and low-key in a lot of places, but it was very controversial."[94] It failed to gel with the broader political consensus, and the nonbinding sense of the Senate resolution (which was not renewed two years later) was "like a small weather system meeting a hurricane."[95] This hurricane had many contributing forces, such as the demands of victims' groups and inner-city advocates concerned with rising urban crime. These were messages that other conservative evangelicals had made their own. It was striking that the Moral Majority, an organization that had not offered nearly the level of constructive engagement on criminal justice matters that Colson had, nevertheless saw the broader cultural consensus and political outcomes align with its earlier lobbying. A few years later, Cal Thomas even indicated his own support for decarceration in a column that called for a reconsideration of the Nunn-Armstrong bill.[96] But the damage had already been done. The effect of the sentencing portion of the Comprehensive Crime Control Act was a set of guidelines that stressed "certainty and severity"—the use of mandatory minimum sentences became standard and, as one report put it, "greatly increased both the percentage of individuals receiving prison sentences and the length of sentences for many offenses."[97] Hatfield's prediction about the core legislation had come true, and his warnings about prison overcrowding would prove prescient as well, as incarceration rates rose exponentially over the following decade.[98]

Over the rest of the 1980s, Colson and his allies at Prison Fellowship made some significant changes in their approach. Some were organizational. In 1983 Prison Fellowship incorporated its reform efforts under the separate entity of Justice Fellowship, distinct from its prison ministry work.[99] Dan Van Ness was appointed Justice Fellowship president a year later. But the major change was what Justice Fellowship staff called a "paradigm shift," one that placed the needs of crime victims at the forefront and intentionally framed the cause as criminal justice reform, not prison reform. It also was an attempt to circumvent the inefficiencies and unpredictability of governmental bureaucracy, the very system that had bitten them in the Nunn-Armstrong ordeal. They called it "restorative justice." This paradigm shift gave evangelicals a framework to address humanitarian ills, while also ameliorating the concerns of a public that had placed the needs of crime victims at the center of debates about crime and punishment.

The restorative justice model was not the invention of Colson or Van Ness. Colson and his evangelical allies had instead drawn from an unlikely source as they looked to reframe their political engagement: the Anabaptist tradition. From their origins in the sixteenth century, Anabaptists differed from the Catholic and the magisterial Reformed traditions in their commitments to adult baptism, pacifism, suspicion (or even rejection) of civil authority, congregational polity, and a literal emphasis on the commands of Jesus. They accordingly developed ecclesiological systems and theological rationale to address peacefully matters of church conflict. For example, assorted Anabaptist traditions practiced "binding and loosing," a communally driven form of confrontation of offenders and discipline drawn from Jesus's commands to his followers in Matthew 18 to bring unresolved disputes before the church. The hope was that offenders would be reconciled to those they had harmed and be restored to the earthly Christian community. This presaged their eternal reconciliation. As Jesus said, "Whatever you bind on earth will be bound in heaven, and whatever you loose on earth will be loosed in heaven" (Matthew 18:18, New International Version). Anabaptist groups often disagreed on how to apply these general theological principles. However, they shared an overarching goal: restore the health of the community after a violation and leave the door open to the reintegration of the offender into community life. Both approaches also rejected violent punishment of offenders and downplayed the obligations of offenders to civil authority.[100]

In the North American context, Anabaptist groups continued restorative disciplinary practices, and in the twentieth century they began increasingly arguing for their public value beyond ecclesial concerns. Anabaptist voices in conversations on crime and punishment were often eschewed, such as in the 1960s when neo-evangelicals at *Christianity Today* indicated their preference for more Reformed modes of thought over that of Mennonite theologian John Howard Yoder on criminal justice matters. But beginning in the late 1970s, the Mennonite scholar and activist Howard Zehr began renewing the Anabaptist-style disciplinary vision. In 1978 he worked with social workers and probation staff to develop the Victim-Offender Reconciliation Program. This program emphasized conflict resolution through face-to-face meetings and restitution agreements with the aid of trained third parties, often as a partial or total substitute for prison time.[101] He eventually began contending for restorative justice's import in broader evangelical circles, publishing an article in the journal of the Christian Legal Society that argued for a recovery of forgiveness: "[Christ] urges us to love those who offend us, to welcome them back, to reconcile them to the community, to forgive and to restore, to move beyond legal retaliation to no retaliation."[102] A truly Christian vision of justice, according to Zehr, depended on Christlike restoration of wrongdoers.[103]

Love and forgiveness (even of criminals) were not unfamiliar concepts to evangelicals. But under Mennonite supervision, the restorative approach would have limitations. This was evident in the rest of Zehr's Christian Legal Society piece, where he spoke about American criminal injustice in terms of the moral problems of militarism. With arms buildups and law and order, "the reasoning process is exactly the same. . . . Both rely upon threat and force, upon the 'big stick' approach." The message was emblazoned in large bold letters in a Mennonite Central Committee–designed graphic that the journal published as an accompaniment to Zehr's article: "Crime is a peace issue."[104] This may have been a compelling message for certain Christian social justice advocates, particularly the small evangelical left, who were no strangers to antiwar activism and militarist skepticism. But this vision would be harder to sell to most evangelicals, who were far more comfortable with America's capacity to mobilize violence at home and abroad.

Colson and the staff of Justice Fellowship believed that they had something to add to the Mennonite restorative justice equation: popularity and the possibility of large-scale integration with the state. Zehr and his allies had largely toiled in relative obscurity, with their activism restricted primarily to Mennonite enclaves in Indiana and Virginia, a reflection of the denomination's limited widespread appeal. Besides lending his own name to the movement, Colson brought a Reformed sensibility to restorative justice, one that allowed for the more positive role of governmental authority and power in the theologically rooted equation of reconciliation and restoration. As Van Ness put it, "We saw all the restorative justice work going among the Mennonites, but also recognized that they weren't really saying much about the state. Justice Fellowship could come in and make it possible for policy to be implemented."[105] The hope was that Colson's high profile and political savvy could help move a small Mennonite movement to new heights.

Just as Colson had something to offer, restorative justice likewise gave Colson the framework to name victims as his foremost concern and to circumvent the state's burdensome obligations and procedures. According to restorative justice theory, American legal procedure was flawed in how it framed the stakeholders in a criminal case as "state v. defendant." This framework was an attempt to satisfy the state's inherent demand for justice (represented by the common image of the balance of the scales in courtrooms), but it tragically overlooked the victim of the crime. By contrast, restorative justice framed an offense as a wrong against the immediate victim and the community more generally. The restoration was not a rebalancing of the metaphysical scales as much as it was an attempt to make tangible human relationships right. Restorative justice practitioners therefore sought ways for victims to enter into guided conversation with offenders so that their needs could be discussed and met. This often meant financial restitution. But it could also result in direct conversation with offenders about *why* they committed a crime and what its damaging effects had been.[106]

While keeping the broader contours of the restorative approach intact, Colson and his allies added their own rhetorical twist. Restorative justice allowed them a way to frame crime to the public as a harrowing matter and criminals as feared enemies. In 1981 Zehr had lamented the recent turn in American culture to identifying criminals as "an alien 'enemy' who is sharply differentiated from us. . . . Viewing offenders as objects rather than persons allows them to be treated in inhumane ways without pangs of conscience."[107] By contrast, when Justice Fellowship's Van Ness published his restorative justice book *Crime and Its Victims* in 1986, InterVarsity Press placed an image on the cover of a frightening criminal figure reaching through a broken house window to undo a latch. The gloved hand of the criminal and his glaring countenance were a stark contrast to the flowery wallpaper visible around the window. Matching the artwork was the title itself: "CRIME," in large text at the top of the cover, followed by "VICTIMS" in significantly smaller text at the bottom. Van Ness initially disliked the cover, but the evangelical InterVarsity Press knew its audience (and the book went on to win several evangelical publishing awards).[108] By foregrounding criminals, crime, and the needs of victims, restorative justice enabled Colson to move away from the prison inmate as the sole object of humanitarian compassion. Justice Fellowship, as one internal description of the organization's mission and history read, had moved from prison reform to criminal justice reform.[109] With fear of crime continually on the rise, possible converts to the reform cause were simply not going to see the humane treatment of prisoners as an issue of primary concern. But framing the issue in mutualistic terms, linking prisoners' rights with victims' rights, offered a way forward.

Restorative justice was an attempt to triangulate numerous strands of evangelical social engagement at one time, in one package. The cover of Van Ness's *Crime and Its Victims* was emblazoned with laudatory blurbs from Cal Thomas, Carl F. H. Henry, and Mark Hatfield, respectively representing the religious right (Thomas had only recently left the Moral Majority), the moderate evangelical center, and its liberal wing. This kind of triangulation continued into the 1990s. Colson wrote a lead article on restorative justice for the law review of Pat Robertson's Regent University. He framed restorative justice not as a progressive social activist agenda or program but as a recovery of biblical values and "objective truth," precisely what Ed Meese had identified as Regent's legal tradition in his introductory piece in the school's first law review a few years earlier. Colson used the biblical example of the tax collector Zacchaeus, who made restitution to victims he had defrauded after meeting Jesus. If the events had happened today, Colson argued, Zacchaeus would have pled not guilty, the victims would not have been reimbursed, and Zacchaeus would sit in prison (and likely reoffend upon release). Instead, "Jesus' response was so much better. Justice was done. Truth was acknowledged. Peace was established."[110] Here was Colson, a conservative evangelical with strong humanitarian sympathies, translating an Anabaptist ethical vision into terms that future lawyers from a Christian right icon's law school could find appealing.

Remaining Tensions

The careful articulation and implementation of restorative justice had seemingly enabled Colson and Prison Fellowship to become all things to all people in their criminal justice reform efforts. On paper, restorative justice made sense; victims received justice, offenders paid back their debts, neighborhoods became safer, and the government saved prison space. And when tried, it often worked. Van Ness and other Justice Fellowship staff made progress lobbying local leaders on the efficacy of the model. They set up task forces in twenty-two states in order to promote restorative principles to churches and legislatures. In 1991 these task forces helped pass twenty-one separate bills that aimed to reduce prison overcrowding while also mandating offender restitution to victims. In conservative Alabama, Justice Fellowship helped provide a "middle road between imprisonment and routine probation for nonviolent offenders." In Maryland, Justice Fellowship successfully lobbied for three new laws (in partnership with victims' rights groups) that expanded victim eligibility for compensation. Restorative justice also gave the reform effort cover to push for legislation that was more prisoner focused, such as a Justice Fellowship–sponsored bill in Minnesota that kept juveniles from adult facilities.[111] With victim-focused restorative justice as its driving paradigm, it seemed at the turn of the 1990s that Colson and his reform-minded allies might have found a model for shifting the tide of American law and order.

And yet, into the 1990s, prison populations still grew. Sentences continued to toughen.[112] Politicians bent over backward to appear tough on crime. Indeed, punitive anticrime politics became such a bipartisan affair that it seemed as if Democrats might outdo Republicans. One famous example was Governor Bill Clinton's refusing clemency for convicted murderer Ricky Ray Rector, who had a severely limited mental capacity, as a way to engender sympathy from voters during the 1992 presidential primary.[113]

What happened? Why did the careful lobbying from Colson and like-minded evangelical humanitarians repeatedly fail to gain broader traction? Part of the answer has to do with expediency, not ideology. It was simply easier and cheaper for politicians and their supporters (at least, in the short term) to construct justice systems that locked offenders away. By their very nature, restitution and restorative justice efforts were challenging to implement. They were resource intensive and required the buy-in of victims, law enforcement, and offenders. It was easier for most involved to plea bargain away any given case so as to move through the criminal court docket as quickly as possible.[114]

In terms of religious engagement, something else occurred. Though the Moral Majority dissipated in 1989, the Christian Coalition emerged the same year and quickly became the leading religious right lobbying organization. It made crime one of its key issues. Unlike earlier Christian law-and-order activism, however, the Christian Coalition's platform reflected some of the new elements that Colson had helped introduce into conservative politics. Ralph Reed, the head of the Christian Coalition, knew Colson's testimony and work well. After Reed has his own radical Christian conversion experience as a young Republican activist, Colson's *Born Again* was the first book (other than the Bible) that he read.[115]

In 1995 the Christian Coalition debuted its *Contract with the American Family* in a room in the capitol, with several members of Congress in tow, including Speaker of the House Newt Gingrich. The "contract" contained ten points that were a combination of religious right concerns from a decade earlier (restricting pornography and abortions) and new additions drawn from the new compassionate conservative agenda (encouraging support of private charities over governmental programs). The contract's tenth point was titled "Punishing Criminals, Not Victims." Parts of it were classic law and order. It urged the personal responsibility of criminals, noted the dangers of rising crime, and advocated "swift, sure punishment" as a response. It warned that not enough criminals saw prison time. But the contract then pivoted to the positive possibilities of community service. It quoted Colson as the authority, using a story that he regularly told about a doctor he had met while at Maxwell who he believed should have been allowed to practice medicine as a form of community service. It then moved to a discussion of victims' rights and criminal justice that "restores the victim" in addition to punishing the offender. Though it never used the term "restorative justice," the contract drew partly on the framework that restorative justice often represented, highlighting the need to reframe criminal justice by shifting the focus away from the offender's obligations to the state and toward the offender's obligations to the victim. But unlike restorative justice, the contract saw the restorative stress as a desirable net loss for offenders. The heading of this section was "Criminal Rights versus Victim Rights," suggesting that the two were in direct conflict (a point restorative justice advocates like Colson did not make).[116]

It was this kind of activism that produced punitive legislation in the mid-1990s, not only in terms of pushing conservatives to act but also leading liberals to take up the anticrime cause as well. One of President Bill Clinton's landmark pieces of legislation was the Violent Crime and Law Enforcement Act of 1994, which built on Reagan's legacy by further cementing incarceration as the primary governmental response to crime through regulations that further lengthened prison terms and increased the likelihood of imprisonment.[117] To justify tougher crime policy, Clinton and his allies cited political scientist John DiIulio Jr.'s concept of "superpredators," which warned of a growing cadre of "radically impulsive, brutally remorseless youngsters." The only correct response to these "superpredators," DiIulio argued, was to put more people in prison, or, as First Lady Hillary Clinton argued at the time with direct reference to the term, to "bring them to heel."[118] Democrats obliged, having DiIulio testify on behalf of their legislation, while conservatives likewise concurred. Former Reagan cabinet member William Bennett coauthored DiIulio's book *Body Count* (which helped popularize the superpredator argument), while the Christian Coalition cited DiIulio in its *Contract with the American Family* on the necessity to consider criminals as moral agents deserving punishment in the face of rising crime.[119]

Restorative justice was lost in this storm. It was a compelling program, but easily co-opted or eclipsed for more simplistic solutions. As Dan Van Ness put it, restorative justice was like classical music, and law-and-order politics like rock 'n' roll: if you have both on at the same time, even at the same volume, people will hear the beat-driven sound of rock. Restorative justice had dynamics that were appealing to many, but its implementation required a level of nuance that was hard to attain, particularly for politicians seeking votes.[120]

This was the paradoxical legacy of Colson's criminal justice reform efforts: like the prisoners he ministered to, he advocated solutions that met fellow conservatives (particularly Christian conservatives) where they were, on their own terms. The downside was that Colson sometimes gave conservatives ways to wriggle out of thinking too critically about their own positions on crime and punishment. This not only occurred on issues related directly to restorative justice. Colson's use of Yochelson and Samenow's theories to frame the crime problem in terms of individual choice made more systemic analyses difficult. He was not always clear on this issue himself. Colson would speak of his own understanding that crime was a challenging problem because people often faced difficult economic choices; he said regularly that every person, no matter how moral, was only a few missed meals away from becoming a thief.[121] But his emphasis on personal responsibility, while useful for framing offender obligations in restorative matters and the depths of God's grace, made it easier for fellow conservatives who mobilized his ideas (such as Reed) to ignore socioeconomic problems that underpinned behavior deemed criminal.

Critics of Yochelson and Samenow's work, the theoretical foundation of Colson's approach, had anticipated this in the late 1970s. Academic reviewers expressed concern that Yochelson and Samenow's work, by discounting rehabilitation, would play into a punitive penal philosophy. It would be "grist for hard-liners," as an otherwise sympathetic reviewer in *Science* put it.[122] Reviewers noted that the Yochelson and Samenow did not actually advocate retribution in their study but contended that this would be the broader effect if their theory was implemented.[123] This was analogous to what happened with Colson. By advocating for a similar understanding of the fully rational, morally determinative "criminal personality," he again made it easier for others to accept that theory while rejecting his own compassionate solutions. Law, without gospel.

Economics was a comparable issue. Colson regularly complained that the government was spending too much money building new prisons. He attracted the interest of fiscal conservatives who believed the same thing, particularly when faced with tightening state budgets. When asked by a Washington State reporter about what impact budget cuts would have on his reform program, Colson replied, "In a sense, that sort of thing has helped. . . . The answer is not more prisons. The answer is more alternatives to prison." However, Colson left the door open for conservatives to embrace his fiscal skepticism but do little to address other issues at stake. The result was political cover to defund what in-prison programs did exist, hoping that churches and prison ministries could pick up the slack. When they did not, there was little accountability. The same reporter who observed Colson's delight in the defunding of prison programs also noted that the reform picture in Washington State as a whole was still far from ideal. Though Colson had pushed some reforms, prison program budgets were still getting slashed and some facilities remained overcrowded.[124]

Moments like this exemplified how compassionate conservatives were unable to fathom or address the structural inequities linked to the rise of neoliberalism more broadly. Colson's rhetoric about prisons regularly eclipsed his ability to offer a constructive response. This was a problem facing other religious social service providers emerging at the same time as well. As Jason Hackworth has shown, Habitat for Humanity made a devastating public critique of governmental housing projects possible. It showed how inefficient governmental housing programs were by offering the same services more cheaply and effectively, a development that the media and politicians trumpeted. As a private organization, though, it was never able to fill the housing void itself, but it effectively (if unintentionally) lodged the self-fulfilling prophecy into the public mind that the governmental effort was doomed to fail (and therefore worthy of being cut).[125]

Colson's mind also changed in important ways that played into problematic accommodations and compromises. Beginning in the late 1980s, Colson consciously adopted the "worldview" ministry mantle, speaking out on a host of cultural and theological issues from a conservative evangelical perspective, such as abortion, religious liberty, postmodernism, and feminism.[126] Though he had always held strong views on many of these issues personally (and sometimes referenced them in print), now he made opining on them a key part of his public ministry. The most prominent example was Colson's public advocacy for US entry into Iraq in 2002, under the rationale that a preemptive strike was "charitable" and accorded with "just war" requirements.[127]

Certain aspects of Colson's understanding of crime and punishment sharpened or were thrown into stark relief as he waded deeper into these other cultural and political battles. His change of heart on the death penalty was one prominent example. In 1982 Colson received a note from a Prison Fellowship staff member that the famed serial killer John Wayne Gacy had written the organization from death row. Gacy had been given a Prison Fellowship newsletter and wanted more ministry literature. Sensing the seriousness of this exchange, Colson began corresponding with Gacy directly, sending him books and eventually meeting with him in person. Gacy's replies included a pencil drawing he had completed of Jesus crowned with thorns, captioned "Christ has Risen."[128] Though Colson was on record as being against the death penalty as late as 1990, just a few years later he reported that the experience had disgusted him.[129] He believed Gacy to be arrogant and without "a hint of remorse," despite claiming to be a Christian. It was this experience that led Colson to evolve on capital punishment: "There was simply no other appropriate response than execution if justice was to be served." He acknowledged flaws in administration of the death penalty but ultimately came to believe it was the biblical solution to crimes of premeditated murder. If Colson was to commit fully to defending the "sanctity of life" on matters like abortion, then he believed he had to support the execution of offenders like Gacy out of respect for the lives of his victims. From the mid-1990s on, Colson regularly returned to the Gacy story and the "conversion" it had prompted. Even as Prison Fellowship remained internally divided on the issue, evangelical publications and websites broadcast Colson's new message in direct opposition to anti–death penalty appeals from other Christians.[130]

Race was a similarly complicated and consequential matter. Throughout his career, Colson struggled to navigate racial issues. He admitted in *Life Sentence* that in the early days of Prison Fellowship, he had been "insensitive" to John Staggers, an African American ministry partner. Even worse, Colson confessed he had spoken to a large group of black prisoners and repeatedly referred to one of his fellow Maxwell inmates as a "black boy." Staggers was aghast that Colson did not understand the troubling nature of racialized language like this. Colson confessed his "clumsy" actions and the "little honest effort" he had made to understand "black attitudes and concerns."[131]

Though Colson acknowledged his own limitations, he nonetheless believed racism was less of a structural matter and something that could be overcome through faith and fellowship. Elsewhere in *Life Sentence*, Colson told stories of racial reconciliation, his refreshed racial understanding paralleling that of black nationalists and Klan members coming to Christ and learning to treat each other respectfully.[132] This general approach, one that persisted throughout his career, led other African American prison ministry leaders to note that Colson's leadership on justice issues, while helpful in many ways, "must be qualified." In an op-ed published after Colson's death in 2012, Harold Dean Trulear called Colson's relationship with black churches "uneasy" and said that these congregations had been frustrated by Prison Fellowship's "paternalistic" approach. Real partnerships, Trulear argued, should look less like smoothed-over stories of "soul-winning" and entail more investment of predominantly white national ministry organizations in local black congregations.[133] Prison Fellowship responded, calling Trulear's words "food for thought," but complained that his critique was "ideologically loaded" and unhelpful. Instead, "both sides" of the race divide had to come together.[134] This was the stock reply of color-blind evangelicalism, and in line with Colson's own approach.

Though he saw racism as sinful, Colson critiqued black voices and progressive positions that appeared to him to be divisive or distracting, or that did not toe what he saw as the obviously correct political lines. This approach intensified in the late 1980s and the following years. In 1991 Colson coauthored a book with former drugstore chain CEO Jack Eckerd, entitled *Why America Doesn't Work*, that bemoaned the loss of the national work ethic and the rise of welfare programs. He singled out African Americans as susceptible, contending that they needed to recover the "rich tradition of family and work" that had characterized their communities before Great Society–style welfare intruded, leaving in its wake an underclass of black mothers who bore illegitimate children just to keep their food stamp benefits. Colson thought he was offering a critique of the welfare state that would empower black Americans (and ultimately drive down the incarceration rate), but his analysis reveled in the racialized "welfare queen" tropes that were common in Reagan-era conservatism, which played into harmful stereotypes and justified divestment in black communities. After all, he argued, "the problems of the inner cities are less structural and institutional than they are behavioral." The success of black self-starters like Clarence Thomas proved to Colson that the limitations of unjust racial and economic structures were able to be overcome, and perhaps even illusory altogether.[135]

Similarly, in a 1996 *Christianity Today* column, Colson discussed the "chill" he felt when black and white inmates separated themselves at a prison ministry event. He said it was the same chill he felt when watching Louis Farrakhan decry the "separate and unequal" America or when he heard people say, in the aftermath of the O. J. Simpson trial, that "whites and blacks do not see things the same way." Colson believed postmodernism was tearing apart America's common culture of liberty, seen in the "proponents of 'Black English'" and the desire of African Americans and Native Americans to drop the "American" modifier in their identities. As he attacked the idea that there were "black truths" and "white truths," Colson echoed the common evangelical worry about the loss of objective truth. But the fact that the targets in this column were racial minorities was illuminating. In discounting particularity, refusing to acknowledge the ways race continued to shape American life, and dismissing those who pointed this fact out, Colson's confident argument for a racially neutral, "objective" Christian worldview ran the risk of simply reifying whiteness.[136]

The implications of Colson's racial consciousness, understanding of crime, and renewed sense of appreciation for the role of civil authority coalesced in his immensely popular book *How Now Shall We Live* (and later in *Justice That Restores*). The book sounded familiar tones on the need for justice reform and for a religious reckoning with a secularizing, postmodern society. But new here was Colson's endorsement of "broken windows"–style policing as a way to restore God's peace to urban neighborhoods. This model of policing assumed that signs of social disorder in neighborhoods (such as broken windows) invited more crime, and therefore law enforcement should be proactive in prosecuting crimes (often misdemeanors) that might spark further disorder, such as loitering or panhandling. Critics of the model pointed out that this mode of "order-maintenance policing" increased police power of surveillance (seen most famously through controversial "stop-and-frisk" strategies and antiloitering laws targeting gangs) and, ultimately, the number of arrests and people put behind bars. The practice's power to actually reduce crime has been questioned as well.[137] Colson nevertheless championed the theory. Linking crime to "a flawed worldview," he argued that communities that did away with laws against vagrancy and loitering had bought into the secular mythology of civil libertarianism. Broken-windows theory was therefore a religious breakthrough, a "fundamental biblical truth" of *shalom,* a "rightly ordered community" that prevented crime before it happened.

Colson believed this was actually an argument *against* reactionary law-and-order politics, citing Saint Augustine to explain how focus on achieving *tranquillitas ordinis* (tranquility produced by order) kept the state more focused on developing peaceful community life rather than "chas[ing] down criminals." But he ignored how vagrancy, loitering, and other crimes could be easily racialized and how expanded police power would inevitably affect people of color. Colson knew that activists and scholars had challenged the practice, but he stuck with the theory. Though he hailed nonpunitive private community development initiatives as well, he praised the New York Police Department directly for developing an expansive vision of crime fighting, where traffic violators, turnstile jumpers, and panhandlers were brought to heel in service of *shalom.* Presumably these arrestees would have found themselves among the inmates Colson and his colleagues ministered to, adding to the ever-growing number of

American prisoners.[138] Arguments like these alienated Colson from progressives and people of color who shared his prison concerns, and activists who wished to place race, inequality, and skepticism of law enforcement at the center of their analysis of justice issues. Though Colson had never seen himself as walking in lockstep with the likes of the ACLU, by the end of his career he was increasingly framing his ministry in direct opposition to progressives on various non–prison related matters.

Colson and his conservative allies believed there was an upside, however. By fostering trust with fellow conservatives and by making his own shifts into more traditionally conservative ideological territory, Colson was able to soften some hardline hearts over the long run. Prison populations continued to grow into the 2000s, but after the 2008 financial crisis it became apparent to many lawmakers that the cost was unsustainable. Colson had continued to cultivate relationships and preach his reform cause, and he ventured deeper into other conservative political and ideological battles. It further endeared him to conservative activists and politicians. Chief among them was Pat Nolan, a former California Republican legislator who had been imprisoned in 1994 for crimes relating to illicit payments from campaign donors. While in prison, Nolan became acquainted with Prison Fellowship, and Colson invited him to lead Justice Fellowship when he was released. As political scientists David Dagan and Steven Teles have noted, Colson (who was nearing the end of his career) and Nolan "were able to form a genuine reform cadre, one with power at the highest levels of the Republican party."[139]

In contrast to Dan Van Ness, who was a political independent and concentrated Justice Fellowship's work on connections to progressive evangelicals like Howard Zehr, Nolan guided Justice Fellowship to directly engage with conservative elites. Though Nolan repudiated the punitive policy he had advocated for as a legislator, he still had the Republican bona fides that allowed him to reach figures like Newt Gingrich.[140] He and Gingrich penned a *Washington Post* op-ed in 2011 that declared, "The criminal justice system is broken, and conservatives must lead the way in fixing it."[141] The op-ed also publicized the new Right on Crime Campaign, a collection of conservative signatories (such as antitax crusader Grover Norquist and family values activist Tony Perkins) who urged focus on the "huge costs in dollars and lost human potential" as a result of overincarceration. Nolan's influence in forming the coalition had been instrumental. The result, as Dagan and Seles put it, was "a new conventional wisdom" for conservatives on criminal justice. The political consequences could be seen in red states like Georgia, where Republican governor Nathan Deal, at the behest of conservative lobbyists affiliated with the Right on Crime movement and evangelical pastors organized by Prison Fellowship, pushed legislation that allowed for reduced sentencing options for key nonviolent offenses and increased funding for drug treatment. Other conservative states followed suit with similar programs.[142]

The story of John DiIulio Jr., the scholar who had previously provided the ideological foundation for punitive crime policy in the mid-1990s with his "super-predator" warnings, was emblematic of this broader political shift. In the early 1990s DiIulio met Colson at a dinner for conservative leaders and began to debate prison policy. As DiIulio put it, it was a battle between "me as the young get-tough hawk and him as the old pro-reform dove." DiIulio undercut Colson by challenging his use of statistics (DiIulio himself had authored some of the reports Colson regularly cited). But instead of taking the move personally or renouncing his ideological nemesis, over the next few years Colson continued to gently push DiIulio. By the end of the decade, with a "renewed Catholic heart," DiIulio had "joined Colson's pro-reform 'restorative justice' chorus" and begun advocating for rapid decarceration, increased funding for treatment programs, and the end of mandatory-minimum drug laws. Colson, according to DiIulio, "softened and spiritualized my views on crime."[143] This was classic Colson: careful outreach to a key influencer, pushing him to a change of heart that could, in turn, lead to a change in prisons.

Colson died in 2012, but his reform legacy persisted. The 2016 election was emblematic of the simultaneous hope and peril of his work on criminal justice and prison reform issues. In 2016 voters passed several important criminal justice reform referenda in states across the country. Many of these referenda passed in red states, with Republican voters leading the push. They were the product of concentrated Right on Crime lobbying from figures like Pat Nolan (who had since left Justice Fellowship to become the director of the American Conservative Union Foundation's Center for Criminal Justice Reform) and Prison Fellowship (which had reintegrated Justice Fellowship under its organizational umbrella as an advocacy division). At the same time, however, these voters also pushed a Republican into the White House: Donald Trump, the self-proclaimed "law and order candidate" who regularly mobilized racist tropes concerning crime, particularly that of migrants and Muslims.[144] Trump installed the like-minded Jeff Sessions, one of the country's most vocal proponents of tougher antidrug prosecution measures, as his attorney general. Even within Trump's own administration, however, a tension could be seen. Because of the influence of conservative evangelical criminal justice reform advocates, in his 2018 State of the Union address Trump urged prison reform and "second chances" for inmates and signed the First Step Act later that year, the most expansive piece of federal justice reform legislation in years.[145]

The contemporary cause of prison and criminal justice reform remains in doubt, for many of the same reasons that efforts in the mid-1980s were stymied. Progressive activists have targeted "the new Jim Crow" with vigor, pushing liberal political consensus away from Clintonian law and order. Some progressive critics have pointed out that the First Step Act is far too modest in scope or that its advocates do not represent the concerns of people of color.[146] But if mass incarceration is to be combatted with any degree of consensus in the current divisive political and cultural climate, it will be because figures like Chuck Colson made the issue viable for a broad spectrum of middle America. More than this, Colson was the most prominent voice in making sure Americans understood that prisons and criminal justice were religious issues, ones that people of faith needed to take seriously. Michelle Alexander, lawyer, author of *The New Jim Crow,* and the leading public authority on mass incarceration, recently joined the faculty of Union Theological Seminary because she came to see the religious valences of the issue. She said, "I would like to imagine that a wide range of people of faith and conscience who sing songs from different keys may be able to join in a common chorus that shakes the foundations of our unjust political, legal and economics systems, and ushers in a new America."[147] If this wide-ranging social movement that can change the hearts and minds of Americans is someday fully realized, it will be linked to the legacy of Colson, a compassionate conservative who also knew something about the power of conversion.

CONCLUSION

On February 21, 2018, Billy Graham died at his home in Montreat, North Carolina, at the age of ninety-nine. Graham's son Franklin had procured two caskets a few years earlier, one for his father and one for his mother, Ruth (who died in 2007). The caskets were simple, made of inexpensive wood and lined only with a mattress pad. They cost $215 apiece. Though they were economical, viewers would have noticed the caskets had been handcrafted with care. If they looked closely, they would have seen three names burned into the side: Richard Liggett, Paul Krolowitz, and Clifford Bowman. These were three men who had built the caskets while incarcerated at Louisiana State Penitentiary, popularly known as Angola. Several other inmates assisted with the project as well, all part of a carpentry program that Angola warden Burl Cain had helped initiate in order to provide caskets for inmates at the prison.

Graham's burial in this casket was significant for two reasons. First, it was physical evidence of the long-established linkage of Graham's public identity with particular conceptions of crime, punishment, and redemption. Though Graham had not regularly preached in prisons, it seemed perfectly natural to his son (and journalists reporting his burial) to have him buried in a casket built by the hands of prisoners. It was a symbol of the evangelical piety that he represented, a faith that stressed God's love and forgiveness of sin. The casket was a symbol of Graham's message of the gospel's capacity to transform individual lives through the power of conversion, even those in the depths of prisons. The Angola carpenters themselves realized this. Graham "showed us the love of God," one of the men said. "Nobody is beyond redemption. I've been redeemed."[1]

Second, the casket indicated the moral complications of this same linkage. Though the inmates counted it "a great honor and a privilege" to build Graham's casket, they were nonetheless caught up in a prison system filled with inequality and problems. Angola's inmate population was 80 percent African American.[2] Louisiana's correctional system budget reportedly dedicated only 1 percent of its funds to comparable rehabilitation programs for inmates.[3] The inmates' work was a form of low-cost convict labor that Louisiana and other states regularly utilized, what critics often named as exploitative and a form of modern-day slavery (as of 2017, the pay scale for inmates in Louisiana ranged from four cents to one dollar per hour).[4] Cain himself was an overseer in this system even as he was an evangelical hero. He was the facilitator of the spread of the gospel even as he presided over the execution process, including the lethal injection of his brethren. Even when read in the most positive light possible, the story of evangelicals' fascination with places like Angola threatened to obscure these troubling realities. For the Graham family, the coffins were a testimony to God's power of forgiveness and love. This power, however, was easily spiritualized and streamlined. The tension between these two aspects of Graham's burial in an Angola casket was one that evangelicals had wrestled with over the past half century as they made concern about crime, punishment, and prisons a key marker of their public identity.

Recent evangelical activity suggests a continuation of Graham's legacy, with attendant complications. Not long after a very public evangelical-style conversion in 2019, hip-hop star Kanye West traveled to the Harris County jail in Houston to perform songs for inmates from his new chart-topping *Jesus Is King* album. "This is a mission, not a show," he reportedly told jail residents. Performing next to a correctional officer, across from a large group of orange-jumpsuit-clad inmates who bobbed to the music, West rapped lines from his 2004 hit "Jesus Walks" that acquired a particular poignancy given the setting: "To the hustlers, killers, murderers, drug dealers, even the strippers, Jesus walks for them." Inmates, almost all of whom were people of color, raised their hands, wept, and knelt in prayer, while members of West's Sunday Service collective invited inmates to accept Jesus as their personal Lord and Savior.

Law enforcement officials and conservative politicians hailed West. The Harris County sheriff saw the performance as complementary to his own office's goals. "We need to be firm with crime, we want our communities safe, but we don't have to lose our compassion," he remarked in comments to West and his fellow performers, a video of which was subsequently released via the Sheriff's Office. Channeling past conversionist anticrime tropes, Greg Abbott, the Republican governor of Texas, tweeted, "What Kanye West does to inspire the incarcerated is transformative. Saving one soul at a time. Inmates who turn to God may get released earlier [because] of good behavior & may be less likely to commit future crimes." Ending crime, in league with the state (or at least perceived to be), one soul at a time—West was a new convert, but he was acting and being interpreted in a manner with a long history.[5]

Evangelicals have not only continued to minister in prisons; some have sought to operate prisons themselves. As scholars like Winnifred Sullivan have shown, evangelicals associated with Prison Fellowship ran an entire wing of an Iowa prison in the early 2000s in an attempt to introduce inmates to spiritual, rehabilitative programming.[6] Though the effort was struck down by a judge for establishment clause violations in 2006, similar "faith-based" and "character-based" state programs that utilize broader language but remain open to evangelical influence have continued. These mobilize religion as an official part of the prison itself.[7] Arguments that "more God" equals "less crime," though perhaps dismissed by secular elites and social scientists, will no doubt continue to exert influence in the management of prisons and correctional programs. Indeed, these programs have been exported abroad to Latin America, where resource-strapped governments have welcomed evangelical influence in their prisons and anti-gang programs.[8]

Though they remain leading voices in criminal justice reform, white evangelicals have also retained their fervor for crime fighting, policing, and security. Popular refrains urging Christians to "back the blue," particularly in the aftermath of publicized instances of police brutality, showcase evangelical support for law and order even in the midst of controversy. In the aftermath of high-profile instances of police killings of African American men in 2015, Franklin Graham posted a message on Facebook to his numerous followers: "Most police shootings can be avoided. It comes down to respect for authority and obedience. The Bible says to submit to your leaders and those in authority 'because they keep watch over you as those who must give an account.'" Polling around this time showed high white evangelical support for law enforcement, with 71 percent saying police were doing an "excellent" or "good" job. Only 45 percent of black Protestants agreed. Each group's rating of police treatment of racial minorities was even more stark, with 68 percent of white evangelicals offering a positive rating, compared with 25 percent of black Protestants. Urban church planter Efrem Smith explained the difference to *Christianity Today*, complicating Graham's apologia: "African Americans, especially in under-resourced urban communities, have had a very different relationship with police departments than most white evangelical communities. . . . Many white evangelicals who have never had a negative experience with the police based on their skin color can have an imbalanced view."[9]

Contemporary evangelical crime concern goes beyond American policing and prisons. Organizations like International Justice Mission, a Christian anti–human trafficking organization with substantial evangelical connections, works overseas with state authorities to rescue victims and bring offenders to justice. Highly professional in its push for social concern and sophisticated in its rhetoric about the Christian responsibility to end slavery, it nonetheless depends on partnership with the coercive powers of the state as they "bring criminals to justice" and "strengthen justice systems" by providing training for police and judges.[10] In its early years, International Justice Mission and similar operations embraced their role as "Cops for Christ" as they led brothel raids in countries like Thailand, though more recently they have worked to increase awareness of structural dimensions underlying trafficking and have toned down their militant language. However, as historian David Swartz has shown, there remains a market for militancy. Evangelical antitrafficking organizations desperate for American donors still promote a story that, in the words of one Chiang Mai activist, "appeals to people back home . . . good guys, bad guys, kick down doors, show smiles on face."[11] Other evangelicals, such as former Los Angeles police leader Robert Vernon, have worked to train law enforcement and government officials all over the world in "character-based leadership." Vernon's Pointman Leadership Institute has led such seminars in over seventy countries, for seventy thousand attendees, and he has spoken openly about his strategy of including biblical principles within these sessions (including the Ten Commandments, coded instead as "Ten Ancient Principles") and evangelizing interested officials at the conclusion of the program in an "optional module" on how to have a personal relationship with Jesus.[12] Other contemporary crises, such as mass shootings, have prompted evangelicals to partner with police or, in some cases, actually deploy their own armed guards or contract with religiously themed security services operating as "sacred security" and "God's watchmen."[13] Security and crime prevention, whether of one's suburban church or a village in Southeast Asia, remain animating evangelical concerns.

As the foregoing examples indicate, evangelical law and order is complicated. In many cases, support of crime fighting and religious prison programs indicates deeply held assumptions both about evangelicalism's comfort with state power and about the use of force. Vocal and often un-questioning support for police and recurring law-and-order sloganeering from politicians who court evangelical voters are also cultural markers that reinforce evangelicalism's associations with whiteness and further its divide from movements that posit the value of black lives in the face of oppression.

But this is not the whole story. Evangelicals visit prisoners, write let-ters, work to find offenders jobs upon reentry, minister to the children of inmates, and mobilize for criminal justice reform. Evangelicals, as a non-evangelical prison chaplain put it to me once, are the ones who show up. I was reminded of this recently when I attended an orientation session for volunteers at a local prison. Along with seven or eight other academics, I was there to teach as part of the prison education program for a large, secular university. But the room for the orientation was filled with about fifty to sixty other people as well. By looking at their T-shirts embla-zoned with Christian slogans and church logos, hearing them introduce themselves as connected to local evangelical ministries, and listening to their plans for the various Bible studies and Christian programs they hoped to run at the prison, it was clear that this was an overwhelmingly evangelical group. Some of them spoke in ways that made the academics in the room obviously uncomfortable, as when a few evangelical volun-teer trainees repeatedly asked staff questions about whether they would have to tolerate LGBT inmates' life choices. But it was clear they cared about the prisoners and were willing to dedicate their time to them. In a world prone to forget incarcerated people, they showed up.

Just over a decade after Burl Cain's chapel message at Wheaton Col-lege in 2005, another prominent speaker arrived on campus to deliver a talk. Bryan Stevenson, the founder of the Equal Justice Initiative, had come to speak about the problems in American criminal justice that he had seen firsthand as an advocate for incarcerated children and death-row inmates (some of whom had been incarcerated at Cain's Angola prison). Stevenson was no stranger to evangelicalism. He had attended college at Eastern Uni-versity, a school best known for various socially engaged, progressive evangelical professors and alumni (such as Tony Campolo, Ron Sider, and Shane Claiborne). He had written a best-selling memoir laced with Chris-tian themes, entitled *Just Mercy,* and become a sought-after speaker at prominent evangelical churches and gatherings, including Willow Creek, Redeemer Presbyterian Church, and the Q Conference.[14] This was all in addition to his burgeoning secular public profile as a MacArthur "Genius"

Fellow, a TED talk speaker, a guest on innumerable television and radio programs, and the subject of glowing profiles in publications like the *New Yorker*.[15]

At Wheaton, Stevenson shared some difficult details about the current realities of American criminal justice. He also had tough words for the packed room of evangelical students and professors: though the Christian church had a responsibility to care for a broken world, it had regularly failed in "increasing the justice quotient." Unlike most evangelicals over the past half century, Stevenson placed race and inequality at the forefront of his discussion of the ills of criminal justice. An African American, he had experienced racist police misconduct as a young man. His law career had shown him firsthand how the justice system disproportionately enveloped and harmed poor people of color. The answer for Stevenson was not found in prison sermons, in incremental reforms, or through pushing the system toward neutral, "color-blind" status. Instead, he wanted to see a full-on national confession of the injustice woven into the fabric of America through its racial history, its constitutional amendments (most obviously the Thirteenth Amendment, which allowed for forced labor of prisoners), and its contemporary expressions of retribution.[16] "We [as Christians] have an insight on what is on the other side of repentance, what is on the other side of acknowledgement of wrongdoing—which is repair," Stevenson told *Christianity Today* in a cover story that profiled his work. "And if we give voice to that, maybe we can encourage our nation to do better at recovering and acknowledging and responding to this history of bigotry and discrimination that has burdened us for so long."[17] To that effect, Stevenson advocated for a large monument to black lynching victims in Montgomery, Alabama. He undoubtedly shared many of the same sensibilities and critiques of American criminal justice as Colson had, as well as many of the same religious dispositions. But his cause was not a simple conservative recovery. It was instead an invitation to a new future.

In making an argument about the mainstream quality of the inhumanity in American criminal justice, Stevenson picked up on a potential challenge for evangelicals that this book has also sought to highlight. America's system of mass incarceration does great harm to poor and minority communities nationwide. Despite recent reforms, it still locks people away for long periods (regularly in inhumane conditions) and offers little in the way of opportunities for restoration. But postwar evangelicals saw their lobbying for tougher forms of criminal justice, like the very evangelical innovation of the penitentiary itself in early America, as a needed intervention, fully in step with the spirit of the age. Evangelicals were able to make this argument successfully because so many other people saw crime as an issue of public concern and proposed similar solutions. Those who wish to challenge mass incarceration or save evangelicalism from enmeshment with punitive politics even in this current moment must reckon with this history, a story of believers being fully in and of the world around them.

Stevenson also urged the Wheaton community to "get proximate" to problems of injustice, to enter difficult situations and embrace their discomfort. As they had with Burl Cain, students responded positively to Stevenson's address, offering him a standing ovation. One student told the college's newspaper, "I think we do need to care about our world, and I think God wants us to do so. . . . I'm going to be mulling over a lot of the things he said and trying to discuss it with friends and get more perspective."[18] Proximity as a driver for caring about a broken world was an appealing notion, likely because it represented a continuation of aspects of evangelical fascination with matters of crime and punishment. "Get proximate" was the call that evangelicals like David Wilkerson, Consuella York, Ray Hoekstra, and Chuck Colson had heeded as they moved into crime-troubled neighborhoods and prisons. Theirs was a religion built to travel, easily mobilized and adapted for innumerable circumstances. It was a gift for ministering to those who were suffering or lonely. And since emphasis on personal conversion via proximity could make things truly *personal,* it also could be an important starting point for new social consciousness. Jim Vaus advocated for Harlem's delinquent youths not because of his politics, but because they were his neighbors. For Colson, getting proximate was the impetus of his reform work. He could not forget his imprisoned brothers whom he had shared life with, or the faces of the desperate looking at him through the bars after his in-prison ministry events had concluded. This proximity was a parallel to that of Jesus himself, who in his death was named as a criminal and executed between two convicted offenders.[19]

For many offenders and inmates, this evangelical work of proximity was good news. And it is ongoing today, as evangelicals continue to pursue fellowship with offenders, visit and write letters to those on the inside, head up programs to bring Christmas presents to the children of prisoners, and welcome formerly incarcerated people into their churches and workplaces, all legacies of the 1970s prison ministry surge. This is work, as

Billy Graham's casket carpenters put it, that shows the love of God and the promise of redemption. If evangelicals do manage to participate in the full dismantling of America's system of mass incarceration, it will likely be because they have continued to invest in and learn from experiences like these, experiences that can interrupt the seemingly natural order of punitive politics and gesture toward an alternative way of life built on grace, restoration, and second (and third, and fourth . . .) chances.

If this way of life is to be more than just a gesture, however, evangelicals must not restrict the radical political implications of proximity, prayer, and friendship with fellow believers on the inside. After all, God's incarnational ministry not only began with Jesus's declaration that the Spirit of the Lord was now upon him but also, as he told a gathered crowd, that the Spirit had sent him to "proclaim freedom for the prisoners" (Luke 4:18, New International Version). As it did with Jesus, this work may push American evangelicals to be at odds with the spirits of the age, particularly if it means confronting head-on the ways race remains determinative in coding perceptions of criminality. For evangelicals already engaged in prison ministry work, this call should not be too burdensome. Even if they are not politically active, most prison ministers today know something is wrong in American criminal justice. They want to see prisoners treated humanely and restored to society, and they know that it is a problem that the inmates with whom they work are disproportionately people of color. For other evangelicals, particularly those who feel the pull of law-and-order politics, proclaiming freedom to the captives will be a taller order. There will need to be, as Stevenson argued, widespread repentance of past punitive sins. This will be particularly hard for those evangelicals who want to believe in their movement's internal integrity and a timeless gospel witness. But repentance like this might better be seen as a conversion. And conversions are what evangelicals do best.

ABBREVIATIONS

Manuscript Collections

BGCA   Billy Graham Center Archives, Wheaton College, Wheaton, IL

CL   Records of Champions for Life, Collection 455, Billy Graham Center Archives, Wheaton College, Wheaton, IL

CLC   Christian Life Commission Resource Files, Collection 138-2, Southern Baptist Historical Library and Archives, Nashville, TN

CM   Carl [Charles Curtis Jr.] McIntire Manuscript Collection, Princeton Theological Seminary, Princeton, NJ

CTR   Records of *Christianity Today*, Collection 8, Billy Graham Center Archives, Wheaton College, Wheaton, IL

CY   Papers of Consuella York, Collection 397, Billy Graham Center Archives, Wheaton College, Wheaton, IL

DPC   Duane Pederson Collection, Collection 66, Archives and Special Collections, David Allan Hubbard Library, Fuller Theological Seminary, Pasadena, CA

EMJ   Evangelism and Missions Journals, Wheaton College Archives and Special Collections, Wheaton, IL

FPHC   Flower Pentecostal Heritage Center, Springfield, MO

HOD   Records of the *Hour of Decision* Radio Program, Billy Graham Evangelistic Association, Collection 191, Billy Graham Center Archives, Wheaton College, Wheaton, IL

HT   Papers of Herbert J. Taylor, Collection 20, Billy Graham Center Archives, Wheaton College, Wheaton, IL

IPM   Records of International Prison Ministries, Collection 320, Billy Graham Center Archives, Wheaton College, Wheaton, IL

JA   John B. Anderson Papers, Abraham Lincoln Presidential Library and Museum, Springfield, IL

JV   Papers of Jim Vaus, Collection 693, Billy Graham Center Archives, Wheaton College, Wheaton, IL

NAE   Papers of the National Association of Evangelicals, Collection 113, Wheaton College Archives and Special Collections, Wheaton, IL

PF   Records of Prison Fellowship Ministries, Collection 274, Billy Graham Center Archives, Wheaton College, Wheaton, IL

RR   Ronald Reagan Governor's Papers, Ronald Reagan Presidential Library, Simi Valley, CA

TS   Papers of Tom Skinner, Collection 430, Billy Graham Center Archives, Wheaton College, Wheaton, IL

WS   Interviews with William Leonard Skinner by Robert Shuster, Collection 443, Billy Graham Center Archives, Wheaton College, Wheaton, IL

Periodicals

AC   *Atlanta Constitution*

ADW   *Atlanta Daily World*

AJC   *Atlanta Journal-Constitution*

AP   Associated Press

BP   *Baptist Press*

BS   *Baltimore Sun*

CC   *Christian Century*

CD   *Chicago Defender*

CDT   *Chicago Daily Tribune*

CH   *Christian Herald*

CL   *Christian Life*

CT   *Christianity Today*

CTR   *Chicago Tribune*

LAT   *Los Angeles Times*

MM   *Moody Monthly*

NYT   *New York Times*

PE   *Pentecostal Evangel*

PJ   *Presbyterian Journal*

PRE   *Prison Evangelism*

UEA   *United Evangelical Action*

WP   *Washington Post*

NOTES

Introduction

1. Burl Cain, chapel address, Edman Chapel, Wheaton College, 2005, recording in author's possession. A parallel account is found in Dennis Shere, *Cain's Redemption: A Story of Hope and Transformation in America's Bloodiest Prison* (Chicago: Northfield, 2005), chap. 1.

2. "Warden Burl Cain to Step Down, Adamantly Denies Allegations against Him," WGNO, December 10, 2015, http://wgno.com/2015/12/10/warden-burl-cain-to-step -down-adamantly-denies-allegations-against-him/.

3. James Ridgeway, "God's Own Warden," *Mother Jones,* August 2011.

4. Wilbert Rideau, *In the Place of Justice: A Story of Punishment and Deliverance* (New York: Alfred A. Knopf, 2010).

5. Cain Burdeau, "Longtime Warden of Angola Prison in Louisiana to Resign," *Shreveport Times,* December 9, 2015, https://www.shreveporttimes.com/story/news /2015/12/09/longtime-warden-angola-prison-louisiana-resign/77067760/.

6. Quoted in Jeffrey Goldberg, "The End of the Line: Rehabilitation and Reform in Angola Penitentiary," *Atlantic,* September 9, 2015.

7. Quoted in Shere, *Cain's Redemption,* 26.

8. For example, see Stephanie Gaskill, "Moral Rehabilitation: Religion, Race, and Reform in America's Incarceration Capital" (PhD diss., University of North Carolina at Chapel Hill, 2017); Tanya Erzen, *God in Captivity: The Rise of Faith-Based Prison Ministries in the Age of Mass Incarceration* (Boston: Beacon, 2017), 59–83; and Michael Hallett et al., *The Angola Prison Seminary: Effects of Faith-Based Ministry on Identity Transformation, Desistance, and Rehabilitation* (New York: Routledge, 2018).

9. National Research Council, Committee on Causes and Consequences of High Rates of Incarceration, *The Growth of Incarceration in the United States: Exploring Causes and Consequences,* ed. Jeremy Travis, Bruce Western, and Steve Redburn (Washington, DC: National Academies Press, 2014), 33.

10. James Forman Jr., "Racial Critiques of Mass Incarceration: Beyond the New Jim Crow," *New York University Law Review* 87, no. 1 (2012): 22; National Research Council, Committee on Causes and Consequences of High Rates of Incarceration, *Growth of Incarceration,* 13.

11. Steven P. Miller, *The Age of Evangelicalism: America's Born-Again Years* (New York: Oxford University Press, 2014). Some key texts that have been critical to my approach here in detailing the origins of mass incarceration and its resonances with currents in American culture and politics are Marie Gottschalk, *The Prison and the Gallows: The Politics of Mass Incarceration in America* (New York: Cambridge University Press, 2006); Naomi Murakawa, *The First Civil Right: How Liberals Built Prison America* (New York: Oxford University Press, 2014); Elizabeth Hinton, *From the War on Poverty to the War on Crime: The Making of Mass Incarceration in America* (Cambridge, MA: Harvard University Press, 2016); William J. Stuntz, *The Collapse of American Criminal Justice* (Cambridge, MA: Harvard University Press, 2011); James Forman Jr., *Locking Up Our Own: Crime and Punishment in Black America* (New York: Farrar, Straus and Giroux, 2017); John Pfaff, *Locked In: The True Causes of Mass Incarceration—and How to Achieve Real Reform* (New York: Basic Books, 2017); Michael W. Flamm, *Law and Order: Street Crime, Civil Unrest, and the Crisis of Liberalism in the 1960s* (New York: Columbia University Press, 2007); Ruth Wilson Gilmore, *Golden Gulag: Prisons, Surplus, Crisis, and Opposition in Globalizing California* (Berkeley: University of California Press, 2007); Max Felker-Kantor, *Policing Los Angeles: Race, Resistance, and the Rise of the LAPD* (Chapel Hill: University of North Carolina Press, 2018); Victor M. Rios, *Punished: Policing the Lives of Black and Latino Boys* (New York: New York University Press, 2011); and Lawrence M. Friedman, *Crime and Punishment in American History* (New York: Basic Books, 1993). Though I came across this essay after I was well into my research, the late William Stuntz's "Law and Grace" offers some interesting provocations about evangelicalism and punitive politics that gave me confidence I was on the right track. William J. Stuntz, "Law and Grace," *Virginia Law Review* 98, no. 2 (2012): 367–84.

12. Axel R. Schäfer, *Countercultural Conservatives: American Evangelicalism from the Postwar Revival to the New Christian Right* (Madison: University of Wisconsin Press, 2011), 5. Interestingly, this term is also used by Ruth Wilson Gilmore to describe the form of American governance that sits on the foundations of the prison state. Gilmore, *Golden Gulag*, 245.

13. Eduardo Bonilla-Silva, *Racism without Racists: Color-Blind Racism and the Persistence of Racial Inequality in America*, 5th ed. (Lanham, MD: Rowman and Littlefield, 2018).

14. Keeanga-Yamahtta Taylor, *From #BlackLivesMatter to Black Liberation* (Chicago: Haymarket Books, 2016), 72.

15. Alessandro Arcangeli, *Cultural History: A Concise Introduction* (New York: Routledge, 2012), 16.

16. David Hall, *Worlds of Wonder, Days of Judgment: Popular Religious Belief in Early New England* (Cambridge, MA: Harvard University Press, 1990), 18.

17. Miller, *Age of Evangelicalism*, 5.

18. Elliott Currie, *Crime and Punishment in America* (New York: Macmillan, 1998), 21.

19. For discussion of the limits of the backlash thesis, see the introduction to Schäfer, *Countercultural Conservatives*.

20. Gilmore, *Golden Gulag*, 10–11.

21. Erzen, *God in Captivity;* Winnifred Fallers Sullivan, *Prison Religion: Faith-Based Reform and the Constitution* (Princeton, NJ: Princeton University Press, 2009); Joshua Dubler, *Down in the Chapel: Religious Life in an American Prison* (New York: Farrar, Straus and Giroux, 2013); James Samuel Logan, *Good Punishment? Christian Moral Practice and U.S. Imprisonment* (Grand Rapids, MI: Eerdmans, 2008). Garrett Felber's *Those Who Know Don't Say* and Joshua Dubler and Vincent Lloyd's *Break Every Yoke* (both released as this book was going to press) promise to be important explorations of religion, activism, and the carceral state. Garrett Felber, *Those Who Know Don't Say: The Nation of Islam, the Black Freedom Movement, and the Carceral State* (Chapel Hill: University of North Carolina Press, 2020); Joshua Dubler and Vincent Lloyd, *Break Every Yoke: Religion, Justice, and the Abolition of Prisons* (New York: Oxford University Press, 2020).

22. Douglas A. Sweeney, *The American Evangelical Story: A History of the Movement* (Grand Rapids, MI: Baker Academic, 2005), 24.

23. For a helpful overview of the stakes of this debate, see Milton G. Sernett, "Black Religion and the Question of Evangelical Identity," in *The Variety of American Evangelicalism,* ed. Donald W. Dayton and Robert K. Johnson (Knoxville: University of Tennessee Press, 1991), 135–47.

24. For example, see "Inmate. Prisoner. Other. Discussed," Marshall Project, April 3, 2015, https://www.themarshallproject.org/2015/04/03/inmate-prisoner-other-discussed.

1. Churchdom's War on Crime

1. Quoted in Paula S. Fass, "Making and Remaking an Event: The Leopold and Loeb Case in American Culture," *Journal of American History* 80, no. 3 (1993): 925.

2. Simon Baatz, *For the Thrill of It: Leopold, Loeb, and the Murder That Shocked Jazz Age Chicago* (New York: Harper Perennial, 2009); Edward J. Larson, "An American Tragedy: Retelling the Leopold-Loeb Story in Popular Culture," *American Journal of Legal History* 50, no. 2 (2008): 119–56.

3. "Hang the Slayers, Billy Sunday Says," *Chicago Herald and Examiner,* June 5, 1924, quoted in in Baatz, *For the Thrill of It,* 319. See also Harold Andrews, "Billy Sunday Says Gibbet Should Punish Boy Killers," *AC,* June 5, 1924.

4. David J. Rothman, *The Discovery of the Asylum: Social Order and Disorder in the New Republic,* rev. ed. (New York: Aldine de Gruyter, 2002), 3–15; Marie Gottschalk, *The Prison and the Gallows: The Politics of Mass Incarceration in America* (New York: Cambridge University Press, 2006), 52–53; Robert C. Wadman and William Thomas Allison, *To Protect and to Serve: A History of Police in America* (Upper Saddle River, NJ: Pearson Prentice Hall, 2004), 1.

5. Adam J. Hirsch, *The Rise of the Penitentiary: Prisons and Punishment in Early America* (New Haven, CT: Yale University Press, 1992), 4–7.

6. Hirsch, 52; Rothman, *Discovery of the Asylum.*

7. Scott D. Seay, *Hanging Between Heaven and Earth: Capital Crime, Execution Preaching, and Theology in Early New England* (DeKalb: Northern Illinois University Press, 2009), 14.

8. Jennifer Graber, *The Furnace of Affliction* (Chapel Hill: University of North Carolina Press, 2011), 22, 36–37, 87.

9. Quoted in Graber, 3–4. For broader discussion of Tocqueville and Beaumont's prison visits, see George Wilson Pierson, *Tocqueville in America* (Baltimore: Johns Hopkins University Press, 1996).

10. Graber, *Furnace of Affliction*, 103–34.

11. Gottschalk, *Prison and the Gallows*, 53–55.

12. James Finley, *Memorials of Prison Life* (Cincinnati: L. Swormstedy and J. H. Power, 1850); Richard P. Heitzenrater, *Wesley and the People Called Methodists*, 2nd ed. (Nashville: Abingdon, 2013), 137.

13. Norris Magnuson, *Salvation in the Slums: Evangelical Social Work, 1865–1920* (Grand Rapids, MI: Baker, 1977), 103–8; Maud Ballington Booth, *After Prison—What?* (New York: F. H. Revell, 1903), http://www.gutenberg.org/files/45234/45234-h/45234-h.htm.

14. Elizabeth R. Wheaton, *Prisons and Prayer; or A Labor of Love* (Chas. M. Kelley, 1906), chap. 1, http://www.gutenberg.org/ebooks/41720.

15. Susie C. Stanley, *Holy Boldness: Women Preachers' Autobiographies and the Sanctified Self* (Knoxville: University of Tennessee Press, 2002), 150.

16. "The International Christian Police Association," *Christian Union,* January 16, 1892.

17. "For a Christian Police Association," *WP,* November 11, 1891; "Christian Activities in New York," *New York Observer and Chronicle,* August 8, 1907; "Interested in the Police," *Philadelphia Inquirer,* January 18, 1897.

18. "Christian Police," *Quiver,* January 1888, 172. See also Don Axcell, *Where Duty Calls: Building Bridges of Hope over 130 Years* (n.p.: DEAX, 2016).

19. "Policemen's Christmas," *NYT,* December 5, 1897.

20. J. L. Spicer, "Going to Church in Revolutionary Canton," *New York Observer and Chronicle,* April 4, 1912.

21. J. L. Spicer, "The Police Force of Greater New York," *Sunday School World,* May 1898.

22. J. L. Spicer, "Protecting Our Protectors: New York Branch International Christian Police Association," *New York Observer and Chronicle,* May 30, 1912.

23. Douglas A. Blackmon, *Slavery by Another Name: The Re-enslavement of Black People in America from the Civil War to World War II* (New York: Doubleday, 2008).

24. *Report on Slavery and Racism in the History of the Southern Baptist Theological Seminary* (Southern Baptist Theological Seminary, December 12, 2018), 7, 35–38, http://www.sbts.edu/wp-content/uploads/2018/12/Racism-and-the-Legacy-of-Slavery-Report-v3.pdf; Derrell Roberts, "Joseph E. Brown and the Convict Lease System," *Georgia Historical Quarterly* 44, no. 4 (1960): 399–410.

25. Donald G. Mathews, *At the Altar of Lynching: Burning Sam Hose in the American South* (New York: Cambridge University Press, 2017), 49–50.

26. Zoe Trodd, "Social Progressivism and Religion in America," in *Oxford Research Encyclopedia of Religion,* 2017, http://oxfordre.com/religion/view/10.1093/acrefore/9780199340378.001.0001/acrefore-9780199340378-e-462; Mathews, *At the Altar of Lynching,* 49.

27. Mathews, *At the Altar of Lynching,* 1–2, 127; Orlando Patterson, *Rituals of Blood: Consequences of Slavery in Two American Centuries* (New York: Basic Civitas Books, 1998), 171–232.

28. On the former, see Mary Beth Mathews, "African Americans Speak to Spectacle Lynchings," *Journal of Southern Religion* 17 (2015). For examples of the latter, see W. E. B. Du Bois, *Darkwater: Voices from within the Veil* (New York: Harcourt, Brace, 1920); Mathews, *At the Altar of Lynching*, 258–60.

29. For an overview of Protestant reactions to lynching, see Robert Moats Miller, "The Protestant Churches and Lynching, 1919–1939," *Journal of Negro History* 42, no. 2 (April 1957): 118–31. For expanded discussion of the white Protestant perception of lynching's threat to law and order, see Aaron Griffith, " 'The Real Victim of Lynch Law Is the Government': American Protestant Anti-lynching Advocacy and the Making of Law and Order," *Religions* 10, no. 2 (February 2019).

30. Michael J. Pfeifer, *Rough Justice: Lynching and American Society, 1874–1947* (Urbana: University of Illinois Press, 2004), 2–3.

31. "Ministers Plead for the Preservation of Our Civilization, Now in Peril Because of Lawlessness and Mob Violence," n.d., series I, subseries II, box 2, folder 7, Judge George Hillyer Papers, Kenan Research Center at the Atlanta History Center, Atlanta, 4.

32. Gregory Mixon and Clifford Kuhn, "Atlanta Race Riot of 1906," New Georgia Encyclopedia, 2015, https://www.georgiaencyclopedia.org/articles/history-archaeology/atlanta-race-riot-1906; "Rioting Goes On, Despite Troops," *NYT*, September 24, 1906.

33. H. K. Pendleton, "Restrain Negro from Crime by Making Him Respect Self," *AC*, October 13, 1906.

34. "Ministers Plead," 6–7.

35. E. T. Wellford, *The Lynching of Jesus: A Review of the Legal Aspects of the Trial of Christ*, 2nd ed. (Newport News, VA: Franklin Printing, 1905), 13.

36. Wellford, 101–2. See also Brian James Hallstoos, "Windy City, Holy Land: Willa Saunders Jones and Black Sacred Music and Drama" (PhD diss., University of Iowa, 2009), 102–4.

37. Khalil Gibran Muhammad, *The Condemnation of Blackness: Race, Crime, and the Making of Modern Urban America* (Cambridge, MA: Harvard University Press, 2010), 35–36.

38. Muhammad, 47–51.

39. F. J. Sypher, ed., *Frederick L. Hoffman: His Life and Works* (n.p.: Xlibris, 2002), 63–65, 99.

40. Froude quoted in Frederick L. Hoffman, *Race Traits and Tendencies of the American Negro* (New York: published for the American Economic Association by Macmillan, 1896), 238–39.

41. Hoffman, 238, 310–12. For a discussion of the history of Christian scripture, race, and the legacy of the Enlightenment in the development of scientific racism, see Colin Kidd, *The Forging of Races: Race and Scripture in the Protestant Atlantic World, 1600–2000* (New York: Cambridge University Press, 2006), chaps. 4–6.

42. Muhammad, *Condemnation of Blackness*, 50.

43. John Roach Straton, "Will Education Solve the Race Problem?," *North American Review* 170, no. 523 (June 1900): 785–801.

44. Booker T. Washington, "Education Will Solve the Race Problem: A Reply," *North American Review* 171, no. 525 (August 1900): 221–32.

45. Muhammad, *Condemnation of Blackness*, 130–31.

46. Wheaton, *Prisons and Prayer*, chap. 12.

47. Clarissa Olds Keeler, *The Crime of Crimes; or, The Convict System Unmasked* (Washington, DC: Pentecostal Era, 1907).

48. S. B. Shaw, *Touching Incidents and Remarkable Answers to Prayer* (Lansing, MI: J. W. Hazelton, 1893).

49. Wheaton, *Prisons and Prayer*, chap. 12.

50. Keeler here was quoting a Department of Labor official on the particular evils of southern prisons. Clarissa Olds Keeler to W. E. B. Du Bois, June 11, 1905, MS 312, W. E. B. Du Bois Papers, Special Collections and University Archives, University of Massachusetts Amherst Libraries, http://credo.library.umass.edu/view/full/mums312-b003-i152; W. E. B. Du Bois to Clarissa Olds Keeler, June 19, 1905, MS 312, W. E. B. Du Bois Papers, Special Collections and University Archives, University of Massachusetts Amherst Libraries, https://credo.library.umass.edu/view/full/mums312-b003-i153.

51. Keeler, *Crime of Crimes*, 3.

52. Gottschalk, *Prison and the Gallows*, 59; Jeffrey S. Adler, "Less Crime, More Punishment: Violence, Race, and Criminal Justice in Early Twentieth-Century America," *Journal of American History* 102, no. 1 (June 2015): 36. See also Justice Research and Statistics Association, "Historical Data," in *Crime and Justice Atlas 2000* (Washington, DC: Justice Research and Statistics Association, 2000), 38–39, http://www.jrsa.org/projects/Historical.pdf.

53. Jeffrey S. Adler, "'It Is His First Offense. We Might as Well Let Him Go': Homicide and Criminal Justice in Chicago, 1875–1920," *Journal of Social History* 40, no. 1 (Autumn 2006): 5.

54. "Public Aid Asked in War on Crime," *NYT*, November 20, 1925.

55. James D. Calder, *The Origins and Development of Federal Crime Control Policy: Herbert Hoover's Initiatives* (Westport, CT: Praeger, 1993), 1–24.

56. Gottschalk, *Prison and the Gallows*, 64–68.

57. Gottschalk, 74.

58. William J. Stuntz, *The Collapse of American Criminal Justice* (Cambridge, MA: Harvard University Press, 2011), 186.

59. See Margaret Werner Cahalan, *Historical Corrections Statistics in the United States, 1850–1984* (Washington, DC: US Department of Justice, December 1986), 30 (table 3.3), http://www.bjs.gov/content/pub/pdf/hcsus5084.pdf.

60. Franklin Delano Roosevelt, "Address to the Attorney General's Crime Conference," December 10, 1934, Franklin D. Roosevelt Master Speech File, box 20, number 756, Franklin D. Roosevelt Presidential Library and Museum, Hyde Park, NY, http://www.fdrlibrary.marist.edu/_resources/images/msf/msf00777.

61. "Church Called to Join Fight on U.S. Crime," *WP*, December 10, 1934; "Bishop Freeman Endorses War on Crime; Pledges Church Support at Capital Service," *NYT*, December 10, 1934; "The Program of the Attorney-General's Conference on Crime," *Journal of Criminal Law and Criminology* 25, no. 5 (1935): 793–94.

62. George M. Marsden, *Fundamentalism and American Culture*, 2nd. ed. (New York: Oxford University Press, 2006), 66; Matthew Avery Sutton, *American Apocalypse: A History of Modern Evangelicalism* (Cambridge, MA: Belknap Press of Harvard University Press, 2014), 184.

63. "The Thrill Mania," *Baptist and Reflector*, August 7, 1924.

64. "Pastor Points Way to Decrease Crime," *NYT*, September 21, 1925.

65. Baatz, *For the Thrill of It,* 319; Ernest B. Gordon, *The Leaven of the Sadducees; or, Old and New Apostasies* (Chicago: Bible Institute Colportage Association, 1926), 172.

66. Marsden, *Fundamentalism and American Culture,* 213; William Jennings Bryan, "Closing Statement of William Jennings Bryan at the Trial of John Scopes," in *Evangelicalism and Fundamentalism: A Documentary Reader,* ed. Barry Hankins (New York: New York University Press, 2008), 92.

67. Mark K. Bauman, "John T. Scopes, Leopold and Loeb, and Bishop Warren A. Candler," *Methodist History* 16, no. 2 (January 1978): 99.

68. "Leopold and Loeb Called Modernists," *NYT,* September 15, 1924.

69. Cover, *King's Business,* March 1925.

70. "God Committed Death Penalty into Hands of State, Says Pastor," *Chicago Herald and Examiner,* August 4, 1924, cited in Baatz, *For the Thrill of It,* 319–20.

71. W. B. Norton, "Many Pastors Give Views on Franks Verdict," *CDT,* September 15, 1924; "Ministers Attack Caverly for Franks Case Decision," *WP,* September 15, 1924.

72. "Pastor Sees Noose as 'Only Salvation' of Loeb and Leopold," *CDT,* June 9, 1924. See also W. B. Norton, "Pastor Defends Penalty; Warns of Laxity," *CDT,* September 22, 1924; Simon Peter Long, *The Wounded Word: A Brief Meditation on the Seven Sayings of Christ on the Cross* (Columbus, OH: F.J. Heer Printing, 1908), 34–35; and J. E. Conant, "Capital Punishment and Human Rights," chap. 3 in *The Growing Menace of the "Social Gospel"* (Chicago: Bible Institute Colportage Association, 1937), reprinted in Joel A. Carpenter, ed., *Fighting Fundamentalism: Polemical Thrusts of the 1930s and 1940s* (New York: Garland, 1988).

73. Carl McIntire, "America Builds a City," January 11, 1927, box 304, folder 10, CM. McIntire's manuscript contains some grammatical irregularities. I have chosen to quote his speech as it was written.

74. Markku Ruotsila, *Fighting Fundamentalist: Carl McIntire and the Politicization of American Fundamentalism* (New York: Oxford University Press, 2016), 20.

75. *Crime Must Go* (United States Flag Association, 1933), pamphlet collection, New York Historical Society.

76. *Crime Must Go.*

77. Newman F. Baker, "Current Notes," *Journal of Criminal Law and Criminology* 24, no. 5 (Winter 1934): 973.

78. "Criminal Aided by Tolerance," *LAT,* October 14, 1933; Marcus Kavanagh, *The Criminal and His Allies* (Indianapolis: Bobbs-Merrill, 1928).

79. "Lone Island Picked to Imprison Worst of Our Criminals," *NYT,* October 13, 1933; David Ward and Gene Kassebaum, *Alcatraz: The Gangster Years* (Berkeley: University of California Press, 2010), 49.

80. "Backs Federal Aid in War on Crime," *NYT,* October 15, 1933.

81. John A. Campbell, *A Biographical History, with Portraits, of Prominent Men of the Great West* (Chicago: Western Biographical and Engraving Company, 1902), 218; "Criminal Aided by Tolerance"; Kavanagh, *Criminal and His Allies,* 370–78.

82. "Priest Lauds Jury Convicting Capone," *BS,* October 19, 1931; Edmund A. Walsh, "The Church and Crime" (National Anti-Crime Conference, Washington, DC, 1933), Patrick J. Hurley Collection, box 55, folder 12, University of Oklahoma Western History Collection.

83. "Backs Federal Aid."

84. "Church Groups Mass Forces to Fight Crime," *WP*, April 28, 1934.

85. On the rise of the "era of the crime commission," see Wadman and Allison, *To Protect and to Serve*, 96.

86. *Building a Moral Reserve, or, The Responsibilities of the Christian Citizen* (Chicago: University of Chicago Press and the American Institute of Sacred Literature, 1930), 63–72; Dennis E. Hoffman, *Scarface Al and the Crime Crusaders: Chicago's Private War against Capone* (Carbondale: Southern Illinois University Press, 1993), 13–15; Laurence Bergreen, *Capone: The Man and the Era*, repr. ed. (New York: Simon and Schuster, 1996), 366; Thomas Reppetto, *American Mafia: A History of Its Rise to Power* (New York: Holt, 2005), 126–27; "Editorial Notes: Chicago Crime Commission," *MM*, April 1922; Virgil W. Peterson and Chicago Crime Commission, *Crime Commissions in the United States* (Chicago: Chicago Crime Commission, 1945), 1, 27–28.

87. "Churches Back Drive on Crime," *LAT*, February 14, 1923.

88. "United States in Hell of a Mess, Says Rev. A. Clayton Powell," *Baltimore Afro-American*, December 16, 1933.

89. "Group Meets to Fight Crime," *CD*, October 7, 1933.

90. "Darrow Is Negro's Worst Enemy—Rev. Ross," *Pittsburgh Courier*, August 1, 1931.

91. "Churchdom Unrelenting in War on Community Crime," *CD*, October 26, 1935; "Churchdom to Open War on Community Crime Wednesday," *CD*, October 19, 1935.

92. James Campbell, *Crime and Punishment in African American History* (New York: Palgrave Macmillan, 2013), 122.

93. "Anti-crime Meet Begins with Small Crowd; Homicides Hit," *ADW*, September 2, 1940. See also J. Raymond Henderson, "Anti Crime Effort Is Commendable, Pastor Says in Article," *ADW*, September 7, 1936; and "Pastor Begins Blitzkrieg on Crime in City: Launch Program Today in Front of Radcliffe," *ADW*, August 23, 1941.

94. Estelle B. Freedman, *Their Sisters' Keepers: Women's Prison Reform in America, 1830–1930* (Ann Arbor: University of Michigan Press, 1981), 73.

95. Rebecca M. McLennan, *The Crisis of Imprisonment: Protest, Politics, and the Making of the American Penal State, 1776–1941* (New York: Cambridge University Press, 2008), 195. Also see David J. Rothman, *Conscience and Convenience: The Asylum and Its Alternatives in Progressive America*, 2nd ed. (New York: Aldine Transaction, 2002).

96. Heath W. Carter, *Union Made: Working People and the Rise of Social Christianity in Chicago* (New York: Oxford University Press, 2015); Walter Rauschenbusch, *Christianity and the Social Crisis* (New York: Macmillan, 1907).

97. Donald K. Gorrell, *The Age of Social Responsibility: The Social Gospel in the Progressive Era, 1900–1920* (Macon, GA: Mercer University Press, 1988), 2.

98. Barry Hankins, *Jesus and Gin: Evangelicalism, the Roaring Twenties and Today's Culture Wars* (New York: Palgrave Macmillan, 2010), 22–23, 30.

99. Elesha J. Coffman, *The Christian Century and the Rise of the Protestant Mainline* (New York: Oxford University Press, 2013), 80–110; Marni Davis, *Jews and Booze: Becoming American in the Age of Prohibition* (New York: New York University Press, 2012).

100. Heather D. Curtis, *Holy Humanitarians: American Evangelicals and Global Aid* (Cambridge, MA: Harvard University Press, 2018), 9.

101. Franklin S. Billings, "The Christian Conscience Crusade: 'Law Enforcement or Chaos,'" *CH*, April 18, 1925; Alfred E. Smith, "The Christian Conscience Crusade: New York's Governor Heartily Approves," *CH*, April 25, 1925.

102. "Leopold and Loeb Called Modernists"; John Roach Straton and Charles Francis Potter, *Fundamentalist versus Modernist: The Debates between John Roach Straton and Charles Francis Potter*, ed. Joel A. Carpenter, Fundamentalism in American Religion, 1880–1950 (New York: Garland, 1988).

103. "Minister Protests Cohen Gang Penalty," *BS*, September 29, 1924.

104. "Crime Cause Found in Maladjustment," *NYT*, May 6, 1932.

105. Sanford Bates, "Crime and Christianity: What Can the Church Do about It?," *Christian Register*, January 7, 1926.

106. William R. Hutchison, *The Modernist Impulse in American Protestantism* (Cambridge, MA: Harvard University Press, 1976).

107. "Asks Church Aid on Crime," *NYT*, September 29, 1929.

108. "Tuttle Bids Church Aid Study of Crime," *NYT*, March 5, 1930.

109. "Tuttle Urges Fight on Crime by Church," *NYT*, December 27, 1930.

110. "Prison Convention Opens Today," *BS*, October 18, 1931; "Priest Lauds Jury."

111. "Prison Convention Opens Today"; "Penologists Blame Society for Crime," *NYT*, October 19, 1931.

112. "27 Students of Crime Will Speak in City," *BS*, October 4, 1931.

113. Stephanie Muravchik, *American Protestantism in the Age of Psychology* (New York: Cambridge University Press, 2011), 28–29.

114. Charles E. Hall, *Head and Heart: The Story of the Clinical Pastoral Education Movement* (Decatur, GA: Journal of Pastoral Care Publications, 1991), 2–3.

115. Susan E. Myers-Shirk, *Helping the Good Shepherd: Pastoral Counselors in a Psychotherapeutic Culture, 1925–1975* (Baltimore: Johns Hopkins University Press, 2009).

116. Hall, *Head and Heart*, 7–8.

117. Hall, 15.

118. Hall, 66–67.

119. Edgardo Rotman, "The Failure of Reform: United States, 1865–1965," in *The Oxford History of the Prison: The Practice of Punishment in Western Society*, ed. Norval Morris and David J. Rothman (New York: Oxford University Press, 1995), 173–79. See also Andrew Skotnicki, *Religion and the Development of the American Penal System* (Lanham, MD: University Press of America, 2000).

120. "Respect for Law Urged by Rabbis," *NYT*, September 18, 1926.

121. Will Herberg, *Protestant, Catholic, Jew: An Essay in American Religious Sociology*, rev. ed. (Garden City, NY: Anchor Books, 1960), 75.

122. Kevin M. Schultz, *Tri-faith America: How Catholics and Jews Held Postwar America to Its Protestant Promise* (New York: Oxford University Press, 2011).

123. Asa Keyes, "The Part of the Church in Law Enforcement," *Bridal Call*, July 1924.

124. "Cardinal Rallies All Faiths in Fight on Youthful Crime," *NYT*, March 7, 1927.

125. *Proceedings of the Governor's Conference on Crime, the Criminal and Society, September 30 to October 3, 1935* (Albany, NY: n.p., 1936).

126. Ronit Y. Stahl, *Enlisting Faith: How the Military Chaplaincy Shaped Religion and State in Modern America* (Cambridge, MA: Harvard University Press, 2017), 11, 17.

127. Winnifred Fallers Sullivan, *A Ministry of Presence: Chaplaincy, Spiritual Care, and the Law* (Chicago: University of Chicago Press, 2014), 78, 150.

128. By contrast, Britain maintained its explicitly Christian (Anglican) framing of prison spaces and leadership. For more on the differences between modern American prisons and those in Great Britain, see James A. Beckford and Sophie Gilliat, *Religion in Prison: "Equal Rites" in a Multi-faith Society* (New York: Cambridge University Press, 2005), 177–84; and Rotman, "Failure of Reform," 192.

129. Lillian McLaughlin, "U.S. Prison Chaplains: 'I'm Not Much Good for a Day or Two after an Execution,'" *Des Moines Tribune*, October 1, 1955.

130. David S. Kennedy, "A Survey of the Present Crisis," *MM*, October 1921.

131. "Penologists Blame Society for Crime."

132. Clarence Darrow, *Attorney for the Damned: Clarence Darrow in the Courtroom*, ed. Arthur Weinberg (Chicago: University of Chicago Press, 2012), 76.

133. Nicole Rafter, "Origins of Criminology," in *What Is Criminology?*, ed. Mary Bosworth and Carolyn Hoyle (New York: Oxford University Press, 2011), 143–54; Peter J. Hutchings, *The Criminal Spectre in Law, Literature and Aesthetics* (New York: Routledge, 2001), 184.

134. Cesare Lombroso, *Crime: Its Causes and Remedies* (London: William Heinemann, 1911), 138–44.

135. Max Huhner, "Crime Does Pay," *Journal of Criminal Law and Criminology* 30, no. 4 (1939): 497.

136. John R. Miner, "Do the Churches Prevent Crime?," *American Journal of Police Science* 2, no. 6 (1931): 468–72; Nathaniel Cantor, "The Causes of Crime," *Journal of Criminal Law and Criminology* 23, no. 6 (1933): 1029–34; Ledger Wood, "Responsibility and Punishment," *Journal of Criminal Law and Criminology* 28, no. 5 (1938): 630–40.

137. Raffaele Garofalo, *Criminology* (Boston: Little, Brown, 1914), 142.

138. Courtland Nixon, "Crime Is Our Crown of Thorns," *Journal of Criminal Law and Criminology* 23, no. 2 (1932): 276–79.

139. Peterson and Chicago Crime Commission, *Crime Commissions*. I have made minor corrections to typos in this original text.

140. L. A. Rutledge, "Pastor Preaches Vigorously against Crime in Sermon," *ADW*, September 9, 1936; S. Parkes Cadman, "Our National Shame: A Searching Discussion of the Crime Problem," *CH*, May 29, 1926.

141. Charles H. Tuttle, "Responsibility of the Bar and the Public in Suppressing Crime," *New York State Bar Association Bulletin* 7, no. 1 (1935): 10–17.

142. "Crime as a National Problem," *CC*, August 13, 1933; "Concurrent Jurisdiction over Major Crimes," *CC*, August 23, 1933. Also see Coffman, *Christian Century*, chap. 5.

143. Harry Emerson Fosdick, "Dare We Break the Vicious Circle of Fighting Evil with Evil!" (sermon, Riverside Church, New York, 1939).

144. "Churches Back Drive on Crime"; *Building a Moral Reserve*, 50–51.

145. Charles Sheldon, "Missionary Police," *CH*, August 1, 1925; Charles Sheldon, "How Much Crime?," *CH*, July 10, 1926.

146. "Clerics Back Move to Halt Criminals," *NYT*, April 20, 1926.

147. Franklin Delano Roosevelt, "Address to Federal Council of Churches of Christ," December 6, 1933, Master Speech File, box 16, number 669, Franklin D. Roosevelt Presidential Library and Museum, Hyde Park, NY, http://www.fdrlibrary.marist.edu/_resources/images/msf/msf00689.

148. Athan G. Theoharis, ed., *The FBI: A Comprehensive Reference Guide* (Westport, CT: Greenwood, 1999), 14, 175.

149. Charles H. Tuttle, "Society's Responsibility for Crime," *American Bar Association Journal* 20, no. 10 (1934): 631–35.

150. Philip Kinsley, "Leaders of Bar Map Campaign against Crime," *CDT*, August 30, 1934; "Bar Adopts Plan to Combat Crime," *BS*, August 30, 1934; "Bar Rallies to Rout 'Black Army' of Crime," *WP*, August 30, 1934.

151. Charles H. Tuttle, "Perjury: A Crime or a Privilege," *Century*, November 1927; John Lodge, "Why 2,000,000 Americans Are Dope Fiends," *Popular Science*, June 1930.

152. Muhammad, *Condemnation of Blackness*, 276–77.

153. Sylvester A. Johnson, "The FBI and the Moorish Science Temple of America, 1926–1960," in *The FBI and Religion: Faith and National Security before and after 9/11*, ed. Sylvester A. Johnson and Steven Weitzman (Oakland: University of California Press, 2017), 55–66.

154. Muhammad, *Condemnation of Blackness*, 91.

155. "A Frightful Homicide Record," *Annual of the Southern Baptist Convention*, 1929, 94.

156. Kavanagh, *Criminal and His Allies*, 145.

157. Muhammad, *Condemnation of Blackness*, 245.

158. Kavanagh, *Criminal and His Allies*, 136–46, 306.

159. "Judge Brings Dixie Style to Chicago," *CD*, February 23, 1929.

160. "Two Killers, Due to Die on Feb 25, Given Legal Aid," *CDT*, February 17, 1929; "Judge Brings Dixie Style."

161. David Stricklin, *A Genealogy of Dissent: Southern Baptist Protest in the Twentieth Century* (Lexington: University Press of Kentucky, 1999).

162. George Hillyer et al., "Hillyer Resolutions" (Chattanooga, TN, 1906), Southern Baptist Convention, http://www.sbc.net/resolutions/688/hillyer-resolutions. See also George Hillyer, "Criminal Law & Law Reform Speeches, 1910–1911," n.d., series 1, subseries IV, box 1, folder 5, Judge George Hillyer Papers, Kenan Research Center at the Atlanta History Center, Atlanta, GA.

163. "Recommendation on Law and Order" (Richmond, VA, 1907), Southern Baptist Convention, http://www.sbc.net/resolutions/665/recommendation-on-law-and-order; "Resolution on Law and Order" (Jacksonville, FL, 1911), Southern Baptist Convention, http://www.sbc.net/resolutions/666/resolution-on-law-and-order; "Social Service Commission Recommendation on Law and Order" (Memphis, 1929), Southern Baptist Convention, http://www.sbc.net/resolutions/667/social-service-commission-recommendation-on-law-and-order-adopted; "Social Service Commission Recommendation concerning

Law Enforcement and Observance" (New Orleans, 1930), Southern Baptist Convention, http://www.sbc.net/resolutions/668/social-service-commission-recommendation-concerning-law-enforcement-and-observance-adopted; "Resolution on Lynching on Mob Violence" (Saint Louis, MO, 1936), Southern Baptist Convention, http://www.sbc.net/resolutions/692/resolution-on-lynching-on-mob-violence; "Resolution on Lynching and Mob Violence" (New Orleans, 1937), Southern Baptist Convention, http://www.sbc.net/resolutions/693/resolution-on-lynching-and-mob-violence; "Resolution concerning Crime and Law Enforcement" (Oklahoma City, OK, 1939), Southern Baptist Convention, http://www.sbc.net/resolutions/669/resolution-concerning-crime-and-law-enforcement; "Resolution concerning Race Relations" (Birmingham, AL, 1941), Southern Baptist Convention, http://www.sbc.net/resolutions/881/resolution-concerning-race-relations.

164. E. T. Wellford, *Crime and Cure: A Review of This Lawless Age and the Mistrial of Christ* (Boston: Stratford, 1930), 5, 10–15.

165. For discussion of the "small-scale and daily" white violence against black Americans around this time and its intersections with police brutality, see Shannon King, "'Ready to Shoot and Do Shoot': Black Working-Class Self-Defense and Community Politics in Harlem, New York, during the 1920s," *Journal of Urban History* 37, no. 5 (September 2011): 757–74.

166. Thorsten Sellin, "Race Prejudice in the Administration of Justice," *American Journal of Sociology* 41, no. 2 (September 1935): 212–17.

167. For example, see George C. Dorsch, "Negro Leaders Map Program against Crime," *BS*, January 30, 1953; "'Thou Shall Not Kill' Mass Meet in Chattanooga Attracts Throng," *ADW*, March 1, 1941; "Lack of Education Causes Crime Wave, Says Negro Pastor," *AC*, September 19, 1921; and "Must Find Remedy for Crime Conditions Rev. Fortune Tells Douglas Day Crowd," *New Journal and Guide* (Norfolk, VA), March 4, 1939.

168. John Roach Straton, "The Menace of Skepticism, Worldliness and Lawlessness," *National Baptist Voice*, October 14, 1922. For more on Straton's racial paternalism, see Mary Beth Mathews, *Doctrine and Race: African American Evangelicals and Fundamentalism between the Wars* (Tuscaloosa: University of Alabama Press, 2017), 35.

169. "Ku Klux Must Go, Says Dr. Straton," *NYT*, December 4, 1922; Hillyer H. Straton, "John Roach Straton and the Ku Klux Klan," *Andover Newton Quarterly* 9, no. 2 (November 1968): 124–34.

170. George Stoll, *The Layman Helps the Warden* (Louisville, KY: Paul's Workshop, 1947), box 1, folder 19, CLC.

171. Kavanagh, *Criminal and His Allies*, 257, 371; McLaughlin, "U.S. Prison Chaplains."

172. On the perils and prospects of consensus history, see Leo P. Ribuffo, "What Is Still Living in 'Consensus' History and Pluralist Social Theory," *American Studies International* 38, no. 1 (February 2000): 42–60; Derek H. Davis, "God and the Pursuit of America's Self-Understanding: Toward a Synthesis of American Historiography," *Journal of Church and State* 46, no. 3 (Summer 2004): 461–78.

173. Michelle Alexander, *The New Jim Crow: Mass Incarceration in the Age of Colorblindness* (New York: New Press, 2010).

174. Naomi Murakawa, *The First Civil Right: How Liberals Built Prison America* (New York: Oxford University Press, 2014), 3, 10–11, 40–42. See also Elizabeth Hinton,

From the War on Poverty to the War on Crime: The Making of Mass Incarceration in America (Cambridge, MA: Harvard University Press, 2016); and James Forman Jr., *Locking Up Our Own: Crime and Punishment in Black America* (New York: Farrar, Straus and Giroux, 2017).

175. Homer Cummings, "Organized Religion and Crime Prevention" (speech, Williamstown Institute of Human Relations, Williamstown, MA, 1935), https://www.justice.gov/sites/default/files/ag/legacy/2011/09/16/08-29-1935.pdf.

176. Daniel K. Williams, *God's Own Party: The Making of the Christian Right* (New York: Oxford University Press, 2010), 18.

177. Robert Wuthnow, *The Restructuring of American Religion* (Princeton, NJ: Princeton University Press, 1988).

2. Jesus Christ Is the Only Control

1. David Frost, *Billy Graham: Candid Conversations with a Public Man* (Colorado Springs, CO: David C. Cook, 2014), 22–23. Graham related a similar version of this story in a sermon at his 1957 Madison Square Garden crusade. Billy Graham, "Spiritual Blindness," August 30, 1957, box 11, folder 9, Papers of Torrey Maynard Johnson, Collection 285, Billy Graham Center Archives, Wheaton College, Wheaton, IL.

2. "Evangelist Converts Vaus, Sound Engineer in Vice Probe," *Los Angeles Examiner,* November 8, 1949, Collection 360, scrapbook 5, BGCA; Cutler B. Whitwell, "The Great Awakening in Los Angeles," *Sunday School Times,* December 7, 1949; Frost, *Billy Graham,* 24.

3. Billy Graham, "Why a Revival?" (sermon, Los Angeles, 1949), tape 5702, BGCA.

4. Grant Wacker, *America's Pastor: Billy Graham and the Shaping of a Nation* (Cambridge, MA: Belknap Press of Harvard University Press, 2014), 12.

5. For example, see George M. Marsden, *Reforming Fundamentalism: Fuller Seminary and the New Evangelicalism* (Grand Rapids, MI: Eerdmans, 1987) and Molly Worthen, *Apostles of Reason: The Crisis of Authority in American Evangelicalism* (New York: Oxford University Press, 2014), 24–35.

6. On evangelicalism as an American folk tradition, see Randall Balmer, *Mine Eyes Have Seen the Glory: A Journey into the Evangelical Subculture in America* (New York: Oxford University Press, 1989), 229–40.

7. James Gilbert, *A Cycle of Outrage: America's Reaction to the Juvenile Delinquent in the 1950s* (New York: Oxford University Press, 1986), 4–5.

8. Worthen, *Apostles of Reason,* 36–37, 84.

9. The Assemblies of God, for example, affiliated with the National Association of Evangelicals in 1943 with these concerns in mind. Edith Blumhofer, *Restoring the Faith: The Assemblies of God, Pentecostalism, and American Culture* (Urbana: University of Illinois Press, 1993), 180–90.

10. On conversionism as a "special mark" of evangelicalism, see David Bebbington, *Evangelicalism in Modern Britain: A History from the 1730s to the 1980s* (London: Unwin Hyman, 1989), 16–29.

11. On the transition of the "born again" movement from subculture to mainstream in the "seventies evangelical moment," see Steven P. Miller, *The Age of Evangelicalism: America's Born-Again Years* (New York: Oxford University Press, 2014), chap. 1.

12. Bruce L. Shelley, "The Rise of Evangelical Youth Movements," *Fides et Historia* 18, no. 1 (January 1986): 48–49.

13. Joel A. Carpenter, "Youth for Christ and the New Evangelicals," in *Reckoning with the Past: Historical Essays on American Evangelicalism from the Institute for the Study of American Evangelicals,* ed. D. G. Hart (Grand Rapids, MI: Baker, 1995), 354–58. "Coming in from the cold" is Carpenter's reference to Richard John Neuhaus, *The Naked Public Square: Religion and Democracy in America* (Grand Rapids, MI: Eerdmans, 1984), 356.

14. Eileen Luhr, "Cold War Teenitiative: American Evangelical Youth and the Developing World in the Early Cold War," *Journal of the History of Childhood and Youth* 8, no. 2 (Spring 2015): 298.

15. Gilbert, *Cycle of Outrage,* 66–71.

16. Joel A. Carpenter, *Revive Us Again: The Reawakening of American Fundamentalism* (New York: Oxford University Press, 1999), 168.

17. Torrey Johnson and Robert Cook, *Reaching Youth for Christ* (Chicago: Moody, 1944), 34.

18. "Minutes of the Second Annual Convention of Youth for Christ International, Inc.," July 22, 1946, Collection 48, box 13, folder 37, BGCA.

19. Youth for Christ International, "What's the Answer?," n.d., box 72, folder 22, HT; Bob Cook, "Youth for Christ International, Inc.," n.d., box 72, folder 22, HT.

20. Carpenter, "Youth for Christ," 363–64.

21. "Minutes of the Second Annual Convention."

22. Carpenter, "Youth for Christ," 365–66. See also "Revolt in the American High School," n.d., box 72, folder 24, HT; and Joseph N. Bell, "God's Teenage Commandos," *Coronet,* November 1957.

23. Johnson and Cook, *Reaching Youth for Christ,* 20.

24. "Teen-Agers on the Rampage," *CL,* February 1954. See also "Evangelist Speaks in School; Board Plans Investigation to Determine Constitutionality," *St. Louis Star-Times,* December 4, 1943; "Bible Called Only Delinquency Cure," *Minneapolis Star,* May 7, 1946; and John G. Turner, *Bill Bright and Campus Crusade for Christ: The Renewal of Evangelicalism in Postwar America* (Chapel Hill: University of North Carolina Press, 2008), 23, 169.

25. Graham here was not specifically addressing crime (instead gesturing toward the general philosophy undergirding the approach of YFC and his preaching), but the topic was clearly on his mind. Just a few pages earlier in the same chapter, he referenced statistics showing rising crime and quoted a warning of J. Edgar Hoover regarding increased youth lawlessness. Billy Graham, *Calling Youth to Christ* (Grand Rapids, MI: Zondervan, 1947), 29, 20. See also Jon Pahl, *Youth Ministry in Modern America: 1930 to the Present* (Peabody, MA: Hendrickson, 2000), 59.

26. Graham, *Calling Youth to Christ,* 113–14. According to Graham, this story originally came from Canadian pastor and evangelist Oswald J. Smith.

27. Luhr, "Cold War Teenitiative," 300.

28. Lloyd G. Hamill, "God Works in San Francisco," *Youth for Christ,* September 1949, quoted in Pahl, *Youth Ministry in Modern America,* 63.

29. Harold Fey, "What about 'Youth for Christ'?," *CC,* June 20, 1945.

30. William Randolph Hearst to Editors of Hearst Papers, June 10, 1945, box 29, folder 2, Papers of Torrey Maynard Johnson, Collection 285, Billy Graham Center Archives, Wheaton College, Wheaton, IL.

31. Elesha Coffman, "'You Cannot Fool the Electronic Eye': Billy Graham and Media," in *Billy Graham: American Pilgrim,* ed. Andrew Finstuen, Anne Blue Wills, and Grant Wacker (New York: Oxford University Press, 2017), 197–215; Wacker, *America's Pastor,* 74–75.

32. Hearst editorial wire service, "New Tide of Faith," November 4, 1949, Collection 360, scrapbook 5, BGCA.

33. Andrew S. Finstuen, *Original Sin and Everyday Protestants: The Theology of Reinhold Niebuhr, Billy Graham, and Paul Tillich in an Age of Anxiety* (Chapel Hill: University of North Carolina Press, 2009), 130.

34. Wacker, *America's Pastor,* 231.

35. AP, "Evangelist Back Home Warns of Delinquency," *Battle Creek (MI) Enquirer,* November 30, 1955. Elsewhere he frequently named delinquency as a "major social problem." AP, "Billy Graham Cites Crime as Top Problem," *Pensacola (FL) News Journal,* August 5, 1955; AP, "Billy Graham Hits at Delinquency during Crusade," *Kingsport (TN) Times,* September 3, 1954.

36. Billy Graham, "What's Wrong with American Morals," *WP,* May 12, 1957.

37. "Text of Billy Graham's Sermon Opening His Crusade in Madison Square Garden," *NYT,* May 16, 1957.

38. Harold Hutchings, "Sins Curb Our Fight on Crime, Says Graham," *CDT,* May 17, 1957.

39. Billy Graham, "God's Delinquent," June 6, 1957, Collection 265, box 17, folder 30, BGCA.

40. See Curtis Mitchell, *God in the Garden: The Story of the Billy Graham New York Crusade* (Garden City, NY: Doubleday, 1957), chap. 16. The pistols are on display at the Billy Graham Library. "God in the Garden," Billy Graham Library, June 22, 2012, http://billygrahamlibrary.org/god-in-the-garden/.

41. George Dugan, "Graham Tells Off Gangs in Harlem," *NYT,* October 9, 1960.

42. Wacker, *America's Pastor,* 233–39.

43. Billy Graham, "God and Crime" (sermon, *Hour of Decision* radio program, 1956), tape 328f, HOD.

44. Billy Graham, "God, Crime, and the Devil" (sermon, *Hour of Decision* radio program, 1957), tape 402g, HOD.

45. "Church Leaders Pledge Aid in Drive on Crime," *LAT,* February 17, 1951.

46. AP, "Bill Graham Attacks Crime in St. Louis," *Dixon Evening Telegraph,* April 21, 1953.

47. Robert W. Ruth, "Crowd Hears Billy Graham Preach from Capitol Steps," *BS,* February 4, 1952.

48. "Kefauver Probes Aided Moral Rebirth, Graham Says," *Tennessean,* February 7, 1954; Emanuel Perlmutter, "Tobey Casts Spell over Crime Inquiry," *NYT,* March 15, 1951.

49. Billy Graham, "My Answer," *Courier-Journal* (Louisville, KY), August 19, 1956.

50. Will Vaus, *My Father Was a Gangster: The Jim Vaus Story* (Washington, DC: Believe Books, 2007), 101.

51. Dick Ross, dir., *Wiretapper* (World Wide Pictures, 1955).

52. "4,000 Cons Hear Graham at Quentin," *Daily Independent Journal* (San Rafael, CA), May 16, 1958; Lawrence DaViess, "Graham Drawing Crowds on Coast," *NYT,* May 18, 1958; "Billy Graham Ends Rally in San Francisco," *CDT,* June 16, 1958; "Billy in San Quentin," *Time,* May 26, 1958.

53. Shelley, "Rise of Evangelical Youth Movements," 51–52; "Revolt in the American High School" and Wendy Collins's Lifeline report in "Youth for Christ International Board of Directors Meeting Minutes," April 28, 1959, box 72, folder 6, HT.

54. "Mass Murder Trial of a Teen-Age Gang," *Life,* February 24, 1958.

55. David Wilkerson, John Sherrill, and Elizabeth Sherrill, *The Cross and the Switchblade* (New York: Bernard Geis Associates, 1963), 3–13. Wilkerson has told this story countless times over his career. For another early account, see W. Clement Stone, "How You Can Get the Good Things of Life," *Chicago Sunday Tribune Magazine,* March 17, 1963.

56. Jack Roth, "Girl Testifies She Hid Knives for Two in Gang after Killing," *NYT,* March 1, 1958.

57. Stone, "How You Can Get," 21.

58. David Batty and Ethan Campbell, *Teen Challenge: 50 Years of Miracles* (Springfield, MO: Teen Challenge, 2008), 11–12, 17.

59. See Wilkerson, Sherrill, and Sherrill, *Cross and the Switchblade,* chaps. 12–13; and David Wilkerson, "Counterattack for Christ," *PE,* October 30, 1960.

60. Bill Ep   ridge and James Mills, "Drug Addicts, Part 2," *Life,* March 6, 1965; Batty and Campbell, *Teen Challenge,* 20–21.

61. Will Vaus, *My Father Was a Gangster,* 145–47; "Interview with Jim Vaus by Bob Crossley: Session 1," April 11, 1967, box 2, folder 7, JV, 4–5, 11.

62. Wilkerson, "Counterattack for Christ."

63. "Interview with Jim Vaus by Bob Crossley: Session 1," 12.

64. "Two-Man Attack on Harlem's Asphalt Jungle," *Ebony,* June 1961.

65. Dave Palmeter, "2 Teen 'Hoods' Trade Weapons for Bible," *Star-Gazette* (Elmira, NY), August 1, 1958; David Wilkerson, "Too Strange to Be Coincidence, Part II," *Guideposts,* December 1961; Hiley H. Ward, "Little Nicky Finds God: Former Teen-Gang Terror Now Is Fighting the Devil," *Detroit Free Press,* February 25, 1963; "Interview with Jim Vaus by Bob Crossley: Session 2," April 26, 1967, box 2, folder 7, JV, 18–22.

66. Palmeter, "2 Teen 'Hoods.'"

67. Jim Vaus to Samuel Rettinger, May 13, 1959, box 1, folder 1, JV.

68. Peter Braestrup, "Former Rackets Man Fights Delinquency," Herald Tribune News Service, *Rapid City Journal,* July 15, 1959.

69. Conrad E. Jensen, *Juvenile Delinquency or Adult?* (New York: American Tract Society, n.d.).

70. "Two-Man Attack," 32; Will Vaus, *My Father Was a Gangster,* 159; Louis Cottell, "'Miracle' of the 23rd Precinct," n.d., box 2, folder 3, JV.

71. Wilkerson, Sherrill, and Sherrill, *Cross and the Switchblade,* 155–57.

72. "Interview with Jim Vaus by Bob Crossley: Session 4," May 22, 1967, box 2, folder 8, JV, 1–18.

73. Louis Cassels, "'Greater Love Hath No Man Than This . . .': Lou Marsh Gave His Life to Help N.Y. Youth Gang," *New Journal and Guide* (Norfolk, VA), February 16, 1963; Dean Peerman, "Death down a Dark Street," *CC,* February 6, 1963.

74. The *Post* did not actually agree with these assessments, calling the public hysteria "nonsense." Gertrude Samuels, "Death of a Youth Worker," *Saturday Evening Post,* April 6, 1963. See also William Stringfellow, *My People Is the Enemy: An Autobiographical Polemic* (Eugene, OR: Wipf and Stock, 2005), 143–44.

75. Phil Ochs, "The Ballad of Lou Marsh," *Broadside,* no. 21, 1963. See also "Lou Marsh," *Shadows That Shine* (blog), May 27, 2012, https://philochsthing.wordpress.com/tag/phil-ochs-lou-marsh/.

76. "Interview with Jim Vaus by Bob Crossley: Session 4." For newspaper coverage of the verdict, see "Four Youths Found Guilty in Slaying of Youth Worker," *NYT,* February 20, 1964.

77. Dave Palmeter, "'We're Mau Maus; He's Our Preacher,'" *Star-Gazette* (Elmira, NY), July 30, 1958.

78. "Excerpts from the 'Testimony' of a Former Drug Addict: Benny Torrez," appendix 3 in Russell Melvin Spangler, "A Rhetorical Study of the Preaching of Pastor David Wilkerson" (PhD diss., Michigan State University, 1969), 257–62.

79. Tom Skinner, *Black and Free* (Grand Rapids, MI: Zondervan, 1968), 36–37; Tom Skinner, interview by Bob Shuster, June 13, 1990, tape 1, TS.

80. Tom Skinner, *Tom Skinner, Top Man of the Lords and Other Stories,* ed. James R. Adair (Grand Rapids, MI: Baker Book House, 1967), 9.

81. Skinner, 9–11; Tom Skinner, interview by Bob Shuster, June 13, 1990, tape 2, TS.

82. McCandlish Phillips, "Evangelist Finds Harlem Vineyard," *NYT,* August 16, 1964.

83. For example, see Wilkerson, Sherrill, and Sherrill, *Cross and the Switchblade,* chap. 18.

84. Palmeter, "2 Teen 'Hoods.'"

85. David Wilkerson, "Rock and Roll—the Devil's Heartbeat," *PE,* July 12, 1959; Wilkerson, "Counterattack for Christ"; David Wilkerson, "Teen Challenge: What God Is Doing at the Teen-Age Evangelism Center in New York City," *PE,* December 31, 1961.

86. Randall Balmer, "Peale, Norman Vincent," in *The Encyclopedia of Evangelicalism* (Waco, TX: Baylor University Press, 2004).

87. John L. Sherrill, "Too Strange to Be Coincidence, Part I," *Guideposts,* November 1961; Wilkerson, "Too Strange."

88. See Gary Wilkerson and R. S. B. Sawyer, *David Wilkerson: The Cross, the Switchblade, and the Man Who Believed* (Grand Rapids, MI: Zondervan, 2014), chap. 6.

89. *Chicago Tribune Magazine of Books,* June 2, 1963, sec. 9; "Book Reviews," *Religious Education* 58, no. 4 (July 1, 1963): 395–408; *WP,* June 20, 1963.

90. "Tips: Previews, Promotions, Sales," *Publisher's Weekly,* April 22, 1963.

91. Batty and Campbell, *Teen Challenge,* 35.

92. "Sales Notes," *Publisher's Weekly,* October 19, 1964; "Christian Recovery Center—History," Adult and Teen Challenge, accessed June 10, 2017, https://www .teenchallengeusa.com/about/history; David R. Wilkerson, John Sherrill, and Elizabeth Sherrill, *Beyond the Cross and the Switchblade* (New York: Pillar Books, 1976), 8.

93. *CTR,* June 2, 1963, sec. 9.

94. Robert L. Kirsch, "'Sex and Single Girl' Falls Short of Its Promising Title," *LAT,* July 6, 1962; "Helen's Book Was a Shock to Her Mother," *LAT,* June 24, 1962; Jennifer Scanlon, "Sensationalist Literature or Expert Advice?," *Feminist Media Studies* 9, no. 1 (March 1, 2009): 1–15.

95. Riva D. Atlas, "Bernard Geis, Celebrity Publisher, Dies at 91," *NYT,* January 10, 2001.

96. "Media," *Publisher's Weekly,* August 5, 1963.

97. Mary Ann Callan, "L.A. Teen-Age Gangs Feed U.S. Dope Rings," *LAT,* July 21, 1963.

98. David Wilkerson, John Sherrill, and Elizabeth Sherrill, "The Cross and the Switchblade," *Good Housekeeping,* July 1963.

99. "Media."

100. For example, see David Wilkerson and Leonard Ravenhill, *Twelve Angels from Hell* (Westwood, NJ: F. H. Revell, 1965); David Wilkerson and Phyllis Murphy, *The Little People* (Westwood, NJ: F. H. Revell, 1966); David Wilkerson and Phyllis Murphy, *Parents on Trial: Why Kids Go Wrong or Right* (Westwood, NJ: F. H. Revell, 1966); and David Wilkerson, *Hey, Preach—You're Comin' Through!* (Westwood, NJ: F. H. Revell, 1968).

101. Nicky Cruz and Jamie Buckingham, *Run Baby Run* (Plainfield, NJ: Logos International, 1968), vii.

102. Jim Vaus, *Teenage Rampage* (Grand Rapids, MI: Zondervan, 1956); Jim Vaus, *The Inside Story of Narcotics* (Grand Rapids, MI: Zondervan, 1953).

103. Robert P. Crossley, "The Two Lives of Jim Vaus," *Reader's Digest,* July 1961; "Two-Man Attack"; "Merv: 8:00 P.M.," *Minneapolis Star,* August 11, 1972; "TV Magazine," *Cincinnati Enquirer,* July 10, 1966; Will Vaus, *My Father Was a Gangster,* xix.

104. Jim Weaver, "Former Gangster Ham Operator Is Saved by Graham," *Cincinnati Enquirer,* March 5, 1972.

105. Ed Townsend and Glen Spey, "Romney Whirlwinds Youth Camp in Sullivan," *Times Herald-Record* (Middletown, NY), September 18, 1967; Les Rodney, "Ex-Aide to Gangsters Speaking Here," *Independent Press-Telegram* (Long Beach, CA), November 21, 1965.

106. Tom Skinner, "I Preach the White Man's Religion," *CL,* July 1966; Skinner, *Tom Skinner;* Skinner, *Black and Free;* Tom Skinner, "Why We Must Win the American Negro," *MM,* April 1968; Tom Skinner, *Now I'm Free!* (Seattle: Life Messengers, n.d.); Tom Skinner, *Top Man of the Lords* (Oradell, NJ: American Tract Society, n.d.).

107. For a discussion of an earlier version of middlebrow book culture, see Matthew S. Hedstrom, *The Rise of Liberal Religion: Book Culture and American Spirituality in the Twentieth Century* (New York: Oxford University Press, 2013), chap. 2.

108. Lloyd Young, dir., *An Epistle from the Koreans* (Film Productions, International, 1959).

109. James R. Adair, "Blood on the Sidewalk," *The Mennonite,* May 7, 1963.

110. Hannah Kim, "Ties That Bind: People, Policy, and Perception in U.S.-Korean Relations, 1905–1965" (PhD diss., University of Delaware, 2011), 334–36.

111. Mel White, *To Forgive a Thief* (Cathedral Films, 1966), film 209, Collection 307, BGCA.

112. "Young Pastor Trying to Hook Hoods on God," *Springfield (MO) Leader-Press,* October 29, 1963.

113. "Narcotics Addicts Find a Cure through Religion," *NYT,* February 16, 1964. See also Dorothy Townsend, "A Religious Approach to Dope Addiction," *LAT,* September 9, 1965.

114. Various success rate claims appear throughout Teen Challenge's promotional literature and in news reports about the ministry. For an early example, see John G. Anderson, "Hawaii Drug Center Thrives," *Honolulu Star-Advertiser,* June 23, 1973. For a broader scholarly discussion of Teen Challenge's effectiveness, see Charles L. Glenn, "Interlude: Teen Challenge," in *The Ambiguous Embrace: Government and Faith-Based Schools and Social Agencies* (Princeton, NJ: Princeton University Press, 2000), 62–73.

115. See, for example, Laurie Goodstein, "Church-Based Projects Lack Data on Results," *NYT,* April 24, 2001.

116. Frank Reynolds, *Is There a God?* (Lenexa, KS: 3CrossPublishing, 2006), 10–11.

117. Skinner, *Now I'm Free!*

118. "Is God Dead?," *Time,* April 8, 1966. For an account of the perceived threat of "big science," see Benjamin E. Zeller, *Prophets and Protons: New Religious Movements and Science in Late Twentieth-Century America* (New York: New York University Press, 2010), 5.

119. Sherrill, "Too Strange"; Wilkerson, "Too Strange."

120. Thelma L. Snell, "'Bad Kids' Analyses Ring True," *WP,* August 4, 1963.

121. Leland Wilkinson, "Is the Church Reaching Teen-Agers?," *Woman's Day,* August 1967.

122. "Roman Catholic Leader Praises Work of Teen Challenge," *PE,* March 16, 1969.

123. Nathan O. Hatch, *The Democratization of American Christianity* (New Haven, CT: Yale University Press, 1989).

124. *The Story of Teen Challenge New York* (Brooklyn: Teen Challenge, 1967), FPHC, 26.

125. Steven P. Miller, *Billy Graham and the Rise of the Republican South* (Philadelphia: University of Pennsylvania Press, 2009), 44.

126. Quoted in Miller, 47–48.

127. Graham, "God, Crime, and the Devil."

128. Jim Vaus, *Why I Quit Syndicated Crime* (Los Angeles: Scripture Outlet, 1951), 17. Vaus's son Will has noted that this book was actually composed by a ghostwriter, though it is largely accurate. Will Vaus, *My Father Was a Gangster,* 91.

129. Spangler, "Rhetorical Study," 37.

130. Will Vaus, *My Father Was a Gangster,* 198.

131. "Serving Jesus Christ at Hell Gate Station," *UEA,* April 1967.

132. For a broader history of this movement, see Kevin M. Kruse, *One Nation under God: How Corporate America Invented Christian America* (New York: Basic Books, 2015).

133. "Lessons of Leadership: Preaching What You Practice," *Nation's Business,* March 1967; Wacker, *America's Pastor,* 116.

134. "Young Pastor."

135. This letter, addressed to Wilkerson, was reprinted in Teen Challenge promotional materials. *Story of Teen Challenge,* 2.

136. "Gangs in Elmira? Police Know of None," *Star-Gazette* (Elmira, NY), August 22, 1958.

137. Callan, "L.A. Teen-Age Gangs." See also Ward Cannel, "Farm to Help Save Gang Boys," *News Journal* (Wilmington, DE), November 20, 1962.

138. Will Vaus, *My Father Was a Gangster,* 171ff.

139. Youth Development, *Crossroads Center,* n.d., box 1, folder 4, JV.

140. Omri Elisha, "Taking the (Inner) City for God: Ambiguities of Urban Social Engagement among Conservative White Evangelicals," in *The Fundamentalist City? Religiosity and the Remaking of Urban Space,* ed. Nezar AlSayyad and Mejgan Massoumi (New York: Routledge, 2011), 235, 237.

141. Darren Dochuk, "'Praying for a Wicked City': Congregation, Community, and the Suburbanization of Fundamentalism," *Religion and American Culture* 13, no. 2 (Summer 2003): 180–85.

142. Thomas J. Sugrue, *The Origins of the Urban Crisis: Race and Inequality in Postwar Detroit,* rev. ed. (Princeton, NJ: Princeton University Press, 2005); Kevin M. Kruse, *White Flight: Atlanta and the Making of Modern Conservatism* (Princeton, NJ: Princeton University Press, 2005); Elizabeth Hinton, *From the War on Poverty to the War on Crime: The Making of Mass Incarceration in America* (Cambridge, MA: Harvard University Press, 2016).

143. Phillips, "Evangelist Finds Harlem Vineyard."

144. Skinner, *Black and Free,* 134.

145. Skinner, 67–68, 92–96.

146. Skinner, "I Preach."

147. As Soong-Chan Rah has put it in his study of Skinner and African American evangelicalism, "The power of the Evangelical gospel would be spoken by someone from the unreached community, proving the exceptional power of the Evangelical message." Soong-Chan Rah, "In Whose Image: The Emergence, Development, and Challenge of African-American Evangelicalism" (ThD diss., Duke Divinity School, 2016), 219.

148. Skinner, *Black and Free,* chap. 7, 11, 12.

149. Skinner, "Why We Must Win."

150. Kim, "Ties That Bind," 293–95, 313, 342–58.

151. "An Epistle from the Koreans," *Gospel Messenger,* September 22, 1962.

152. AP, "Funeral Services Held for Slain Korean Student in Phila.," *Standard-Sentinel* (Hazleton, PA), April 30, 1958; H. B. Sissel to Harry Walrond, May 3, 1961, Record Group 78, box 11, folder 19, Presbyterian Historical Society, Philadelphia.

153. Carl F. H. Henry, *The Uneasy Conscience of Modern Fundamentalism* (Grand Rapids, MI: Eerdmans, 1947).

154. Dick Humphrey (United Press International), "Former Grants Pass Rancher Helps with Juvenile Problems," *Medford (OR) Mail Tribune,* September 18, 1959.

155. David Lester, "My Son Was a Drug Addict," *Good Housekeeping,* January 1965, 114.

156. David Wilkerson, "Should Marijuana Be Legalized," *PE: International Edition,* February 1968.

157. Emily Dufton, "The War on Drugs: What's God Got to Do with Fighting Addiction?," *Atlantic,* March 27, 2012.

158. Christian Smith, quoted in Brian Steensland and Philip Goff, *The New Evangelical Social Engagement* (New York: Oxford University Press, 2013), 11. See also Michael O. Emerson and Christian Smith, *Divided by Faith: Evangelical Religion and the Problem of Race in America* (New York: Oxford University Press, 2000), 118.

159. Curtis J. Evans, "A Politics of Conversion: Billy Graham's Political and Social Vision," in Finstuen, Wills, and Wacker, *Billy Graham,* 147.

160. Robert W. Snyder, "A Useless and Terrible Death: The Michael Farmer Case, 'Hidden Violence,' and New York in the Fifties," *Journal of Urban History* 36, no. 2 (February 2010): 226–50.

161. Wilkerson, Sherrill, and Sherrill, *Cross and the Switchblade,* 18–19.

162. Wilkerson, Sherrill, and Sherrill, 29.

3. Religion Is a Real Weapon

1. National Inter-religious Task Force on Criminal Justice, Work Group on the Death Penalty, "What the Religious Community Has to Say on Capital Punishment," n.d., box 38, folder 20, NAE; Henry Schwarzschild to Floyd Robinson [Robertson], September 1, 1976, box 38, folder 20, NAE.

2. For a discussion of the NAE's importance during the 1940s–1960s, see Axel R. Schäfer, *Countercultural Conservatives: American Evangelicalism from the Postwar Revival to the New Christian Right* (Madison: University of Wisconsin Press, 2011), 10.

3. Henry Schwarzschild to Floyd Robinson [Robertson], September 1, 1976.

4. Floyd Robertson to Henry Schwarzschild, September 11, 1976, box 38, folder 20, NAE.

5. Floyd Robertson and Henry Schwarzschild, "Capital Punishment: An Exchange," *Christianity and Crisis* 37, no. 2 (February 21, 1977): 30–32.

6. John P. Adams and Carol J. Ross, "Letter from Board of Church and Society of the United Methodist Church," January 10, 1978, box 38, folder 20, NAE.

7. Andrew S. Finstuen, *Original Sin and Everyday Protestants: The Theology of Reinhold Niebuhr, Billy Graham, and Paul Tillich in an Age of Anxiety* (Chapel Hill: University of North Carolina Press, 2009).

8. Grant Wacker, *America's Pastor: Billy Graham and the Shaping of a Nation* (Cambridge, MA: Belknap Press of Harvard University Press, 2014), 263–66.

9. Blake Morgan, "There Are Plenty of Useful Themes for Prayer as Atlanta Prepares for the Graham Revival," *AJC,* October 15, 1950.

10. W. Stanley Mooneyham, "Evangelicals—Divisive or Dynamic?," *PJ,* April 8, 1964. A later study showed drops in crime during Graham's 1959 Australian crusade.

Stuart Piggin, *Word and World Spirit: Evangelical Christianity in Australia* (Brunswick East, Melbourne: Acorn, 2012), 97–98.

11. Papers of Roy Lundquist, n.d., Collection 2, folders 1–15, BGCA.

12. Billy Graham, "Billy Graham Makes Plea for an End to Intolerance," *Life*, October 1, 1956.

13. See Steven P. Miller, *Billy Graham and the Rise of the Republican South* (Philadelphia: University of Pennsylvania Press, 2009), chap. 2.

14. See Miller, chap. 3; and Wacker, *America's Pastor*, chap. 3.

15. Wacker, *America's Pastor*, 120–26; Miller, *Billy Graham*, 56.

16. "Faubus in Integrated Audience Hears Plea to Believe in Christ," *ADW*, September 15, 1959.

17. Mark Newman, *Getting Right with God: Southern Baptists and Desegregation, 1945–1995* (Tuscaloosa: University of Alabama Press, 2001), 119; Miller, *Billy Graham*, 59.

18. Religion News Service, "Nashville Clergy Condemn Acts of Violence," *Biblical Recorder*, September 21, 1957; "600 Atlanta Churches Pray for Orderly Desegregation," *AC*, August 28, 1961; "Law and Order Sabbath," *ADW*, August 27, 1961.

19. Miller, *Billy Graham*, 59.

20. Wacker, *America's Pastor*, 21–22.

21. J. Edgar Hoover, "The Challenge of the Future," *CT*, May 26, 1958.

22. Quoted in Richard Gid Powers, *G-Man: Hoover's FBI in American Popular Culture* (Carbondale: Southern Illinois University Press, 1983), 253.

23. For example, see "Teen-Agers on the Rampage," *CL*, February 1954.

24. "Why Christianity Today?," *CT*, October 15, 1956.

25. "In the Beginning: Billy Graham Recounts the Origins of Christianity Today," *CT*, July 17, 1981. See also Mark G. Toulouse, "Christianity Today and American Public Life: A Case Study," *Journal of Church and State* 35, no. 2 (March 1, 1993): 241–84.

26. J. Edgar Hoover, "Statement of Director J. Edgar Hoover," *FBI Law Enforcement Bulletin*, June 1, 1961, 1–2. I am grateful to Lerone Martin for bringing this document to my attention.

27. M. A. Jones to Cartha DeLoach, November 21, 1960, https://archive.org/stream/FernC.Stukenbroeker/Stukenbroeker%2C%20Fern%20C.-2#page/n273/mode/2up.

28. Michael S. Weaver, "The Bitter Enemy of Religion: J. Edgar Hoover and Anti-Communist Rhetoric in Christianity Today (1956–1971)" (unpublished paper, April 26, 2011), in author's possession.

29. L. Nelson Bell to J. Howard Pew, February 8, 1961, box 1, folder 58, CTR.

30. V. R. Edman and J. Edgar Hoover, May 28, 1958, https://archive.org/details/WheatonCollegeHQ9412695951pp/page/n15/mode/2up.

31. J. Edgar Hoover, "Communist Menace: Red Goals and Christian Ideals," *CT*, October 10, 1960; J. Edgar Hoover, "What Does the Future Hold?," *CT*, June 19, 1961.

32. J. Edgar Hoover, "Spiritual Priorities: Guidelines for a Civilization in Peril," *CT*, June 22, 1962.

33. L. Nelson Bell, "A Layman and His Faith: Delinquency—There Is a Cause," *CT*, February 3, 1958.

34. Pitirim A. Sorokin, "Demoralization of Youth: Open Germs and Hidden Viruses," *CT*, July 6, 1959; Russell Fornwalt, "For They Have Sown the Wind," *CT*, July 6, 1959. Other articles from the issue included Emma Fall Schofield, "Will Alcohol Destroy Our Youth?"; Talbot Ellis, "A Judge Speaks"; J. Marcellus Kik, "Combating Juvenile Delinquency"; and "The Delinquent Church."

35. "Evers' Murder Signals Eventual Burial of Segregation," *CT*, July 5, 1963.

36. "Law and Reformation," *CT*, October 27, 1958.

37. Lawrence Chenoweth, "The Rhetoric of Hope and Despair: A Study of the Jimi Hendrix Experience and the Jefferson Airplane," *American Quarterly* 23, no. 1 (1971): 28.

38. "Delinquent Church."

39. Carl F. H. Henry, *Aspects of Christian Social Ethics* (Grand Rapids, MI: Eerdmans, 1964), 92–94. Henry's published work here was originally a set of lectures delivered at Fuller Theological Seminary in 1963.

40. Henry, 96, 166.

41. Stuart Barton Babbage, "Review of Current Religious Thought," *CT*, January 19, 1959.

42. Carl Henry to Gordon H. Clark, November 26, 1959, box 15, folder 12, CTR.

43. Jacob J. Vellenga, "Is Capital Punishment Wrong?," *CT*, October 12, 1959; John Howard Yoder, Charles S. Milligan, and Gordon H. Clark, "Capital Punishment and the Bible," *CT*, February 1, 1960; "The Modern Debate on the Death Penalty," *CT*, February 1, 1960.

44. William C. Placher, *A History of Christian Theology: An Introduction* (Louisville, KY: Westminster John Knox, 1983), 221.

45. Quotes from Molly Worthen, *Apostles of Reason: The Crisis of Authority in American Evangelicalism* (New York: Oxford University Press, 2014), 65–66, 84–86.

46. Chuck McFadden, *Trailblazer: A Biography of Jerry Brown* (Berkeley: University of California Press, 2013), 30–31; Christopher S. Kudlac, *Public Executions: The Death Penalty and the Media* (Westport, CT: Praeger, 2007), 30–31; "Let Caryl Chessman Live," *CC*, April 27, 1960.

47. McFadden, *Trailblazer*.

48. Kudlac, *Public Executions*, 31.

49. "Governor Brown Compounds the Caryl Chessman Travesty," *CT*, March 14, 1960; "The Real Lesson of the Chessman Case," *CT*, May 23, 1960; "When Justice Ceases to Be Justice," *Southern Presbyterian Journal*, March 9, 1960.

50. Christian Smith, *American Evangelicalism: Embattled and Thriving* (Chicago: University of Chicago Press, 1998).

51. "The Basic Sinfulness of the 'Freedom Riders' Riots," *CT*, June 5, 1961; "The Love of Freedom and Judicial Determination," *CT*, July 17, 1961.

52. L. Nelson Bell, "A Plea for Communication and an Examination of Long-Held Opinions," *UEA*, August 1963.

53. Miller, *Billy Graham*, 94.

54. "The Crowded Coliseum," *CT*, September 27, 1963. See also "Graham Raps High Court," *WP*, August 30, 1963.

55. Christopher Alan Hickman, "The Most Dangerous Branch: The Supreme Court and Its Critics in the Warren Court Era" (PhD diss., George Washington University, 2010), 172–77.

56. "Miranda v. Arizona," Oyez, accessed January 26, 2017, https://www.oyez.org /cases/1965/759.

57. "Mallory v. United States," Oyez, accessed January 26, 2017, https://www .oyez.org/cases/1956/521.

58. "Technicality a Vicious Device for Outwitting the Law," *CT,* January 6, 1958. See also "We Must Stop," *UEA,* June 1967; "The Warren Court Era," *CT,* July 19, 1968.

59. Washington Seminar Folder, n.d., box 62, folder 12, NAE.

60. Clyde W. Taylor, "A Washington Seminar for Pastors and Laymen," *UEA,* December 1963; Clyde W. Taylor, "Capital Commentary: Law Enforcement," *UEA,* March 1966.

61. Hickman, "Most Dangerous Branch," 263.

62. Naomi Murakawa, *The First Civil Right: How Liberals Built Prison America* (New York: Oxford University Press, 2014), 76.

63. Darren Dochuk, *From Bible Belt to Sunbelt: Plain-Folk Religion, Grassroots Politics, and the Rise of Evangelical Conservatism* (New York: W. W. Norton, 2011), 251.

64. Michael W. Flamm, *Law and Order: Street Crime, Civil Unrest, and the Crisis of Liberalism in the 1960s* (New York: Columbia University Press, 2007), 44; Kathleen Hall Jamieson, *Packaging the Presidency: A History and Criticism of Presidential Campaign Advertising* (New York: Oxford University Press, 1996), 212–15; "'Choice' [1964 Barry Goldwater Campaign Film]," posted May 22, 2011, YouTube video, 28:32, https://www.youtube.com/watch?v=xniUoMiHm8g.

65. Wacker, *America's Pastor,* 210–11. For more on Goldwater's southern and Sunbelt appeal, see Dochuk, *From Bible Belt to Sunbelt,* chap. 9.

66. Hinton, *From the War on Poverty,* 81.

67. Robert Esbjornson, *A Christian in Politics, Luther W. Youngdahl: A Story of a Christian's Faith at Work in a Modern World* (Minneapolis: T. S. Denison, 1955).

68. "Outspoken Judge: Luther Wallace Youngdahl," *NYT,* June 16, 1961.

69. Alfred E. Clark, "Youngdahl Urges More Probation," *NYT,* June 1, 1963; "Judge Youngdahl Urges Improved Detention Systems: Minister Sees Need for Prayer Solution," *WP,* May 16, 1966.

70. Murakawa, *First Civil Right,* 82; Hinton, *From the War on Poverty,* 83–84.

71. "Crime and Christianity," *CT,* March 26, 1965; "The War on Crime," *CT,* April 14, 1967; "The Criminal Code: Reform or Retreat," *CT,* May 26, 1967.

72. "Crime Commission Member Says Report Omitted Place of Religion," *UEA,* April 1967; Christian Crusaders Class of the Evangelical United Brethren Church of Waterloo, "From the Study: Notes and Quotes," *Waterloo Press,* November 21, 1968; John B. Anderson, "Word from Washington: Is There a Cure for the Cancer of Crime?," *Christian Times,* March 19, 1967.

73. Murakawa, *First Civil Right,* 77–78; Hinton, *From the War on Poverty,* 63–64.

74. Albert Watson, "The Los Angeles Situation," *Congressional Record* 111 (August 17, 1965): 20792; Billy B. Hathorn, "The Changing Politics of Race: Congressman Albert William Watson and the S.C. Republican Party, 1965–1970," *South Carolina Historical Magazine* 89, no. 4 (1988): 227–41.

75. Flamm, *Law and Order.*

76. Bill Henry, "By the Way: Capital Nervous about L.A. Riots," *LAT,* August 17, 1965; "Leaders at Odds over L.A. Riot," *CD,* August 21, 1965; "Curfew Lifted in Los Angeles," *NYT,* August 18, 1965.

77. Billy Graham, "Saved or Lost?," August 15, 1965, Collection 265, box 28, folder 8, BGCA. In the archived copy of this sermon, many of the parts having to do with rioting and crime are crossed out. Graham likely used the Montreat sermon as the basis for a Houston crusade sermon that he preached several weeks later. The Houston sermon manuscript followed the Montreat version except in the crossed-out sections of the original version. Billy Graham, "Saved or Lost?," November 24, 1965, Collection 265, box 28, folder 9, BGCA. See also "Get Tough Policy Urged by Graham," *AJC,* August 15, 1965.

78. "Schmitz Commutes to Special Session," *La Habra (CA) Star,* September 15, 1965; "Riots Are Subsidized as Well as Organized: Barron's Weekly," *CTR,* August 6, 1967.

79. D. Leroy Sanders, "Violence: Its Cause and Cure," *PE,* October 17, 1965.

80. Samuel H. Sutherland, "A Glimmer of Light," *King's Business,* November 1965; Adam Laats, *Fundamentalist U: Keeping the Faith in American Higher Education* (New York: Oxford University Press, 2018), 231.

81. "3-Day Crusade by Graham Group to End in Watts," *LAT,* December 4, 1965; Miller, *Billy Graham,* 128.

82. Hinton, *From the War on Poverty,* 73.

83. Murakawa, *First Civil Right,* 77.

84. Hinton, *From the War on Poverty,* 75.

85. Allen F. Bray III, "Try Them with Truth," *CT,* April 24, 1964.

86. "Why Did They Riot?," *CT,* March 29, 1968.

87. Quoted in David Edwin Harrell Jr., *White Sects and Black Men in the Recent South* (Nashville: Vanderbilt University Press, 1971), 57–66.

88. "Why Did They Riot?"; "U.S. Crime: Beyond the Law," *CT,* September 11, 1970; Robert C. Cunningham, "Watts—a Year Later," *PE,* July 17, 1966.

89. For a broader history of "family values" evangelical activism, see Seth Dowland, *Family Values and the Rise of the Christian Right* (Philadelphia: University of Pennsylvania Press, 2015).

90. E. R. Kimball, "The Home and National Order/Disorder," *Evangelical Beacon,* August 13, 1968.

91. Clyde W. Taylor, "War on Obscenity?," *UEA,* June 1965.

92. Representative John B. Anderson, speaking on House Resolution 729: Penalties for Inciting Riots, *House Congressional Record* 113 (July 19, 1967): 19350.

93. "Lyndon B. Johnson: Proclamation 3796—National Day of Prayer and Reconciliation," July 27, 1967, American Presidency Project, https://www.presidency.ucsb.edu/node/306179.

94. W. Barry Garrett, "LBJ Calls for Prayer and Action for Justice," *BP,* July 28, 1967.

95. "LBJ Appeals to Nation for Change in Hearts," *BP,* March 27, 1968.

96. Barry Hankins, *Uneasy in Babylon: Southern Baptist Conservatives and American Culture* (Tuscaloosa: University of Alabama Press, 2002), 175.

97. "American People Need Desire for Justice," *BP*, March 28, 1968.

98. Jim Newton, "Carmichael, Race Oppression Blamed for Nashville Rioting," *BP*, April 20, 1967.

99. "Positive Actions in Race Relations Urged by Baptists," *BP*, January 10, 1968.

100. James F. Findlay, *Church People in the Struggle: The National Council of Churches and the Black Freedom Movement, 1950–1970* (New York: Oxford University Press, 1993), 4.

101. "Unity of Mission Conference Draws 143 Participants to Chicago," Diocesan News Service, June 5, 1968, http://www.episcopalarchives.org/cgi-bin/ENS/ENSpress_release.pl?pr_number=66-19.

102. Weldon Wallace, "Bishops Warn against 'Law and Order' Cloak," *BS*, October 25, 1968; Diane Stepp, "Law and Order and Justice Urged by Episcopal Bishops," *AC*, October 25, 1968.

103. James L. Adams, "Race and Riots Engage United Church," *CT*, July 21, 1967.

104. Findlay, *Church People in the Struggle*, 64–65.

105. "Church Leaders Take 'Hardline' Position on Death Penalty," *BP*, July 10, 1969.

106. Martin B. Bradley, "Baptist VIEWpoll Report: Baptist Leaders Prefer Appointment of 'Conservatives' to High Court," *BP*, July 23, 1969.

107. Floyd Craig, "Survey Lists Race, War, Crime as Top Baptist Moral Issues," *BP*, December 5, 1969.

108. "Criswell Challenges First, Dallas, to Reach All Races," *BP*, June 11, 1968.

109. "Death Penalty Repeal Killed in NC Senate," *PJ*, March 27, 1963; "Punishment Study Is Killed by Legislature," *PJ*, July 10, 1963.

110. "The 1966 General Assembly!," *Concerned Presbyterian*, June 1966; "Religion's Impact Waning," *Concerned Presbyterian*, September 1968; "The 1969 Mobile General Assembly," *Concerned Presbyterian*, July 1969.

111. Elizabeth White Sevier, "Ministers, Listen to Laymen," *Cumberland Presbyterian*, June 11, 1968.

112. Randall Balmer and John R. Fitzmier, *The Presbyterians* (Westport, CT: Greenwood, 1993), 107.

113. Daniel Sack, "A Divided House," in *The Future of Mainline Protestantism in America*, ed. James Hudnut-Beumler and Mark Silk (New York: Columbia University Press, 2018), 119–20.

114. Bradley J. Longfield, *Presbyterians and American Culture: A History* (Louisville, KY: Westminster John Knox, 2013), 195.

115. John R. Fry, *The Trivialization of the United Presbyterian Church* (New York: Harper and Row, 1975), 47; "There's No Excuse," *PJ*, June 23, 1971.

116. Fry, *Trivialization*, 38.

117. "Of Crime and Punishment X," *PJ*, January 23, 1974.

118. Barry Hankins, "Southern Baptists and Northern Evangelicals: Cultural Factors and the Nature of Religious Alliances," *Religion and American Culture* 7, no. 2 (Summer 1997): 271–98.

119. "How to Lick a Problem," *PJ*, January 12, 1966.

120. James DeForest Murch, "The Protestant Position Today," 1963, box 53, folder 1, NAE.

121. G. Archer Weniger, "God Commands Death Penalty for Murder," *Sword of the Lord,* October 8, 1965; Dochuk, *From Bible Belt to Sunbelt,* 232.

122. John Fea, *The Bible Cause: A History of the American Bible Society* (New York: Oxford University Press, 2016), 290–92.

123. Carl McIntire, "Key 73 vs. Revival '76" (*20th Century Reformation Hour,* n.d.), box 555, folder 86, CM; "Revival '76" (*20th Century Reformation Hour,* n.d.), box 152, folder 39, CM.

124. "What Do Churches Really Think about Capital Punishment?," *CT,* July 18, 1960.

125. Philip Jenkins, *Decade of Nightmares: The End of the Sixties and the Making of Eighties America* (New York: Oxford University Press, 2006), 136.

126. L. Nelson Bell, "A Layman and His Faith: Civil Disobedience," *CT,* April 26, 1968.

127. "H. Law and Order," 1966, Policy Resolutions Adopted by the National Association of Evangelicals, 1956–1967, box 175, folder 19, NAE; National Association of Evangelicals, "Resolutions Adopted in 1968: Law and Order," 1968, Collection 584, box 36, folder 6, BGCA; Robert C. Cunningham, "Iniquity Abounding," *PE,* July 14, 1968; "Evangelicals Call for 'Unique' Crisis Help," *PJ,* May 8, 1968.

4. God's Law and Order

1. Ronald N. Jacobs, *Race, Media, and the Crisis of Civil Society: From Watts to Rodney King* (New York: Cambridge University Press, 2000), 86.

2. Robert L. Vernon, *L.A. Justice* (Colorado Springs, CO: Focus on the Family, 1993), 50–51, 172, 238, 155.

3. James Forman Jr., "Racial Critiques of Mass Incarceration: Beyond the New Jim Crow," *New York University Law Review* 87, no. 1 (2012): 114–15. Forman rebuts critiques leveled by Michelle Alexander and others that FBI crime-reporting methods are not trustworthy.

4. Naomi Murakawa, *The First Civil Right: How Liberals Built Prison America* (New York: Oxford University Press, 2014), 82, 85.

5. Sherry Laymon, *Fearless: John L. McClellan, United States Senator* (Mustang, OK: Tate, 2011), 189–96, 200, 262; Kenneth O'Reilly, "The FBI and the Politics of the Riots, 1964–1968," *Journal of American History* 75, no. 1 (June 1988): 91–114.

6. N. M. Camardese, "God—or the Supreme Court?," *Senate Congressional Record* 114 (May 21, 1968): 14142.

7. "We Must Stop," *UEA,* June 1967; Marvin Mayers, "Crime and Violence," in *Facing Today's Problems* (Wheaton, IL: Scripture Press, 1970), 72. McClellan contributed a back-cover blurb for M. L. Moser, *Capital Punishment: Christian or Barbarian?* (Little Rock, AR: Challenge, 1972).

8. Vesla M. Weaver, "Frontlash: Race and the Development of Punitive Crime Policy," *Studies in American Political Development* 21 (Fall 2007): 230–65.

9. "Congressman Cited as 'Layman of Year,'" April 8, 1964, box 53, folder 3, NAE.

10. Jim Mason, *No Holding Back: The 1980 John B. Anderson Presidential Campaign* (Lanham, MD: University Press of America, 2011), 8–20.

11. "Can We Reclaim the American Dream? An Interview With Congressman John B. Anderson," *MM,* July–August 1968. Portions of this interview were aired on WMBI, the Moody Bible Institute radio station. The interview was also reprinted in *Evangelical Beacon,* August 13, 1968.

12. Numerous letters on civil rights from mainline church leaders and members, particularly Methodists and Lutherans, can be found in John Anderson's papers, box 39, Legis. Judiciary—Civil Rights I folder, JA. As of this writing, the John Anderson Papers have not been fully processed, and therefore box numbers may differ in the future.

13. John B. Anderson to Richard N. Ostling, April 30, 1968, box 39, Legis. Judiciary—Civil Rights I folder, JA.

14. Constituent to John B. Anderson, April 23, 1968, box 39, Legis. Judiciary—Civil Rights I folder, JA.

15. For example, see Myron P. Fitzhenry to John B. Anderson, February 20, 1970, box 51, Judiciary—Courts folder, JA.

16. Constituent to John B. Anderson, March 12, 1968, box 39, Legis. Judiciary—Civil Rights I folder, JA.

17. Mason, *No Holding Back,* 19.

18. "Can We Reclaim the American Dream?"

19. Representative John B. Anderson, speaking on "Providing for Agreeing to Senate Amendment to H.R. 5037, Law Enforcement and Criminal Justice Assistance Act of 1967," *Congressional Record* 114 (June 6, 1968): 16275–76.

20. Aldo Beckman, "Anti-crime Bill May Face Long Delay," *CTR,* June 2, 1968; Aldo Beckman, "House Clears Way for Stiff Crime Bill," *CTR,* June 6, 1968; Frank Eleazer, "House Clears Way for Anti-crime Bill," *AC,* June 6, 1968.

21. Kevin M. Kruse, *One Nation under God: How Corporate America Invented Christian America* (New York: Basic Books, 2015), 228–73.

22. Weaver, "Frontlash," 255; Murakawa, *First Civil Right,* 86.

23. Aldo Beckman, "LBJ Urged to Sign, Veto Anti-crime Bill," *CTR,* June 8, 1968; "Crime-Control Bill," *LAT,* June 9, 1968; Max Frankel, "President Signs Broad Crime Bill, with Objections," *NYT,* June 20, 1968.

24. Billy Graham, "A Nation Rocked by Crime" (sermon, *Hour of Decision* radio program, 1966), tape 880b, HOD; Billy Graham, "Rioting, Looting, and Crime" (sermon, *Hour of Decision* radio program, 1967), tape 916, HOD; Billy Graham, *Rioting or Righteousness* (Minneapolis: Billy Graham Evangelistic Association, 1967).

25. Representative Robert T. Ashmore, speaking on Law Enforcement and Criminal Justice Assistance Act of 1967, *Congressional Record* 113 (August 8, 1967): 21822; Representative George W. Andrews, "Graham versus Rioting," *Congressional Record* 113 (August 8, 1967): 21924.

26. Steven P. Miller, *Billy Graham and the Rise of the Republican South* (Philadelphia: University of Pennsylvania Press, 2009), 130–34.

27. Charles P. Henderson, *The Nixon Theology* (New York: Harper and Row, 1972), 4.

28. Billy Graham, "1969 Inaugural Prayer," n.d., Clipping File, January 1969 folder, BGCA, http://www2.wheaton.edu/bgc/archives/inaugural05.htm; Kruse, *One Nation*

under God, 246; Nancy Gibbs and Michael Duffy, *The Preacher and the Presidents: Billy Graham in the White House* (New York: Center Street, 2007), chap. 18.

29. Elizabeth Hinton, *From the War on Poverty to the War on Crime: The Making of Mass Incarceration in America* (Cambridge, MA: Harvard University Press, 2016), 140.

30. Hinton, 138–66.

31. Religion News Service, "Trouble with Preachers Cited by Police Group," *PJ,* January 27, 1971; Conrad S. Jensen, *Twenty-Six Years on the Losing Side* (Oradell, NJ: American Tract Society, 1964), 6, 15, 63.

32. "Letter to a Police Chief," *PJ,* September 10, 1969.

33. Here Hargis was quoting CIA official Lyman B. Kirkpatrick, Jr. He also quoted J. Edgar Hoover at length on the regularly "unfounded and irresponsible" charges of police brutality. Billy James Hargis, *Rising Crime in the U.S.* (Tuscaloosa, OK: Christian Crusade, n.d.), 6–10.

34. Richard Wolff, *Riots in the Streets* (Wheaton, IL: Tyndale, 1968); Bruce Shelley, "Racism," in *Facing Today's Problems* (Wheaton, IL: Scripture Press, 1970), 156–74. See also H. Bruce Chapman, "Law and Order . . . and Justice and Mercy," *Evangelical Beacon,* February 11, 1969.

35. John B. Anderson, *Between Two Worlds: A Congressman's Choice* (Grand Rapids, MI: Zondervan, 1970), 1–10.

36. Anderson, 46–57.

37. Anderson, 58–60.

38. Anderson, 122–23, 128.

39. Representative John B. Anderson, speaking on Law Enforcement Assistance Amendments, *Congressional Record* 116 (June 29, 1970): 21848–49.

40. Anderson, *Between Two Worlds,* 130.

41. "Harlem's 'Billy Graham' Preaching in Revival," *Pittsburgh Courier,* January 16, 1965.

42. *Freedom Now,* December 1968; David R. Swartz, *Moral Minority: The Evangelical Left in an Age of Conservatism* (Philadelphia: University of Pennsylvania Press, 2012), 34–35.

43. Tom Skinner, "The U.S. Racial Crisis and World Evangelism," Urbana, accessed June 28, 2017, https://urbana.org/message/us-racial-crisis-and-world-evangelism; Swartz, *Moral Minority,* 34–35.

44. "Black Clergy Ask Understanding," *Sacramento Observer,* September 25, 1969.

45. Soong-Chan Rah, "In Whose Image: The Emergence, Development, and Challenge of African-American Evangelicalism" (ThD diss., Duke Divinity School, 2016), 220, 226.

46. William E. Pannell, "To Free the Oppressor," *World Vision,* May 1971, box 1, folder 4 (Clippings, 1968–1979), TS.

47. "Controversial Black Preacher Putting Stress on Social Issues," *NYT,* September 2, 1973.

48. Randall Balmer, "Skinner, Thomas 'Tom,'" in *Encyclopedia of Evangelicalism* (Waco, TX: Baylor University Press, 2004).

49. Tom Skinner, *If Christ Is the Answer, What Are the Questions?* (Grand Rapids, MI: Zondervan, 1974), 183–94.

50. "Richard Nixon Denounced by Pastor," *Baltimore Afro-American*, November 10, 1962; Steven Miller, *Billy Graham*, 128.

51. Darren Dochuk, *From Bible Belt to Sunbelt: Plain-Folk Religion, Grassroots Politics, and the Rise of Evangelical Conservatism* (New York: W. W. Norton, 2011), 288.

52. E. V. Hill, interview by Mark Joseph, accessed June 28, 2017, https://web.archive.org/web/20010518042150/http://www.mjmgroup.com/Transcripts/EV_Hill.htm.

53. Russell Chandler, "Hang in There Brother: Edward Victor Hill," in *The Overcomers* (Old Tappan, NJ: F. H. Revell, 1978), 52–63.

54. For more on Yorty's anticrime efforts, see Michael W. Flamm, *Law and Order: Street Crime, Civil Unrest, and the Crisis of Liberalism in the 1960s* (New York: Columbia University Press, 2007), 70–71.

55. Lerone Martin, "Bureau Clergyman: How the FBI Colluded with an African American Televangelist to Destroy Dr. Martin Luther King, Jr.," *Religion and American Culture* 28, no. 1 (Winter 2018): 1–51.

56. Graham, *Rioting or Righteousness*.

57. "Get Tough Policy Urged by Graham," *AJC*, August 15, 1965.

58. Thomas A. Johnson, "Negro Leaders See Bias in Call of Nixon for 'Law and Order,'" *NYT*, 1968.

59. Dochuk, *From Bible Belt to Sunbelt*, 334–35.

60. Michael Javen Fortner, "'Must Jesus Bear the Cross Alone?' Reverend Oberia Dempsey and His Citizens War on Drugs," *Journal of Policy History* 27, no. 1 (January 2015): 118–56; "Churchmen Differ as to Punishment for Pushers," *PJ*, February 14, 1973.

61. James Forman Jr., *Locking Up Our Own: Crime and Punishment in Black America* (New York: Farrar, Straus and Giroux, 2017).

62. Jim Cleaver, "Local Leaders Plan Crime War," *Los Angeles Sentinel*, December 23, 1976.

63. "Churches in Harlem Hurt by Crime," *Baltimore Afro-American*, January 25, 1969.

64. Dochuk, *From Bible Belt to Sunbelt*, 288.

65. Edward Gilbreath, "Jesus Was Not a White Man," *Christian History*, 2014, https://www.christianhistoryinstitute.org:443/magazine/article/jesus-was-not-a-white-man/.

66. Robert Leo Heinemann, "The 'Social Gospel' of Black Evangelicals, 1968–1975: A Study of a Rhetorical Attempt to Alter Three Race-Related Images" (PhD diss., Ohio State University, 1975), 245–46; Howard O. Jones, *For This Time: A Challenge to Black and White Christians* (Chicago: Moody, 1968), 155.

67. Howard O. Jones, *White Questions to a Black Christian* (Grand Rapids, MI: Zondervan, 1975), 97, 121, 125–34, 194–96.

68. W. S. McBirnie to Ronald Reagan, November 30, 1965, Gubernatorial Campaign Files, series IV, box C31, 66: The Creative Society, RR.

69. Ronald Reagan, "The Creative Society" (speech, University of Southern California, April 19, 1966), http://www.freerepublic.com/focus/news/742041/posts. See also Ronald Reagan, *The Creative Society: Some Comments on Problems Facing America* (New York: Devin-Adair, 1968).

70. Citizens Committee to Elect Ronald Reagan Governor, "News Release," August 11, 1966, Gubernatorial Campaign Files, series IV, box C34, Legal Affairs: Law & Order 66 folder, RR.

71. Friends of Ronald Reagan, "Statement of Ronald Reagan," 1966, Gubernatorial Campaign Files, series IV, box C34, Legal Affairs: Watts folder, RR.

72. Dochuk, *From Bible Belt to Sunbelt*, 259–92.

73. Seymour Korman, "Reagan Enters Governor Race," *CTR*, January 5, 1966; Seymour Korman, "Reagan Plans Police School If Elected," *CTR*, August 29, 1966.

74. Gerard DeGroot, *Selling Ronald Reagan: The Emergence of a President* (New York: I. B. Tauris, 2015), 215.

75. Dochuk, *From Bible Belt to Sunbelt*, 269.

76. John Elmer, "Crime Top Issue: Reagan," *CTR*, September 29, 1967.

77. Ronald Reagan, "Message to Legislature—Criminal Justice," April 10, 1969, Gubernatorial Papers, 1966–74: Press Unit, box P18, Speeches—Governor Ronald Reagan, 1969 [01/01/1969–04/28/1969], RR, https://www.reaganlibrary.gov/sites/default/files/digitallibrary/gubernatorial/pressunit/p18/40-840-7408624-p18-002-2017.pdf.

78. Herbert Ellingwood, "Law Enforcement Planning and Coordination, 1969–1974," an oral history conducted 1981, 1983, interview by Gabrielle Morris, 1985, Law Enforcement and Criminal Justice in California, 1966–1976, Regional Oral History Office, Bancroft Library, University of California, Berkeley, 6.

79. Herbert Ellingwood, Billy Graham Oral History Program, interview by Lois Ferm, May 5, 1986, Collection 141, box 32, folder 2, BGCA.

80. Herbert Ellingwood, "Christianity and Social Action," *Voice of Bethel*, August 1968, found in Ellingwood, "Law Enforcement Planning and Coordination," 50.

81. Ellingwood, "Law Enforcement Planning and Coordination," 41.

82. Herbert Ellingwood, "Riots," n.d., Governor's Office, 1967–1975, box GO72, Legislation—Riot, 1967–70, folder 2, RR.

83. Ellingwood, "Law Enforcement Planning and Coordination," 14–15; Pat Sauer and Capitol News Service, "Governor Faces Rule," *Desert Sun*, August 4, 1973.

84. Phil Hanna, "Moscone Fears for Personal Privacy!," Capitol News Service, August 23, 1973, Governor's Office, 1967–1975, box GO191, Research file, Legal Affairs—Law Enforcement Task Force, RR.

85. Ellingwood, "Law Enforcement Planning and Coordination," 37–38.

86. For more on the "liberal" history of mandatory minimums, see Murakawa, *First Civil Right*, 92–111.

87. Ellingwood, "Law Enforcement Planning and Coordination," 39.

88. "Judge Heads Crime Panel," *Los Angeles Sentinel*, May 19, 1977; Marie Gottschalk, *The Prison and the Gallows: The Politics of Mass Incarceration in America* (New York: Cambridge University Press, 2006), 77–80.

89. Vernon Grose, "Making the Appellate Process Relevant to the Public" (presented at the Fourth California Conference on the Judiciary Task Force on the Appellate Process, Los Angeles, CA, October 13, 1977), box 32, folder 1, PF.

90. Ellingwood, "Law Enforcement Planning and Coordination," 39.

91. Randy Moore, *Evolution in the Courtroom: A Reference Guide* (Santa Barbara, CA: ABC-CLIO, 2002), 65, 125.

92. Grose, "Making the Appellate Process."

93. Ellingwood, "Riots."

94. W. S. McBirnie, *The Attack on Your Local Police* (Glendale, CA: n.p., n.d.), 16, 14.

95. George S. Goshorn, "McBirnie Claims Smear, Calls Governor 'Liar,'" *Glendale News-Press*, October 13, 1966, Campaign Files, Series IV, Box C31, 66: The Creative Society, RR.

96. McBirnie, *The Attack on Your Local Police*, 25, 27, 4–5, 28; Eric Malnic, "Minority Group Asks More, Not Fewer Police," *LAT*, August 17, 1968.

97. State of California Governor's Office, *To Keep Our People Safe and Free* (Sacramento: State of California Governor's Office, n.d.), Governor's Office, 1967–1975, box GO190, Research file, Legal Affairs—Law and Order (Molly Sturges Tuthill) folder, RR.

98. Hinton, *From the War on Poverty*, 143.

99. "Law Enforcement," April 15, 1969, Governor's Office, 1967–1975, box GO190, Research file, Legal Affairs—Law Enforcement (Molly Sturges Tuthill) folder, RR.

100. State of California Governor's Office, *To Keep Our People Safe*.

101. Joan Petersilia, "California's Prison Policy: Causes, Costs, and Consequences," *Prison Journal* 72, no. 1–2 (June 1, 1992): 9.

102. Stephen Martini, *Onward and Upward: A History of the Fellowship of Christian Peace Officers* (Cleveland, TN: Dry Ice, 2011), 39, 60; "Our History," Fellowship of Christian Peace Officers—USA, accessed June 30, 2019, https://fcpo.org/102.11/history-of-the-fellowship-of-christian-peace-officers; Nevin F. Miller, "Peace Officers Gather to Study Christ's Teachings," *San Bernardino Sun*, March 8, 1979.

103. AP, "Hardened Police Officers Form Fellowship to Further Religion," *San Bernardino Sun*, August 13, 1977.

104. Nevin Miller, "Peace Officers Gather."

105. Mayerene Barker, "Officers Carry the Word as Well as Guns," *LAT*, April 15, 1980.

106. Kenneth Hansen, "Officer's Hymns End Siege with Gunman," *LAT*, August 6, 1971; Michael Barrett, "How an LAPD Officer Kept a Man from Becoming a Killer," *Los Angeles Magazine*, April 14, 2016, https://www.lamag.com/longform/soundcityhostage/; *Barrett* (Johnson-Nyquist Productions and Outreach Films, 1976); Ethel Barrett, *Barrett: A Street Cop Who Cared* (Old Tappan, NJ: F. H. Revell, 1978).

107. Martini, *Onward and Upward*, 71.

108. Robert C. Cunningham, "Watts—a Year Later," *PE*, July 17, 1966, 4; Dan L. Thrapp, "Answer to Civil Rights Is in Heart, Fisk Says," *LAT*, February 13, 1967.

109. Ernest A. Schonberger, "Church Urged to Open Eyes on Race Problem," *LAT*, September 25, 1966; Martin J. Schiesl, "Behind the Badge: The Police and Social Discontent in Los Angeles since 1950," in Norman M. Klein and Martin J. Schiesl, eds., *20th Century Los Angeles: Power, Promotion, and Social Conflict* (Claremont, CA: Regina Books, 1990), 166–71; AP, "Deputy Chief Davis Named LAPD Head," *Sun-Telegram* (San Bernardino, CA), August 16, 1969.

110. "CBM Group Officers to Install," *Independent Star-News* (Pasadena, CA), November 30, 1968.

111. Jerry Belcher, "3 Chief Candidates More Alike Than Not," *LAT*, February 24, 1978; Bob Vernon, *L.A. Cop: Peacemaker in Blue* (Nashville: Impact Books, 1977), 144.

112. Bob Vernon (speech at NAE Convention, 1985), box 121, item 55 #173, NAE.

113. Vernon, *L.A. Cop,* 135–36.

114. Vernon, 140.

115. Skip Ferderber, "Team 28 Policing Success Prompts Expansion," *LAT,* March 22, 1973.

116. Skip Ferderber, "Venice Police Team 28 Will Open Headquarters in Palms," *LAT,* June 29, 1972; Erwin Baker, "L.A. Police Go Citywide with Venice Crime Project," *LAT,* February 13, 1975.

117. See Dochuk, *From Bible Belt to Sunbelt,* chap. 8.

118. Robert L. Vernon, "Team 28: A Team-Policing Experiment in Los Angeles" (MBA thesis, Pepperdine University, 1974), 4–6.

119. Ferderber, "Venice Police Team 28"; Max Felker-Kantor, *Policing Los Angeles: Race, Resistance, and the Rise of the LAPD* (Chapel Hill: University of North Carolina Press, 2018), 57–59.

120. Ferderber, "Team 28 Policing Success."

121. Nancy Baltad, "77th St. Division: Hate Is Giving Way to Amity," *LAT,* January 11, 1974.

122. Baltad.

123. Felker-Kantor, *Policing Los Angeles,* 57–58.

124. Skip Ferderber, "A Policeman's Lot: Damned If You Do—or If You Don't," *LAT,* February 25, 1971; Jim Cleaver, "The Results of a Changing Tide and Public Opinion," *Los Angeles Sentinel,* November 28, 1974.

125. Felker-Kantor, *Policing Los Angeles,* 114.

126. Michael K. Brown, *Working the Street: Police Discretion and the Dilemmas of Reform* (New York: Russell Sage Foundation, 1981), 301.

127. Felker-Kantor, *Policing Los Angeles,* 120–21.

128. Data come from "Prisoners under the Jurisdiction of State or Federal Correctional Authorities, December 31, 1978–2016" and the "Imprisonment Rate of Sentenced Prisoners under the Jurisdiction of State or Federal Correctional Authorities per 100,000 U.S. Residents, December 31, 1978–2016" tables, in E. Ann Carson and Joseph Mulako-Wangota, "Corrections Statistical Analysis Tool (CSAT)—Prisoners," Bureau of Justice Statistics, accessed July 8, 2019, https://www.bjs.gov/index.cfm?ty=nps.

129. Cary J. Rudman and John Berthelsen, *An Analysis of the California Department of Corrections' Planning Process: Strategies to Reduce the Cost of Incarcerating State Prisoners* (Sacramento: California State Assembly Office of Research, 1991), i. See also Ruth Wilson Gilmore, *Golden Gulag: Prisons, Surplus, Crisis, and Opposition in Globalizing California* (Berkeley: University of California Press, 2007), 88.

130. Petersilia, "California's Prison Policy," 10–18.

131. Herbert Ellingwood, "Crime Hurts: The Christian's Role in Relieving the Pain," *New Wine,* May 1977, DPC.

132. Herbert Ellingwood, "Ronald Reagan: God, Home and Country," *CL,* November 1980.

133. Dochuk, *From Bible Belt to Sunbelt,* 374–87.

134. Ronald Reagan, "Transcript of Speech at the Newport Beach Exchange Club," February 14, 1969, Gubernatorial Papers, 1966–74: Press Unit, box P18, Speeches—Governor Ronald Reagan, 1969 [01/01/1969–04/28/1969], RR https://www.reaganlibrary

.gov/sites/default/files/digitallibrary/gubernatorial/pressunit/p18/40-840-7408624-p18
-002-2017.pdf.

135. Bob Vernon and C. C. Carlson, *The Married Man* (Old Tappan, NJ: F. H. Revell, 1980), 23–31.

136. Larry Christenson, *The Christian Family* (Minneapolis: Bethany Fellowship, 1970), 94.

137. James C. Dobson, *Dare to Discipline* (Wheaton, IL: Tyndale House, 1970), 12–14, 21, 100–103, 126–31, 187, 190–217.

138. Dale Buss, *Family Man: The Biography of Dr. James Dobson* (Carol Stream, IL: Tyndale, 2005), 45. For more background on Dobson and his work, see Hilde Løvdal Stephens, *Family Matters: James Dobson and Focus on the Family's Crusade for the Christian Home* (Tuscaloosa: University Alabama Press, 2019).

5. A Sermon in Your Cell

1. B. G. Allison to A. C. Miller, January 21, 1957; Bill Lutker to A. C. Miller, February 21, 1958; Jack W. Manning to A. C. Miller, January 24, 1957; Joseph Stiles to A. C. Miller, January 25, 1957; Bill Lutker, "Friends Incorporated Newsletter," January 1958, all in box 1, folder 17, CLC.

2. Russell Chandler, "Inmates 'Reborn': Conversions to Christ—a Prison Revival," *LAT,* March 15, 1976. Reprints included Russell Chandler, "Guards, Cells Don't Bar Prisoners from Religion," *Anniston (AL) Star,* March 20, 1976; and Russell Chandler, "Prison Inmates Getting Religion," *Lansing (MI) State Journal,* March 27, 1976.

3. "Counting Souls," *Time,* October 4, 1976; Kenneth Woodward and John Barnes, "Born Again!," *Newsweek,* October 25, 1976.

4. In total the directory listed nearly five hundred entries, but many of them were branches of other ministries or did not have a founding date noted. Ivan Fahs, *Prison Ministry Directory 1986 Edition* (Wheaton, IL: Institute for Prison Ministries, Billy Graham Center, n.d.).

5. For an overview of these tensions throughout missionary history, see William R. Hutchison, *Errand to the World: American Protestant Thought and Foreign Missions* (Chicago: University of Chicago Press, 1993), esp. chap. 7.

6. Consuella York, interview by Robert Shuster, November 21, 1988, tape 3, CY. See also Paul Galloway, "Saint of the Cell," *CTR,* February 2, 1989.

7. Gordon P. Gardiner, *Out of Zion into All the World* (Shippensburg, PA: Companion, 1990), 147–48, 157–60; Mother Daisy Robinson, *How a Lifer Received Life* (Gospel Publishing House, n.d.), FPHC; *PE*, November 8, 1964.

8. York, interview, November 21, 1988, tape 3, CY.

9. Consuella York, interview by Robert Shuster, July 19, 1988, tape 2, CY; York, interview, November 21, 1988, tape 3, CY.

10. Paul Galloway, "Obituaries: Rev. Consuella York, 72; Jail Minister," *CTR,* December 13, 1995.

11. York, interview, November 21, 1988, tape 3, CY.

12. York, interview, July 19, 1988, tape 2, CY; York, interview, November 21, 1988, tape 3, CY.

13. York, interview, November 21, 1988, tape 3, CY.

14. Tanya Erzen, *God in Captivity: The Rise of Faith-Based Prison Ministries in the Age of Mass Incarceration* (Boston: Beacon, 2017), 5.

15. In addition to newspaper reports, the national news program *20/20* featured York in 1989. See Rick Kogan, "'20/20' to Feature Jailhouse Minister," *CTR*, April 7, 1989.

16. Wolfgang Saxon, "Elton Trueblood, 94, Scholar Who Wrote Theological Works," *NYT*, December 23, 1994; "Declares Small Colleges Better for the Students," *Franklin (IN) Evening Star,* August 22, 1956.

17. R. Alan Streett, "Carnell, Edward John (1919–1967)," in *Evangelical America: An Encyclopedia of Contemporary American Religious Culture,* ed. Timothy J. Demy and Paul R. Shockley (Santa Barbara, CA: ABC-CLIO, 2017); D. Elton Trueblood, *Philosophy of Religion* (Grand Rapids, MI: Baker, 1973); D. Elton Trueblood, "The Self and the Community," in *Quest for Reality: Christianity and the Counter Culture,* ed. Carl F. H. Henry (Downers Grove, IL: InterVarsity, 1973).

18. Tony Campolo, "The Quiet Revolutionary," *CT,* February 11, 1991.

19. Campolo.

20. Elton Trueblood, *While It Is Day* (New York: Harper and Row, 1974), 109–14; Timothy Gloege, *Guaranteed Pure: The Moody Bible Institute, Business, and the Making of Modern Evangelicalism* (Chapel Hill: University of North Carolina Press, 2015).

21. Trueblood, *While It Is Day,* 120; "Force of Yokefellow Prison Ministry Related at Parley," *Palladium-Item* (Richmond, IN), March 21, 1976.

22. Bob Terrell, "A Prison Ministry," *Asheville (NC) Citizen-Times,* November 12, 1975.

23. Florence Lawson, "Prison Ministry a Focal Point of 24th Yokefellow Conference," *Palladium-Item* (Richmond, IN), March 20, 1977.

24. Cheri A. Felts, "Yokefellows Prison Ministry Helps," *Gettysburg (PA) Times,* May 22, 1987; Barbara Fussell, "Yokefellow Ministry: Outside Force Gives Missing Ingredient," *Evening Telegram* (Rocky Mount, NC), April 1, 1979.

25. "Force of Yokefellow Prison."

26. Fussell, "Yokefellow Ministry."

27. Terrell, "Prison Ministry."

28. McNeil Brothers and Daniel Smith, "Cops and Robbers Revival at McNeil Island," *PRE,* Winter 1979, FPHC.

29. Robert Wuthnow, "Appendix: Small Groups—a National Profile," in *I Come Away Stronger: How Small Groups Are Shaping American Religion* (Grand Rapids, MI: Eerdmans, 2001), 378–81.

30. "Trueblood, David Elton, 1900–1994," *CT,* February 6, 1995.

31. Tape 1, June 21, 1991, WS.

32. Tape 1, WS; Tape 2, June 21, 1991, WS.

33. Tape 2, WS.

34. Tape 2, WS.

35. Tape 3, June 21, 1991, WS.

36. Tape 2, WS.

37. Helen Altonn, "Prison's Chaplain Leads Busy Life," *Honolulu Star-Bulletin,* May 6, 1976.

38. Nadine W. Scott, "Good News Mission Program: State Prison Gets Spiritual Aid," *Honolulu Star-Bulletin*, February 26, 1977.

39. For standard treatments of this dynamic in evangelical history, see Harry S. Stout, *The Divine Dramatist: George Whitefield and the Rise of Modern Evangelicalism* (Grand Rapids, MI: Eerdmans, 1991); Nathan O. Hatch, *The Democratization of American Christianity* (New Haven, CT: Yale University Press, 1989); George M. Marsden, *Fundamentalism and American Culture*, 2nd ed. (New York: Oxford University Press, 2006); and Grant Wacker, *America's Pastor: Billy Graham and the Shaping of a Nation* (Cambridge, MA: Belknap Press of Harvard University Press, 2014).

40. Robert Wuthnow, *The Restructuring of American Religion* (Princeton, NJ: Princeton University Press, 1988).

41. John G. Turner, *Bill Bright and Campus Crusade for Christ: The Renewal of Evangelicalism in Postwar America* (Chapel Hill: University of North Carolina Press, 2008), 3, 73.

42. On "new paradigm churches," see Donald E. Miller, *Reinventing American Protestantism: Christianity in the New Millennium,* rev. ed. (Berkeley: University of California Press, 1999).

43. David King, "The New Internationalists: World Vision and the Revival of American Evangelical Humanitarianism, 1950–2010," *Religions* 3, no. 4 (2012): 922–49.

44. Good News Jail and Prison Ministry, "The Good News Mission Story—1981," posted February 11, 2014, YouTube video, 28:54, https://www.youtube.com/watch?v=wTlkb7HILNs.

45. Tape 2, WS; Scott, "Good News Mission Program."

46. "Our History," Good News Jail and Prison Ministry, accessed November 30, 2017, https://goodnewsjail.org/history/.

47. Bill Glass, interview by author, September 24, 2018.

48. Bill Glass, *Free at Last* (Waco, TX: Word Books, 1976), 23–24.

49. Glass, 29–33; Glass, interview.

50. Gary D. Kinder to Board Members of the Bill Glass Evangelistic Association, September 27, 1972, box 2, folder 3, CL; Watson Spoelstra, "'You Came to Prison to Visit,'" *Goalposts,* February 1973, box 13, folder 9, CL.

51. Glass, *Free at Last,* 60.

52. "Bill Glass Evangelistic Association Crusades," n.d., box 13, folder 9, CL; John Rainwater to Bunny Martin, August 25, 1982, box 14, folder 2, CL.

53. "Tentative Schedule for Prison Crusade, Marion, Ohio," July 28, 1972, box 3, folder 15, CL; Glass, *Free at Last,* 41–45.

54. Rick Nielsen and Ron Kuntz, *Doin' Time: An In-Depth Look at Life behind Bars through a Window of Hope* (Grand Island, NE: Cross Training, 2001), 72.

55. Glass, *Free at Last,* 36–37.

56. "Crusade Promotion Stickers," n.d., box 13, folder 8, CL.

57. Glass, *Free at Last,* 13.

58. Bill Glass, "See-Thru Views," n.d., box 14, folder 3, CL.

59. Nielsen and Kuntz, *Doin' Time,* 70–71.

60. Bill Glass, "Recreation in Prison Evangelism," *Church Recreation Magazine,* December 1983, Southern Baptist Historical Library and Archives, Nashville.

61. Spoelstra, "'You Came to Prison to Visit.'"

62. Nielsen and Kuntz, *Doin' Time,* 71.

63. Glass, *Free at Last,* 43–45.

64. Jack Heard to Bill Glass, March 26, 1975, box 14, folder 3, CL.

65. Tony Ladd and James A. Mathisen, *Muscular Christianity: Evangelical Protestants and the Development of American Sport* (Grand Rapids, MI: Baker, 1999), 13–16.

66. Ladd and Mathisen, 62, 78–81, 96.

67. Quoted in Ladd and Mathisen, 126–27.

68. "Defends Sports: Glass, Ex-Pro Gridder, Now a Crusader," *LAT,* August 6, 1972.

69. Ladd and Mathisen, *Muscular Christianity,* 11–13.

70. Ladd and Mathisen, 79.

71. Bill Glass and Terry Pluto, *Champions for Life: The Power of a Father's Blessing* (Deerfield Beach, FL: Faith Communications, 2005).

72. Nancy Madsen, "The Power of a Father's Blessing: What Former NFL Pro Bill Glass Has Learned after 36 Years of Prison Ministry," *CT,* January 2006; Glass, interview.

73. Glass and Pluto, *Champions for Life,* x; Glass, interview.

74. Glass and Pluto, *Champions for Life,* 18.

75. John P. Bartkowski, "Breaking Walls, Raising Fences: Masculinity, Intimacy, and Accountability among the Promise Keepers," *Sociology of Religion* 61, no. 1 (2000): 35–50.

76. See Estelle B. Freedman, *Their Sisters' Keepers: Women's Prison Reform in America, 1830–1930* (Ann Arbor: University of Michigan Press, 1981), chap. 3.

77. Erzen, *God in Captivity,* 151.

78. Glass, interview.

79. Spoelstra, "'You Came to Prison to Visit.'"

80. Glass, *Free at Last,* 45, 68.

81. Nielsen and Kuntz, *Doin' Time,* 26.

82. Glass, *Free at Last,* 45, 52.

83. Glass, 118.

84. "About Us," Bill Glass: Behind the Walls, accessed May 4, 2020, via the Internet Archive Wayback Machine, https://web.archive.org/web/20160506152339/https://www.behindthewalls.com/about-us.

85. Charles Hillinger, "'Chaplain Ray' Serves Big Captive Audience," *LAT,* November 14, 1979.

86. Chaplain Ray [Hoekstra] and Walter Wagner, *God's Prison Gang* (Old Tappan, NJ: F. H. Revell, 1977), 10.

87. [Hoekstra] and Wagner, 17.

88. Hillinger, "'Chaplain Ray.'"

89. Matthew Avery Sutton, *Aimee Semple McPherson and the Resurrection of Christian America* (Cambridge, MA: Harvard University Press, 2009), 2–3.

90. Peter Manseau, "Religion News on the Radio," in *The Oxford Handbook of Religion and the American News Media,* ed. Diane Winston (New York: Oxford University Press, 2012), 130.

91. Manseau, 132.

92. Daniel Vaca, "Book People: Evangelical Books and the Making of Contemporary Evangelicalism" (PhD diss., Columbia University, 2012), 200.

93. Tona J. Hangen, *Redeeming the Dial: Radio, Religion, and Popular Culture in America* (Chapel Hill: University of North Carolina Press, 2002), 123.

94. AP, "'Radio Chaplain' Reaches Prison Inmates," *Santa Fe New Mexican,* June 5, 1972.

95. Edmund K. Gravely Jr., "Religious Radio Proves a Blessing—Even in New York," *NYT,* June 23, 1974.

96. "Chaplain Ray Radio Logs," *PRE,* 1971, FPHC.

97. AP, "'Radio Chaplain.'"

98. Ray Hoekstra, "Restitution—Forgotten Justice," n.d., tape 22, IPM.

99. Ray Hoekstra and Corrie ten Boom, "Side One: Corrie ten Boom Speaks to Prisoners with Chaplain Ray," n.d., tape 14, IPM.

100. Vaca, "Book People," 192–93.

101. Robert A. Johnson, *Disciple in Prison* (Dallas: International Prison Ministry, 1975), 17.

102. Johnson, 87–88.

103. AP, "'Radio Chaplain.'"

104. Don Morris to Bill Glass, n.d., box 14, folder 3, CL.

105. AP, "'Radio Chaplain.'"

106. Charles E. Lasage and Michael Leiby, "Prisoners Touched by 'Life Changing Books,'" *PRE,* Winter 1979, FPHC.

107. "Cards from Prisoners," 1988, box 1, folder 1, CY.

108. Altonn, "Prison's Chaplain."

109. Bill Glass Evangelistic Association, "Friend of a Prisoner," n.d., box 14, folder 3, CL.

110. Cecil Baker, "Quit Coddling!," *PJ,* January 14, 1976; R. W. Childs, "Rehabilitation Too!," *PJ,* February 11, 1976.

111. "The Goal," *PRE,* 1971, FPHC.

112. Ray Hoekstra, "From the Chaplain's Desk," *PRE,* 3rd qtr. 1978, FPHC.

113. Ray Hoekstra, "Side Two: Ministry to the Small Jails," n.d., tape 22, IPM.

114. Harry Howard and Ray Hoekstra, *Changed Lives in San Quentin* (Dallas: Acclaimed Books, 1985), 173–93.

115. Altonn, "Prison's Chaplain."

116. Glass, interview.

117. Phil Wagner, "Congress of Prison Ministries," n.d., box 50, tape 6, DPC.

118. Duane Pederson, "Congress of Prison Ministries 1978: Opening Prayer, Welcome," n.d., box 50, cassette from Duane Pederson, Bill McCoy, Corrie ten Boom, Jim Collier, DPC.

119. "Corrie ten Boom's Prison Ministry to Be Carried on by Duane Pederson," n.d., box 56, folder 7, DPC.

120. Ann Sibel, "Clubs," *Tampa Bay Times,* November 9, 1988.

121. "Kairos Prison Ministry—the History of Kairos," Kairos Prison Ministry, accessed December 11, 2017, http://www.kairosprisonministry.org/history.php.

122. Selwyn Crawford, "Kairos Inc. Helps Inmates Cope with Life in Prison," *Orlando Sentinel,* January 1, 1982; Marvin Wamble, "Getting High on God's Love," *Reno Gazette-Journal,* July 21, 1982.

123. Charles W. Colson, *Born Again* (Peabody, MA: Hendrickson, 1995), 58.

124. Charles W. Colson, *Life Sentence* (Lincoln, VA: Chosen Books, 1979), 154–60.

125. Tape 3, WS; "Colson Tells of Prison Ministry," *BP,* April 29, 1976; Colson, *Life Sentence,* 60.

126. Lawson, "Prison Ministry a Focal Point." For more on Colson's awareness of other prison ministries around the time of Prison Fellowship's founding, even as he describes their limitations, see Colson, *Life Sentence,* 277–78.

127. Kendrick Oliver, "'Hi, Fellas. Come on In.' Norman Carlson, the Federal Bureau of Prisons, and the Rise of Prison Fellowship," *Journal of Church and State 55,* no. 4 (Autumn 2013): 740–57.

128. For example, see Winnifred Fallers Sullivan, *Prison Religion: Faith-Based Reform and the Constitution* (Princeton, NJ: Princeton University Press, 2009); Tanya Erzen, "Testimonial Politics: The Christian Right's Faith-Based Approach to Marriage and Imprisonment," *American Quarterly 59,* no. 3 (September 1, 2007): 991–1015; Oliver, "'Hi, Fellas'"; David Dagan and Steven Teles, *Prison Break: Why Conservatives Turned against Mass Incarceration* (New York: Oxford University Press, 2016); and Erzen, *God in Captivity.*

129. Fahs, *Prison Ministry Directory.*

130. "New Prison Ministries," *Eternity,* May 1977, DPC.

131. John Wigger, *PTL: The Rise and Fall of Jim and Tammy Faye Bakker's Evangelical Empire* (New York: Oxford University Press, 2017), 1, 135–36.

132. Bill Powell, "PTL Shows Are Going to Inmates at Eddyville," *Courier-Journal* (Louisville, KY), March 14, 1983; Wigger, *PTL,* 136.

133. Fahs, *Prison Ministry Directory.*

134. Hanna Rosin, "Jim Bakker's Revival," *WP,* August 11, 1999.

135. "Unedited Transcript, Billy Graham and Phil Donahue Show, Women's Prison, Marysville, Ohio," February 1972, Collection 580, box 193, folder 4, BGCA, 3, 1, 27–28.

136. Clara Miller, "Off the Hook," *Marysville Journal-Tribune,* February 11, 1972; Betty Harris, "Billy Graham Visits Ohio Prison to Tape TV Show," *Muncie Evening Press,* February 19, 1972; Clara Miller, "Dr. Graham Answers Many Questions for Inmates," *Marysville Journal-Tribune,* February 11, 1972.

137. "Unedited Transcript, Billy Graham and Phil Donahue Show, Women's Prison, Marysville, Ohio," 18–19.

138. "Unedited Transcript, Billy Graham and Phil Donahue Show, Women's Prison, Marysville, Ohio," 33–34.

139. AP, "Billy Graham Says Prisons Need Reforms," *Charleston Daily Mail,* February 11, 1972; "Prisoner Spoke Briefly, but to Point," *Miami Herald,* February 12, 1972.

140. Hutchison, *Errand to the World,* 13.

141. *Chaplaincy Ministries—1941–2014* (AG Chaplaincy, 2015), 21, 24.

142. Paul R. Markstrom, *Volunteers in Prison Manual,* 1977, FPHC; Paul R. Markstrom, *Prison Ministry and Your Church* (Assemblies of God Division of Home Missions, 1982), FPHC.

143. Preface to Paul R. Markstrom, ed., *Chaplain's Manual* (Springfield, MO: General Council of the Assemblies of God, 196?). See also Duane Pederson, *How to Establish a Jail and Prison Ministry* (Nashville: Thomas Nelson, 1979), 23–25, 59, 61.

144. Dale K. Pace, *A Christian's Guide to Effective Jail and Prison Ministries* (Old Tappan, NJ: F. H. Revell, 1976), 13.

145. Pace, 19–22.

146. Pace, 136–37, 143–45.

147. Philip B. Taft Jr., "Whatever Happened to That Old-Time Prison Chaplain," *Corrections,* December 1978, box 9, folder 9, PF.

148. I am grateful for Kendrick Oliver's work on prison ministry for helping me understand this broader contested landscape, as seen through the controversy over this article. Oliver, "'Hi, Fellas,'" 748.

149. Gregory J. McMaster, "Hole Time," *Journal of Prisoners on Prisons* 10, nos. 1 and 2 (1999): 87–97.

150. Philip Jenkins, *Decade of Nightmares: The End of the Sixties and the Making of Eighties America* (New York: Oxford University Press, 2006), 134–45.

151. John H. Allan, "Profits of 'The Godfather,'" *NYT,* April 16, 1972.

152. Chaplain Ray [Hoekstra], foreword to *Holes in Time: The Autobiography of a Gangster,* by Frank Costantino (Dallas: Acclaimed Books, 1979).

153. Jenkins, *Decade of Nightmares,* 149.

154. Howard and Hoekstra, *Changed Lives in San Quentin,* 1.

155. Patrick A. Langan, *Race of Prisoners Admitted to State and Federal Institutions, 1926–86* (Washington, DC: Bureau of Justice Statistics, Office of Justice Programs, US Department of Justice, May 1991), 5, https://www.ncjrs.gov/pdffiles1/nij/125618.pdf.

156. Howard and Hoekstra, *Changed Lives in San Quentin,* 14–15.

157. Glass, interview.

158. John M. Leighty, "Entertainers and Athletes Spread the Word in Prison," *LAT,* December 7, 1986.

159. Glass, *Free at Last,* 84–85, 100.

160. Glass, 160–61.

161. Michelle Alexander, *The New Jim Crow: Mass Incarceration in the Age of Colorblindness* (New York: New Press, 2010), 97–139.

162. Heather Ann Thompson, *Blood in the Water: The Attica Prison Uprising of 1971 and Its Legacy* (New York: Pantheon Books, 2016), 6–7.

163. "Likely Attica Prison Riot Shooters Named, 45 Years Later," CBS News, August 24, 2016, https://www.cbsnews.com/news/likely-attica-prison-riot-shooters-named-45-years-later/; Heather Ann Thompson, "Attica: It's Worse Than We Thought," *NYT,* November 19, 2017.

164. For a discussion of the impact of Attica on evangelical prison ministry, see Kendrick Oliver, "Attica, Watergate, and the Origin of Evangelical Prison Ministry, 1969–1975," in *American Evangelicals and the 1960s,* ed. Axel R. Schäfer (Madison: University of Wisconsin Press, 2013), 121–38.

165. Ray Hoekstra, "Interview with Chaplain Jeff Carter of Attica Prison," n.d., tape 1, IPM; Douglas C. Lyons, "Spreading the Gospel behind Bars," *Ebony,* July 1988.

166. In some IPM materials, the special was listed under other names, such as "The Public Enemies," but it was eventually marketed under *God's Prison Gang.* Art Linkletter and Ray Hoekstra, *God's Prison Gang,* n.d.; "Attica Television Special," *PRE,* February 1981, FPHC.

167. "Shelocta Church Shows 'God's Prison Gang,'" *Indiana (PA) Gazette*, May 14, 1983; "Sheriff Saw TV Special," *PRE*, February 1981, FPHC; "Former Prisoner Saw Attica TV Special," *PRE*, 2nd qtr. 1981, FPHC.

168. "Attica Prison TV Special Honored with Angel Award," *PRE*, 2nd qtr. 1981, FPHC.

169. Thompson, *Blood in the Water*, xv, 6–7, 229.

170. Glass, *Free at Last*, 88.

171. Glass, "See-Thru Views."

172. W. S. McBirnie to Ronald Reagan, November 30, 1965, Gubernatorial Campaign Files, series IV, box C31, 66: The Creative Society, RR; Ronald Reagan, "The Creative Society" (speech, University of Southern California, April 19, 1966), http://www.freerepublic.com/focus/news/742041/posts.

173. Herbert Ellingwood, "Making Faith Work—across Two Worlds," 1972, box 111, folder 6, NAE. See also "Bethelites Go to Prison," *PE*, July 23, 1972.

174. Herbert Ellingwood, Mike Khaled, and John Nichels, "Congress of Prison Ministries, Special Attorney General State of California, 'Your Turn,'" n.d., box 50, tape 2, DPC.

175. *Set Free*, 1977, Collection 631-18, box 32, folder 7, Southern Baptist Historical Library and Archives, Nashville.

176. Carl A. Robins, "An 'Inside' View of Prison Ministries," *Houston Chronicle*, December 30, 1978.

177. Ray Hoekstra, "The Three Causes of Crime, and the One Sure Cure," n.d., tape 24, IPM. Transcriptions of Chaplain Ray's recordings are my own.

178. Hoekstra, "Restitution—Forgotten Justice."

179. Ray Hoekstra, "Interview with Dallas County Sheriff Carl Thomas," n.d., tape 13, IPM.

180. Ray Hoekstra, *The Victim, The Offender: A Discussion of the Forgotten Part of Justice—Biblical Restitution* (Dallas: Acclaimed Books, 1983).

6. There Are Better Ways

1. Charles W. Colson, "Notebook #4," January 9 and 10, 1975, box 10, folder 6, Papers of Charles Wendell Colson, Collection 275, Billy Graham Center Archives, Wheaton College, Wheaton, IL.

2. Charles W. Colson, "Notebook #1," October 13 and 17, 1974, box 10, folder 6, Papers of Charles Wendell Colson, Collection 275, Billy Graham Center Archives, Wheaton College, Wheaton, IL. Colson also related the air force jacket and dye story in Charles W. Colson, *Born Again* (Grand Rapids, MI: Chosen Books, 1976), chap. 25.

3. Colson, *Born Again*, chap. 24; Charles W. Colson, *Life Sentence* (Lincoln, VA: Chosen Books, 1979), 24.

4. "Ministry Goals for 1982 in Comparison with 1980 and 81," *Jubilee*, February 1982, EMJ. Scholars who discuss Colson and Prison Fellowship generally focus on prison ministry or his influence in the "born again" subculture of the 1970s and evangelical public life in later decades. For examples of the former, see Winnifred Fallers Sullivan, *Prison Religion: Faith-Based Reform and the Constitution* (Princeton, NJ: Princeton University Press, 2009); Tanya Erzen, "Testimonial Politics: The Christian

Right's Faith-Based Approach to Marriage and Imprisonment," *American Quarterly* 59, no. 3 (September 1, 2007): 991–1015; Tanya Erzen, *God in Captivity: The Rise of Faith-Based Prison Ministries in the Age of Mass Incarceration* (Boston: Beacon, 2017), 59–83; Kendrick Oliver, "Attica, Watergate, and the Origin of Evangelical Prison Ministry, 1969–1975," in *American Evangelicals and the 1960s*, ed. Axel R. Schäfer (Madison: University of Wisconsin Press, 2013), 121–38; and Kendrick Oliver, "'Hi, Fellas. Come on In.' Norman Carlson, the Federal Bureau of Prisons, and the Rise of Prison Fellowship," *Journal of Church and State* 55, no. 4 (Autumn 2013): 740–57. For the latter, see Kendrick Oliver, "How to Be (the Author of) Born Again: Charles Colson and the Writing of Conversion in the Age of Evangelicalism," *Religions* 5, no. 3 (September 11, 2014): 886–911; Steven P. Miller, *The Age of Evangelicalism: America's Born-Again Years* (New York: Oxford University Press, 2014), 13; and Jeff Sharlet, *The Family: The Secret Fundamentalism at the Heart of American Power* (New York: HarperCollins, 2008).

5. Two works have discussed Colson's reform efforts. Cultural theorist Andrea Smith focuses on the various discourses present within conservative evangelicalism more generally on prison issues, with the aim of developing an account of the "unlikely alliances" available to marginalized people groups (chiefly Native Americans). Political scientists David Dagan and Steven Teles have shown how Colson was a key influencer in more recent conservative criminal justice reform work. This chapter builds on some of their arguments and nuances and challenges others, such as Smith's general equation of Colson with rising "Christian right" forces in the 1980s. Andrea Smith, *Native Americans and the Christian Right: The Gendered Politics of Unlikely Alliances* (Durham, NC: Duke University Press, 2008); David Dagan and Steven Teles, *Prison Break: Why Conservatives Turned against Mass Incarceration* (New York: Oxford University Press, 2016).

6. Conservative journalist Marvin Olasky was the first to use the term "compassionate conservatism," beginning in his work in the late 1980s and early 1990s. His early articulation of compassionate conservatism typically focused on issues related to poverty and the welfare state. See Marvin Olasky, *Compassionate Conservatism: What It Is, What It Does, and How It Can Transform America* (New York: Free Press, 2000), chap. 1; and Marvin Olasky, *The Tragedy of American Compassion* (Washington, DC: Regnery, 1994).

7. Elliott Currie, *Crime and Punishment in America* (New York: Macmillan, 1998), 21.

8. D. Michael Lindsay, *Faith in the Halls of Power: How Evangelicals Joined the American Elite* (New York: Oxford University Press, 2007), 59.

9. For example, see Billy Graham, "My Answer," *Pensacola News Journal*, October 18, 1975.

10. Colson, *Life Sentence*, 181–90.

11. Garry Wills, "'Born Again' Politics," *NYT Magazine*, August 1, 1976. See also Oliver, "Attica, Watergate," 134; and Marie Coutu, "Colson Group Shares the Faith," *Waterbury American*, June 14, 1977.

12. Michael Cromartie to Charles W. Colson, April 21, 1978, box 10, folder 12, PF.

13. Colson and his associates regularly told stories about other troubling prison visits in the late 1970s and early 1980s that motivated him finally to seek reform, such as those in Santa Fe, New Mexico; Stillwater, Minnesota; and Walla Walla, Washington.

It is not clear that one was *the* actual turning point, but since Atlanta was the one selected by Colson himself for his second book, it became one of the most prominent. Colson, *Life Sentence,* 291–301; David Peterson, "Stillwater Prison Improved, Colson Says," *Minneapolis Star,* April 26, 1979; Daniel W. Van Ness, *Crime and Its Victims* (Downers Grove, IL: InterVarsity, 1986), 12; Jonathan Aitken, *Charles W. Colson: A Life Redeemed* (New York: Doubleday, 2005), 320.

14. Alice Murray, "Colson Says Inmates Hot, Not Scared," *AC,* June 28, 1978.

15. Rita Gillmon, "Colson Asks Aid for Inmates," *San Diego Union,* July 7, 1978.

16. Sally Clower, *Justice Fellowship Case History* (Prison Fellowship Research and Development, January 1992), 1–2. I am grateful to Dan Van Ness for sharing this document with me.

17. Clower, 2.

18. Murray, "Colson Says Inmates Hot."

19. Bob Stanley, "Colson Urges Prayer to Open Texas Prisons," *BP,* June 13, 1979.

20. Jim Newton, "Colson Opposes Capital Punishment," *BP,* June 13, 1979.

21. Colson, *Born Again* (1976), 224.

22. Stanton E. Samenow, "The Criminal Personality: New Concepts and New Procedures for Change," *Humanist* 38, no. 5 (September 1, 1978): 18; Samuel Yochelson and Stanton E. Samenow, *The Criminal Personality* (New York: J. Aronson, 1976); Richard A. Dienstbier, "Exceptions to the Rule: A Review of *The Criminal Personality, Volume I: A Profile for Change,*" *Law and Human Behavior* 1, no. 2 (1977): 207–16.

23. Dienstbier, "Exceptions to the Rule," 215–16.

24. Samenow, "Criminal Personality," 18.

25. Gordon Loux to Charles W. Colson, August 24, 1977, box 10, folder 12, PF.

26. Phil McCombs, "Colson Crusades to Free Inmates, Build No Prisons," *WP,* December 2, 1981; William F. Buckley Jr., "The Reformation of Charles Colson," *WP,* April 20, 1982.

27. Charles W. Colson and Ellen Santilli Vaughn, *Kingdoms in Conflict* (Grand Rapids, MI: Zondervan, 1987), 333–41. Colson also cited Ellul throughout his earlier work, Colson, *Life Sentence.*

28. C. S. Lewis, "The Humanitarian Theory of Punishment," *Res Judicatae* 6, no. 2 (June 1, 1953): 226, 227, 230.

29. Charles W. Colson to David Bovenizer, "Purdy Women's Prison at Gig Harbor, Washington," 1980, box 16, folder 6, PF.

30. George H. Nash, *The Conservative Intellectual Movement in America since 1945* (New York: Basic Books, 1976).

31. Michael W. Flamm, *Law and Order: Street Crime, Civil Unrest, and the Crisis of Liberalism in the 1960s* (New York: Columbia University Press, 2007), 78; William F. Buckley Jr., "Police Review Boards: Whose Delinquencies Concern Us?," *LAT,* October 26, 1966.

32. "Where to Go on Prison Reform," *Firing Line,* April 15, 1982, Firing Line broadcast records, Hoover Institution Archives, https://digitalcollections.hoover.org /objects/6681; Buckley, "Reformation of Charles Colson"; William F. Buckley Jr., "On the Right: Prison Reform," *National Review,* May 14, 1982. I am grateful to Alexander E. Callaway for bringing Colson's presence on *Firing Line* to my attention.

33. Robert Martinson, "What Works? Questions and Answers about Prison Reform," *Public Interest* 35 (Spring 1974): 25.

34. Charles W. Colson to David Bovenizer, January 29, 1980, box 16, folder 6, PF.

35. McCombs, "Colson Crusades"; Colson to Bovenizer, "Purdy Women's Prison."

36. Gordon Loux to Floyd Robertson, March 11, 1980, box 35, folder 34, NAE.

37. Two early pieces are Charles W. Colson, "Watergate or Something like It Was Inevitable," *CT*, March 12, 1976; and Charles W. Colson, "Religion Up, Morality Down," *CT*, July 21, 1978.

38. For example, see Larry R. Isitt, "Willie: Maximum Freedom in a Maximum-Security Prison," *CT*, April 6, 1984.

39. Norris Magnuson, *Salvation in the Slums: Evangelical Social Work, 1865–1920* (Grand Rapids, MI: Baker, 1977).

40. Charles W. Colson, September 7, 1978, box 11, folder 1, PF.

41. Charles W. Colson to David Bovenizer, February 23, 1980, box 16, folder 6, PF.

42. Randall Balmer, *Redeemer: The Life of Jimmy Carter* (New York: Basic Books, 2014), 59–61.

43. Clower, *Justice Fellowship Case History*, 3–4.

44. Colson to Bovenizer, "Purdy Women's Prison," 6–7.

45. Colson and Vaughn, *Kingdoms in Conflict*, 293–300; Charles W. Colson to Ralph Veerman, November 14, 1978, box 48, folder 28, PF; Colson to Bovenizer, "Purdy Women's Prison," 6–7; AP, "Colson Says Give Cons a Hand in Running Prison," *Oregon Statesman*, October 24, 1979; Janet Evenson, "Must Learn More of Inmates: Colson," *Oregon Statesman*, October 25, 1979; Betty Stevens, "Colson Praises Prison Ministry," *Lincoln Journal*, May 16, 1985; Richard W. Larsen, "Chuck Colson's Visit—Words of Hope for Our Prisons," *Seattle Times*, April 9, 1985.

46. Richard W. Larsen, "Aftermath of a Stickup—a One Eyed Angel," *Seattle Times*, April 14, 1985; Colson and Vaughn, *Kingdoms in Conflict*, 300–301.

47. Charles W. Colson, "Is There a Better Way? A Perspective," *Christian Legal Society Quarterly* 2, no. 3 (Summer 1981): 13.

48. Charles W. Colson, statement, *Federal Criminal Law Revision, Part 1: Desirability of Reduced Use of Incarceration to Punish Criminals, Particularly Nonviolent Offenders; Potential for Alternative Forms of Punishment for Crime: Hearings before the Subcommittee on Criminal Justice, Committee on the Judiciary, US House of Representatives* (February 5, 1982).

49. Colson.

50. Charles W. Colson, "Taking a Stand When Law and Justice Conflict," *CT*, February 4, 1983.

51. Daniel K. Williams, *God's Own Party: The Making of the Christian Right* (New York: Oxford University Press, 2010), 3.

52. Jerry Falwell, "Perspective: America's Shameful State," *CTR*, April 16, 1982.

53. Moral Majority, *What Is the Moral Majority?*, n.d., General Materials of the Moral Majority, box 1, series 1, folder 1, Liberty University Archive.

54. Ronald S. Godwin, statement, *Federal Criminal Law Revision, Part 1: Objections to H.R. 1647, H.R. 4711, and S. 1630 Reductions of Jail Sentences and Other Provisions Liberalizing Federal Treatment of Various Crimes: Hearings before the Sub-*

committee on Criminal Justice, Committee on the Judiciary, US House of Representatives (December 14, 1981).

55. Beth Spring, "Moral Majority Aims at the Criminal Code," *CT*, February 5, 1982.

56. Ronald L. Gainer, "Report to the Attorney General on Federal Criminal Code Reform," *Criminal Law Forum* 1, no. 1 (September 1, 1989): 173; Albert P. Melone, "The Politics of Criminal Code Revision: Lessons for Reform," *Capital University Law Review* 15 (1986): 191–204; Steve Snider, "Moral Majority: Potent Non-lobby," *St. Louis Post-Dispatch,* April 21, 1982.

57. Barbara Ann Stolz, "Interest Groups and Criminal Law: The Case of Federal Criminal Code Revision," *Crime and Delinquency* 30, no. 1 (January 1984): 91–106.

58. AP, "Moral Majority Eyes Ohio's Judges," *Akron Beacon Journal,* July 28, 1981; Bob Weston, "Leis to Offer Records on Judicial Decisions to Moral Majority," *Cincinnati Enquirer,* July 28, 1981.

59. Jon East, "Moral Majority Rally Attracts 25 Candidates," *St. Petersburg Independent,* August 20, 1980.

60. Marie Gottschalk, *The Prison and the Gallows: The Politics of Mass Incarceration in America* (New York: Cambridge University Press, 2006), 77–80.

61. Edwin Meese, "Introduction," *Regent University Law Review* 1, no. 1 (Spring 1991): 2.

62. David John Marley, "Ronald Reagan and the Splintering of the Christian Right," *Journal of Church and State* 48, no. 4 (Autumn 2006): 851–68.

63. "CBN President Member of Crime Task Force," *New Journal and Guide* (Norfolk, VA), August 11, 1982.

64. Lois Haight Herrington et al., *Final Report of President's Task Force on Victims of Crime* (Washington, DC, December 1982), 17.

65. Herrington et al., 29–31.

66. Doris L. Dolan et al., "Task Force Roundtable Interview Transcript," interview by Anne Seymour, 2002, Oral History of the Crime Victim Assistance Field, http://vroh .uakron.edu/transcripts/TaskForceRoundtable.php.

67. Herrington et al., *Final Report,* 95–96.

68. Kissette Bundy, "Reagan Backs Crime Fight of Christians," *Philadelphia Tribune,* April 27, 1984.

69. Bundy; "Crime Fighter," *Philadelphia Daily News,* April 5, 1984; Walter F. Naedele, "Rev. B. Sam Hart, 80, Broadcaster," *Philadelphia Inquirer,* January 26, 2012; assorted photos, box 612, folder 26, CM.

70. Gottschalk, *Prison and the Gallows,* 131.

71. Gottschalk, 89–90.

72. Ashton N. Burruss, "Making Excuses," *Free Lance-Star* (Fredericksburg, VA), September 18, 1982.

73. For example, see Americans for Robertson, "'Robertson for President' Advertisement," *Quad-City Times* (Davenport, IA), January 10, 1988.

74. William C. Hammack and Robert Crook, "Pro-con: The Governor's Task Force on Corrections," *Mississippi Lawyer* 29, no. 3 (December 1982): 20–23; "Colson Backs Prison Ideas," *Clarion-Ledger* (Jackson, MS), October 15, 1982; AP, "Corrections Leaders Impressed by Colson," *Greenwood (MS) Commonwealth,* October 15, 1982.

75. AP, "Labelled as Soft on Crime . . . Prison Release Bill Killed," *Laurel (MS) Leader-Call,* February 9, 1982.

76. Hammack and Crook, "Pro-con," 23.

77. Spring, "Moral Majority."

78. Charles W. Colson to David Bovenizer, August 13, 1980, box 16, folder 7, PF; Charles W. Colson to David Bovenizer, January 29, 1980, box 16, folder 6, PF; Charles W. Colson to David Bovenizer, February 23, 1980, box 16, folder 7, PF; Charles W. Colson to David Bovenizer, September 12, 1980, box 16, folder 7, PF.

79. Charles W. Colson to Jerry Falwell, March 14, 1983, box 31, folder 1, PF.

80. Jerry Falwell to Charles W. Colson, March 2, 1983, box 31, folder 1, PF; Mark DeMoss to Charles W. Colson, November 15, 1984, box 31, folder 1, PF.

81. Charles W. Colson to Jerry Falwell, August 20, 1981, box 31, folder 1, PF; Charles W. Colson to Jerry Falwell, March 4, 1986, box 31, folder 1, PF.

82. Cal Thomas to Charles W. Colson, November 8, 1982, box 31, folder 1, PF.

83. Charles W. Colson to Daniel W. Van Ness, November 19, 1982, box 31, folder 1, PF.

84. "Senators Propose Alternative Sentencing Bill," *Jubilee,* January 1983, EMJ; Clower, *Justice Fellowship Case History,* 6.

85. Sentencing Improvement Act of 1983, S. 1644 (1983), https://www.congress .gov/bill/98th-congress/senate-bill/1644; William L. Armstrong, "Prudent Use of Prison Space: The Sentencing Improvement Act," *Journal of Legislation* 11, no. 2 (1984): 237–48.

86. Prison Fellowship, "Questions and Answers on the Nunn-Armstrong Sentencing Improvement Act of 1982," October 1982, box 45, folder 36, CLC; "Justice Fellowship Update," *Jubilee,* October 1963, EMJ.

87. Kenneth S. Kantzer, "A New Solution to the Crisis in Our Prisons," *CT,* June 17, 1983; Larry Braidfoot to William Armstrong, December 2, 1982, box 45, folder 36, CLC; Larry Braidfoot to Sam Nunn, December 2, 1982, box 45, folder 36, CLC; "Legislation on the Federal Agenda," *Criminal Justice Update,* Fall 1983, box 45, folder 36, CLC; "Sentencing Reform," National Association of Evangelicals, 1983, https://www .nae.net/sentencing-reform/.

88. Charles W. Colson, "Another Point of View: 'A Struggle for Justice,'" *Jubilee,* March 1984, EMJ.

89. Senator Mark Hatfield, speaking on S. 1644, *Congressional Record* 129 (July 20, 1983): 19861–62.

90. For the broader history behind this general legislative thrust, see Naomi Murakawa, *The First Civil Right: How Liberals Built Prison America* (New York: Oxford University Press, 2014), 99–104; and Katie Stith and Steve Y. Koh, "The Politics of Sentencing Reform: The Legislative History of the Federal Sentencing Guidelines," *Wake Forest Law Review* 28, no. 2 (1993): 223–90.

91. William L. Armstrong and Sam Nunn, "Alternatives to Incarceration: The Sentencing Improvement Act," in *Crime and Punishment in Modern America,* ed. Patrick B. McGuigan and Jon S. Pascale (Washington, DC: Free Congress Research and Education Foundation, 1986); Senators Sam Nunn and William Armstrong, speaking on Amendment No. 2684, *Congressional Record* 130 (January 31, 1984): 991–95.

92. Senator Mark Hatfield, speaking on Amendment No. 2684, *Congressional Record* 130 (January 31, 1984): 999–1001.

93. Colson, "Another Point of View."

94. Clower, *Justice Fellowship Case History,* 91.

95. Daniel W. Van Ness, interview by author, February 19, 2018.

96. Cal Thomas, "Building More Prisons Is No Way to Fight Crime," *LAT* Syndicate, May 26, 1989.

97. National Research Council, Committee on Causes and Consequences of High Rates of Incarceration, *The Growth of Incarceration in the United States: Exploring Causes and Consequences,* ed. Jeremy Travis, Bruce Western, and Steve Redburn (Washington, DC: National Academies Press, 2014), 78.

98. Sentencing Project, "Trends in U.S. Corrections," June 2017, https://sentencing project.org/wp-content/uploads/2016/01/Trends-in-US-Corrections.pdf.

99. Clower, *Justice Fellowship Case History,* 7.

100. Clifford K. Dorne, *Restorative Justice in the United States: An Introduction* (Upper Saddle River, NJ: Pearson Prentice Hall, 2008), 167–69.

101. Mark Umbreit and Marilyn Peterson Armour, *Restorative Justice Dialogue: An Essential Guide for Research and Practice* (New York: Springer, 2010), 37; Howard Zehr and Mark Umbreit, "Victim Offender Reconciliation: An Incarceration Substitute," *Federal Probation* 46, no. 4 (December 1982): 63–68.

102. Howard Zehr, "Our Military Mentality Approach to Criminal Justice," *Christian Legal Society Quarterly* 2, no. 3 (Summer 1981): 11.

103. As scholars of American indigenous peoples' movements have shown, there is a much longer and diverse history of restorative practices in North America beyond Zehr and Anabaptism. However, most scholars of restorative justice identify Zehr as a key figure in formalizing the approach in terms of Western legal norms. Smith, *Native Americans,* 50–51.

104. Zehr, "Our Military Mentality Approach," 9–11.

105. Van Ness, interview, February 19, 2018.

106. Zehr and Umbreit, "Victim Offender Reconciliation," 68; Howard Zehr, *The Little Book of Restorative Justice* (Intercourse, PA: Good Books, 2002).

107. Zehr, "Our Military Mentality Approach," 9.

108. In 1987 the book won the Eternity Book of the Year and Evangelical Christian Publishers Association Gold Medallion awards. Van Ness, *Crime and Its Victims;* Van Ness, interview, February 19, 2018.

109. Clower, *Justice Fellowship Case History,* 9.

110. Charles W. Colson, "Truth, Justice, Peace: The Foundations of Restorative Justice," *Regent University Law Review* 10 (1998): 9.

111. Clower, *Justice Fellowship Case History,* appendix A.

112. Sentencing Project, "Trends in U.S. Corrections."

113. Peter Applebome, "Death Penalty; Arkansas Execution Raises Questions on Governor's Politics," *NYT,* January 25, 1992.

114. Regarding the import of plea bargaining and prosecutors, see John Pfaff, *Locked In: The True Causes of Mass Incarceration—and How to Achieve Real Reform* (New York: Basic Books, 2017).

115. Ralph Reed, "Colson's Life and Legacy," *National Review* (blog), April 23, 2012, https://www.nationalreview.com/2012/04/colsons-life-and-legacy-nro-symposium/.

116. Christian Coalition, *Contract with the American Family* (Nashville: Moorings, 1995), 121–29. See also Smith, *Native Americans,* 62.

117. National Research Council, Committee on Causes and Consequences of High Rates of Incarceration, *Growth of Incarceration,* 70–71.

118. William J. Bennett, John J. DiIulio, and John P. Walters, *Body Count: Moral Poverty . . . and How to Win America's War against Crime and Drugs* (New York: Simon and Schuster, 1996); James Traub, "The Criminals of Tomorrow," *New Yorker,* November 4, 1996; John J. DiIulio, "Arresting Ideas: Tougher Law Enforcement Is Driving Down Urban Crime," *Policy Review* 74 (Fall 1995): 12–16; C-SPAN, "Hillary Clinton on 'Superpredators,'" 1996, posted February 25, 2016, YouTube video, 2:02, https://www.youtube.com/watch?v=j0uCrA7ePno.

119. Christian Coalition, *Contract with the American Family,* 125.

120. Daniel W. Van Ness, interview by author, January 19, 2018.

121. Smith, *Native Americans,* 56.

122. Constance Holden, "The Criminal Mind: A New Look at an Ancient Puzzle," *Science* 199, no. 4328 (February 3, 1978): 514.

123. Gene Stephens, "Review of *The Criminal Personality, Volumes I and II,*" *American Journal of Criminal Justice* 3, no. 1 (March 1978): 80–82; Holden, "The Criminal Mind," 511–14.

124. Larsen, "Chuck Colson's Visit."

125. Jason R. Hackworth, *Faith Based: Religious Neoliberalism and the Politics of Welfare in the United States* (Athens: University of Georgia Press, 2012), 63–85.

126. Charles W. Colson, *Born Again* (Grand Rapids, MI: Chosen Books, 2008), 374.

127. Charles Colson, "Just War in Iraq," *CT,* December 9, 2002.

128. John Wayne Gacy Correspondence, 1980–1982, box 31, folder 6, PF.

129. Charles Colson, "Voting for the Executioner," *CT,* October 8, 1990.

130. Randy Frame, "A Matter of Life and Death," *CT,* August 14, 1995; Charles W. Colson, "Preserving the Dignity of Man," BreakPoint, June 8, 2001, http://www.leaderu.com/socialsciences/colson-dignity.html; Charles W. Colson and Harold Fickett, *The Faith: What Christians Believe, Why They Believe It, and Why It Matters* (Grand Rapids, MI: Zondervan, 2008); Charles W. Colson, "Why I Support Capital Punishment," Gospel Coalition, accessed February 28, 2018, https://www.thegospelcoalition.org/article/why-i-support-capital-punishment/.

131. Colson, *Life Sentence,* 81–86.

132. Colson, 161–73.

133. Harold Dean Trulear, "Prison Ministry in the Post-Colson Era," *Capital Commentary,* May 25, 2012.

134. Steve Rempe, "Serving Prisoners, Post Chuck," Prison Fellowship, May 29, 2012, https://www.prisonfellowship.org/2012/05/serving-prisoners-post-chuck/.

135. Charles Colson and Jack Eckerd, *Why America Doesn't Work* (Dallas: Word, 1991), 75–89.

136. Charles Colson, "Quit the Babel-ing," *CT,* January 8, 1996.

137. Bernard E. Harcourt, *Illusion of Order* (Cambridge, MA: Harvard University Press, 2001), 1–11; Bernard E. Harcourt and Jens Ludwig, "Broken Windows: New Evi-

dence from New York City and a Five-City Social Experiment," *University of Chicago Law Review* 73, no. 1 (2006): 271–320.

138. Charles Colson and Nancy Pearcey, *How Now Shall We Live?* (Carol Stream, IL: Tyndale, 1999), 203–9; Charles Colson, *Justice That Restores* (Wheaton, IL: Tyndale, 2001), 116–19.

139. Dagan and Teles, *Prison Break,* 45–46.

140. Smith, *Native Americans,* 65.

141. Dagan and Teles, *Prison Break,* 105; Newt Gingrich and Pat Nolan, "Prison Reform: A Smart Way for States to Save Money and Lives," *WP,* January 7, 2011.

142. Dagan and Teles, *Prison Break,* 106–36.

143. John J. DiIulio Jr., *Godly Republic: A Centrist Blueprint for America's Faith-Based Future* (Berkeley: University of California Press, 2007); John J. DiIulio Jr., "Chuck Colson and Second Chances," *Wall Street Journal,* April 24, 2012.

144. Louis Nelson, "Trump: 'I Am the Law and Order Candidate,'" Politico, July 7, 2016, https://www.politico.com/story/2016/07/trump-law-order-candidate-225372.

145. Donald J. Trump, "State of the Union Address," January 30, 2018, https://www.whitehouse.gov/briefings-statements/president-donald-j-trumps-state-union-address/; Emma Green, "Trump's Evangelical Advisers Could Help Him Secure a Win on Sentencing Reform," *Atlantic,* December 12, 2018. For a discussion of this seemingly paradoxical development, see the preface to Pfaff, *Locked In.*

146. Rachel Kushner, "Is Prison Necessary? Ruth Wilson Gilmore Might Change Your Mind," *NYT,* April 17, 2019.

147. "Michelle Alexander Joins Union Theological Seminary," Union Theological Seminary, September 12, 2016, https://utsnyc.edu/michelle-alexander-joins-union-theological-seminary/.

Conclusion

1. Anna Douglas, "The Story behind Billy Graham's Casket and the Prison Inmates Who Made It," *Charlotte Observer,* March 1, 2018, http://www.charlotteobserver.com/news/special-reports/billy-graham-life/article202833794.html.

2. Jeffrey Goldberg, "The End of the Line: Rehabilitation and Reform in Angola Penitentiary," *Atlantic,* September 9, 2015.

3. James Ridgeway, "God's Own Warden," *Mother Jones,* August 2011.

4. "Prison Wages: Appendix," Prison Policy Initiative, accessed March 17, 2018, https://www.prisonpolicy.org/reports/wage_policies.html; Michelle Alexander, *The New Jim Crow: Mass Incarceration in the Age of Colorblindness* (New York: New Press, 2010), 157.

5. Jessica Napoli, "Kanye West Performs at Houston Jails: 'This Is a Mission, Not a Show,'" Fox News, November 16, 2019, https://www.foxnews.com/entertainment/kanye-west-performs-houston-jails; "Kanye West Performs with Choir at Harris County Jail in Houston," TMZ, November 15, 2019, https://www.tmz.com/2019/11/15/kanye-west-harris-county-houston-jail-joel-osteen/; Alaa Elassar, "Kanye West Performed a Surprise Concert for Inmates in Houston Jail," CNN, November 16, 2019, https://www.cnn.com/2019/11/16/us/kanye-west-texas-prison-concert-trnd/index.html.

6. Winnifred Fallers Sullivan, *Prison Religion: Faith-Based Reform and the Constitution* (Princeton, NJ: Princeton University Press, 2009).

7. Sasha Volokh, "Do Faith-Based Prisons Work?," *WP*, February 10, 2014.

8. Byron Johnson, *More God, Less Crime: Why Faith Matters and How It Could Matter More* (West Conshohocken, PA: Templeton, 2011); Kevin Lewis O'Neill, *Secure the Soul: Christian Piety and Gang Prevention in Guatemala* (Oakland: University of California Press, 2015); Robert Brenneman, *Homies and Hermanos: God and Gangs in Central America* (New York: Oxford University Press, 2011); Andrew Johnson, *If I Give My Soul: Faith behind Bars in Rio de Janeiro* (New York: Oxford University Press, 2017).

9. Kate Shellnutt, "Black, White, and Blue: How Christians Rate the Police," *CT*, February 17, 2017.

10. International Justice Mission homepage, accessed January 14, 2020, https://www.ijm.org/.

11. David R. Swartz, "'Rescue Sells': Narrating Human Trafficking to Evangelical Populists," *Review of Faith and International Affairs* 17, no. 3 (2019): 99.

12. "About Pointman," Pointman Leadership Institute, accessed January 14, 2020, http://pointmanglobal.org/about; Fellowship of Christian Peace Officers—USA, "2014 FCPO-USA Nation Conference—Robert Vernon," October 17, 2014, posted May 1, 2017, YouTube video, 44:53, https://youtu.be/c00aa3GYfKg.

13. Randolph Lewis, *Under Surveillance: Being Watched in Modern America* (Austin: University of Texas Press, 2017), 164.

14. For example, see Redeemer Center for Faith and Work, "Grace, Justice, and Mercy: An Evening with Bryan Stevenson and Rev. Tim Keller," posted June 1, 2016, Vimeo video, 1:10:53, https://vimeo.com/168964644; "Q Contributors: Bryan Stevenson," Q, accessed March 13, 2018, http://qideas.org/contributors/bryan-stevenson; and Bryan Stevenson, *Just Mercy: A Story of Justice and Redemption* (New York: Spiegel and Grau, 2014).

15. "Bryan Stevenson," Equal Justice Initiative, accessed March 14, 2018, https://eji.org/bryan-stevenson; Jeffrey Toobin, "The Legacy of Lynching, on Death Row," *New Yorker*, August 15, 2016.

16. "Prison Labor and the Thirteenth Amendment," Equal Justice Initiative, accessed March 17, 2018, https://eji.org/history-racial-injustice-prison-labor.

17. D. L. Mayfield, "Facing Our Legacy of Lynching," *CT*, August 18, 2017. For an account of Stevenson's visit to Wheaton, see "Renowned Activist Bryan Stevenson Visits Campus," *Wheaton Record*, October 24, 2016.

18. "Renowned Activist."

19. As theologian Karl Barth writes, "If anyone identified himself with prisoners it was [Jesus Christ]. . . . That is the Lord who has mercy on you: this prisoner who is your liberator, the liberator of us all." Karl Barth, *Deliverance to the Captives* (New York: Harper Brothers, 1961), 75–84.

ACKNOWLEDGMENTS

This book could not have been written without the support of so many colleagues, friends, and family members. My doctoral mentors Kate Bowler and Grant Wacker pushed me to think big, write well, and listen to the voices of the past with critical empathy. I could not have asked for better teachers. I am also grateful to teachers and graduate student colleagues from Duke Divinity School and the University of North Carolina–Chapel Hill. Molly Worthen and Lauren Winner rounded out my dream team of a committee. Yaakov Ariel, Brandon Bayne, Luke Bretherton, Douglas Campbell, Brendan Case, Mark Chaves, Edgardo Colón-Emeric, Matt Dougherty, Craig Dykstra, Susan Eastman, Curtis Freeman, Brenna Keegan, Xi Lian, Tito Madrazo, Brett McCarty, Scott Muir, Wen Reagan, Russ Richey, Meredith Riedel, Brook Wilensky-Lanford, Cari Willis, Josh Young, and Colin Yuckman all offered me insights or encouragement.

I had a number of other valuable conversation partners while writing this book: Uta Balbier, Spencer Bradford, Christina Bryant, Elesha Coffman, Lorraine Cuddeback, Brad East, Andrew Finstuen, Brantley Gasaway, Layla Karst, Kyle Lambelet, Devin Manzullo-Thomas, Gustavo Maya, Arlene Montevecchio, Kathleen O'Connor, Amanda Pittman, Paul Putz, Jason Sexton, Daniel Silliman, Tim Snyder, David Swartz, Amber Thomas, Noah Toly, Isaac S. Villegas, Anne Blue Wills, and Neil Young, to name only a few. Stephanie Gaskill, Max Felker-Kantor, Matt Jantzen, Andrew Jones, David Kirkpatrick, David Komline, Zac Koons, Leah Payne, Kevin Whelan, and Kelsey Woodruff read portions of the manuscript at various stages and offered incredibly helpful feedback. Heath Carter, Darren Dochuk, Jennifer Graber, and Elizabeth Hinton read the entire manuscript and pushed me to make changes that improved the book immensely.

I was fortunate to spend a year as a postdoctoral fellow at the John C. Danforth Center on Religion and Politics at Washington University in Saint Louis. The Danforth Center not only provided me space, time, and funding for research and writing, it also offered a wonderful community: Fannie Bialek, Marie Griffith, John Inazu, Sandy Jones, Deborah Kennard, Dana Lloyd, Laurie Maffly-Kipp, Lerone Martin, Charlie McCrary, Cyrus O'Brien, Sheri Peña, Leigh Schmidt, Mark Valeri, Abram Van Engen, and the regular attendees at the center's colloquium, particularly Amy Gais, Elena Kravchenko, and Adam Park.

I am grateful to my colleagues at Sattler College, who are a delight to work with. A special thanks to Zack Johnson, Hans Leaman, Michael Miller, and Jesse Scheumann, who have all offered much support and encouragement.

My students challenge and inspire me in new ways every semester. I am particularly grateful to students in my Religion and Mass Incarceration courses at Duke, my Religion and American Society course at Missouri Eastern Correctional Center (taught through Washington University's Prison Education Project), and Kenneth Godoy and Lois Friesen from Sattler.

I am grateful for the generous financial support from the Kenan Institute for Ethics; Duke University Chapel; the Center for the Study of Philanthropy and Voluntarism at Duke's Sanford School of Public Policy; and Duke Divinity's Baptist House of Studies. I was also the beneficiary of research and travel grants from the Southern Baptist Historical Library and Archives; the Torrey M. Johnson, Sr. Scholarship Fund at the Billy Graham Center Archives; the Religion in North Carolina Digital Collection, Duke Divinity's Office of Black Church Studies; and Wheaton College's Institute for Prison Ministries. The Louisville Institute has been a particularly important source of funding and support. I am grateful to Edwin Aponte, Jessica Bowman, Pamala Collins, Keri Liechty, and Don Richter for their dedication and investment in scholars like me. I workshopped an early version of a chapter at a stimulating Religion and Incarceration Workshop hosted by the Central New York Humanities Corridor, the Andrew Mellon Foundation, and Syracuse University Religion Department. I am grateful to Joshua Dubler and Vincent Lloyd for organizing this gathering.

This book could likewise not have been written without archivists and librarians. The teams at the Billy Graham Center Archives and Wheaton College Archives and Special Collections deserve special mention: Keith Call, Paul Ericksen, Katherine Graber, and Bob Shuster accommodated numerous requests and answered countless questions. Chris Schnell at the Abraham Lincoln Presidential Library graciously provided me access to the John B. Anderson Papers. Taffey Hall and her team at the Southern Baptist Historical Library and Archives were particularly helpful and generous with their time. I also want to thank Wayne Sparkman at the PCA Historical Center; Glenn Gohr, Alice Harris, and Darrin Rodgers at the Flower Pentecostal Heritage Center; Tim Grasso, Emilio A. Núñez, Esther Park, and Alyson Thomas in Archives and Special Collections at Fuller Theological Seminary; Kelly Barton, Michael Pinckney, and Ray Wilson at the Reagan Presidential Library; Ken Henke at Princeton Theological Seminary's Special Collections and Archives; Abigail Sattler at Liberty University Archives; Sarah Patton at the Hoover Institution Library and Archives; Mariam Touba at the New York Historical Society; Steve Zeleny at the Foursquare Heritage Archives; Leah Lefkowitz at the Atlanta History Center; and Lisa Jacobson, Charlene Peacock, and the rest of the team at the Presbyterian Historical Society. Alexander Callaway, Amber Thomas, and Elga Zalite did excellent work as proxy researchers.

Librarians at Duke University, Duke Divinity School, Washington University, and the Boston Public Library offered me crucial assistance throughout. I am particularly grateful to Ryan Denniston at Duke, Michael Schaefer at Washington University, and the interlibrary loan staff at all three institutions.

Several prison ministers, reform advocates, and religious leaders graciously took time to speak with me. Patty Baker, Dave Batty, David Carlson, Manny Cordero, Craig DeRoche, Bill Glass, Lennie Spitale, Harold Dean Trulear, and Howard Zehr all offered crucial personal and professional insights. Steve Lowe, Karen Swanson, and Dan Van Ness deserve special mention as incredibly kind and thoughtful conversation partners. Will Vaus and Gary Wilkerson graciously answered numerous questions I had about their fathers' ministries.

I would like to thank my editor, Kathleen McDermott, Stephanie Vyce, Kathi Drummy, Mihaela-Andreea Pacurar, and the rest of the team at Harvard University Press for their investment in this project. I also want to thank Don Yerxa and *Fides et Historia* for publishing an earlier portion of my work. Chapter 1 builds on ideas I first discussed in "The Real Victim of Lynch Law Is the *Government:* American Protestant Anti-lynching Advocacy and the Making of Law and Order," *Religions* 10, no. 2 (2019): 116. Much of Chapter 2 was first published as "'Jesus Christ Is the Only Control': Crime, Delinquency, and Evangelical Conversion in the Early Postwar Era," *Fides et Historia* 50, no. 1 (2018): 35–59. Ideas presented in this article also inform Chapter 3.

Friends and family members have supported me in countless ways. My parents, Jim and Laurel, always believed in me and showed me unconditional love. My children, Sam, Evelyn, and Franklin, are ever-present sources of joy. Luke, Emory, Camilla, Meaghan, Eileen, David, Luke, John, Kelsey, and Phil—thank you all for cheering me on and for tolerating my apparently constant need to write and talk about religion during family holidays. Friends from Durham Mennonite Church, Third Baptist Church, Alamance-Orange Prison Ministry, and Orange Correctional Center always had my back. Other friends, such as Randy, Griff, Elizabeth, Jonathan, Beth, David, Kelli, Amy, Ashley, Dustin, James, Jennifer, Mike, Adam, Andrew, Kevin, Alex, Dan, and Nathaniel, were always ready with words of encouragement. Most of all, I want to thank my wife, Eliza. She has been an unending source of love and support, and she inspires me every day with her laughter, friendship, and grace.

INDEX